P9-DFO-323

IRETON LIBRARY
MARYMOUNT UNIVERSITY
Presented by
RASKOB FOUNDATION

ORGANIZATIONAL FUNCTIONING IN A CROSS-CULTURAL PERSPECTIVE

ORGANIZATIONAL FUNCTIONING IN A CROSS-CULTURAL PERSPECTIVE

Edited by

George W. England
University of Minnesota and
International Institute of Management, Berlin

Anant R. Negandhi
Kent State University and
International Institute of Management, Berlin

Bernhard Wilpert
Padagogische Hochschule Berlin and
International Institute of Management, Berlin

ISBN: 0-87338-225-0

Library of Congress Cataloging in Publication Data

Main entry under title:

Organizational Functioning in a cross-cultural perspective.

Includes bibliographies and index.
1. Comparative management—Congresses. I. England, George William. II. Negandhi, Anant R. III. Wilpert, Bernhard, 1936- IV. Ohio. State University, Kent. Comparative Administration Research Institute.
HD29.073 658.4 78-31169
ISBN 0-87338-225-0

Published by:
Comparative Administration Research Institute
Kent State University, Kent, Ohio 44242

Distributed by:
The Kent State University Press
Kent State University, Kent, Ohio 44242

Photosetting by:
Thomson Press (India) Limited, New Delhi

PREFACE

Since the publication of Harbison-Myers' book, *Management in the Industrial World*, in 1959, Cross-Cultural Organization Studies and *Comparative Management* have become "respected" fields of endeavors for scholarly efforts. Consequently, during the last three decades, scores of articles and about a dozen books on the subject have been published. And yet, the many serious teachers and researchers in this area have expressed doubts about what we have learned from this honorable exercise.

As with so many events in life, the optimist would respond by saying 'a great deal' while the pessimist would say 'nothing.'

To ponder these extreme viewpoints and perspectives and to compare them with the "realities" of the present situation, we, the three of us from the two different continents, representing three different national origins and cultural milieus combined our energies and invited 40 scholars from 10 countries to discuss their research studies at where East meets West— Hawaii— under the shadows of the College of Business Administration of the University of Hawaii. The result is this volume.

The occasion of this gathering was also a celebration of the 10th anniversary of the Comparative Administration Research Institute of Kent State University (CARI) and a "temporary" but lovable marriage of CARI with the International Institute of Management, Science Center Berlin and the College of Business Administration of the University of Hawaii. These three institutions provided the financial and moral support for this gathering. We owe a deep sense of gratitude and sincere thanks to three sponsoring institutions and their leaders, Dr. David Heenen, Dean, College of Business Administration, University of Hawaii; Dr. Walter Goldberg, Director, International Institute of Management, Science Center Berlin; and Anant R. Negandhi, Director of CARI.

The organization of logistics, hotel rooms, meals, conference room, gathering and coordinating and distribution of papers fell on the shoulders of Professors Lane Kelley of the University of Hawaii and Ram Baliga, University of Wisconsin, Eau Claire. Their dedication and hard work made all the difference between 'success' and failure of our own efforts. We owe a million thanks to both of them.

As usual, we three are solely responsible for all the shortcomings and failures in our efforts. But we tried, and we will do it again.

Two Continents
December 1978

GWE
ARN
BW

In Memory of T.A. Martyn Johns
Who left us so suddenly.

CONTRIBUTORS

Mary E. Beres
Temple University
James S. Blandin
Naval Postgraduate School
Erhard Blankenburg
International Institute of Management, Berlin
Warren B. Brown
University of Oregon
Gunter Endruweit
University of the Säär
George W. England
University of Minnesota/IIM, Berlin
Luis G. Flores
Escuela de Administracion de Negocios para Graduados (ESAN)
Peter J. Frost
University of British Columbia
David C. Hayes
University of British Columbia
Frank Heller
Tavistock Institute
J. Duane Hoover
Texas Tech University
T. A. Martyn Johns
University of Hong Kong
Jean de Kervasdoue
Ecole Polytechnique, France
John Kimberly
Yale University
Anant R. Negandhi
Kent State University/IIM, Berlin
James Portwood
Temple University
Gordon Redding
University of Hong Kong
Roger M. Troub
Texas Tech University
Carlton J. Whitehead
Texas Tech University
William T. Whitely
University of Kansas
Bernhard Wilpert
International Institute of Management/Padagogische Hochschule, Berlin

COMMENTATORS

B. R. Baliga
University of Wisconsin, Eau Claire
Keith Davis
Arizona State University
George W. England
University of Minnesota/IIM
J. Faison
University of Hawaii
Pjotr Hesseling
Erasmus University
James Miller
Georgia State University
John Miner
Georgia State University
William H. Money
Kent State University
F. Musschoot
Rijksuniversiteit Ghent
Naoto Sasaki
Sophia University, Japan
Wolfgang Staehle
Technical University Darmstadt
Makoto Takamiya
International Institute of Management, Berlin

CONTENTS

Preface v

List of Contributors and Commentators vii-viii

1. Cross-Cultural Studies on Organizational Functioning 1

SECTION I: VALUES, GOALS, AND DECISION MAKING 17

2. A Cross-National Test of England's Model of Manager's Value Systems and their Relationship to Behavior 19
   William Whitely

3. Managerial Decision Making: An International Comparison 49
   F. A. Heller and B. Wilpert

4. Organizational Goals in the Peruvian Co-determination and the Yugoslav Self-determination Systems 73
   J. Duane Hoover, Roger M. Troub, Carlton J. Whitehead and Luis G. Flores

5. Managerial Responses and Organizational Adaptation to Environmental Uncertainty in Denmark and the U. S. 89
   Warren B. Brown and James S. Blandin

6. Paradigm Differences and their Relation to Management, with Reference to South-East Asia 103
   S. G. Redding and T. A. Martyn-Johns

7. Studies on Values, Goals, and Decision-Making: A Critical Evaluation 127
   James Miller, Keith Davis, Wolfgang H. Staehle, Naoto Sasaki, and J. Faison

SECTION II: TECHNOLOGICAL VERSUS CULTURAL IMPERATIVES 137

8. Explaining Cultural Differences in the Perceived Role of Work: An Intranational Cross-Cultural Study 139
   Mary Elizabeth Beres and James D. Portwood

9. National Contexts and Technology as Determinants of Employee's Perceptions 175
   George W. England and Anant R. Negandhi

10. Are Organization Structures Culture-Free? The Case of Hospital Innovation in the U.S. and France 191
Jean de Kervasdoue and John R. Kimberly

11. Technological versus Cultural Imperatives: A Critical Evaluation 211
John B. Miner, Pjotr Hesseling, and William H. Money

SECTION III: INSTITUTIONAL GOALS AND ORGANIZATIONAL FUNCTIONING 223

12. Relations Between Organizational Goals and Structures: A Comparison of German and U.S. Police Organizations 225
Günter Endruweit

13. An Exploration in Two Cultures of a Model of Political Behavior in Organizations 251
Peter J. Frost and David C. Hayes

14. Comparing the Incomparable—Study of Employment Agencies in Five Countries 273
Erhard Blankenburg

15. Institutional Goals and Organizational Functioning: A Critical Evaluation 299
William H. Money, B. R. Baliga, F. Musschoot, and Makoto Takamiya

16. Problems and Prospects 307

INDEX 317

NAME
SUBJECT

Cross-Cultural Studies on Organizational Functioning

This volume presents current cross-cultural organizational studies. In so doing, it attempts to take stock of where we are and where we seem to be going in terms of efforts directed toward understanding organizational functioning through cross-cultural and/or cross-national studies. The empirical content of the studies in the volume speaks for itself. The studies are presented individually along with accompanying discussion. The purpose of this chapter is to raise a series of general issues or questions that seem relevant to what is being done in this area:

1. Why study organizational functioning in different countries and/or cultures?
2. What evidence do the studies suggest about a "convergence hypothesis" of organizational functioning?
3. What substantive and methodological suggestions flow from the reported studies?
4. What theoretical and methodological shortcomings exist in the field as it currently stands?
5. Where do we go from here?

On the following pages we present a brief historical perspective on the field; identifying major variables, issues and range of coverage of the studies presented; and consider the issues raised in the first three questions cited above. The issues involved in questions 4 and 5 and the relevant papers are dealt with in the concluding chapter of the volume.

HISTORICAL PERSPECTIVE[1]

The emerging field of cross-cultural studies on organizational functioning is largely a result of partial integration between the cross-cultural comparative management field and organization theory areas. Although some cross-cultural organization studies were conducted prior to the 1950s, the large-scale projects on industrialization of developing countries at four major universities,

[1] The historical perspectives on cross-cultural studies outlined in the following pages are based on Anant R. Negandhi "Comparative Management and Organization Theory: A marriage Needed," *Academy of Management Journal*, Vol. 18, No. 2, 1975

namely MIT, Chicago, California and Princeton, during the 1950s provided a major impetus to the comparative management area. Scholars from various social disciplines—psychology, sociology, social and cultural anthropology, economics and political sciences—contributed towards these efforts. The differing backgrounds of these scholars are reflected in their conceptualizations and methodologies as well as in their specific findings. The conceptual and methodological approaches utilized by the comparative management theorists can be divided roughly into the following groups: (a) economic development; (b) environmental approach; and (c) the behavioral approach.

Economic Development Orientation

This concern can be traced to the initial large-scale projects undertaken at the four universities noted above in the 1950s. The basic premise was simple: managerial input plays an important role in achieving rapid industrial and economic development in underdeveloped countries. The approach was essentially a macro or aggregate approach and, accordingly, it concentrated on the examination of basic trends of managerial development rather than analysis of specific management practices at the micro or firm level.

This level of concern in cross-cultural management studies leads to a link, theoretically and empirically, with economic development theorists. The area or discipline of economic development itself, if not vague, is too general to be suitable for testing the well-conceptualized hypotheses necessary for building any discipline. As a result, with the economic development thrust, the cross-cultural management field itself did not progress far beyond identifying and noting the importance of managerial input in economic development.

Environmental Approach

Utilizing economic development concern as a main premise, the environmental approach in cross-cultural management studies attempted to highlight the impact of external environmental factors, e.g., socio-economic, political, legal, and cultural, on management practices and effectiveness. It is essentially a macro approach. The work of Farmer and Richman (1965) exemplifies this concern. The underlying hypothesis here is that managerial practices and effectiveness are the functions of external environmental variables and, accordingly, interfirm differences in both practices and effectiveness can be explained on the basis of differences in environmental conditions facing firms in different locations and/or countries.

The classification of environmental variables provided by Farmer and Richman (1965) and others (Schollhammer, 1969) has been useful in drawing attention to the significant external variables affecting the workings of complex organizations. The over-emphasis on environmental factors, however, has led to the belief that individual enterprises are basically passive agents of external environments. This may not be so. A manager is not necessarily a passive agent. Both an organization and a decision maker (manager) interact with environmental stimuli and attempt to mold them in order to achieve desired goals and objectives (Parsons, 1961; Schollhammer, 1969). As Boddewyn has aptly remarked, "A real danger exists . . . of letting environment crowd the comparative analysis. Comparisons are somewhat precariously balanced between management itself and its environment" (1966:12). One therefore needs to take care "not to throw out the management baby with the environment bath or smother it in a blanket of social context" (1966:12).

Conceptually and operationally, the environment approach has not progressed beyond providing arbitrary classifications for separating environmental factors into certain groups, e.g., economic, social and cultural. In other words, various environmental factors have not been operationalized, nor have testable hypotheses emerged from this approach.

The Behavioral Approach

The behavioral approach in cross-cultural management studies attempts to explain behavioral patterns between individuals and groups in organizational settings. Here, basically, authors have concentrated on three different aspects:

1. Understanding the "National Character Profiles" and deducing from this knowledge certain aspects of organizational behavior patterns (Davis, 1971; Narain, 1967).
2. Attitudes and perceptions of managers concerning some key management concepts and activities (Barrett, 1970; H. Barrett, 1969; Haire, 1966; Nath, 1969; Ryterband, 1970; Thiagarajan, 1968).
3. Prevalent beliefs, value systems, and need hierarchies in a given society (Davis, 1971).

The basic assumption here is that attitudes, beliefs, value systems, and need hierarchies are functions of a given culture. Therefore, by establishing relationships between these concepts and managerial practices and effectiveness, one can deduce the impact of cultural variables on management practices and effectiveness.

From the massive data generated during the last decade or so, one can easily be convinced that the attitudes, beliefs, values and need hierarchies are different in different societies. They are even different among different subgroups (ethnic and/or occupational) within a given society. However, the claim regarding the linkage between *culture* and *attitudes*, *attitudes* and *behavior*, and *behavior* and *effectiveness*, raises a variety of conceptual and methodological problems. First, most of these concepts are ill-defined, and their operational measures are poorly conceived. For example, as Ajiferuke and Boddewyn (1970) have stated, "Culture is one of those terms that defy a single all-purpose definition, and there are almost as many meanings of culture as people using the term". It appears that culture, although used as independent variable in most cross-cultural management studies, has a most obscure identity and often is used as a residual variable. Second, if one is interested in understanding and explaining interfirm differences in managerial practices and effectiveness, as is presumed in the comparative management area, there is increasing evidence to support the contention that management practices, behavior and effectiveness are as much, if not more so, functions of such contextual variables as size, technology, location, and market conditions as they are of socio-cultural variables (Ajiferuke and Boddewyn, 1970:26–27).

In summary, an understanding of the impact of socio-cultural variables on management practices and effectiveness should include attention to the relevant developments and findings in the organization theory discipline.

Recent Changes in the Organization Theory Area

The last two decades have brought many fundamental changes in the area of organization theory. These changes have resulted in a proliferation of different approaches (Koontz, 1968) and in shifts in basic orientations for the study of complex organizations (Negandhi, 1973). Although the Weberian model of bureaucracy still dominates the literature on complex organizations, the shift from a descriptive to an analytical level is not only noticeable, but it has become necessary for scholars aspiring to publish in reputable journals. Starting from a mere characterization of the bureaucratic phenomenon, research efforts to study complex organizations have advanced to the point of seeking an explanation for the causes of specific structural arrangements and tracing the consequences of particular structures on behavior patterns and the effectiveness of an organization. The emphasis now is to establish empirically the reasons why different degrees of variations exist in the hierarchial structure of individual organizations and to examine the impact of different structural patterns on behavior and effectiveness.

In addition to the shift from a descriptive to an analytical level, the perspective for studying complex organizations has changed. Organizational studies undertaken during the last decade were concentrated primarily on examining the impact of such internal variables as size, technology, work-flow, leadership style, managerial strategies and location on organizational structures, behavior patterns and effectiveness. This so-called closed systems approach can easily be discerned in the studies by Indik (1963), Caplow (1957), Woodward (1965, 1970), Harvey (1968), Perrow (1967, 1969) Hickson and his colleagues (1969), and the Ohio State University and University of Michigan studies on leadership (Stogdill, 1965 and Likert, 1967).

Briefly, scholars utilizing the closed-systems approach conceive the units of their specific studies as independent of external environmental influences. As Emery and Trist (1969) have stated, "Thinking in terms of a closed system . . . allows most of its problems to be analyzed without reference to its external environment." In contrast, an open-systems approach, by its very name, requires consideration of the influence of the external environment of an organization on the internal properties of the organization (Dill, 1958; Emery, 1965; Emery, 1969; Miller, 1955; Negandhi, 1973 and 1974; Thompson, 1967; Thompson, 1958; Thorelli, 1967 and Von Bertalanffy, 1950). In order to understand the open-systems perspective, one needs, to examine the overall systems and general systems concepts and the usefulness of these concepts in studying complex organizations. A system has been defined as "a regularly interacting or interdependent group of items forming a unified whole" which "is in or tends to be in equilibrium." Alternately, it is defined as "a set of objects together with relationships between the objects and between their attributes" (Webster's Dictionary, 1967). The interlinking of various parts of subsystems within a given system seem to be the main differentiating attributes of a system. These attributes thus force one to think in terms of a *multiple causation*, rather than in terms of single causes.

The general systems approach, conceived at a still higher level of abstraction, visualizes the study of all living organisms within this singular framework in order to test hypotheses at cross-levels of living systems, which include the cell, organ, organism, group, organization, society, and the supernational system (Miller, 1955). The key attributes of general systems are: subsystems or different components in a given system: holism, open systems, input-transformation-output phenomenon, system boundaries, negative entropy, steady state, dynamic equilibrium, feedback mechanism, cybernetics, hierarchy, internal elaboration, multiple goal-seeking, and equifinality (Kast, 1972).

It is indeed challenging to utilize such abstract attributes in understanding the functioning of complex organizations. However, the present state of knowledge, as well as the understanding of these concepts, is so minimal that the utilization of them has created considerable confusion among scholars of different disciplines. Until such time as these general systems concepts are fully developed and operationalized, the so-called mid-range approach, contingency theory, seems to provide a realistic means of utilizing some of the salient attributes of the systems' concept for the study of complex organizations. As Kast and Rosenzweig have stated:

> The general tenor of the contingency view is somewhere between simplistic, specific principles and complex, vague notions. It is a mid-range concept which recognizes the complexity involved in managing modern organizations but uses patterns of relationships and/or configurations of subsystems in order to facilitate improved practice. The art of management depends on a reasonable success rate for actions in a probabilistic environment. Our hope is that systems' concepts and contingency views, while continually being refined by scientists/researchers/theorists, will also be made more applicable (1972:28).

By utilizing the contingency perspective, scholars such as Lawrence and Lorsch (1969), Burns and Stalker (1961), and Woodward (1965, 1970), have made considerable contributions to our understanding of the structuring and functioning of complex organizations. It is this very perspective in organization theory which may well provide a bridge for anchoring the cross-cultural management area within the overall organization theory discipline. To facilitate such an integration, however, the contingency theory perspective needs broadening and enlarging by including consideration of socio-cultural factors. The papers presented in this volume reflect this so-called mid-range or contingency approach.

BRIEF REVIEW OF PAPERS

The papers presented attest to the diversity and range of efforts directed toward understanding organizational functioning through cross-cultural and/or cross-national studies. Authors in this volume come from ten different countries, while the studies reported cover samples of individuals or institutions from twenty-three countries. Nearly 20,000 respondents are represented in the studies including individuals from all levels of management, supervisors, skilled workers, semi-skilled workers, unskilled workers, police officers, and administrators, academic administrators and faculty, government workers at professional levels, health-care personnel and a national probability sample of employed individuals. A wide range of the industrial sector is covered including private industry, cooperatives and governmental units. The studies deal with 36 major variables or variable complexes which can be roughly categorized into environmental variables, organizational variables and variables dealing with behavior, attitudes and perceptions as shown in Table 1.

Table 1

VARIABLES

Environmental Variables

- Ecological environment
- Demographic environment
- Historical environment
- Personal environment
- Environmental uncertainty
- Social structure
- Country or culture as a variable

Organizational Variables

- Job performance requirements
- Organizational skill levels
- Management functions
- Organizational goals
- Organizational structure variables
- Organizational differentiation
- Organizational integration methods
- Organizational centralization–decentralization
- Organizational democracy
- Degree of legalism
- Organizational networks
- Organizational instruction
- Management practices

Behavior, Attitudes, and Perceptions

- Decision-making
- Administrative behavior
- Discretionary behavior
- Political behavior
- Information search behavior
- Management attitudes
- Job attitudes and Job satisfaction
- Personal values
- Personal value systems
- Personal value orientations
- Work values
- Cognitive patterns
- Workers perceptions about public issues
- Workers perceptions about importance of job characteristics
- Workers perceptions about employee participation in decision-making
- Workers perceptions about factors in promotion opportunities

A thumb-nail sketch of the countries covered, groups studied, and major variables considered by each paper is shown in Table 2.

Table 2

SUMMARY OF STUDIES

Study	*Countries*	*Groups Studied*	*Major Variables*
Whitely	India Australia	Managers (N=768)	Personal values, value systems, value orientations and choice behavior.
Heller and Wilpert	France Germany Israel Netherlands Spain Sweden United Kingdom United States	Managers (N=1500)	Decision-making, centralization, job performance requirements, and skill acquisition time.
Brown and Blandin	Denmark United States	Managers (N=118)	Managerial perceptions of environmental uncertainty as influencing information search behavior, degree of organizational differentiation and use of a variety of integration methods.
Hoover, Troub, and Whitehead	Peru Yugoslavia	Chief Executive Officers (N=67)	Perceptions of goal hierarchies (stability and change) as a result of power equalization efforts.
Redding and Martyn-Johns	Hong Kong Indonesia Japan Malaysia Philippines Singapore Thailand Vietnam	Managers (N=800)	Paradigm differences and hypothesized differences in management functions.
Beres and Portwood	United States	Blacks and Whites from a national sample (N=6835)	Work values as influenced by ecological, demographic, environment, past environment, personal environment, and social structure.

Table 2 (*Contd.*)

Study	*Countries*	*Group Studied*	*Major Variables*
England and Negandhi	India United States	Supervisors and rank and file (N = 535)	Compares inter-country differences with intracountry differences on worker perceptions about public issues, importance of job characteristics, employee participation in decision making, factors in promotional opportunities and levels of worker satisfaction.
Endruweit	Germany United States	Police Officers (N = 6200)	Differences in 15 structural variables between the two countries.
Kervasdoue and Kimberley	France United States	Hospitals (N = 1100)	Compares the relationship between organization structure variables and innovation adopted in the two countries.
Blankenburg	France Germany Italy Sweden England	Individuals and institutions concerned with labor market policy	Comparison of employment agencies around three comparison criteria: decentralization—centralization; degree of legalism; organizational networks.
Frost and Hayes	Australia Canada	Two institutes of technology. Academic administrators, faculty and service personnel (N = 20)	Conceptual basis and pilot-study of forms of behavior within organizations (administrative behavior, discretionary behavior, political behavior)

While there is great diversity in the studies reported, one is still able to view them in terms of a series of major issues or questions that are generally relevant to cross-cultural research in organizational functioning. It is to this task we now turn.

1. Why study organizational functioning in different countries and/or cultures?

The papers identify four major answers to this question. First is the notion of developing generalizations or universals that apply everywhere. This might be stated as follows: the science of organizations seeks to establish propositions that apply universally across time and space. Systematic cross-national and cross-cultural studies are very much needed in order to build the science of organizations. Whitehall's comments on this issue are worth noting:

> It seems to me that country and culture as prior conditioning variables, may influence significantly individuals who, though able to give unanimous support to a proposition at a sufficient level of abstraction, nevertheless are

> seeing, feeling, and responding to quite different stimuli. I do not question the usefulness of the universal proposition, but only wonder about the commonality of meaning to people with quite different cultural conditioning. The point I am attempting to make is that industrial, or organizational, determinism, while it may lead to certain universal relationships at a sufficient level of abstraction, may be both the outcome *and* forerunner of perceptions and events which carry a heavy load of cultural determinism. A knowledge of these country-specific perceptions and events is essential if we are to understand, and work within, a culture quite different from our own.[2]

A second major reason for studying organizational functioning in different countries and/or cultures is identified as determining if general cultural or national distinctions found in the literature lead to observed differences in organizational functioning. While many of the papers share to some extent this rationale, it seems most central to the work reported by Redding and Martyn-Johns and expressed as follows:

> It is proposed to deal with what seems a fundamental issue in comparative management and one which is rarely examined. It is summed up in the commonest of the phrases used by the western practicing manager dealing with his Asian equivalents . . . 'They think differently.' What I want to examine are the ways in which they think differently, and the possible effects on managerial behavior and organization . . . . we proceed to examine what might otherwise be termed cognitive structures or ways of thinking and look at their effects on managerial behavior. The aim is to indicate cross-cultural differences in ways of seeing reality and the inevitable differences in behavior which result.

A variant of this rationale is the reverse procedure of determining if observed differences in organizational functioning are supported by general or national distinctions found in the literature.

A third rationale for studying organizational functioning cross-nationally or cross-culturally is to identify differences that are large enough and potentially meaningful enough to warrant additional work. This reason is central to the England and Negandhi paper which states:

> We are interested in examining, then, only relatively large differences in employee perceptions where there is reference group support for the assertion that this appears to be an area of significant country difference. It is only these differences that merit the painstaking effort required to show that they are 'culturally or environmentally determined' differences and to trace these elements of culture and/or environment that seem to produce them.

Such a procedure is clearly only the first step in a sequential process.

The fourth reason suggested for studying organizational functioning cross-nationally or cross-culturally is to identify practices, techniques or relationships that can be "transported from one country to another or from one culture to another."

[2] Unpublished manuscript, College of Business Administration, University of Hawaii, 1977.

> In attempting to draw policy conclusions from two economies such as Britain and Germany, a critical issue is the extent to which a management approach which appears to be successful in one society can be expected to take root and flourish if transplanted to the other society. Is our conception one of structural contingency by which we believe that it is possible to find a recipe for success which suits a given stage of economic development regardless of the social setting? Or is our view that the mode of formulating and implementing industrial policies necessarily derives from and, to be acceptable, must conform with the cultural expectations to each society?

2. What evidence do the studies suggest about the "convergence hypothesis" of organizational functioning?

While different study purposes, variables employed, samples and methodological procedures make it difficult to answer this question with any degree of precision, we interpret the studies in toto as severely questioning the convergence hypothesis. Only two studies (Frost and Hayes, and England and Negandhi) seem to indicate that country makes little difference in the variables studied. The remaining ten studies generally find that country and/or culture does make a significant difference in many of the variables studied. Perhaps the situation was best summarized by Professor Davis:

> There are so many variables, and management situations are so fluid that what we have is a condition of *equifinality* in which there are many different combinations of decision making and management practice that will lead to optimum results for an organization. This condition of equifinality appears to be the situation with comparative management at the present time. We can identify a multitude of variables, and we can relate them in combinations with some predictive probability; however there is no one best way. A number of different combinations appear to have approximately equal success, as in different practices in Japan, Germany, and the United States. Perhaps an appropriate academic term for this concept is the *equifinal model of comparative* management. It clearly implies that there is no one best way to managerial effectiveness.

3. What substantive and methodological suggestions flow from the reported studies for researchers interested in cross-cultural organizational functioning?

Models of culture: Two models of culture and how they affect behavior are presented. Beres and Portwood define culture as follows: "Culture is a cognitive frame of reference and a pattern of behavior transmitted to members of a group from previous generations of the group." Through this definition it is suggested that the cultural process involves several dimensions of behavior.

(a) A psychological dimension in the learning and use of a mindset;
(b) A social dimension in the interactions among group members; and
(c) An historical dimension in the transmission of mindsets and practices across generations of a group.

The authors are clearly drawing on the disciplines and theoretical formulations of anthropology, psychology and sociology in articulating and developing their model of culture.

Redding and Martyn-Johns place cognitive systems or paradigms at a central point in their view of the cultural process.

> Three mental states are envisaged between the impinging of information on the person and the eventual motivation to behave. Firstly, the process of perception which acts via selectivity, interpretation and closure to take information and transmit it in an amplified, distorted, filtered or relatively 'pure' form. This information is then worked on in the stage 2 cognitive processes of imagination, thinking, reasoning and decision-making, and is then processed into a way of seeing reality. This latter stage is seen as a set of cognitive systems, or paradigms, which are relatively stable over time. They are the 'maps by which we steer', the systems of both belief and understanding, whether articulated or subconscious, which become the main guides to behavior.

In several respects, these two models are similar, and both clearly illustrate the tremendous complexity of research that tries to directly estimate the influence of culture.

Qualifications about cultural explanations: Two studies clearly point out the need for controlling or taking account of ecological/demographic and social/organizational variables before attributing differences to the variable culture. As Beres and Portwood indicate:

> . . . the proposed model identifies culture as having a direct influence on the cognitive frame of reference and patterns of behavior of individuals. Through this influence, it affects individual's actions, and in an interactive process, the structure and effectiveness of organizations. The process is complex, in that culture's influence is mingled with the effects of the contemporary ecological and social environment.

The last sentence suggests that one must disentangle the contributions due to cultural factors and those due to contemporary ecological and social environment factors.

England and Negandhi make the same point by arguing:

> . . . let's not get excited about observed national differences unless they are rather large in magnitude in an *absolute sense* and in a *relative sense* when compared to observed within country differences. It is only when national differences are large in both an absolute and a relative sense that it seems worthwhile to pursue the very difficult issues surrounding the reasons (cultural and others) why such differences exist and what the consequences of such differences are.

Thus, what appear as cultural differences on the surface may well be a function of multiple causation. The moral is simple and could be phrased as: all that appears cultural may, in fact, also be due to other causes.

Management practices and culture: German and British management practices differ in ways consistent with general cultural distinctions between the two countries (issue of the relationship of the individual to the collectivity). Management practices workable in Germany could not be easily transferred to Britain. Exceptions to this pattern of transfer difficulty are management practices dealing with a "marketing orientation" and expectation that "reward is linked to performance" (Child and Kieser).

Where culture is most likely to have an impact: The closer one focuses onto actual behavior and practice, the more one is likely to find cultural effects. In other words, the cultural factor will have most bearing upon modes of interpersonal relationships and individual conduct (Child and Kieser).

Sub-cultural differences within a country: Wide intranational variations in one aspect of work meaning are present in the United States, and some of these variations may well have their origins in the earlier cultures of Africa and Europe (Beres and Portwood).

National differences in decision-making patterns: National differences account for 10–15 per cent of the variance in decision-making patterns while sector differences (dominant technology) account for 5–10 per cent of the variance. United Kingdom, Israeli, German and United States managers have the most centralized regimes of decision-making, while Swedish and French managers employ decentralized models of decision-making. Service companies and electronic companies with highly developed technologies tend to make decisions in a generally decentralized fashion, while continuous flow technology companies appear on the side of higher decentralization. Data does not support

(1) the cultural cluster thesis of Haire, Ghiseli, and Porter (1966);
(2) German—Anglo Saxon difference expectations; or
(3) the managerial-gap thesis of Servan-Schreiber (1968).

Skill emerges as a major factor in all countries in explaining variations of centralized or participative decision-making between dyads of boss-subordinates. In general, it can be said that when skills are low or seen to be low, centralized decision-making is preferred to participation (Heller and Wilpert).

Organizational goals and organizational structure: There is a clear and continuing challenge to structural theory in organizational functioning. Organizational structure does not follow directly from organizational goals, but comes as well from socio-cultural factors operating as intervening variables (Enderweit).

Managerial values and managerial choice behavior: There is moderate relationship between personal value systems and choice behavior of managers. Value orientation differences moderate the relationship between value systems and choice behavior. There are differences in the subsystems of values of a particular group of managers (by country and by orientation) as related to choice behavior (Whitely).

Level of analysis: It may be that we are moving to a stage of development in modern industrial society where to focus on management practice as opposed to government policy is to examine the wrong level in accounting for comparative industrial performance (Child and Kieser).

With this brief introduction to the volume, the studies themselves are reported along with accompanying discussion. The reader is reminded that the final summary chapter will consider two important questions:

(1) What theoretical and methodological shortcomings exist in the field as it stands today?
(2) Where do we go from here?

Whether one views the present status of the field of comparative organization studies positively or negatively, it does seem clear that we have two major choices before us. We can continue along the present lines by conducting largely eclectic studies that may have very different theoretical, methodological, domain, and intent basis, and hope that individually and collectively they are sufficient and sufficiently additive to make a science of organizations. There are many virtues and many proponents of such an approach. Conversely, a sufficient number of scholars and researchers could decide that the field is essentially floundering and needs integrative model building and conceptualizing before research can become meaningful and additive. This would imply that many of our best minds should focus on the search for and development of such integrative models which would hopefully move us to another level of research. This notion also has many virtues and some proponents.[3] The extent to which these proponents can and will do the job is certainly problematical. Nevertheless, the alternatives are clearly before us.

[3] See Negandhi, 1975 and Roberts, 1970.

REFERENCES

Ajiferuke, M., and Boddewyn, J. "Culture and Other Explanatory Variables in 1970 Comparative Management Studies." *Academy of Management Journal*. 13: 153–163.

Barrett, G. V., and Bass, B. M. "Comparative Surveys of Managerial Attitudes and 1970 Behavior," in Boddewyn J. (Ed.), *Comparative Management: Teaching, Research, and Training*. New York: Graduate School of Business Administration, pp. 179–207.

Barrett, G. V., and Ryterband, E. C. "Cross-Cultural Comparisons of Corporate 1968 Objectives on Exercise Objectives" (Paper presented at the 66th Annual Convention, American Psychological Association, San Francisco, September).

Barrett, G. V., and Ryterband, E. C. "Life Goals of United States and European 1969 Managers," *Proceedings, XVI International Congress of Applied Psychology*. Amsterdam: Swets and Zeitlinger, pp. 413–418.

Boddewyn, Jean. "Comparative Concepts in Management Administration and 1966 Organization," *Memo* (New York: Graduate School of Business Administration), 12.

Burns, T., and Stalker, G. M. *The Management of Innovation* (London: Tavistock). 1961

Caplow, Theodore. "Organizational Size," *Administrative Science Quarterly*. 1: 1957 484–505.

Davis, Stanley M. *Comparative Management: Cultural and Organizational Perspectives*. 1971 Englewood Cliffs: Prentice-Hall.

Dill, William R. "Environment as an Influence on Managerial Autonomy," *Administrative* 1958 *Science Quarterly*. 2: 409–443.

Emery, F. E., and Trist, E. L. "The Causal Texture of Organizational Environments," 1965 *Human Relations*. 18: 21–32.

Emery, F. E., and Trist, E. L. "Socio-Technical Systems," *Systems Thinking*. 1969 Harmondsworth, England: Penguin Books, 281.

Farmer, R. N., and Barry M. Richman, *Comparative Management and Economic* 1965 *Progress*. Homewood, Ill: Irwin.

Haire, M., Ghiselli, D. E. and Porter, L. W. *Managerial Thinking: An International Study*. 1966 New York: Wiley.

Harvey, Edward, "Technology and the Structure of Organizations," *American* 1968 *Sociological Review*. 33: 247–259.

Hickson, D., Pugh, D. S. and Pheysey, D. C. "Operations Technology and Organization 1969 Structure: An Empirical Reappraisal." *Administrative Science Quarterly*. 14: No. 3, 378–397.

Indik, Bernard P. "Some Effects of Organization Size on Member Attitudes and 1963 Behavior," *Human Relations*. 16: 369–384.

Kast, Fremont E., and James E. Rosenzweig. "General Systems Theory: Applications for 1972 Organization and Management," *Academy of Management Journal*. 15: No. 4, 463.

Koontz, H., and O'Donnell, C. *Principles of Management*. New York: McGraw-Hill. 1968

Lawrence, Paul R., and Jay W. Lorsch. *Organization and Environment*. Homewood, 1969 Ill: Irwin.

Likert, Rensis. *The Human Organization: Its Management and Value*. New York: 1967 McGraw-Hill.

Miller, J. G. "Toward a General Theory for the Behavioral Sciences," *American*
1955 *Psychologist*. 10: 513–551.

Narain, Dhirendra. *Annals*, March, 124–132.
1967

Nath, R. "A Methodological Review of Cross-Cultural Management Research," in J.
1969 Boddewyn (Ed.), *Comparative Management and Marketing*. Glenview. Ill: Scott, Foresman, pp. 195–222.

Negandhi, Anant R. *Management and Economic Development: The Case of Taiwan*. The
1973 Hague: Martinus Nijhoff.

Negandhi, Anant R. (Ed.) *Modern Organizational Theory*. Kent, Ohio: Kent State
1973 University Press, pp. 102–131.

Negandhi, Anant R. *Organization Theory in an Open System Perspective*. New York: The
1974 Dunellen Co., Inc.

Negandhi, Anant R., and Reimann, B. C. "Correlates of Decentralization: Closed- and
1973 Open-Systems Perspectives," *Academy of Management Journal*. 16: No. 4, 570–582.

Parsons, Talcott, et al. *Theories of Society*. New York: Free Press, 38–41.
1961

Perrow, Charles: "A Framework for the Comparative Analysis of Organization,"
1967 *American Sociological Review*. 32: 192–208.

Ryterband, E. C., and Barrett, G. V. "Managers' Values and Their Relationship to the
1970 Management of Tasks: A Cross-Cultural Comparison," in B. M. Bass, Cooper R. C. and Hass, J. A. (Eds.), *Managing for Accomplishment*. Lexington, Mass.: Heath Lexington.

Schollhammer, Hans. "Comparative Management Theory Jungle," *Academy of*
1969 *Management Journal*. 12: 81–97.

Servan-Schreiber J. J., The American Challenge. New York: Athenoum House, Inc
1968

Stogdill, Ralph M. *Managers, Employees, Organizations*. Columbus, Ohio.: The Ohio
1965 State University Bureau of Business Research.

Thiagarajan, K. M. *A Cross-Cultural Study of the Relationships Between Personal Values*
1968 *and Managerial Behavior*. Technical Report 23, NONR NOOO 14–67A, Rochester, N. Y.: University of Rochester, Management Research Center.

Thompson, James D. *Organizations in Action*. New York: McGraw-Hill.
1967

Thompson, J. D., and McEwen, W. J. "Organizational Goals and Environment: Goal-
1958 Setting as an Interaction Process," *American Sociological Review*. 13: No. 1, 23–31.

Thorelli, Hans B. "Organizational Theory: An Ecological View," *Proceedings of the*
1967 *Academy of Management*. pp. 66–84.

Von Bertalanffy, L. "The Theory of Open Systems in Physics and Biology," *Science*.
1950 3: 23–29.

Webster's Seventh New Collegiate Dictionary. Springfield, Mass.: Merriam, p. 895.
1967

Woodward, Joan. *Industrial Organization: Theory and Practice*. London: Oxford
1965 University Press.

Woodward, Joan. "Technology, Managerial Control, and Organizational Behavior," in
1970 Negandhi, A. R. et al. (Eds.), *Organizational Behavior Models*. Kent, Ohio.: Bureau of Economic and Business Research, Kent State University.

Section I

VALUES, GOALS, AND DECISION MAKING

A Cross-National Test of England's Model of Manager's Value Systems and Their Relationship to Behavior

WILLIAM WHITELY
University of Kansas

England's Model of Values, Decision Behavior, and Moderator Variable Categories

England's model (1968) has stimulated a great deal of the comparative research on manager's personal values and the correlates of values in recent years which he recently summarized (England, 1976). The intent of the present study is to provide a test of certain properties and relationships specified in this model and in doing so provide a comparative test. This model, presented in Figure 1, includes personal value systems as an important source of influence on decision behavior, but includes several other classes of variables which moderate or mediate this relationship. There are two major classes of values, non-relevant or weak values and conceived values, within the universe of values or potential value space for an individual or a specific group. The distinction between these classes of values is in terms of their likely impact on behavior. Non-relevant or weak values are unlikely to influence behavior and three overlapping categories of conceived values are more likely to have an impact, but vary in their impact. Operative values are likely to have the most significant influence on behavior. Intended values are likely to have a moderate relationship to behavior. Adopted values affect behavior only because of situational factors. Situational characteristics are hypothesized to have a major effect on intended and adopted values and their relationship to behavior. These characteristics dampen the relationship for intended values and enhance the relationship for adopted values.

Value systems influence behavior in two major ways; through behavioral channeling and perceptual screening. Behavioral channeling represents a more direct influence of value systems on behavior than perceptual screening. That is, alternative generation and testing and decision making or choice are more direct and information processing more diffused examples of the influence of value

Figure 1

THEORETICAL MODEL OF THE RELATIONSHIP OF VALUES TO BEHAVIOR

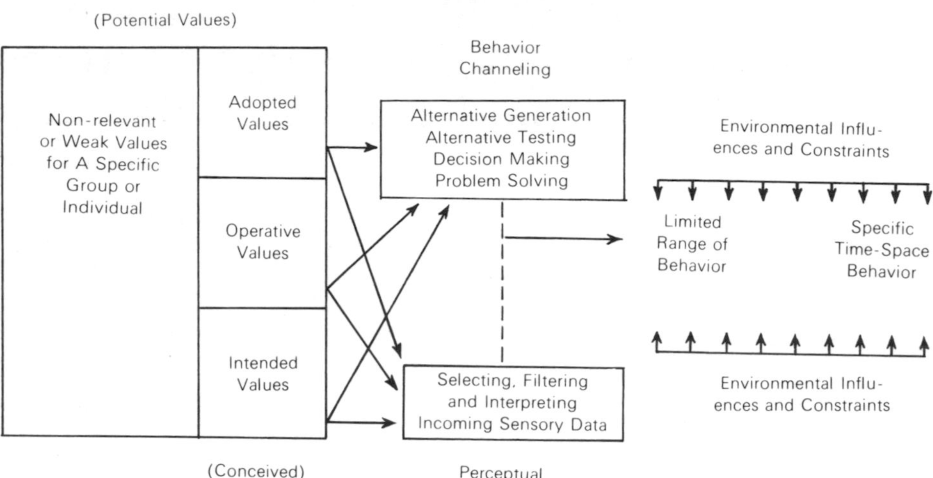

systems on behavior. The arrows in Figure 1 indicate that value systems have multiple effects on several of the sub-processes identified as components of decision making.

The environmental context incorporated in the model summarizes important sources of influence on the relationship between value systems and behavior. As the model indicates, environmental conditions influence and constrain the behavioral expression of value systems. Thus value systems are not the whole study and phenomena like the j-shaped curve in compliance research may eliminate any relationship between value systems and behavior. The story to date does indicate, however, significant relationships between managers' values and choice behavior, decision process variables, success, and perceptions of work unit effectiveness (England, 1976).

The inclusion of the term "specific time-space behavior" is an acknowledgment of mediators of relationships, such as the value issues in the problem and choices, posed for the manager. Problems, in other words, include situationally specific values such as priorities among their properties. A consequence of the issues posed is that different subsystems of the entire personal value system are likely to relate to the selection of choices due to the differences in the value issues posed in the particular alternatives or problems.

Considerations in the Present Test of England's Model

England's (1976) recent monograph summarizes much of the research where the unit of analysis was individual values. A second unit of analysis suggested by his model as the independent variable is systems of values. Cross-national comparisons of managers' value systems have previously used value systems as a unit of analysis. Value systems incorporate additional properties such as value integration absent from individual values. The integration of values into systems and subsystems indicates, as one example, the influence of socialization and social learning (Bem, 1970). To use values as the unit of analysis implies that no such integration occurs. By using value systems as the unit of analysis it is easier to develop conceptual linkages between England's research and the models and research of others (Locke, 1976). March and Simon (1959) identify the cognitive limitations of man as being one of man's limitations as a decision maker. A more parsimonious value structure seems to be sympathetic to this limitation. Finally, Mintzberg (1973) suggests that managers have simplified models of the world. Value systems provide a potential grain of sand around which managers' simple models of the world crystallize.

Cluster analysis has been the method for testing the value-behavior relationship in previous studies with managers. The result is that these studies have identified homogeneous subgroups of managers, based on their values or behavior, but have not identified the subsystems of values relating to behavior or the magnitude of relationship between values and behavior. These are both important questions that England's model and the present study seek to address.

Finally, no tests of the value systems-behavior relationship have been made which extend this central hypothesis to cover populations of managers, other than the United States managers. The present study seeks to provide an initial bridge across this void.

The Present Test of England's Model among Australian and Indian Managers

The purpose of the present study is to offer a comparative test of the relationship between managers' value systems and their choices, determine the magnitude of the relationship, and identify the subsystems of values accounting for the relationship. Further, this study seeks to identify differences in these relationships for managers from two different countries and two different value orientations. Value orientation is discussed below and operationality defined in the methods section.

The independent variable, personal value systems of managers, includes the entire domain of potential values identified by England and operationalized in his measure discussed subsequently, and the interrelatedness of these values. This is a broader definition than that in prior correlational studies where only a subset of values in the potential value space was used in assessing relationships with success or perceptions of work unit effectiveness. The inclusion of all values in the potential value space in value systems and the correlation of these values systems with behavior, broadens the test of this relationship which is the central hypothesis deducible from England's model.

The dependent variable in the present study is choice behavior. Choice behavior is one element of the process of decision making (March and Simon, 1958; Mintzberg *et al.*, 1976) and is what England refers to as "decision making" in his model.

Value orientation and country differences are viewed as moderators of the value system-choice behavior relationship in the present study. England

(1968:55), like others (Brogden, 1952), identifies pragmatism and moralism as two widely held value orientations. The meaning assigned to stimuli is the basis for distinguishing pragmatism and moralism. Pragmatic managers tend to assign an instrumental meaning to stimuli. Moralist managers tend to assign an ethical meaning to stimuli. England, like Weick (1969) and Silverman (1970), view the knowledge of the assignment of meanings to stimuli as crucial since different meanings are likely to lead to differentiation in behavior. Hence, value orientation is a moderator variable and the resulting expectation is to find differential relationships between value systems and behavior for the two groups of managers within each country.

Values, like attitudes, are generally thought to consist of affective, cognitive, and connotive properties. As indicated above, a particular combination of the affective and cognitive properties, discussed in the methods section, determines the value orientation. Classification of managers into one or the other of these value orientations does not preclude considerable variation between managers within value orientations as to the particular values that are in operative, intended, adopted, or weak categories. The classification of managers as pragmatists or moralists seems justified on two counts. First, in a theoretical sense, as indicated above, the assignment of different meanings to stimuli can relate to differentiated behavior. In addition, value systems can vary greatly despite the value orientation. Value systems are a relatively permanent framework which shapes an individual's perceptions and behavior. These systems are similar to an ideology or philosophy. Value orientations help in identifying the values which are likely to influence behavior the most. The value systems and value orientations of managers account for separate portions of variance in the relationship to behavior. Second, evidence indicates that there is no relationship between situational variables such as span of control, level of management, and functional area and value systems for moralist managers but there is for pragmatist managers (Whitely, 1977); there is a difference in the magnitude of the relationship between value systems and decision making for the two groups (Whitely, 1977); and pragmatic managers are more successful than moralist managers (England and Lee, 1974). These differences occur regardless of the country in which comparisons are made.

Country differences are an instance of environmental influences that moderate value systems-choice relationships. Kluckhohn and Strodtbeck (1961) have identified culture as a major source of influence on the development of value systems. If country, acting as a proxy for cultural considerations, does influence value systems, then, in England's model, structural properties of these systems should differ. If the structure of the value systems differ then their interrelationships with choices can potentially differ. Two structural properties tested in the present study are the interrelatedness of values and the subsystems identified. The effect of these differences would be on the channeling of behavior and would show up in the form of differences in the magnitude of observed multivariate relationships between value systems and choices. England and Lee (1974) did find a stronger relationship between values and success among Australian managers than among Indian managers, an outcome also expected in the present study.

There is some evidence indicating that certain aspects of the two countries, in addition to structural differences in value systems, provide reasons for expecting differences in the magnitude of value systems-behavior relationships. The managerial systems in Australia and India are different in the sense that ownership is more widely diffused in Australia than in India (Wheelright, 1957; Chattopadhyay, 1973). Tandon (1973) sought to tie ownership arrangements to social system characteristics in India suggesting that parochialism· and nepotism accompany these arrangements. These practices of parochialism and nepotism often constrain decision making and personnel practices. If social system and ownership characteristics constrain decision making in India, then individual differences will not relate to Indian managers' decisions as strongly as they would among Australia managers where these constraints are removed. This is consistent with England's model which indicates that environmental constraints reduce the relationship between value systems and behavior.

By way of summary the present study tests the following hypotheses:

Hypothesis One: There is a relationship between value systems and choices of managers.

Hypothesis Two: Value orientation differences moderate the relationship between value systems and choices.

Hypothesis Three: There are differences in the subsystems of values of a particular group of managers related to their choices on different problems.

Hypothesis Four: The magnitude of the relationship between value systems and behavior will be greater for managers from Australia than for managers from India.

METHOD

Sample Design

Stratified random samples of managers were drawn using national directories of managers in private industry in both Australia and India. Stratification was on the basis of size of firm, level of management, and function. The percentage of usable returns was 30 per cent in Australia and 72 per cent in India. The differences in return rate reflect different data collection procedures. Mailed surveys were used in Australia and interviews were used in India. Both samples were well distributed on several demographic and organizational variables as Table 1–3 indicate. The sample statistics for Australian managers are similar to those found by Clark and McCabe (1970) with a sample of Australian managers five times the size of the present one. The final samples include 282 Australian managers (141 pragmatists and 141 moralists) and 486 Indian managers (211 pragmatists and 275 moralists).

The effect of these different data gathering procedures on the differences in the data obtained needs to be addressed. Demand characteristics (Orne, 1969) may differ between the two methods and influence the resulting data. In the present study this is most likely to influence the values data rather than most of the demographic, work history, or organizational data. The effect of demand characteristics would, therefore, be of greatest concern in comparisons between countries such as those needed in the fourth hypothesis. The present study did not explicitly attempt to measure demand characteristics. The procedure used instead was to compare the value systems of managers to the results of other studies using alternative methodologies. These comparisons were limited to Indian managers since demand characteristics are likely to be greater with this method than with the interview method (Rosenthal, 1966). The values data in the present study closely approximate the values data collected by Thiagarajan (1968) on an independent sample of Indian managers using a survey procedure and the same questionnaire. This is at least some evidence indicating that demand characteristics were not playing a major role in the present study. In addition, comparisons of the data on Indian managers in the present study with the attitude data gathered by Haire, Ghiselli, and Porter (1966) using a survey method yield consistent results. While these comparisons are not conclusive since the samples or the measures are not the same, they do lend some confidence to the results of the present study.

Measurement of Values and Choices

Values were measured using England's (1968) personal values questionnaire (PVQ). This instrument measures the cognitive and affective properties of the values of managers to 66 concepts classified into five categories: goals of business organizations, personal goals of individuals, groups of people, ideas associated with people, and ideas about general topics. The cognitive property

Table 1

DEMOGRAPHIC CHARACTERISTICS DESCRIPTIVE STATISTICS

Age	*Australia Pragmatists* %	*Australia Moralists* %	*India Pragmatists* %	*India Moralists* %
20–29	3.5	2.8	6.2	4.4
30–34	9.2	7.1	16.6	11.6
35–39	13.5	11.3	20.4	21.5
40–44	21.3	17.0	27.5	20.7
45–49	20.6	16.3	12.8	15.6
50–54	12.8	19.1	8.1	12.4
55–59	12.8	13.5	5.7	8.7
60 and Over	6.4	12.8	2.4	5.1
No Information	0.0	0.0	0.5	0.0

Education	*Australian Pragmatists* %	*Australian Moralists* %	*Indian Pragmatists* %	*Indian Moralists* %
Some High School	7.8	8.5	0.9	1.8
High School Diploma	14.2	14.2	4.3	7.6
Some College	24.8	38.3	9.5	12.7
Bachelors Degree	36.2	30.5	41.7	32.0
Some Postgraduate	10.6	6.4	15.6	15.6
Postgraduate Degree	5.0	1.4	0.0	0.0
No Information	1.4	0.7	0.0	0.0

Table 1 (*Contd.*)

Annual Income	*Australian Pragmatists* %	*Australian Moralists* %	*Indian Pragmatists* %	*Indian Moralists* %
Under $6,000	4.3	11.3	6.6	10.5
$ 6,000–$ 7,999	11.3	17.0	40.8	42.2
$ 8,000–$ 9,999	21.3	17.7	28.0	22.9
$10,000–$11,999	14.2	17.0	10.9	10.5
$12,000–$14,999	14.9	12.8	5.7	5.1
$15,000–$19,999	22.0	12.8	4.3	2.9
$20,000–$24,999	3.5	5.7	0.9	1.5
$25,000–$34,999	2.8	3.5	0.9	1.8
$35,000–$49,999	2.8	1.4	0.0	0.4
$50,000 and above	2.8	0.7	1.9	2.2

College Major	*Australian Pragmatists* %	*Australian Moralists* %	*Indian Pragmatists* %	*Indian Moralists* %
Did not Attend College	38.3	48.3	4.7	37.6
Humanities	2.8	2.1	7.1	8.4
Fine Arts	1.4	14.9	1.9	5.1
Engineering	10.6	12.8	20.9	13.5
Business Administration	21.3	12.8	11.8	6.5
Physical Sciences	7.1	5.7	9.0	14.9
Social Sciences	13.5	1.4	11.4	13.1
Law	—	—	1.9	1.8
Accounting	—	—	3.8	3.3
Engineering and Business Administration	—	—	3.8	2.5
Other Combinations of Majors	5.0	2.1	23.2	27.5
No Information	13.5	14.9	0.5	0.7

Father's Occupation	*Australian Pragmatists* %	*Australian Moralists* %	*Indian Pragmatists* %	*Indian Moralists* %
Government Service	17.7	18.4	28.0	34.2
Business-Trade	32.6	29.1	36.5	26.2
Business Executive	17.0	14.9	8.5	8.0
Teaching	1.4	2.8	2.4	5.5
Professional	9.9	10.6	18.0	14.5
Other Occupation	19.9	22.7	5.7	11.6
No Information	0.7	1.4	0.9	0.0

Urban-Rural Background	*Australian Pragmatists* %	*Australian Moralists* %	*Indian Pragmatists* %	*Indian Moralists* %
Rural	29.8	32.6	18.0	25.5
Urban	69.5	66.7	80.6	73.5
No Information	0.7	0.7	1.4	1.1

Table 2

WORK HISTORY DESCRIPTIVE STATISTICS

Time in Present Position	*Australian Pragmatists* %	*Australian Moralists* %	*Indian Pragmatists* %	*Indian Moralists* %
Under 1 Year	19.1	14.9	11.4	9.1
2–3 Years	26.2	26.2	24.2	22.9
4–5 Years	18.4	14.9	19.4	16.4
6–10 Years	14.2	17.0	29.4	28.7
11–15 Years	8.5	12.1	8.5	12.4
Over 15 Years	12.1	13.5	6.6	10.2
No Information	1.4	0.7	0.5	0.4

Total Managerial Experience	*Australian Pragmatists* %	*Australian Moralists* %	*Indian Pragmatists* %	*Indian Moralists* %
0–1 Year	0.7	1.4	3.3	1.1
2–3 Years	5.0	3.5	5.2	6.2
4–5 Years	4.3	6.4	13.3	8.7
6–10 Years	20.6	12.1	40.8	25.1
11–15 Years	29.1	23.4	18.5	25.5
16–20 Years	14.9	17.0	10.0	16.4
21–30 Years	14.2	21.3	5.2	11.6
Over 30 Years	10.6	14.2	3.3	5.5
No Information	0.7	0.7	0.5	0.0

Table 3

ORGANIZATIONAL DESCRIPTIVE STATISTICS

Organization Level	*Australian Pragmatists* %	*Australian Moralists* %	*Indian Pragmatists* %	*Indian Moralists* %
Top Management	58.2	56.2	44.5	45.8
Upper Middle Management	26.9	31.9	44.6	44.0
Lower Middle Management	14.2	10.0	10.4	10.2
No Information	.7	1.9	.5	0.0

Department	*Australian Pragmatists* %	*Australian Moralists* %	*Indian Pragmatists* %	*Indian Moralists* %
Production-Operations	13.5	9.9	8.1	6.9
Sales-Distribution	9.9	17.0	19.9	20.7
Engineering	1.4	5.0	3.8	3.3
Finance-Accounting	7.1	12.1	7.6	11.6
Personnel-Ind. Relations	7.1	5.7	9.5	9.5

Table 3 (*Contd.*)

Department	*Australian Pragmatists* %	*Australian Moralists* %	*Indian Pragmatists* %	*Indian Moralists* %
Public Relations-Advertising	0.7	0.0	—	—
Research and Development	1.4	2.1	—	—
Contract Construction	2.1	1.4	—	—
Materials-Purchasing	—	—	0.5	1.5
General Administration	37.6	36.2	45.5	43.6
Consultancy	—	—	1.4	0.4
Other Department	19.1	10.6	3.3	2.5
No Information	0.0	0.0	.5	0.0

Number of Products or Services	*Australian Pragmatists* %	*Australian Moralists* %	*Indian Pragmatists* %	*Indian Moralists* %
Company Produces One Product or Performs One Service	19.1	17.7	15.6	18.2
Company Produces a Few Similar Products or Performs a Few Similar Services	16.4	22.0	29.9	26.9
Company Produces a Few Different Products or Performs a Few Different Services	13.5	14.2	15.2	17.5
Company Produces Many Different Products or Performs Many Different Services	41.8	32.6	34.1	32.4
None of the Above	8.5	12.8	4.7	5.1
No Information	0.7	0.7	0.5	0.0

*Size of Company**	*Australian Pragmatists* %	*Australian Moralists* %	*Indian Pragmatists* %	*Indian Moralists* %
Small	49.0	42.5	40.3	38.9
Medium	29.8	35.5	26.1	26.2
Large	21.3	21.9	33.7	34.9
No Information	0.0	0.0	0.5	0.0

*The size categories were relative to the individual countries and were defined respectively for Australia and India as follows:

Small: Under 250 for both.

Medium: Australia 250 to 1999; India 250 to 999.

Large: Australia 2000 or greater; India 1000 or greater.

Table 3 (*Contd.*)

Type of Position	*Australian Pragmatists* %	*Australian Moralists* %	*Indian Pragmatists* %	*Indian Moralists* %
Line Management	38.3	29.1	21.8	22.9
Staff Management	22.7	26.2	31.8	33.5
Combined line and Staff Management	36.9	44.0	46.4	43.6
No Information	2.1	.7	0.0	0.0
Nature of Ownership	*Australian Pragmatists* %	*Australian Moralists* %	*Indian Pragmatists* %	*Indian Moralists* %
Proprietorship	19.9	26.2	0.9	2.5
Partnership	7.8	4.3	4.3	6.5
Private Limited	24.1	16.3	31.3	27.6
Private Limited: Foreign Subsidiary	—	—	15.6	15.6
Private Limited: Foreign Financed and Managed	—	—	8.5	8.7
Private Limited: Indian Owned and Managed	—	—	35.5	32.4
Public Limited	38.3	40.4	—	—
Other Ownership	9.2	11.3	3.3	6.2
No Information	0.7	0.5	0.5	0.4
Nature of Business	*Australian Pragmatists* %	*Australian Moralists* %	*Indian Pragmatists* %	*Indian Moralists* %
Agriculture	1.4	2.1	0.0	0.7
Mining	1.4	4.3	0.9	0.4
Construction	7.1	3.5	0.0	1.1
Manufacturing	41.8	41.1	62.1	55.6
Transport and Public Utilities	4.3	5.7	2.8	1.1
Wholesale and Retail Trade	12.1	8.5	8.5	13.1
Finance, Insurance, and Real Estate	8.5	8.5	2.4	2.5
Services	2.8	2.8	2.4	3.6
Banking	—	—	0.5	1.5
Other Business	20.6	22.7	0.5	2.2
Manufacturing, Wholesale, Retail	—	—	6.6	8.0
Other Combinations of the Above	—	—	10.4	9.8
No Information	0.0	0.8	0.5	0.4
Total	100.0	100.0	100.0	100.0

is the meaning (successful, right, or pleasant) assigned to concepts by managers. The affective property is the importance (high, medium, or low) assigned to concepts by managers. Managers with pragmatic value orientations tend to assign a "successful" meaning to concepts that they also indicate are highly important. Operationally a moralist value orientation is the tendency to assign a "right" meaning to concepts viewed as being highly important. The assumption is that these two properties of values are two primary determinates of the intentional or connotive property of values. That is, the intention of the manager to behave in certain ways is strongly influenced by the importance and meaning of the values. Intentions are viewed as a primary correlate of actual behavior.

Managers' choices were measured on five short simulation exercises where the problems and alternatives posed the following five value issues: (1) economic costs *versus* human relations costs; (2) loyalty and performance of employees *versus* progress and technological change that has made these employees redundant; (3) expediency *versus* ethical considerations in the acquisition of funds to finance expansion; (4) selection of a task-oriented or an interpersonally oriented subordinate; and (5) the amount of discretion allocated to subordinates in decision making. Alternatives were ordered on a continuum except for the fourth problem which offered two alternatives.

Classification of Managers As Pragmatists or Moralists

The classification of a manager as a pragmatist or moralist results from his responses to all 66 concepts on the use of three rules specified below.

1. Among the concepts a manager reports as being of high importance, identify the proportion classified as successful, as right, and as pleasant and select the largest category. Hence one identifies the largest of the following conditional probabilities: P (Successful/High importance, P(S/Hi); P (Right/High importance, P(R/Hi); and P (Pleasant/High importance), P(P/Hi).
2. Compare the largest of the above conditional probabilities to its complement. For example, if P(S/Hi) is the largest of the three, then its complement is the probability of responding successful given average and low importance, P(S/Ai and Li). If the former is larger than its complement, the individual's primary orientation is tentatively classified as a pragmatist. This rule would operate similarly in classifying managers as moralists and hedonists.
3. After having determined a manager's primary orientation identify his operative value category. For example, for a "pragmatic" individual, the operative value category consists of those concepts which he jointly rates as high importance and successful. If the proportion of concepts in this category, i.e., P(S/Hi) is more than .15 (of the 66 concepts) the individual retains his primary orientation. If the proportion is less than .15 the individual is reclassified to a mixed value orientation. The present study includes only managers with pragmatic or moralistic value orientations.

Given this operational definition of operative values, it is possible to classify the remaining values for the manager. Adopted values are those concepts which fit the primary value orientation of the manager but which he does not regard as being highly important. Thus, for a manager with a pragmatic orientation, adopted values consist of all concepts which are rated as "successful" and either "average importance" or "low importance". Intended values for a pragmatic manager are values toward all those concepts rated by him as "high importance" and "right" or "pleasant". Finally, weak values for a pragmatic manager are all concepts which are neither regarded as highly important nor fitting the primary value orientation of an individual.

In scoring the values for subsequent analysis, operative values were given a score of 4, intended values a score of 3, adopted values a score of 2, and weak values a score of 1. These scores are intentionality scores and are the scores that are factor analyzed. These scores form a scale based on their likely relationship with behavior since they are defined in terms of the two properties of values (importance and meaning) viewed as the main determinants of behavioral intentions.

Data Analysis Design

Initial analysis of the values data consisted of separate principal factor analysis of r correlation matrices for each group with squared multiple correlations as the initial communality estimate. Then varimax rotation was used for all factors exceeding the Kaiser criterion (eigenvalues exceeding 1.0) for each of the four groups of managers (value orientation x country). Factor analysis is an appropriate statistical technique to use in the present study because the unit of analysis investigated is the value systems of managers. Value integration, as one example, has been previously mentioned as one property of value systems. In the present study the presence of integration would be present if clearly interpretable factors emerge.

The number of subjects relative to the number of variables in the present study is approximately 2:1 in Australia and 3.5:1 to 4.1:1 in India. While this may present some concern in Australia, there is little agreement among statisticians as to the desirable ratio. Rummel (1970:220) indicates that the "*minimum* allowable ratio of cases to variables for inference is still a matter of research taste."

Subsequent analysis of a comparison of the four factor structures were done using the coefficient of congruence (Harmon, 1967) in order to test for similarities and differences; a test necessary for an interpretation of the results for the second and third hypotheses. Final analysis consisted of the generation of factor scores. Responses on each of the five exercises were regressed on the factor scores and the beta weights were tested for significance in those equations where the multiple R's were significant. If more than one R is significant any differences in factors with significant beta weights in the equations is evidence for the influence of the value issue.

RESULTS

There were fourteen and thirteen value factors generated from the data for Australian moralist and pragmatist managers respectively. Eleven and seven factors emerged from the data for Indian pragmatic and moralist managers

Table 4

AUSTRALIAN PRAGMATIST MANAGERS
SUMMARY OF SIGNIFICANT FACTOR LOADINGS

Variable Number	*Variable Name*	*Factor Loading*	*Variable Number*	*Variable Name*	*Factor Loading*
	Factor One			Factor Two	
9	Employees	.45	3	Employee Welfare	.43
11	My Co-Workers	.39	4	Organization Stability	.61
12	Craftsman	.51	7	Social Welfare	.50
14	Managers	.36	39	Dignity	.52
16	My Subordinates	.37	46	Security	.53
17	Laborers	.75	50	Prestige	.42
19	Blue Collar Workers	.78			
21	Technical Employers	.56		Factor Three	
23	Labor Union	.42			
24	White Collar Workers	.72	5	Profit Maximization	.39
61	Government	.33	13	My Boss	.39
			22	Me	.41
	Factor Four		25	Ambition	.42
			42	Money	.66
31	Prejudice	.50	47	Power	.47
52	Caution	.46	51	Authority	.47
57	Conservatism	.53	63	Property	.59
60	Force	.54			
62	Liberalism	.56		Factor Five	
66	Risk	.45			
			7	Social Welfare	.35
	Factor Six		8	Organization Growth	.61
			10	Customers	.51

Table 4 (*Contd.*)

Variable Number	*Variable Name*	*Factor Loading*
27	Obedience	.40
28	Trust	.62
30	Loyalty	.64
34	Cooperation	.40
37	Honor	.39
	Factor Eight	
38	Leisure	.37
40	Achievement	.34
53	Change	.35
55	Compromise	.64
	Factor Ten	
26	Ability	.49
33	Skill	.52
35	Tolerance	.38
41	Autonomy	.34
48	Creativity	.49
	Factor Thirteen	
9	Employees	.41
18	My Company	−.37
58	Emotions	.34
65	Religion	.59

Variable Number	*Variable Name*	*Factor Loading*
	Factor Seven	
15	Owners	.75
18	My Company	.35
20	Stockholders	.65
	Factor Nine	
1	High Productivity	.52
49	Success	.53
64	Rational	.44
	Factor Eleven	
16	My Subordinate	.52
40	Achievement	.43
44	Job Satisfaction	.38
54	Competition	.60
	Factor Twelve	
12	Craftsman	−.40
45	Influence	.56
47	Power	.37
56	Conflict	.45
60	Force	.37

Table 5

AUSTRALIAN MORALIST MANAGERS
SUMMARY TABLE OF SIGNIFICANT FACTOR LOADINGS

Variable Number	*Variable Name*	*Factor Loading*
	Factor One	
7	Social Welfare	.36
9	Employees	.47
11	My Co-Workers	.68
12	Craftsman	.71
14	Managers	.55
15	Owners	.49
16	My Subordinates	.42
17	Laborers	.78
19	Blue Collar Workers	.85
20	Stockholders	.44
21	Technical Employees	.70
24	White Collar Employees	.79
	Factor Four	
51	Authority	.39
61	Government	.38
65	Religion	.70
	Factor Six	
22	Me	42
45	Influence	.39
50	Prestige	.66
51	Authority	.40
63	Property	.43

Variable Number	*Variable Name*	*Factor Loading*
	Factor Two	
29	Aggressiveness	.44
31	Prejudice	.35
36	Conformity	.54
46	Honor	.37
57	Conservatism	.49
	Factor Three	
5	Profit Max.	.35
8	Organization Growth	.60
40	Achievement	.45
54	Competition	.53
25	Ambition	.55
59	Equality	.33
	Factor Five	
25	Ambition	.34
41	Autonomy	.67
43	Individuality	.44
47	Power	.35
48	Creativity	.33
53	Change	.47
	Factor Eight	

Table 5 (*Contd.*)

Variable Number	*Variable Name*	*Factor Loading*	*Variable Number*	*Variable Name*	*Factor Loading*
			10	Customers	−.33
	Factor Seven		34	Cooperation	.49
			38	Leisure	.41
4	Organization Stability	.41	49	Success	.38
27	Obedience	.43	64	Rational	.36
35	Tolerance	.34			
55	Compromise	.39		Factor Nine	
58	Emotions	.52			
			3	Employee Welfare	.42
	Factor Ten		7	Social Welfare	.55
			9	Employees	.36
1	High Productivity	.35	32	Compassion	.65
2	Industry Leadership	.35	62	Liberalism	.33
6	Organization Effectiveness	.52	35	Tolerance	.45
26	Ability	.55	59	Equality	.39
33	Skill	.66			
				Factor Twelve	
	Factor Eleven				
			28	Trust	.46
16	My Subordinates	.36	30	Loyalty	.67
66	Risk	−.68	37	Honor	.61
	Factor Thirteen			Factor Fourteen	
15	Owner	.34	1	High Productivity	.34
20	Stockholders	.43	39	Dignity	.43
23	Labor Unions	.43	45	Influence	.42
42	Money	.51	60	Force	.48
47	Security	.37			

Table 6

INDIAN PRAGMATIST MANAGERS
SUMMARY OF SIGNIFICANT FACTOR LOADINGS

Variable Number	*Variable Name*	*Factor Loading*	*Variable Number*	*Variable Name*	*Factor Loading*
	Factor one			*Factor Two*	
27	Obedience	.57	7	Social Welfare	.38
28	Trust	.59	10	Customer	−.36
30	Loyalty	.46	31	Prejudice	.60
34	Cooperation	.41	40	Achievement	−.55
35	Tolerance	.46	49	Success	−.44
36	Conformity	.37			
46	Security	.37		Factor Three	
52	Caution	.43			
			32	Compassion	.47
	Factor Four		36	Conformity	.35
			43	Individuality	.40
2	Industry Leadership	.39	59	Equality	.36
6	Organization Effectiveness	.51	66	Risk	.43
8	Organization Growth	.52			
33	Still	.35		Factor Five	
48	Creativity	.59			
53	Change	.38	9	Employees	.34
			17	Laborers	.71
	Factor Six		19	Blue Collar Workers	.72
			23	Labor Unions	.49
3	Employee Welfare	.64	24	White Collar Workers	.67

Table 6 (*Contd.*)

Variable Number	*Variable Name*	*Factor Loading*	*Variable Number*	*Variable Name*	*Factor Loading*
4	Organization Stability	.38			
18	My Company	.37		Factor Seven	
20	Stockholders	.34			
54	Competition	−.33	44	Job Satisfaction	.55
			56	Conflict	−.38
	Factor Eight				
				Factor Nine	
22	Me	.33			
37	Honor	.52	1	High Productivity	.33
39	Dignity	.52	11	My Co-Workers	.44
41	Autonomy	.33	13	My Boss	.41
42	Money	.42	14	Managers	.43
47	Power	.49	26	Ability	.40
50	Prestige	.57	41	Authority	.34
51	Authority	.41	64	Rational	.53
63	Property	.44			
				Factor Eleven	
	Factor Ten				
			54	Competition	.36
12	Craftsman	−.42	55	Compromise	.42
25	Ambition	.40	57	Conservatism	.34
57	Conservatism	.33	61	Government	.54
58	Emotions	.41	65	Religion	.55

Table 7

INDIAN MORALIST MANAGERS
SUMMARY OF SIGNIFICANT FACTOR LOADINGS

Variable Number	*Variable Name*	*Factor Loading*	*Variable Number*	*Variable Name*	*Factor Loading*
	Factor One			*Factor Two*	
9	Employees	.37	32	Compassion	−.33
17	Laborers	.61	41	Autonomy	.37
19	Blue Collar Workers	.61	43	Individuality	.33
23	Labor Unions	.39	53	Change	.40
24	White Collar Workers	.48	56	Conflict	.40
			58	Emotions	.60
	Factor Three		65	Religion	.36
25	Ambition	.39		Factor Four	
33	Skill	.34			
36	Conformity	.40	27	Obedience	.57
40	Achievement	.46	28	Trust	.46
42	Money	.44	30	Loyalty	.55
45	Influence	.46	34	Cooperation	.40
47	Power	.49	35	Tolerance	.36
49	Success	.49	37	Honor	.35
50	Prestige	.40	39	Dignity	.33
			46	Security	.38
	Factor Five		52	Caution	.35
6	Organization Effectiveness	.43		Factor Six	

Table 7 (*Contd.*)

Variable Number	*Variable Name*	*Factor Loading*
8	Organization Growth	.37
26	Ability	.34
33	Skill	.34
34	Cooperation	.37
40	Achievement	.34
44	Job Satisfaction	.34
48	Creativity	.34
64	Rational	.38
	Factor Seven	
3	Employee Welfare	.50
7	Social Welfare	.58
8	Organization Growth	.32
11	My Co-Workers	.38
32	Compassion	.37
35	Tolerance	.41
55	Compromise	.43
62	Liberalism	.37

Variable Number	*Variable Name*	*Factor Loading*
13	My Boss	.37
15	Owners	.52
18	My Company	.39
22	Me	.33
24	White Collar Workers	.34
63	Property	.40

respectively. Tables 4 through 7 present a summary of the factor analytic results including only the loadings of values toward those concepts that are significant (loading >.325).

Table 8 presents a summary of the results from the comparison of factor structures and includes only a description of the factors found to be similar. The definition of similarity is a coefficient of congruence ≥.75 following Scheewind and Cattell's (1971) recommendation. Given the large number of factors yielded and in the interests of concentrating on data bearing on the four hypotheses, only those factors with significant beta weights in the regression analyses or similar in the coefficient of congruence tests are interpreted. These results indicate the emergence of an "internal reference group" factor for all four groups of managers. The values loading on this factor include, as examples, values toward subordinates, employees, my boss, and craftsman. Among Indian managers two additional similarities were identified. The first is a

Table 8

SIMILAR VALUE FACTORS IDENTIFIED BY COEFFICIENT OF CONGRUENCE

Country and Value Orientation	*Australian Moralist Managers*	*Indian Pragmatist Managers*	*Indian Moralist Managers*
Australian Pragmatist Managers	Factor One for both groups .8819	Factor one Australia and Factor Five India .7871	Factor One Australia and Factor One India .8642
Australian Moralist Managers		Factor One Australia and Factor Five India .7545	Factor One Australia and Factor One India .8418
Indian Pragmatist Managers			Factor One Pragmatist and Factor Four Moralist .7508 Factor Four Pragmatist and Factor Five Moralist .8736 Factor Five Pragmatist and Factor One Moralist .7650

Table 9

OVERALL RELATIONSHIPS BETWEEN VALUE SYSTEMS AND BEHAVIOR FROM REGRESSION ANALYSIS

Predictors and Country	*One*	*Two*	*Job Incident* *Three*	*Four*	*Five*
Value Systems[1]					
1. Australian Pragmatists	.347	.326	.345	.363	.392*
2. Australian Moralists	.250	.424*	.447**	.348	.305
3. Indian Pragmatists	.217	.345**	.258	.365**	.262
4. Indian Moralists	.149	.150	.193	.234*	.159

[1] Degrees of freedom are 13,127; 14,126; 11,199; and 7,267 respectively.
* = .05; ** = .01.

similar paternalistic value factor or subsystem of values. Values loading on this factor include, as examples, obedience, trust, loyalty, cooperation, tolerance, conformity, security, and caution. The second similarity is on a factor that includes values centering around an integration of dynamic organizational goals and personnel competence. Individual values loading on this dimension or subsystem include industry leadership, organizational efficiency, organizational growth, skill, creativity, and change. Beyond this, however, there were no similarities between value systems indicating that there are large differences whether comparisons are made between value orientations, countries, or both.

Results bearing on the first, second, and fourth hypotheses are presented in Table 9. The first hypothesis was supported in all four groups; value systems of managers relate to their choices. There are five significant relationships between organization context variables and choices for pragmatic managers and only one for moralist managers supporting the second hypothesis regarding value orientation differences. The differences in the multiple correlation between the two groups of Australian managers on the second, third, and fifth equations and for the two groups of Indian managers on the second and fourth equations support the second hypothesis; value orientation does influence value systems-behavior relationships. The relationships between value systems and choices are greater for Australian managers than for Indian managers indicating support for country as a moderator variable.

More than one significant relationship between value systems and choices is necessary in order to test the influence of the value issue. Only Australian moralist and Indian pragmatist managers fulfill this condition. The value systems of Australian moralist managers were significantly related to choices on the second and third exercises. Value factors one ($p < .05$), nine ($p < .05$), and fourteen ($p < .05$) have significant beta weights in the relationship with choices in the retention and retraining of redundant employees on the second exercise. The first factor is an "internal reference group" described previously. Factor nine is a socialism-humanism dimension with values toward social welfare, employee welfare, compassion, tolerance, and equality having significant loadings. The fourteenth factor is a social influence dimension that is work based with values toward force, dignity, influence, and high productivity having significant loadings. All three beta weights have positive signs.

The fourth ($p<.05$), ninth ($p<.05$), tenth ($p<.01$), and eleventh ($p<.05$) factors were related to Australian moralist managers' choices on the third exercise. Factor four is an external institutional authority dimension with values toward government and religion having significant loadings. Factor nine is the socialism-humanism dimension. Factor ten is an organization and personal effectiveness subsystem with values toward high productivity, industry leadership, organization effectiveness, ability, and skill having significant loadings. The values with significant loadings on factor eleven are risk and subordinates. Since the sign for risk was negative and subordinates had a positive sign, this was interpreted as a subordinate predictability dimension. The signs of the beta weights were negative on the fourth and ninth factors and positive on the tenth and eleventh factors. The problem and choices proposed dealt with the establishment of a pension fund for employees in lieu of a wage increase with the knowledge that the employees covered would be terminated due to technological changes before they would collect a pension. The money in the pension fund would finance present research and development projects.

The equation between the value factors and choices on job incident two was also significant for Indian pragmatist managers. Factors one ($p<.05$) and six ($p<.05$) had positive signs. Factor one is the paternalism dimension mentioned earlier. Values toward employee welfare, organization stability, and my stockholders have positive loadings and values toward competition a negative loading on factor six. This factor indicates a valuation of a stable social and ownership environment.

The beta weights for the first ($p<.001$) and seventh ($p<.05$) value factors in the fourth equation for Indian pragmatists both have positive signs. Factor one is the paternalism dimension. Two values have significant loadings on the seventh dimension; job satisfaction has a positive loading and conflict has a negative loading. Job satisfaction, it would seem, is partially the absence of conflict. Indian pragmatist managers who tend to have higher scores on the paternalism and job satisfaction dimensions choose a socially oriented assistant who is congenial, well like, and contributes to the department's morale.

The results for the other two groups are important for subsequent discussion. The seventh ($p<.05$), eighth ($p<.05$), and thirteenth ($p<.05$) had negative, positive, and positive signs among Australian pragmatist managers on the fifth exercise. Values loading on the seventh factor include owners, company, and stockholders, suggesting a company ownership dimension. Values toward leisure, achievement, change, and compromise load on the eighth factor suggesting a span of control or implementation focused dimension. Values toward employees, company, emotions, and religion load on the thirteenth factor suggesting an institutional affect subsystem. The problem posed was the amount of delegation and subordinate discretion in decision making. The single value dimension with a significant beta weight on the fourth equation for Indian moralist managers is the paternalism factor previously mentioned. The sign is positive.

DISCUSSION

The results found support and make more explicit the model developed by England. In doing so, the findings strike a note both for universalism and for particularism in relationships between value systems and behavior. Finally, the importance of value systems as a correlate of choices and the content of the value systems provides some initial answers to previously unaddressed questions.

The fundamental conjecture advanced by England is that value systems of managers relate to their decision behavior. This statement received universal support in this study. The relationships are also important ones, with the possible exception of that for Indian moralist managers, if the average amount of variance is taken as an index of importance. The rank order of the four groups in terms of the average amount of variance accounted for across all incidents is Australian moralist managers (13.1 per cent), Australian pragmatist managers (12.6 per cent), Indian pragmatist managers (8.7 per cent), and Indian moralist managers (3.2 per cent). Hage and Dewar (1973) provide additional support for the importance of personal values. They found that the values of members of dominant coalitions and the directors of sixteen health and welfare organizations in the United States accounted for approximately forty per cent of the variance in program innovations over a two-year period. The indication from these two studies is that value systems play an important role in individually and organizationally relevant decisions.

The finding of six significant relationships between value systems and choices in twenty tests (four groups and five dependent variables) far exceeds chance. Further, as indicated above, value systems account for a proportion of the variance that is comparable or greater than the variance often found between other variables and managers' behavior (Campbell, Dunnette, Lawler, and Weick, 1970). If we have learned anything about behavior we have certainly learned that its correlates are multivariate. Throughout the present study other correlates or sources of influence or relationships have been mentioned including the nature of the problem posed, social system constraints, and organizational and role characteristics of managers. Discussion of the relationship between other variables, such as attitudes, and behavior also recognizes that the linkage is far from perfect (Kiesler and Munson, 1975). Much additional research is necessary to disentangle the complexities involved and offer more precise models and explanations. The present results are encouraging, however, and suggest that future research should be conducted to provide better answers.

Against this background of universal support there is a series of particular findings that stand out in relief. First, the value systems of the four groups of managers are very different. Value orientation is a moderator of the structure of value systems. The within-country differences in comparisons using the coefficient of congruence are relevant here. This coefficient is an index of the similarity of the pattern and magnitude of loadings on different factors. The two groups of Australian managers are very different and the two groups of Indian managers are more dissimilar than similar. England has not previously discussed this moderator effect explicitly, but this finding would seem to be consistent with the differentiation in systems of values for managers indicated in his model.

Value orientation as a moderator of value systems-behavior relationships, the conjecture advanced by England, also receives considerable support. There is no test for the significance of the differences in Z scores transformed from multiple correlations. But the differences between the within-country groups are very large on any relationship where the multiple correlation is significant for pragmatists, moralists, or both.

The joint effect of value orientation on both value systems and the relationship of these systems to behavior suggests two conclusions. First, value orientation is important in assessing the structure of value systems. Further, it is possible that the dimensions identified also have the same cognitive and affective properties as individual values. That is, the subsystems identified can also have an instrumental or ethical meaning and differ in importance. Since the meaning-importance structures differ for moralist and pragmatist managers the observed differences are still a function of the cognitive and affective properties. But now these are properties of subsystems of values than individual values.

Differences in value issues are one instance of the multifaceted nature of problems and alternatives. The subsystems of values related to choices can therefore differ considerably if the issues posed are dissimilar. The exercises were purposely constructed to pose different value dilemmas. The results bearing on the third hypothesis support the mediating effect of value issue differences where a test is possible. The issues in the second exercise were employee loyalty and past performance *versus* progress and technological change. Those in the third exercise were expediency *versus* ethical considerations in the acquisition of research and development funds. The fourth exercise pitted the issues of task orientation and social orientation against each other. Between the second and third equations for Australian moralist managers six factors have significant beta weights. Only one factor, socialism-humanism, is common to both equations and even then the signs are opposite. Paternalism was the only factor common to the second and fourth equations for Indian pragmatist managers. A total of three factors had significant beta weights between the two equations.

The particular factors with significant beta weights further support the influence of the value issues. The internal reference group, socialism-humanism and social influence factors for Australian moralist managers on exercise two have a social base in common where the concern is with employees of the organization. In contrast, where expediency and ethics *vie*, an external referent, external institutional authority, a performance dimension, and organizational-personal effectiveness, relate to choices. For Indian pragmatist managers the differences are not sharp but a stable social and ownership environment in the second exercise is more of an organization climate dimension. The job satisfaction or harmony dimension, significant where task and social orientation are the issues, is at the individual level and refers to interpersonal relations.

There are two comparisons that can be made between the managers from the two countries. The first is on the basis of the evidence relating to the fourth hypothesis. The second is a comparison of the general nature of the factors that had significant beta weights in those equations where the overall correlation was significant. The percentage of variance reported earlier is the clearest evidence for stronger relationships between value systems and behavior among Australian than among Indian managers. These are average percentages based on the squared multiple correlations for all five relationships. Again, no significance test is available for assessing these differences. The rationale given earlier for expecting this difference was based on prior research. But, more basically, the explanation is the greater importance of situational characteristics relative to individual differences among Indian managers than among Australian managers. This is a somewhat tenuous explanation at the present time, because there is not a large body of evidence to support it.

But Whitely (1977) did find types of ownership to relate much more to choices of Indian managers than to choices of Australian managers. This is not an altogether surprising finding, but is important because ownership is an organization control variable (Pondy, 1969). In a study cited earlier by Wheelright (1957), wide diffusion of ownership was found among the 102 largest public firms in Australia. This suggests that there has been considerable movement from owner-controlled to management-controlled enterprises. Conversely, the Chattopadhyay (1973) study estimated that there are only half a million stockholders in India and indicates that a large percentage of Indian firms is still owner managed. Further Tandon (1973) sought to link the parochialism and nepotism often accompanying ownership practices in India to decision making and personnel practices. Since both decision making and personnel practices are included in the five job incidents the relationships found between ownership and choices is consistent with these prior observations.

An examination of what values subsystems relate to choices also is consistent with a management control-ownership control explanation. There is a managerial control focus to the company ownership and span of control or implementation factors for Australian pragmatist managers and the organizational-personal effectiveness factor for Australian moralist managers. All the factors significant for the two groups of Indian managers, paternalism, stable social and ownership environment, and job satisfaction, have in common a social control focus. Both groups of Indian managers also opted for social stability in their choice of an assistant.

Several conclusions stem from the results of this research. Value systems of managers do explain enough of the variance in choices on the simulation exercises to warrant further investigation. However, these results are only suggestive and a fuller appreciation of the importance of these systems will have to wait until several research directions have been pursued. The exercises were developed solely to provide an internal validity test of England's model. The tasks were not developed with an eye toward those typically found in managerial work. A future direction then, is for a more balanced concern between internal and external validity and, further, with all of the decision process, not just choice.

A second direction is the issue of the form of the model used in combining situation and individual explanations of behavior that entered, in the present context, in the explanation of country differences. An assumption in the explanation offered for the cross-national differences is that situational and individual differences combine in a linear fashion. There is sufficient research and theory under the rubric of "contingency theory" indicating that interactive models warrant some investigation. Perhaps one of these two models is better in Australia and the other is better in India.

One task dimension treated separately, though rationally, in the present study is value issue. The task issue had the status of a hypothetical construct. Operationalizing this construct by asking the subjects what perceived issues they saw in the exercises when they are debriefed would be one possible procedure to use. This would place the explanation offered on firmer ground.

Finally, prediction is a tricky business with value systems. We need to know more about their development, stability, and degree of integration in order to predict their likely influence on behavior. The development of moral behavior and values has received a great deal of theoretical and empirical inquiry, but little seems to be known about the development of pragmatism, realism, or materialism among managers. This may be a fruitful area for future inquiry. These may be treated as separate value orientations and could build upon the research already conducted. Value orientation has been inductively arrived at so far. We could begin with these orientations as constructs and proceed from there.

Second, stability of value systems is still an important research need. Only one study has been done so far and, in actuality, the issue of stability was only indirectly tested there since it was a replication of England's (1967) study of United States managers. What seems to be needed is a within-subjects, repeated measures design over a significant (e.g., 3–5 years) period of time. An important addendum to such a study would be to trace individuals going through important vocational passages: as business school freshmen; as business school seniors; as graduate students; as management trainees; and as junior managers. It is important, too, to draw a distinction between the structural stability of value systems and the relational stability between value systems and the decision process.

The degree of integration, that is the scope, complexity, and interrelationship of value systems, certainly bears more investigation. In a statistical sense two procedures seem warranted. First, the clarity and theoretical significance of the factor structures, magnitude of loadings, and percentage of common variance need further study. Second, Bartlett's test or Rao's test of the correlation matrices need to be used since the determinant of such matrices can be tested against the null hypothesis (i.e., significantly different from zero).

The degree of integration, as a function of processes influencing integration, needs initial investigation and relates to the stability issue above. England postulates that certain values development from such processes but the effect may be greater; such processes may affect the structure of value systems.

Finally, not only is there a need to extend research to the relationship between value systems and other parts of the decision process, but also to the manner in which the decision process unfolds. Alkers *et al.*, (1972) found that personal values related to decision behavior only when a rational process of making choices was used, not when the process was irrational. Not only is this a provocative result needing further study, but it points out the need for other process-oriented research on the way value systems are translated into behavior and under what conditions.

These are all heady issues. We are not likely to run out of fascinating questions needing inquiry and the need to pose fascinating questions for a long time.

REFERENCES

Alkers, H. A., Rao, V. R., and Hughes, G. D. "Value Consistent and Value Expedient
1972 Decision Making." *Proceedings of the 80th Annual Convention of the American Psychological Association*, San Francisco.

Bem, D. J. *Beliefs, Attitudes, and Human Affairs*. Belmont, Calif.: Brooks-Cole.
1970

Brogden, H. E. "The Primary Personal Values Measured by the Allport-Vernon Test, 'A
1952 Study of Values.'" *Psychological Monographs*. No. 16:66.

Campbell, J. P., Dunnette, M. D., Lawler, E. E., and Weick, K. *Managerial Behavioral,
1970 Performance, and Effectiveness*. New York: McGraw-Hill.

Chattopadhyay, P. "Corporate Personality." In Neelamegham, S. (ed.), *Management
1973 Development: New Perspectives and Viewpoints*: 142–166. Delhi, India: Kalyani.

Clark, A. W., and McCabe, S. "Leadership Beliefs of Australian Managers." *Journal of
1970 Applied Psychology*. 54:1–6.

England, G. W. *The Manager and His Values: An International Perspective from the
1976 United States, Japan, Korea, India, and Australia*. Cambridge, Mass.: Ballinger.

———. "Personal Value Systems of American Managers. *Academy of Management
1968 Journal*. 10, 1:53–68.

England, G. W., and Lee, R. "The Relationship between Managerial Values and
1974 Managerial Success in the United States, Japan, India, and Australia. *Journal of Applied Psychology*. 59, 4:411–419.

Hage, J., and Dewar, R. "Elite Values *versus* Organizational Structure in Predicting
1973 Innovation." *Administrative Science Quarterly*. 18:279–290.

Haire, M., Ghiselli, E., and Porter, L. W. *Managerial Thinking: An International Study*.
1966 New York, N. Y.: Wiley.

Harmon, H.H. *Modern Factor Analysis*. Chicago, Ill.: University of Chicago Press.
1967

Kiesler, C. A., and Munson, P. A. "Attitudes and Opinions." In Rosenzweig, M. R., and
1975 Porter, L. W. (Eds.), *Annual Review of Psychology*: 415–456. Palo Alto, Calif.: Annual Reviews, Inc.

Kluckhohn, F., and Strodtbeck, F. *Variations in Value Orientations*. New York, N. Y.: Row
1961 Peterson and Co.

Locke, E. A. "The Nature and Causes of Job Satisfaction." In Dunnette, M. D. (ed.),
1976 *Handbook of Industrial and Organizational Psychology*. Chicago: Rand McNally.

March, J., and Simon, H. *Organizations*. New York: John Wiley.
1959

Mintzberg, H. *The Nature of Managerial Work*. New York: Harper and Row.
1973

Mintzberg, H., Raisinghani, D., and Théorêt, A. "The Structure of Unstructured Decision
1976 Processes." *Administrative Science Quarterly*. 2:246–275.

Orne, M. T. "Demand Characteristics and the Concept of Quasi-Controls." In
1969 Rosenthal, R., and Rosnow, R. L. (eds.), *Artifacts in Behavioral Research*: 147–181. New York, N. Y.: Academic press.

Pondy, L. R. "Effects of Size, Complexity, and Ownership on Administrative
1969 Complexity." *Administrative Science Quarterly*. 14, 1:47–60.

Rummel, R. J. *Applied Factor Analysis*. Evanston, Ill.: Northwestern University Press.
1970

Scheewind, K. A., and Cattell, R. B. "Zum Problem die Faktor Identification Verteilungen

1971 und Vertrauensintervalle von Kongrung Koeffiguntten fur Personlichkeltsfaktoron im der Beriech Objectivanalytischer Text." *Psykologische Beitrage*, Sonderdrucke, 12:214–220.

Thiagarajan, K. M. "A Cross-Cultural Study of the Relationships between Personal
1968 Values and Managerial Behavior." *Technical Report #23*. University of Rochester, Management Research Center.

Tandon, P. "Professional Management in India." In Neelamegham, S. (ed.),
1973 *Management Development: New Perspectives and Viewpoints*: 77–86. Delhi, India: Kalyani.

Wheelwright, E. *Ownership and Control of Australian Companies A study of 102 of the*
1957 *Largest Public Companies Incorporated in Australia*. Sydney: The Law Book Company of Australia.

Whitely, W. T. "The Relationship of Managerial Values and Decision Making: A Cross-
1977 National Investigation." Unpublished Doctoral Dissertation, University of Minnesota.

Managerial Decision Making: An international comparison*

F. A. HELLER
Tavistock Institute of Human Relations, London
B. WILPERT,
Padagogische Hochschule Berlin
and International Institute of Management, Science Center Berlin, and Research Collaborators**

This paper describes research on influence and power sharing among senior levels of management in successful modern organizations. Results from eight different countries fail to sustain any clear "culturological" explanation. National differences, however, are important and account for 10–15 per cent of the variance, while differences between sectors (dominant technology) account for 5–10 per cent of the variance in decision-making patterns.

Skill emerges as a major factor in all countries in explaining variations of centralized or participative decision-making between dyads of boss-subordinates. We call this a situational or contingency factor. Several ways of measuring skill in relation to job needs are used. Both subjective and objective measures show a very consistent reliable pattern. In general, it can be said that when skills are low or seen to be low, centralized decision making is preferred to participation.

Contingency or situational approaches to organizational behavior are replacing monistic or universalistic positions (Staehle, 1973) but are in some danger of becoming a "bandwagon". It was to be expected, therefore, that they

* The study was financed from several sources. The Social Science Research Council (UK) and the International Institute of Management (Berlin) made the major contributions.

** The following researchers collaborated in this study as the main contributors in addition to the authors of this paper: P. Docherty, The Economic Research Institute at the Stockholm School of Economics, Sweden; P. Fokking, Erasmus University Rotterdam, The Netherlands; J.-M. Fourcade, Centre d'Enseignement Supérieur des Affaires, France; W. t'Hoft, Erasmus University Rotterdam, The Netherlands; B. Roig-Amat, Instituto de Estudios Superiores de la Empresa, Universidad de Navarra, Spain; T. D. Weinshall, Tel-Aviv University, Israel. Each center was responsible for funding and supervising its own field work. Statistical and computing consulting services were provided by R. Mays, Civil Service College, London and M. James, Research Resources Ltd., London.

would soon come under severe criticism. Moberg and Koch (1975) warn against recent precocious and megalomaniac attempts to aggregate different situational approaches and to present them as integrated theoretical positions. Such holistic demands, they argue convincingly, would destroy the very basis of contingency thinking, falling into the universalistic trap instead of contributing "to a mid-range theory of organizations between 'universal truths' and everything depends".

A second criticism advanced against contingency approaches is the claim that they represent a mechanistic, deterministic view of the world where variables such as technology, organizational structure, environmental turbulence, and task characteristics unequivocally define behavioral outputs. The freedom of relevant actors to choose certain strategies in the pursuance of specific goals is seen as either non-existent or at best so limited that people emerge as puppets in a network of contingency relations (Crozier and Friedberg, 1976). Such a view of contingency statements overlooks the fact that most contingency statements are statements of probability rather than all-encompassing iron laws. Besides, it appears to be very virtue of situational propositions that they enable a researcher or actor to include individual needs, strategies and characteristics in an analysis as constituent elements of the situation. Contingency views attempt to probe the specific ranges of applicability of theoretical propositions including the preference structures of actors. They become a means of scanning the environment for significant regularities.

A third attack is launched against contingency approaches on the basis that they are basically conservative. It is alleged that they describe the *status quo* non-prescriptively and assume that it is "the optimal fit" of, let us say, structure and environment. This means that contingency theories accept underlying value premises uncritically (Miller, undated).

Since there are many different contingency models, it is not appropriate to attempt a detailed defense or to make out a case for the intrinsic value of contingency views. One can point out, however, that the ultimate test of any theory is its capacity to predict events, and this is the critical ingredient for facilitating directed, purposeful change. In relation to the present research project, we would claim that the findings, on the role of skill as a mediating variable for instance, help to predict where participation is likely to occur and how to increase its value. In our opinion, the significance of contingency or situational approaches lies in its heuristic modesty (Bass *et al.*, 1975). It could even be argued that, in the last analysis, any good theory must specify the conditions under which it operates and consequently takes on a contingency framework (Moberg and Koch, 1975).

Our research was designed as a way of studying the effects of several sets of variables indirectly or interactively influencing a specific social behavior: the interaction patterns of two interlocking management levels in organizational decision-making. We thereby reverse the traditional approach to leadership and decision-making which tended to inquire into the consequences of certain decision-making styles in terms of their economic and social consequences for the organization and its members. Rather, we intend to identify key contingency relationships and their relative impact on behavior that practitioners and theoreticians consider critical for the survival and growth of organizations.

FRAMEWORK OF THE STUDY

The research spans several systematic levels of analysis (Heller, 1973). It ranges from a macro-level (ω-variables) with countries constituting distinctive units of comparison, moving to meso-level where the effects of industrial sectors or predominant technologies (δ-variables) are studied, and finally includes a micro-level with organizational micro-structure (γ-variables), task (β-variables) and person-related variables (α-variables) serving as focal points for analysis (see figure 1).

METHODS

The whole study comprised over 1,500 senior managers in 129 large companies from eight countries: France, Germany, The Netherlands, Israel, Spain, Sweden, U.K., U.S.A. The sample is made up from economically successful and "progressive"[1] companies from thirteen industrial sectors. The companies were generally chosen from among the largest of their respective industrial sector in each country. They range from continuous-flow production (e.g., refinery, paper production), large batch production (e.g., telecommunication equipment production, packaging industry) to small-batch production (e.g., airplane production) to service industries (e.g., public transport systems, banking) and retailing. (For a detailed description of the sectors cf. Heller, 1971; Wilpert, 1977). Approximately one-half of the managers belong to the highest level immediately below the chief executive, or

Figure 1

MODEL OF ASSUMED CONTINGENCY RELATIONSHIPS*
* (from Wilpert 1977)

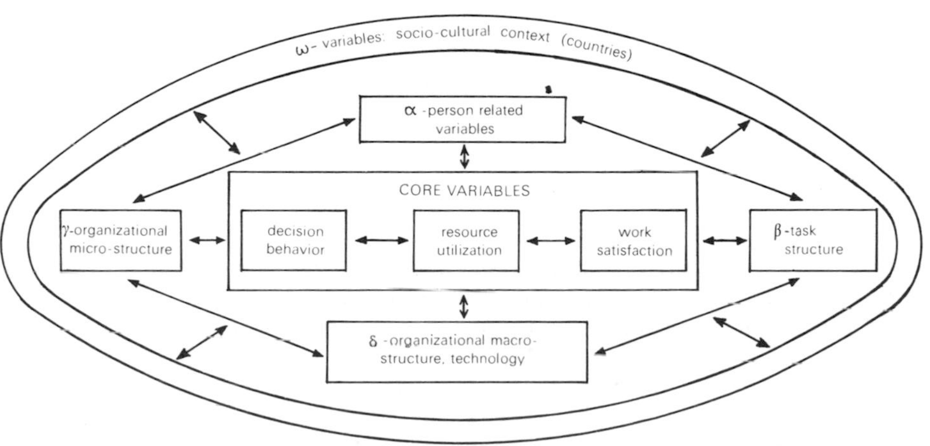

[1] "Progressive" was defined as a combination of techno-economic success and openmindedness of management towards modern managerial practices.

the board of management[2]. A deliberate attempt was made to cover 100 per cent of all managers of this first level (L1). The other half (L2) consists of the most senior immediate subordinate of Level 1, i.e., their formal deputies or closest co-workers. The average of the matched managers in our sample for Level 1 is 46.6 years (L2:42.9), with an average tenure in the company of 16.6 years (L2:14.9 years). On average, they held their present job for 5.7 years (L2:5.1) and had command over 521 (L2:193) employees in their respective departments.

An important and unusual feature of this research is the way the senior-subordinate dyad is used to obtain independent corroboration of behavioral as well as attitudinal measures. The senior level's description of the amount of influence shared between it and the next level down can be checked against the subordinate's description of the same behavior. Similarly, we can compare and contrast the skill judgements of both levels when they relate to the same set of data, namely, the job requirements at L 1 and L 2. The dyadic measurement unit can also be used to obtain independent *cross-level judgments* that avoid "social desirability" distortion. For instance, the senior manager's judgment of job requirements for both levels can be correlated with the senior man's decision styles as described by his subordinate (see Table 7). The senior manager's judgment of his subordinate's potential for promotion can be compared with the subordinate's description of the senior man's power-sharing behavior (see Table 8).

This paper presents only a part of the study. For certain statistical comparisons our international sample is reduced to make it more valid for comparative purposes. When each senior-level manager is matched to his most experienced immediate subordinate, we call this a dyadic sample. Furthermore, when comparisons are made between our sample of countries, we reduce the industrial sectors from thirteen to eight in order to ensure close matching. Our smallest sample consists of seventy comparable companies and 1250 managers in 625 matched dyads of senior and subordinate managers. Sometimes comparison with U.S. data had to be omitted because certain instruments were developed only after the U.S. study had been completed.

The method of data collection was Group Feedback Analysis (Heller, 1969), a combination of structured questionnaire technique and immediate feedback of part of the questionnaire data to the group of respondents from one managerial level in a given company. An extensive discussion of the level's results followed the feedback. The data were fed back anonymously with individual answers, means and distributions so that each participant was aware of his/her answers and could compare them with those of his/her colleagues. The same was later repeated with the participating managers of the other levels. The very lively discussions and interpretations (usually lasting one hour, but sometimes up to four hours) were tape recorded for later content analysis.

The complete research was based on fourteen questionnaires. These are described in Heller, 1976 and Wilpert, 1977. Here we confine ourselves to

[2] In the case of Germany, where sometimes boards of management constitute the chief executive level, the highest level in our study could be perceived as formally reporting to such a board.

findings which relate to six questionnaires, Forms 2, 3, 5, 6, 7, 11.[3]

FORM 2. Job Performance Requirements contains 12 items (5-point Likert-type scales) comparing the job performance requirements of one level with those of the other level and asked which job required more or less of, e.g., technical competence. Both levels answer the same question.

FORM 3. Skill Acquisition Time includes the same 12 items as Form 2, and requested answers from each dyad partner on how much time the L 2 manager would need to acquire the competence needed to do the L 1 job successfully. The subordinate (L 2) estimates how long he needs to acquire the skills needed by the senior manager. The senior (L 1) also estimates the time his subordinate needs to acquire the senior's skills.

FORM 5. Specific Decision Questionnaire[4] contains 12 decision items of general relevance to a manager. The items were grouped according to three decision types: SUB-decisions relating to a senior manager's immediate subordinate; DEPT-departmental decisions; EMP-decisions relating to employees working for L 2. L 1 was asked to report the relative frequency in percentage of his using one of the following decision methods which are assumed to constitute an influence-power sharing continuum (IPC):

I. own decision without detailed explanation to subordinates;
II. own decision with detailed *ex post* explanation to subordinate (in writing or through meetings);
III. own decision with prior consultation of subordinate;
IV. joint decision with subordinate;
V. delegation of decision to subordinate.

L 2 was asked to describe the superior's decision behavior on the same scale.

FORM 6. General Decision Questionnaire askes L 1 and L 2 to describe their own general decision behavior "in all important questions they are responsible for" on the same accumulative percentage scale as in Form 5.

FORM 7. Lateral Decision Questionnaire asks for a similar self-judgement on decision making in cooperation with colleagues on the same level. The senior manager describes his collaboration with colleagues and the subordinate level manager similarly describes his lateral decision behaviour.

The ordinal scales of Forms 5, 6, and 7 were transformed to a continuous variable with a maximum of 5.0 (all decisions taken without explanation or

[3] Analyses of Forms 2 and 3 are conducted with composites based on factor analyses. For internal consistency measures, see Appendix. Form 5 has theoretical composites. Individual items were used from Forms 6, 7 and 11.

[4] This form was an adaptation of a questionnaire devised by Blankenship and Miles, 1968.

consultation with subordinates) and a minimum of 1.0 (delegation of all decisions). The transformation is done through a weighting of the respondents' percentages given for each decision style such that the percentage of style I is multiplied by 5; II by 4 . . . and V by 1. The sum of the products then is divided by 100. A high value, therefore, signifies centralized decision making, that is to say, a lack of power and influence for the subordinates. The distribution of this 'Decision Centralization Score' (DCS) is reasonably smooth with no marked bunching of integer values.

FORM 11.Formal Skill Qualifications is a 12-item questionnaire on training and educational background.

The questionnaires were translated from the English original into the various vernaculars. The translation was checked through independent re-translations and minor accommodations after pretests in each country. Where appropriate, questionnaires were factor analyzed to form composite indices (if the comparison of α-values of composites and overall averages of a form suggested this). In addition, means for all questions were used for further statistical analyses.

The final data base consists of two different sets[5], depending on the purpose of a given analysis: (1) The full population of more than 1500 managers from 129 companies of 13 industrial sectors in several countries; and (2) The subset of data based on 625 complete dyads of managers of eight common industrial sectors[6] in which we were able to collect data in seven participating countries.

In this paper bivariate analysis is used to investigate the different impact of macro-, meso- and micro-levels of decision styles. These results are reported in the next section. Further work is now being done using multivariate analysis including regression to quantify the relative weight necessary to estimate style scores from these levels of variables.[7]

FINDINGS

Macro-level: Country Context

A comparison of the average decision-making patterns of managers from the various countries reveals quite consistent results across the various measures we used. One-way analysis of variance using Decision Centralization Scores (DCS) shows that decision behavior of managers is significantly influenced by their national contexts (Tables 1 and 2). About 10–15 per cent of the variance in decision-making patterns can be explained by overall country effects.

This may be considered as a partial corroboration of the alleged 'cul-

[5] Wherever possible we use also data from a previous U.S. study (Heller, 1971) for comparisons.

[6] For list of sectors, see Tables 4 and 5.

[7] Heller, Mays, and Wilpert, "The Use of Contingency Models in a Multi-national Study of Managerial Behavior." Mimeographed. Tavistock Institute of Human Relations, 1977.

true-bound'' thesis (Child, Kieser, 1975) holding that organizations differ as a consequence of cultural (national) conditions and antecedents. We prefer to use the term national rather than cultural, since in the majority of studies, including our own, culture has not been defined separately from national boundaries (Roberts, 1970).

Given that we find significant differences in the overall regime (managerial power and influence sharing) of comparable organizations in different

Table 1

COUNTRY AND MANAGERIAL DECISION MAKING: L 1
One-way ANOVA, DCS Values. Intl. Dyad File[8]

	Department Decisions (DEPT)	*Employee Decisions (EMP)*	*Subordinate-related Decisions (SUB)*	*All Specific Decisions (SPEC)*	*General Decision Making (F6)*	*Lateral Decision Making (F7)*
U.S.A.	3.31 (62)	2.56 (58)	3.46 (60)	3.09 (48)	2.70 (20)	2.31 (20)
U.K.	3.33 (64)	2.61 (71)	3.40 (59)	3.05 (51)	2.95 (79)	3.20 (79)
Netherlands	2.69 (40)	2.45 (40)	3.20 (42)	2.74 (28)	2.84 (52)	2.24 (52)
Germany	2.99 (53)	2.77 (48)	3.43 (55)	3.03 (39)	2.85 (66)	2.92 (65)
France	2.58 (34)	2.26 (38)	3.15 (38)	2.59 (28)	2.63 (45)	2.40 (42)
Sweden	2.39 (57)	2.27 (54)	3.03 (51)	2.55 (47)	2.53 (60)	3.00 (59)
Israel	2.91 (33)	2.49 (30)	3.36 (31)	2.85 (25)	3.08 (41)	2.79 (41)
Spain	2.68 (36)	2.42 (30)	3.45 (32)	2.75 (25)	3.00 (47)	2.88 (47)
Means (Total N)	2.91 (379)	2.49 (369)	3.32 (368)	2.25 (291)	2.83 (410)	2.92 (405)
F–Ratio	11.105	2.487	4.882	7.346	4.766	3.463
Approximate percentage variance explained by country effect	17	6	8	15	7	5

[8] Number of respondents varies whenever one member of a dyad did not respond to one of the items and due to eight sector reduction. N is given in brackets

TABLE 2

COUNTRY AND MANAGERIAL DECISION MAKING: L 2
One-way ANOVA, DCS Values. Intl. Dyad File[9]

	Department Decisions (DEPT)	*Employee Decisions (EMP)*	*Subordinate-related Decisions (SUB)*	*All Specific Decisions (SPEC)*	*General Decision Making (F6)*	*Lateral Decision Making (F7)*
U.S.A.	3.56 (61)	2.19 (54)	3.23 (50)	3.09 (36)	2.96 (20)	2.41 (20)
U.K.	3.19 (58)	2.44 (64)	3.20 (53)	2.89 (39)	2.98 (76)	3.42 (79)
Netherlands	3.43 (34)	2.30 (36)	2.82 (35)	2.77 (24)	2.78 (52)	3.10 (52)
Germany	2.56 (49)	2.33 (47)	2.86 (33)	2.47 (24)	2.88 (66)	2.96 (65)
France	2.50 (36)	2.21 (39)	3.06 (35)	2.56 (27)	2.68 (45)	2.57 (41)
Sweden	2.18 (57)	2.26 (52)	3.03 (47)	2.50 (41)	2.56 (60)	3.18 (58)
Israel	3.52 (29)	2.38 (27)	3.04 (27)	3.03 (17)	3.19 (41)	3.03 (41)
Spain	1.95 (34)	2.29 (31)	2.90 (24)	2.31 (16)	2.85 (47)	2.63 (47)
ϕ	2.87 (358)	2.30 (350)	3.04 (304)	2.72 (224)	2.85 (407)	3.00 (403)
F–Ratio	23,979	0,803 n.s.	3.131	8.634	4.580	4.943
Approximate percentage variance explained by country effect	32	7	6	22	7	8

countries, the next question to be asked is whether characteristic patterns of differences emerge.

Taking the average DCS scores of the total sample of managers as the dividing line between countries with "participative regimes" and countries with "centralized regimes" we see that the U.K., Israeli and German L 1 managers describe themselves rather consistently as using the most centralized decision methods (Table 3). This self-judgment is corroborated by the judgments of their immediate subordinates describing their superiors' behavior in the case of the U.K. and Israeli managers. British managers are particularly consistent, one could almost say insistent, on describing the decision behavior at the two top

[9] Number of respondents varies whenever one member of a dyad did not respond to one of the items and due to eight sector reduction. N is given in brackets.

Table 3

DEGREE OF DECISION CENTRALIZATION ACCORDING TO COUNTRY
L 1 describes own; L 2 describes decision-making of L 1 (Form 5)

Low Centralization	*L 1* MEAN[10]	*High Centralization*
Netherlands France Sweden* Spain	DEPT	United Kingdom* Germany U.S.A.*
France Sweden Spain	EMP	United Kingdom Germany U.S.A.
Netherlands France Sweden*	SUB	United Kingdom* Germany U.S.A.* Spain
Netherlands France Sweden* Spain	SPEC	United Kingdom* Germany U.S.A.*
France Sweden* U.S.A.	F6	United Kingdom* Israel* Spain*
Netherlands France U.S.A. Israel	F7	United Kingdom Sweden
	L 2	
France* Sweden* Spain* Germany*	DEPT	United Kingdom* Netherlands* Israel* U.S.A.*
France U.S.A.	EMP	United Kingdom Israel
Netherlands Spain Germany	SUB	United Kingdom U.S.A.
France Sweden Spain* Germany	SPEC	United Kingdom* Netherlands Israel* U.S.A.*

[10] Countries with DCS-scores within .05 of MEAN were left out (about one standard error).

Table 3 *(Contd.)*

Low Centralization	*L1 Mean*[10]	*High Centralization*
Netherlands France Sweden* U.S.A.	F6	United Kingdom* Israel*
France* Spain* U.S.A.*	F7	United Kingdom* Netherlands Sweden

* According to Scheffee-Test: Asterisked countries are significantly different from asterisked countries of the opposite group.

levels of their companies as highly centralized! On the basis of the overall DCS values on specific decisions of U.S. managers, we would usually have to locate them among those using the highest degrees of centralized decision making. On the other end of the influence power-sharing continuum appear the Swedish and French managers as employing comparatively decentralized decision-making methods.

Another interesting phenomenon is the difference between the description of decision-making of senior and subordinate levels. There is a tendency for subordinates to describe the dyadic decision pattern as less centralized than the description of the same decision pattern described by the senior manager. In Table 3, this comes out particularly clearly for the German sample of L 2 managers who describe their superior's behavior as relatively decentralized. These results reverse the more usual findings that subordinates describe their superiors' behavior as relatively more centralized than the description given by superiors (for instance, Vroom and Yetton, 1973; Ritchie and Miles, 1970).

A few observations may be appropriate at this stage relating our findings to those of other authors. The cultural cluster thesis of Haire, Ghiselli and Porter (1966), that managerial attitudes seem to fall into recognizable cultural clusters of countries is not supported by our findings. The type of country grouping that emerges from our data suggests that distinctive categories in terms of Nordic, Anglo-Saxon, and Latin-European countries do not exist in decision behavior. German, and sometimes Spanish managers, would have to be grouped with Anglo-Saxon managers; and French, together with Swedish managers, would be grouped together with the Dutch. The marked differences attributed to German and Anglo-Saxon managerial systems in terms of decision centralization and influence power-sharing (cf. Ruedi and Lawrence, 1970; Grosset, 1970; Granick, 1962, 1972; Child and Kieser, 1975) are not verified by our findings. German and British L 1 managers describe their decision behavior basically in similar, namely centralized, terms. If we can use our data for a transatlantic comparison of managerial behavior, we would have to reject the once-famous managerial gap thesis (Servan-Schreiber, 1967) which claims that higher productivity of U.S. firms in comparison to European ones can be explained by the greater degree of delegation and participation among hierarchial levels of U.S. firms. If anything, we would have to group American managers with the most centralized European managers.

Table 4

INDUSTRIAL LABOR (DOMINANT TECHNOLOGY AND MANAGERIAL DECISION MAKING) L1
One-Way ANOVA, DCS-Values, Intl. Dyad File

Sector	*DEPT*	*EMP*	*SUB*	*SPEC*	*F6*	*F7*
1. Electronics	2.82 (73)	2.33 (70)	3.42 (74)	2.88 (67)	2.76 (63)	2.96 (63)
2. Retailing	3.39 (42)	2.64 (40)	3.38 (38)	3.07 (29)	2.94 (39)	2.82 (38)
3. Public Trans.	2.81 (51)	2.59 (48)	3.30 (50)	2.84 (35)	3.04 (63)	3.14 (60)
4. Packaging	3.19 (37)	2.59 (35)	3.27 (37)	2.97 (32)	2.82 (36)	2.52 (36)
5. Banking	3.03 (56)	2.65 (55)	3.31 (58)	2.91 (35)	2.92 (80)	3.22 (80)
6. Tele. Comm.	2.62 (46)	2.30 (45)	2.23 (42)	2.70 (37)	2.77 (49)	2.65 (48)
7. Paper	2.72 (35)	2.34 (39)	3.36 (35)	2.71 (26)	2.69 (38)	2.73 (38)
8. Refinery	2.73 (39)	2.54 (34)	3.21 (34)	2.76 (30)	2.59 (42)	2.96 (42)
Means (Total N)	2.91 (379)	2.49 (369)	3.32 (368)	2.86 (291)	2.83 (410)	2.93 (405)
F-Ratio	4.541	2.735	.92 n.s.	1.894 n.s.	2.903	2.287
Approximate percentage variance explained by sector effect	8	5	1	4	4	3

Meso-level: industrial sector/dominant technology

One of the critical contingency elements for organizational functioning is often assumed to be the dominant technology of an organization (Woodward, 1965; Thompson, 1967; Perrow, 1967, 1970). We have no specific measurements of technology, but the distinct sectors (see Table 4) use, on average, different technologies. Comparing the decision-making of managers in the eight sectors for which we have comparable data, we come to the conclusion that industrial sector or dominant technology does indeed have an impact on managerial behavior (Tables 4–5). Some 5–10 per cent of the variance in decision behavior can be explained on the basis of managers belonging to companies in a particular sector or with a particular technology. Service

Table 5

INDUSTRIAL SECTOR DOMINANT TECHNOLOGY AND MANAGERIAL DECISION MAKING: L 2
One-Way ANOVA, DCS-Values, Intl. Dyad File

Sector	*DEPT*	*EMP*	*SUB*	*SPEC*	*F6*	*F7*
1. Electronics	2,67 (69)	2.11 (70)	2.89 (61)	2.59 (53)	2.62 (63)	2.91 (63)
2. Retailing	3.27 (38)	2.56 (34)	3.14 (36)	2.89 (21)	2.99 (39)	2.72 (38)
3. Public Trans.	2.95 (55)	2.48 (50)	3.17 (40)	2.92 (33)	2.94 (63)	2.72 (60)
4. Packaging	3.17 (31)	2.36 (33)	3.26 (33)	2.88 (20)	2.84 (36)	3.32 (36)
5. Banking	2.84 (51)	2.53 (52)	3.07 (40)	2.72 (24)	2.99 (79)	3.36 (78)
6. Tele. Comm.	2.76 (41)	2.20 (41)	3.05 (35)	2.73 (27)	2.77 (49)	2.85 (48)
7. Paper	2.99 (38)	2.16 (38)	2.97 (31)	2.75 (24)	2.83 (38)	2.93 (38)
8. Refinery	2.48 (35)	2.02 (32)	2.85 (28)	2.42 (22)	2.71 (40)	3.12 (62)
Means (Total N)	2.87 (358)	2.30 (350)	3.04 (304)	2.72 (224)	2.85 (407)	3.00 (403)
F-Ratio	2.572	4.476	2.517	2.649	2.496	3.021
Approximate percentage Variance explained by sector effect	4	8	5	7	4	5

companies, on the whole, tend to have managers who decide in a comparatively more participative fashion, with banking managers taking the lead. The same is true for electronics companies with highly-developed, intensive technologies (Thompson, 1967), while managers dealing with continuous flow technologies appear on the side of higher centralization.

Micro-level: dyadic skill requirements and resources

One of the guiding hypotheses of our research was that objective and perceived skill requirement and skill availability have a major impact on the decision-making process. A non-parametric test of this assumption was employed by splitting the managers into three approximately equal groups on the basis of each variable, for instance "high", "medium" and "low" education, and cross-tabulating with other variables. Table 6 shows the results tabulating

Table 6

THE RELATIONSHIP BETWEEN VARIOUS MEASURES OF SKILL (EDUCATION, etc) AND MANAGERIAL DECISION MAKING[11]

	Level 1 N = 763						*Level 2 N = 783*					
FORM 11	*FORM 5*						*FORM 5:*					
Skills, Education, etc.	*DEPT*	*EMP*	*SUB*	*SPEC*	*FORM 6*	*FORM 7*	*DEPT*	*EMP*	*SUB*	*SPEC*	*FORM 6*	*FORM 7*
Number of professional institutions person belongs to	K0017	C025			C0190 K0000	K0015	K0207	K0001	K0070	K0155	C0000 K0000	
Journals taken	K0001	K0002	K0213	K0141	K0000		K0282	K0000	K0230		K0000	K0107
Journals read	C0003 K0000	K0001	K0005	C0246 K0003			K0082				K0082	
Educational level	C0000 K0000	C0000 K0000	C0218 K0000	C0194 K0000	C0001 K0000	K0145	C0051 K0001	K0013	C0227 K0001	K0133	C0000 K0000	K0019
Number of outside courses attended		K0169		K0092			K0036	K0040			K0043	K0002
Number of inside courses attended	C0010 K0000	K0019	K0008	K0002	C0001 K0000		C0011 K0000	C0163 K0000	K0024	C0155 K0000	C0004 K0000	

[11] This table gives figures only when results are significant above the 5 per cent level. The letter C stands for chi square test; K for Kendall's non-parametric correlation coefficient tau. An entry of K = 0017 means that the correlation is significant at the level of 17 in 10,000. If only noughts are shown, the significance level is better than 1 in 10,000. Similarly for chi square. All relationships shown are negative, i.e. the higher the level of education and skill, the more participative is decision-making (low degree of centralization)

skills and educational background measures against the various assessments of decision styles (Forms 5, 6, and 7: Chi square (C) and Kendall's tau (K)). Results are shown only if they are significant above the 5 per cent level. It can be seen that there is a high degree of consistency in these relationships for both senior levels of management. When skills and educational qualification are high, decision-making is decentralized or participative. This is equally true for both levels and is strongest for the variable measuring formal educational qualifications.

Similar strong evidence comes from the data on the relationship between perceived skill requirements (Form 2), skill availabilities, and decision-making (Table 7). The more demanding a L 1 manager perceives his job to be, compared to his subordinate's job, the more will he be inclined to decide in a centralized rather than in a participative fashion. The result, in Table 7, shows parametric correlations, the non-parametric results being equally consistent and significant.

Table 7 shows results relating to one of the two levels separately. We also have results comparing data from L 1 with data from L 2 (cross-level analysis). In many respects, cross-level data is more reliable since it avoids social desirability and order effect. For instance, we can correlate the senior manager's judgments about job skill differences with his subordinate's description of the decision methods used. Such a table would be the same as Table 7, except that the decision styles on the right-hand side are described by Level 2. The statistical results are very similar, but show slightly smaller correlations coefficients (but all significant above the 1 per cent level).

A substantially different analysis of the relationship between skill and decision making comes from Form 3. Managers are asked to estimate the time it

Table 7

L 1 PERCEPTIONS OF SKILL REQUIREMENTS FOR HIS JOB COMPARED TO THOSE OF HIS SUBORDINATE AN L1 DECISION BEHAVIOR
Correlation Co-efficients (Pearson).
International Dyad File (N=625).

Job performance requirements as judged by L1 (Form 2)	*Decision styles described by L 1*				
	DEPT	*EMP*	*SUB*	*SPEC*	*F6*
Entrepreneurial competence[12]	—.23	—.22	—.20	—.25	—.29
Technical competence	—.17	—.21	—.19	—.22	—.22
Interpersonal competence	—.27	—.21	—.15	—.26	—.28
Average	—.27	—.28	—.24	—.32	—.35

Note: Scale values of skill requirements scales run from 1 = very much more needed to 5 = very much less needed. Significance: all correlations are significant beyond the 1 per cent level.

[12] For items in the various factors, see Appendix.

TABLE 8

L 1 PERCEPTION OF L 2'S PROMOTIONAL FEASIBILITY (SKILL ACQUISITION TIME NEEDED) AND L 1 DECISION BEHAVIOR. Cross-Level Correlation-Coefficients (Pearson). International Dyad File (N = 625).

L 1 perception of skill acquisition time for L 2 (Form 3)	*L 2 perception of L 1 decision making*			
	DEPT	*EMP*	*SUB*	*SPEC*
Entrepreneurial skills	—	.08+		.11++
Technical competence	10+	.12++	.15++	.20++
Interpersonal competence	n.s.	n.s.	n.s.	n.s.
Average	—	.10+	.10+	.16++

Note on significance: + = sign 5 per cent
++ = sign 1 per cent

would take their subordinate to acquire the skills necessary to carry out the senior man's job (promotion feasibility). We hypothesized that when this time estimate was high, centralized decision methods would be used. This assumption is supported by cross-level analysis. (Table 8).

The findings on skill requirements (Form 2) and on skill learning times (Form 3) are complementary. Highly centralized decision making is related to a low estimation of skills needed in a subordinate's job; similarly, it is related to a low estimation of a subordinate's capacities to acquire the skills needed in the L 1 job. Hence, it can be concluded that objectively-measured skills, as well as subjective skill estimates in the dyadic relationship, must be considered to be among the most crucial factors in the understanding of influence and power sharing in modern organizations. These results support the human resources model and the findings of Ritchie and Miles (1970) that a superior's confidence and trust in his subordinates is an important aspect of the participation process.

DISCUSSION AND CONCLUSION

The literature on comparative management and industrial relations is divided between cultural convergence and divergence protagonists (Hofstede and Kassem, 1976; Dore, 1973). It seems likely, however, that, apart from the difficulty of justifying the use of the term "culture", clusters of countries probably vary with the subject matter under investigation and for reasons we do not yet understand fully. Two views are frequently put forward. One suggests that certain countries have traditionally shown similarities of managerial or organizational behavior, for instance, "Latin" countries, or "Nordic" countries. The other view holds that similarities and differences between countries are related to their economic success or stage of development. The first explanation leans towards a natural selection model which "posits that environmental factors select those organizational characteristics that best fit the environment." The second explanation reflects a resource dependence model which claims "that organizations seek to manage or strategically adapt to their environments" (Aldrich and Pfeffer, 1976:79). We do not believe that the evidence in favor of either model is completely convincing. In fact, it may very well be that both models are partially in evidence in every country (Weinshall, 1972).

A previous research team attempted to re-draw the map of the world by revising geographic distances between countries on the basis of their similarity in managerial decision-making attitudes (Haire, Ghiselli and Porter, 1966:ix). The attempt was daring and ingenious, but almost certainly premature (Barrett and Bass, 1976). International comparative work will in future have to pay more attention to different systems levels of organizational functioning (Negandhi and Prasad, 1971). Attention has to be paid to external as well as internal organizational variables at the same time. External indices such as labor market structure, patterns of socialization through family, educational system and on-the-job socialization, turbulence, etc., will have to be considered. One might then discover that similar behavior is not so much a function of "Cultural" likeness (being "Nordic," for instance) as of similar phenotypes based on substantial genotypical differences. An interesting move in this direction was taken by Ajiferuke and Boddewyn (1970) who successfully used eight external indicators (including level of education and life expectancy) in a multiple regressional analysis of the Haire *et. al.* (1966) micro-level data.

The research presented in this paper used two external indicators: country and industrial sector. We see that significant country differences were present, but we cannot yet explain the reason for this. Labelling these differences "cultural" certainly does not help. The significant differences due to the economic-sector variable, however, could bear some resemblence to the "functional niche in the interorganizational division of labor" (Aldrich and Pfeffer, 1976:99), which appears to be a fairly universal explanatory phenomenon that cuts across national boundaries.

We need a framework that links up various explanatory levels from the individual to the wider society. Recent models take a useful step in this direction (Miles *et al.*, 1978; Weinshall, 1976). They postulate a series of relationships between a company's problem-solving activity, its structure, the strategies it adopts in dealing with its environment, and the managerial philosophies which direct choices of behavior. The models do not cover variables such as the economic sectors country or culture, but concentrate on the links among market behavior, organization structure, and managerial processes. One of these models further attempts to relate these variables to managerial choices between human relations and human resources models (Miles, 1965).

Our data gives considerable support to human resources model thinking. Managers seem to adjust their decision behavior to their perception of skills among subordinates. Where skill resources are great, participative decision making is significantly more prevalent than in circumstances when skill resources are low or seen to be low. This finding is now well established in previously published results from American, British and German samples (Heller, 1971; Heller and Wilpert, 1977; Wilpert, 1977).

The relationship between skill and participation is of practical importance for two reasons. In the first place, it prevents or minimizes the practice of using participation to give people "a feeling" of it, rather than the reality which implies a measure of influence sharing (Strauss, 1963). What Etzioni (1969) has called "inauthentic participation" is based on the naive assumption that pretending to give people influence, by consultation for instance, will keep them happy. When the objective is to use people's skills rather than to keep them happy, genuine participation has to be used.

The second practical consequence of our finding relates to training. If participative decision-making is (in part) a function of skill resources, then increasing skills is a way of increasing participation. In contrast, it is probably true that training packages designed to increase participative behavior as such are likely to increase inauthentic participation with all the negative practical and ethical consequences this implies (Clarke and McCabe, 1970; Cummings and Schmidt, 1972).

On the theoretical level, the link between the use of skills and participative decision-making is congruent with the view that skill utilization is a motivating factor. Argyris and Schon (1974) have pointed to this possibility when they argue for the idea that "man is also motivated by a sense of competence and a need to be effective." They see "one source of human energy is psychological success with challenging opportunities; thus, effectiveness may be connected with psychological health" (Argyris and Schon, 1974:x). The connection between skill and utilization, participative decision-making, effectiveness and psychological health is certainly worth exploring.

REFERENCES

Ajiferuke, M., and J. Boddewyn. "Socioeconomic Indicators in Comparative 1970 Management." *Administrative Science Quarterly*. 15:453–458.

Aldrich, H. E., and J. Pfeffer. "Environments of Organizations." *Annual Review of* 1976 *Sociology*. 2:79–105.

Argyris, Ch., and D. A. Schon. *Theory is Practice: Increasing Professional Effectiveness.* 1974 San Francisco: Jossey-Bass, Inc.

Barrett, G. V., and B. M. Bass. "Cross-Cultural Issues in Industrial and Organizational 1976 Psychology." In Marvin Dunnette (ed.), *Handbook of Industrial and Organizational Psychology*: 1639–1686. Chicago, Ill.: Rand McNally.

Bass, B., and E. Valenzi. "Contingent Aspects of Effective Management Styles." In 1974 J. Hunt and L. Larson (eds.), *Contingency Approaches to Leadership*: 130–152. Carbondale and Edwardsville, Southern Ill.: University Press.

Bass, B., E. Valenzi, D. Farrow, and R. Solomon. "Management Styles Associated with 1975 Organizational Task, Personal, and Interpersonal Contingencies." *Journal of Applied Psychology*. 60:720729.

Bavelas, J. B. "Systems Analysis of Dyadic Interaction: The Role of Interpersonal 1975 Judgement." *Behavioral Science*. 20:213–222.

Blankenship, L. V., and R. E. Miles. "Organizational Structure and Managerial Decision 1968 Behavior." *Administrative Science Quarterly*. 13:106–120.

Brossard, M., and M. Maurice. "Betriebliche Organisationsstrukturen im interkulturellen 1974 Vergleich." *Soziale Welt.* 25:432–454.

Child, J., and A. Kieser. "Organization and Managerial Roles in British and West-1975 German Companies—an Examination of the Culture-Free Thesis." Institut für Unternehmensführung, Free University Berlin, Working Paper.

Clarke, A. W., and S. McCabe. "Leadership Beliefs of Australian Managers." *Journal of* 1970 *Applied Psychology*. 54:1–6.

Crozier, M., and E. Friedberg. *L'acteur et le Systēme.* Paris: Le Seuil. 1977

Cummings, L., and St. M. Schmidt. "Managerial Attidues of Greeks: The Roles of 1972 Culture and Industrialization." *Administrative Science Quarterly.* 17:265–272.

Dore, R. *British Factory—Japanese Factory.* London: George Allen & Unwin. 1973

Etzioni, A. "Man and Society: the Inauthentic Condition." *Human Relations.* 1969 22:325–332

Granick, D. *The European Executive.* London: Weidenfeld and Nicholson 1962

Grosset, S. *Management: American and European Styles.* Belmont, Cal.: Wadsworth 1970 Publ.

Haire, M., E. Ghiselli, and L. W. Porter. *Managerial Thinking: An International Study.* 1966 New York, London, Sidney: John Wiley.

Heller, F. A. "Group Feed-back Analysis: A method of field research." *Psychological* 1969 *Bulletin*. 72:108–117.

———. *Managerial Decision Making: A Study of Leadership Styles and Power* 1971 *Sharing among Senior Managers*. London: Tavistock Publications.

———. "The Decision Process: Analysis of Power Sharing at Senior Organizational 1976 Levels." In R. Dubin (ed.), *Handbook of Work, Organization and Society*: 687–745. Chicago: Rand McNally.

———. "Leadership, Decision-Making and Contingency Theory." *Industrial* 1973 *Relations*. 12:183–199.

———. "Infrastructures of Organizational Power: A Process Model", *International* 1974 *Institute of Management*, Preprint I/74–59. Berlin.

Hofstede, G., and S. Kassem. *European Contributions to Organization Theory*. Assen, 1976 Netherlands: Van Gorcum.

Jago, A. G., and V. H. Vroom. "Perceptions of Leadership Style: Superior and 1975 Subordinate Descriptions of Decision-making Behavior." In J. G. Hunt and L. Larson (eds.), *Leadership Frontiers*: 103–120. Kent, Ohio: Kent State University Press.

Jago, A. G., and V. H. Vroom. "Hierarchical Level and Leadership Style." *Organizational* 1977 *Behavior and Human Performance*. 18:131–145.

Marrett, C. B., J. Hage, and M. Aiken. "Communication and Satisfaction in 1975 Organizations." *Human Relations*. 28:611–626.

Miles, R. E. "Human Relations or Human Resources?" *Harvard Business Review*. 1965 43:148–163.

Miles, R. E. and C. C. Snow. *Organization, Strategy, Structure and Process*. New York: 1978 McGraw-Hill.

Millar, J. A. "Contingency Theory, Values and Change." *Mimeographed*, undated.

Moberg, D. J., and J. L. Koch. "A Critical Appraisal of Integrated Treatments of 1975 Contingency Findings." *Academy of Management Journal*. 18:109–124.

Negandhi, A. and B. Prasad. *Comparative Management*. New York: Appleton Century 1971 Croft.

Perrow, C. "A Framework for the Comparative Analysis of Organization." *American*
1967 *Sociological Review*. 32:194–208.

———. *Organizational Analysis: A Sociological View.* Belmont, Cal., London:
1970 Wadsworth Publ.

Pfeffer, J., and G. R. Salancik. "Determinants of Supervisory Behavior: A Role Set
1975 Analysis." *Human Relations*. 28:139–154.

Pye, L. W. "Mao Tse-Tung's Leadership Style." *Political Science Quarterly*.
1976 91:219–235.

Ritchie, J. B. and R. E. Miles. "An Analysis of Quantity and Quality of Participation as
1972 Mediating Variables in the Participative Decision-Making Process." *Personnel Psychology*. 23:347–359.

Roberts, K. "On Looking at an Elephant: An Evaluation of Cross-Cultural Research
1970 Related to Organizations." *Psychological Bulletin*. 74:327–350.

Ruedi, A., and P. R. Lawrence. "Organizations in Two Cultures." In J. W. Lorsch and
1970 P. R. Lawrence (eds.), *Studies in Organizational Design*: 54–83. Homewood, Ill.: Irwin.

Servan-Schreiber, J.-J. *Le Défi Américain*. Paris: Editions Denoel.
1967

Staehle, W. H. *Organisation und Führung sozio-technischer Systeme. Grundlagen einer*
1973 *Situationstheorie.* Stuttgart: Enke Verlag.

Strauss, G. "Some notes on power equalization." In H. J. Leavitt (ed.), *The Social*
1963 *Science of Organizations*: 39–84. Englewood Cliffs, N.J.: Prentice Hall.

Tagiuri, R. and L. Petrullo. *Person Perception and Interpersonal Behavior*. Stanford, Cal.:
1958 Stanford University.

Thompson, J. D. *Organizations in Action: Social Science Basis of Administrative Theory*.
1967 New York: McGraw-Hill.

Vroom, V. H. and Ph. W. Yetton. *Leadership and Decision-Making*. Pittsburgh, Pa.:
1973 University of Pittsburgh Press.

Weinshall, T. D., The Industrialization of a Rapidly Developing Country—Israel, in:
1976 Robert Dubin (ed.), *Handbook of Work, Organization and Society*. Chicago, Ill: Rand McNally.

Weinshall, T. D. (ed.). *Culture and Management*. London: Penguin Books.
1977

Wilpert, B. and F. A. Heller. "Power Sharing at Senior Management Levels." *Omega*.
1973 1:451–464.

Wilpert, B. *Führung in deutschen Unternehmen*. Berlin, New York: W. de Gruyter.
1977

Woodward, J. *Industrial Organization: Theory and Practice*. London: Oxford University
1965 Press.

Appendix
QUESTIONNAIRES AND RELIABILITY MEASURES

Job Performance Requirements
(Form 2)[13]

TO WHAT EXTENT AND HOW DOES THE NATURE OF YOUR OWN JOB DIFFER FROM THAT OF YOUR SUBORDINATE/SUPERIOR (Differences in pay, status, etc., do not form part of this enquiry)

Please put a circle around the item you select.

1. Does your own job require more or less detailed KNOWLEDGE OF TECHNICAL MATTERS?

Very much more	More	About the same	Somewhat less	Much less
1	2	3	4	5

2. Does your own job require CLOSER OR LESS CLOSE CONTACT WITH PEOPLE?
3. Does your own job require more or less KNOWLEDGE OF HUMAN NATURE?
4. Does your own job require more or less IMAGINATION than your subordinate's job?
5. Does your own job require more or less SELF CONFIDENCE?
6. Does your own job require more or less RESPONSIBILITY than your subordinate's?
7. Does your own job require more or less DECISIVENESS?
8. Does your own job require more or less TACT than your subordinate?
9. Does your own job require more or less ADAPTABILITY?
10. Does your own job require more or less FORCEFULNESS than your subordinate?
11. Does your own job require more or less INTELLIGENCE?
12. Does your own job require more or less INITIATIVE than your subordinate?

Skill Acquisition Time
(Form 3)

IF YOU[14] WERE PROMOTED TO ANOTHER JOB TODAY AND YOUR (named)

---

[13] Administered to both managerial levels.
Internal consistency measures (Crombach's α) of composites based on factor analysis:

Entrepreneurial competence	(items 4, 5, 6, 7, 10, 12)	=.850
Technical competence	(items 1, 11)	=.722
Interpersonal competence	(items 2, 3, 8, 9)	=.384
Average of all 12 items		=.866

[14] Filled in by Level 1. Level 2 responds in terms of how much time L 2 would need.
Internal consistency measures (Crombach's α) of composites based on factor analysis:

Entrepreneurial competence	(items 9, 6, 7, 10)	=.841
Technical competence	(items 1, 4, 9, 11, 12)	=.792
Interpersonal competence	(items 2, 3, 8)	=.708
Average of all 12 items		=.886

IMMEDIATE SUBORDINATE WERE TO STEP INTO YOUR SHOES TOMORROW. HOW MUCH TIME—IF ANY—WOULD HE NEED TO ACQUIRE THE NECESSARY SKILL? (For level 2: if you were to step into your Boss's shoes tomorrow, how much time. . .)

Please *circle* the appropriate response:

1. The extent to which the job requires DETAILED TECHNICAL KNOWLEDGE

Almost no time	1 month	3 months	6 months	1 year	3 years	6 years	10 years	15 years	Would never learn
	——— .	——— .	——— .	———	——— .	——— .	——— .	——— .	

2. The extent to which the job requires CLOSE CONTACT WITH PEOPLE.
3. The extent to which the job requires KNOWLEDGE OF HUMAN NATURE.
4. The extent to which the job requires IMAGINATION.
5. How much time would *HE* need to acquire the necessary skills to the extent to which the job requires SELF CONFIDENCE.
6. The extent to which the job requires RESPONSIBILITY
7. The extent to which the job requires DECISIVENESS.
8. How much time would *HE* need to require the necessary skills to the extent to which the job requires TACT.
9. The extent to which the job requires ADAPTABILITY.
10. The extent to which the job requires FORCEFULNESS.
11. The extent to which the job requires INTELLIGENCE.
12. The extent to which the job requires INITIATIVE.

Specific Decision Questionnaire

(Form 5)

Below is a set of decisions. If you[15] do not have the authority to make the final decision, or at least to make a formal recommendation that will usually be accepted, then check the box marked "not applicable." However, if the decision is applicable, then indicate which of the various decision procedures you use to arrive at the decision or recommendation. If you use more than one procedure, split up the percentages accordingly. Most usually, however, you will put 100 next to one of the five alternatives.

1. The decision to increase the salary of your direct subordinate.

( ) Not applicable
1———% Own decision without detailed explanation
2———% Own decision with detailed explanation
3———% Prior consultation with subordinate
4———% Joint decision-making with subordinate
5———% Delegation of decision to subordinate

TOTAL 100%

---

[15] This questionnaire is filled in by Level 1 managers. Level 2 managers answer the same question, but always describing the decision behavior of his immediate superior. DEPT. decisions are: 5, 8; EMP: 2, 3, 6, 7, 9; SUB; 1, 4, 10, 11, 12; SPEC: Average of all twelve decisions.

2. The decision to increase the number of employees working for your subordinate.
3. The decision to hire one of several applicants to work for your subordinate.
4. The decision on the style and lay-out of typed letters in your subordinates office.
5. The decision relating to the purchase of a piece of equipment for your department at a cost within your budgetary discretion.
6. The decision to promote one of the employees working for your subordinate.
7. The decision to give a merit pay increase to one of your subordinate's employees.
8. The decision to change the money allocation for your department during the preparation of the company budget (or next year's planning).
9. The decision to discharge one of your subordinate's staff.
10. The decision to change an operating procedure followed by your subordinate.
11. The decision to assign your subordinate to a different job (on same salary) under your jurisdiction.
12. The decision regarding what goals or standard of performance (or policy) should be set for your subordinate.

Retest reliability: .82 (N = 32) with an interval of seven weeks.

General Decision Questionnaire

(Form 6)[16]

Please consider ALL the IMPORTANT decisions with which you are faced in the course of your job (including those not listed on Form 5).

Indicate in a general and overall way the percentage of cases in which you use each of the five decision procedures. If, in general, you do not use a particular procedure, simply put 0 % next to it. You are still thinking primarily of your interaction with your named subordinate.

1———— % Own decision without detailed explanation

2———— % Own decision with detailed explanation

3———— % Prior consultation with subordinate

4———— % Joint decision-making with subordinate

5———— % Delegation of decision to subordinate

100 %

[16] Filled in by both managerial levels

Lateral Decision Questionnaire
(Form 7)[17]

We now deal with a different issue.

You probably have *colleagues at the same level as yourself* and you may (at times) wish to discuss your pending decision with them. The relationship with your colleagues will depend on many factors and will differ from person to person and firm to firm.

Please think only of your colleagues and NOT your superior(s). Consider all important decisions that you normally make in the course of a year, and state how you make them on average:

1——— % Own decision without explanation to colleagues

2——— % Own decision with explanation to colleagues

3——— % Prior consultations with colleagues

4——— % Jointly with colleagues

5——— % Leave decisions to colleagues to make[18]

100 %

Note: "Decision" includes advice that is usually accepted.

[17] We mean decisions you normally take or could take yourself, if you wished to do so.
[18] Filled in by both managerial levels.

Organizational Goals in the Peruvian Co-Determination and the Yugoslav Self-Determination Systems

J. DUANE HOOVER
ROGER M. TROUB
CARTON J. WHITEHEAD
Texas Tech University

LUIS G. FLORES
Escuela de Administration de Negocios para Graduados
(ESAN) Lima, Peru

In recent years efforts to provide workers with more participation in the determination of general decisions concerning the management of industrial firms have been made in a number of countries. Many writers, such as Fine (1973), Flaes (1973), Karlsson (1973), Mumford (1976), and Zimblist (1976), have commented on the introduction of new industrial organization legislation in different countries. These new forms of organization, adopted in markedly different socio-cultural settings, can be expected to have important impacts on social, economic, and political processes and on the characteristics and organizational behavior of firms (Adizes, 1971; Bernstein, 1976; Kuhne, 1976; Vanek, 1974; Zimblist, 1975). Despite the implications of these different impacts in different settings, there is a paucity of comparative investigation.

The study from which this report is drawn sought to identify, compare and analyze (1) the May, 1975, perceptions of the hierarchy of goals of their firms by chief executive officers operating under the Peruvian co-determination system and the perceptions of their counterparts in the Yugoslav self-determination system; and (2) the May, 1975, perceptions by managers in both countries of their firm's goals hierarchy five years earlier. The Escuela de Administracion de Negocios para Graduados (ESAN) funded and directed the field portion of the research in Peru, and financial assistance from the Ford Foundation made the Yugoslav field work possible. The study was also designed to provide benchmark information for future analyses, particularly future analysis of change over time. The purpose of this article is to report findings which concern the perceptions of goal hierarchies.

The perception of the nature of the organizational goal hierarchy was selected for investigation because of its crucial importance in influencing the nature and behavior of firms and of groups and individuals within firms. Peru was selected because introduction of its co-determination system presented a potential for massive organizational change in its industrial sector and the need for information to assess impacts of the system's introduction. Yugoslavia was chosen for comparative purposes because it served as a partial model for changes in the Peruvian economic system; because it also is a less developed country, but with notably different socio-cultural characteristics; and because it has a much longer period of experience with its system of worker participation. Two manufacturing industries were examined, plastics products and the knitted products section of the textile industry. These industries were examined because they are common to both countries, because of the relatively high degree of similarity of the technologies found in both countries for each of the two industries, and because of the differences between the two—the nature of the plastics industry makes it inherently more dynamic.

In this article, the nature of the Peruvian and Yugoslav approaches to power equalization and the nature of the conceptual context of the investigation will be outlined first. Then the methods and procedures of the study will be described. The findings concerning perceptions of organization goal hierarchies will be presented next, and finally a discussion of the findings will be provided.

THE RESEARCH SETTING

Power Equalization and the Yugoslav and Peruvian Systems

Power equalization efforts can be defined as any attempt to broaden the distribution of decision-making power in an organization by modifying the structure of authority in the management system. Organizational structures involving efforts toward power equalization can vary over a wide range. The Peruvian and Yugoslav efforts toward power equalization have important similarities and have important differences.

Both efforts involve attempts to increase distributional equity and productive efficiency. Both were also conceived as important ingredients in national efforts to increase economic growth and development, both were legislated into existence as a major element in the economic structure of the economy, and both emphasize worker participation in decision-making. The Yugoslav efforts provided a partial model for the Peruvian experiment in the legislative change of the organizational structure of industrial enterprises.

The Yugoslav process toward power equalization began in 1950. The system which has been developed can be termed a self-determination model in which enterprises are owned by the nation, but workers in the enterprise determine production and investment programs, price products, and set the compensation to be received by member workers of the enterprise for their productive contributions.

The Yugoslav experiment involves a management system divided into four levels (Glueck and Kavran, 1973): policy, administrative, advisory, and operating (see Figure 1). The top authority at the policy level is the workers' council

Figure 1

INTERNAL ORGANIZATION OF THE YUGOSLAV MANAGEMENT SYSTEM

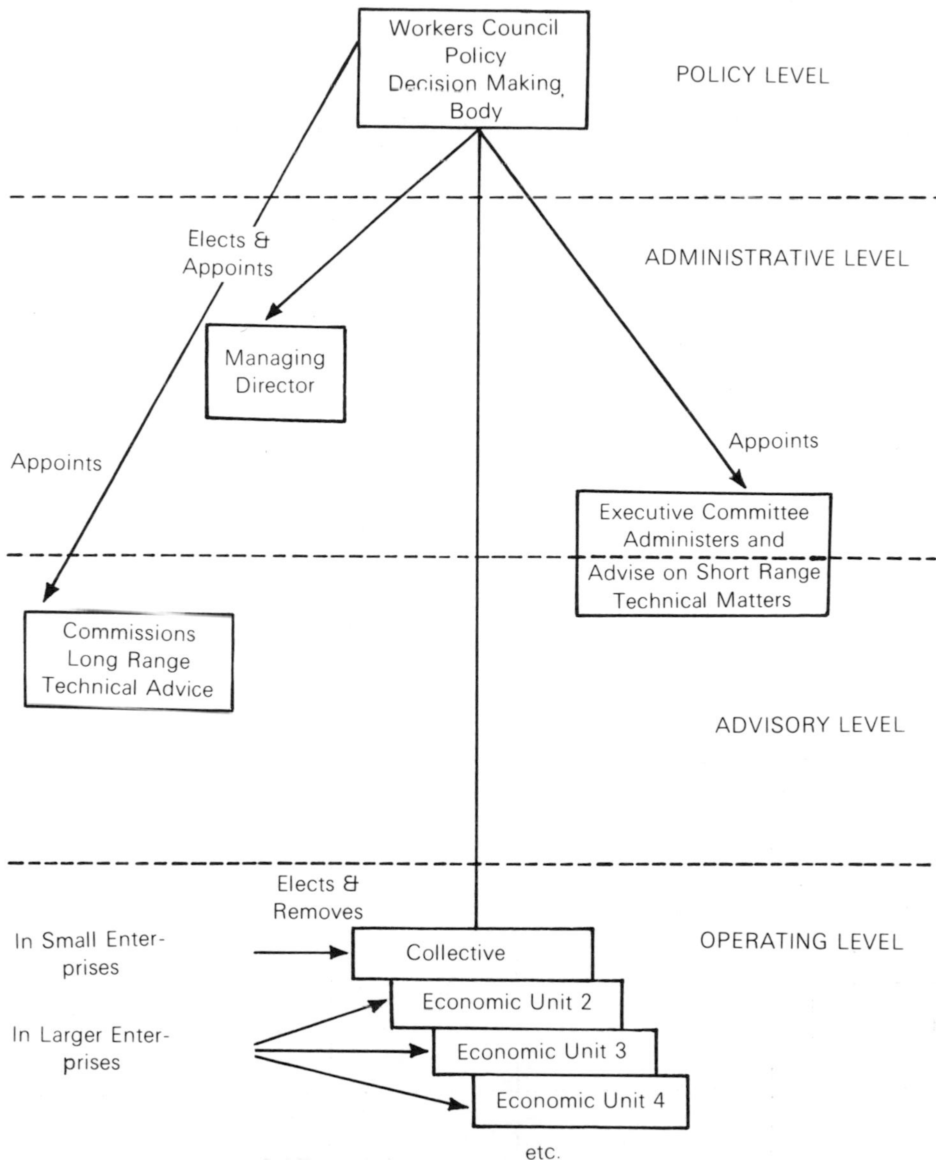

composed for full-time workers elected by all workers in larger enterprises or of all workers in enterprises with fewer than 30 employees. It is the legislative body which formulates long-range policy and protects the interests of the workers.

There are two main divisions at the administrative level: the managing director and the executive committee. The former is elected by the workers' council and is charged with the responsibility of implementation of the decisions of the council. Executive committees are appointed by the council to provide operation and control decisions and short-term planning decisions. At the advisory level, the executive committees also provide advice on long-run matters. Technical advice on long-run considerations is handled by a commission selected by the workers' council. The blue and white collar workers at the

Figure 2

INTERNAL ORGANIZATION OF THE PERUVIAN MANAGEMENT DECISION-MAKING STRUCTURE

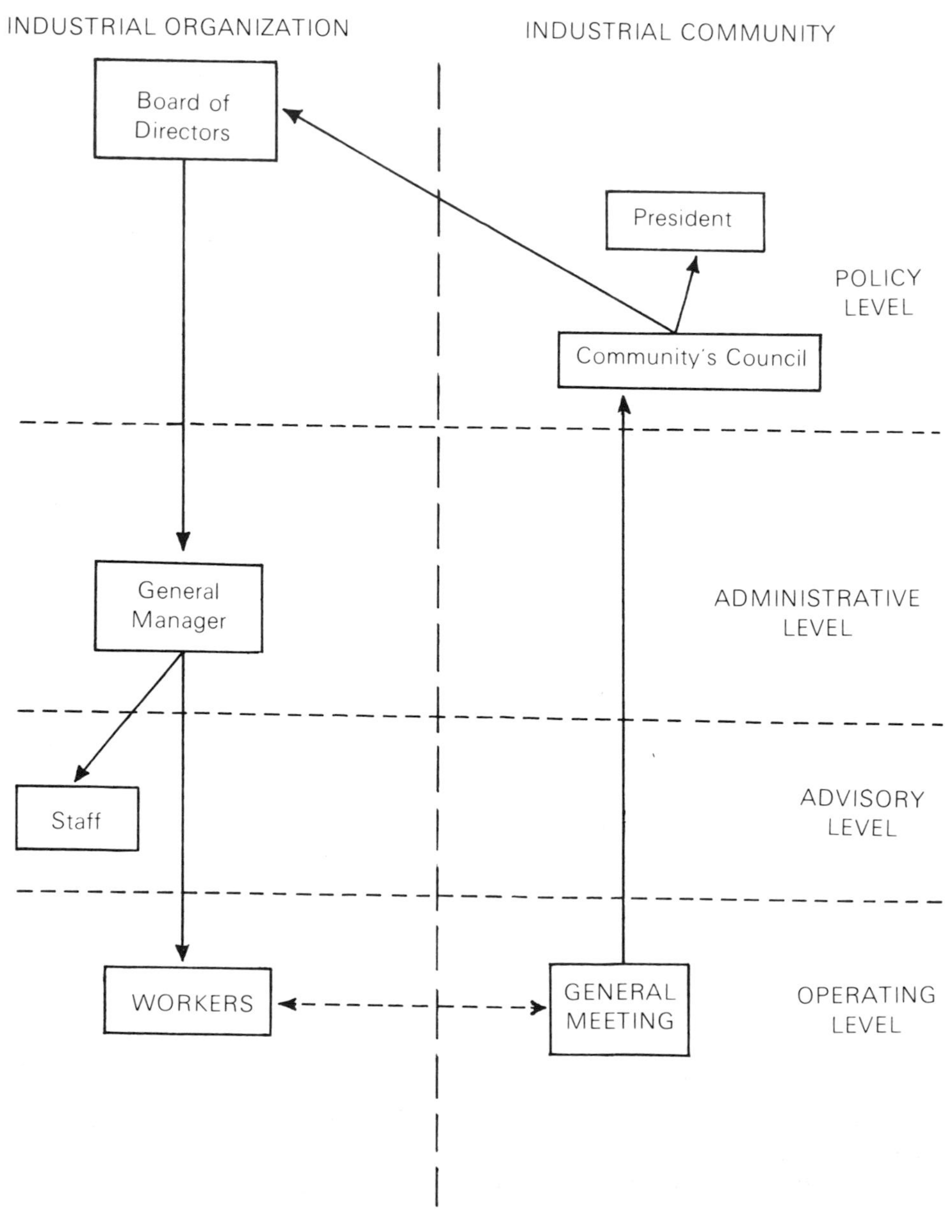

operating level do not hold major administrative positions, but some are members of the workers' council and some are members of the executive committees.

The Peruvian experiment began in 1970 when major legislation was enacted to introduce what was called an economic system of reformed private enterprise ("Ley de Comunidad Industrial" D.L.:18384, 1970). The law provided for the transformation of the structure of industrial firms from that of purely private enterprises to one in which workers and private owners would co-determine control of enterprises in a 50–50 split of decision-making authority through the board of directors as established by the "industrial communities." The co-determination legislation sought to achieve a measure of worker participation in a set of decisions similar to those in which the workers in the Yugoslav self-determination system participate. One of the significant differences is the extent of worker influence in decision-making processes. The Peruvian law specified a bifurcated authority structure (See Figure 2).

In the Peruvian scheme all workers in the firm are members of the industrial community which has its own officers and administration. The industrial community is authorized to name representatives to the firm's board of directors in proportion to the company's shares currently held by the industrial community through the Peruvian law which required firms to set aside a percent of their pre-tax profits. Under the 1970 legislation, two per cent of those profits went to a national research fund, 10 per cent were assigned to an employee profit sharing program and the remaining 15 per cent were to be recapitalized as shares in the firm which belong to the industrial community. It was required that the distribution of the stock continue until the industrial community owned one-half of the firm.

As illustrated in Figure 2, the flow of decision-making authority in the Peruvian scheme can be viewed as a circle from the board of directors (on which the workers are represented), down to the general manager, through the various levels of management to workers in general. The workers form the industrial community which elects a council which, in turn, designates the workers' representatives on the board of directors. Thus, the management of the firm is influenced by the decision-making authority of the people who are being managed.

At the time of the study, most firms in the sample had from 17 to 25 per cent worker ownership, with an average of 22 per cent. Although the Peruvian co-determination system was still in its formative stage, enough change had occurred to provide an opportunity to examine managers' perceptions of aspects of the Peruvian experiment in its early period.

Conceptual Underpinnings

The nature, role and significance of organizational goals and support for the individual elements of the theoretical underpinnings of this study can be derived from several sources (Sills, 1958; Thompson, 1958; Etzioni, 1960; Perrow, 1961; Parsons, 1963; Simon, 1964; Thompson, 1967). The conceptual structure underlying some of the relationships selected for the study can be represented by the following propositions:

(1) Organizations are instrumental social phenomenon. As such their

goals are significant to their legitimacy in and coalignment with their socio-cultural and political environment;

(2) Organizational goals are fundamental influences on organizational behavior. They constitute a basic set of constraints for organizational decisions;

(3) Organizational goals reflect the perspectives, perceived interests, and values of those actors who formulate organizational goals;

(4) The perspectives, perceived interests, and values of actors vary significantly by intra- and inter-country differences in socio-cultural characteristics;

(5) Significant changes in the composition of the set of actors which determine organizational goals can be expected to result in significant changes in the characteristics of the set of organizational goals; and

(6) Different configurations within organizational goal sets can be expected in different socio-cultural settings even though the aims of the establishment of particular organizational structures may be similar and there may be significant similarities in the particular structures established.

Applied to the Peruvian shift in the authority structure of industrial enterprises toward greater worker influence on goals of the firm, these propositions lead to an *a priori* expectation of perceptions of changes in the goal hierarchy by chief executives. At the same time, the perceptions of goal hierarchies by Yugoslavian executives could be expected to be more stable. They also lead to *a priori* expectations of differences in the perceptions of goal hierarchies between Peru and Yugoslavia, since they have markedly different socio-cultural characteristics. The study sought to obtain information about those perceptions.

METHODS AND PROCEDURES

The data for the study were collected by the administration of a questionnaire during a personal interview with chief executive officers (CEOs). If the CEO was unavailable, the second manager in the firm's managerial hierarchy was interviewed. Data were obtained in 1975 for 35 managers in Peru (19 plastics firms and 16 textiles firms) and for 32 managers in Yugoslavia (14 plastics firms and 18 textiles firms). In Peru, the firms examined included all firms in the selected industries with 50 or more workers located in the area of Lima and Callao, areas which account for about 80 per cent of the total industrial output of the country. In Yugoslavia, managers from all of the firms in the selected industries in the Republic of Serbia and the two independent provinces of Viovodina and Kosovo were interviewed.

Among other things, information was solicited concerning the ranking of goals for the firm currently and the current perceptions of the rank order of goals five years earlier, just before the enactment of the Peruvian power equalization legislation. The researchers recognize that the 1970 and 1976 perceptions of individual managers are not independent. However, this procedure did allow the research to focus upon the individual manager's perception of the change in his firm's goal hierarchy relative to the five-year period. Caution was taken to use procedures which would deal with the introduction of statistical biases not related to the information sought. For example, the order of presentation of goals to the managers was randomized each time they were presented to a manager.

A closed response process was employed which required the executives to rank the goals of their firms from among the following alternatives:

(1) Profitability (improvement in the rate of return on investment);
(2) Employment (provision of more and better jobs and/or higher wages and/or more stable employment);
(3) Technological Leadership (leadership in the industry in technological innovation and sophistication in products and in production techniques);
(4) Social Contribution (contribution to the solution of public and social problems including those associated with education, transportation, technology, and health conditions);
(5) Economic Development (accommodation to the economic system of the country in a fashion which contributes to the economic development of the country); and
(6) Production (expansion of physical output to the maximum extent feasible).

Ideal circumstances would have permitted information to be obtained through time concerning all of the various important actors in the system of goal formulation and modification. The conditions almost always confronted in cross-cultural comparative research efforts, however, are far from ideal. For example, in order to gain the cooperation of the participating managers, it was necessary to forego collection of demographic and job-related data. Collection of such data, while highly desirable, could have jeopardized the entire research project. The constraints placed on the research reported here and the nature of the information sought did not permit the use of some of the more sophisticated statistical techniques currently available. Nevertheless, cross-cultural comparative research efforts, even when constrained to the typical conditions, can provide enriched comprehensions of and useful insights into a variety of important phenomena.

THE FINDINGS

The findings of the study reported here are organized in terms of five hypotheses. After presentation of the hypotheses and the data associated with them, discussion of the findings will be provided in the section which follows.

Hypothesis I: There will be no evidence of differences between the Peruvian manager's perceptions of the organizational goal hierarchy at the time of the study (May, 1975) and their May, 1975, perceptions of the organizational goal hierarchy in 1970 (the year before the Industrial Community Law became effective).

The goal hierarchy perceptions of the Peruvian managers, the average rankings of the goals, and the percentage breakdown of responses are provided

Table 1

PERCEPTIONS OF PERUVIAN MANAGERS OF THEIR FIRMS ORGANIZATIONAL GOAL HIERARCHY—MAY, 1975

Organizational Goals	*Hierarchy Based on the Average Ranking*		*Average Ranking*	
	1970	*1975*	*Perceptions Concerning 1970*	*Perceptions Concerning 1975*
Production	1	1	1.70	1.66
Economic Development	2	2	3.00	2.89
Technological Leadership	3	3	3.29	3.43
Profitability	4	4	3.56	3.60
Employment	5	5	4.00	4.00
Social Contribution	6	6	5.44	5.51

in Tables 1 and 2. The data collected do not permit the null hypothesis to be rejected. The average rankings of the goal hierarchy in May, 1975, and of concurrent perceptions of the goal hierarchy in 1970 are strikingly similar, and they result in very high Spearman and Kendall rank order correlation coefficients (Table 3).

The second hypothesis concerned the perceptions of organizational goal hierarchies in Yugoslavia.

Hypothesis II: There will be no evidence of differences between the Yugoslav managers' perceptions of the organizational goal hierarchy of their firms at the time of the study (May, 1975) and their May, 1975, perceptions of the organizational goal hierarchy of their firms in 1970.

In contrast to the Peruvian data, the Yugoslav data indicate perceptions of marked differences in the managers perceptions of the goal hierarchies for their firms (Tables 4 and 5), and the data yielded relatively low rank order correlation coefficients (Table 3) and tended to support the rejection of the hypothesis.

The third hypothesis dealt with the relationships between the perceptions of the selected Peruvian managers and their Yugoslav counterparts.

Hypothesis III: There will be no evidence of differences between the Peruvian managers' perceptions of the organizational goal hierarchy of their firms and the Yugoslav managers' perceptions of the hierarchy of their firms at the time of the study (May, 1975).

A comparison of the average ranking of goals by the Peruvian and Yugoslav managers is provided by the data in Table 6. The average rankings differ somewhat but not greatly. The production and contribution to economic

Table 2

PERCENTAGE RANKING OF INDIVIDUAL ORGANIZATIONAL GOALS: MANAGERS' PERCEPTION IN PERU

*Goals**	*Year*	*Rank 1*	*Rank 2*	*Rank 3*	*Rank 4*	*Rank 5*	*Rank 6*	*Total*
Production	1970	50.0	32.4	14.7	2.9	0.0	0.0	100%
	1975	51.4	34.3	11.4	2.9	0.0	0.0	100%
Economic Developpment	1970	14.7	26.5	23.5	20.6	8.8	5.9	100%
	1975	14.1	28.6	22.9	17.1	8.6	5.7	100%
Technological Leadership	1970	20.6	14.7	17.6	17.6	20.6	8.8	100%
	1975	17.1	14.3	17.1	20.0	22.9	8.6	100%
Profitability	1970	11.8	17.6	11.8	26.5	26.5	5.9	100%
	1975	11.4	14.3	14.3	28.6	27.3	5.7	100%
Employment	1970	0.0	8.8	29.4	20.6	35.3	5.9	100%
	1975	0.0	8.6	28.6	22.9	34.3	5.7	100%
Social Contribution	1970	2.9	0.0	2.9	11.8	8.8	73.5	100%
	1975	2.9	0.0	5.7	8.6	8.6	74.3	100%

*In order of 1975 Average Ranking.

development goals were ranked first and second respectively in both countries. The average ranking data indicate a greater degree of consensus among the Peruvian managers than among the Yugoslav managers. The Spearman and Kendall rank correlation coefficients do not support the notion of an extremely high degree of similarity between the average rankings of the managers in the two countries (Table 2).

The findings associated with the first three hypotheses could be influenced by a variety of factors. Two additional hypotheses were formulated to probe the possible influence of firm size and industry differences. Hypothesis IV was directed to the relationships between the managers' perceptions of the goal hierarchy for their firms and the size of their firms.

Hypothesis IV: There will be no evidence of differences between managers' perceptions of the organizational goal hierarchy in large firms and managers of small firms perceptions of the organizational goal hierarchy for their firms in either Peru or Yugoslavia.

The analysis associated with Hypothesis IV involved ranking the firms by

Table 3

RANK ORDER CORRELATION COEFFICIENTS BETWEEN THE RELATIVE FREQUENCY DISTRIBUTION OF THE ORGANIZATIONAL GOAL HIERARCHIES REPORTED BY PERUVIAN AND YUGOSLAV MANAGERS*

	Peru				*Yugoslavia*			
	May 1975 Perceptions		*Perceptions Concerning 1970*		*May 1975 Perceptions*		*Perceptions Concerning 1970*	
	Spearman	*Kendall*	*Spearman*	*Kendall*	*Spearman*	*Kendall*	*Spearman*	*Kendall*
Peru Perceptions	—	—	.9870	.9493	.3997	.3079	.1990	.1463
May 1975	—	—	(.001)**	(.001)	(.008)	(.004)	(.122)	(.105)
Perceptions Concerning	—	—	—	—	.3771	.3012	.1663	.1161
1970	—	—	—	—	(.122)	(.005)	(.166)	(.160)
Yugoslavia Perceptions	—	—	—	—	—	—	.4733	.3776
May 1975	—	—	—	—	—	—	(.002)	(.001)

* The Frequency distribution is expressed in percentages.
** The numbers in parentheses represent the level of significance of the coefficients.

Table 4

PERCEPTIONS OF YUGOSLAV MANAGERS OF THEIR FIRMS ORGANIZATIONAL GOAL HIERARCHY—MAY, 1975

Organizational Goals	*Hierarchy based on the Average Ranking*		*Average Ranking*	
	1970	*1975*	*Perceptions Concerning 1970*	*Perceptions Concerning 1975*
Production	1	1	2.96	2.78
Economic Development	4	2	3.72	3.25
Technological Leadership	4	2	3.72	3.25
Employment	3	4	3.34	3.69
Social Contribution	6	5	4.13	3.81
Profitability	2	6	3.13	4.22

size in terms of the number of employees and comparison of the data for the managers of firms in the upper and lower quartiles. The Spearman and Kendall rank order correlation coefficients for the average rankings between managers of large and small firms are provided in Table 7 for the Peruvian and the Yugoslav managers separately. Some association is indicated for the rankings of the managers of large and small firms in Peru, but the data do not tend to support the null hypothesis. The degree of association among the Yugoslav managers is low and supports the rejection of the hypothesis in the Yugoslav case.

Hypothesis V: There will be no evidence of differences in the average goal hierarchy rankings between managers of firms in the plastics products industry and managers of firms in the textiles industry in either Peru or Yugoslavia.

Some support was found for the hypothesis applied to Peruvian managers (Table 6). The degree of association indicated between the rank order of goals by Yugoslav managers in the plastics products industry and Yugoslav managers in the textiles industry, however, was low.

DISCUSSION OF THE FINDINGS

The findings provided by the study were surprising. The *a priori* expectation that the managers of the Peruvian firms would have perceived notable shifts in the goal hierarchies of their firms prior to the introduction of the Peruvian co-determination system was not confirmed. Indeed, the data indicated perceptions of almost no change in the ranking of goals for that period. The *a priori* expectation of differences between the average ranking of the Yugoslav and Peruvian managers was confirmed, but the degree of difference was less

Table 5

PERCENTAGE RANKING OF INDIVIDUAL ORGANIZATIONAL GOALS: MANAGERS' PERCEPTION IN YUGOSLAVIA

*Goals**	*Year*	*Rank 1*	*Rank 2*	*Rank 3*	*Rank 4*	*Rank 5*	*Rank 6*	*Total*
Production	1970	25.0	25.0	15.6	12.5	6.3	15.6	100 %
	1975	37.5	18.8	3.1	21.9	6.3	12.5	100 %
Economic Development	1970	18.8	12.5	12.5	18.8	9.4	28.1	100 %
	1975	21.9	18.8	18.8	12.5	9.4	18.8	100 %
Technological Leadership	1970	6.3	28.1	15.6	12.5	12.5	25.0	100 %
	1975	12.5	34.4	12.5	12.5	12.5	15.6	100 %
Employment	1970	12.5	18.8	21.9	21.9	18.8	6.3	100 %
	1975	6.3	12.5	31.3	15.6	25.0	9.4	100 %
Social Contribution	1970	6.3	6.3	18.8	15.6	43.8	9.4	100 %
	1975	15.6	9.4	12.5	18.8	28.1	15.6	100 %
Profitability	1970	31.3	9.4	15.6	18.8	6.3	18.8	100 %
	1975	6.3	6.3	21.9	18.8	18.8	28.1	100 %

* In order of 1975 Average Ranking.

than what might have been expected. Although the data provided evidence of different degrees of consensus on the goal rankings (with notably higher consensus in Peru than in Yugoslavia), data for the hierarchies of the firms in Peru and Yugoslavia are not highly dissimilar.

That the Peruvian managers perceived little difference in the goal hierarchies of their firms from before the co-determination legislation to almost five years of movement toward greater influence by workers in decision-making might be partially explained by a hypothesis which indicates that they did not expect the trend toward greater worker influence to be effective or relatively permanent. If this was what happened, the findings reported here could not be interpreted as being necessarily in conflict with the conceptual propositions upon which the investigation rested.

Indeed, the Peruvian legislation has recently been modified in a fashion which tends to reduce the growth of worker influence in decision-making. The structure described in Figure 2, based upon "Ley de Comunidad Industrial: Decreto Ley 18384", has recently been supplemented by "Ley de Comunidad

TABLE 6

PERCEPTIONS OF PERUVIAN AND YUGOSLAV MANAGERS OF THEIR FIRMS ORGANIZATIONAL GOAL HIERARCHY—MAY, 1975

Organizational Goals	*Hierarchy Based on the Average Ranking*		*Average Ranking*	
	Peru	*Yugoslavia*	*Peru*	*Yugoslavia*
Production	1	1	1.66	2.78
Economic Development	2	2	2.89	3.25
Technological Leadership	3	2	3.43	3.25
Profitability	4	6	3.60	4.22
Employment	5	4	4.00	3.69
Social Contribution	6	5	5.44	3.81

Industrial: Decreto Ley 21789". This new law, described in detail in *El Peruano* (February 2, 1977:1, 3–5) changes many of the equity ownership considerations of the industrial community, while basically retaining the internal organizational structure of the 1970–1975 Peruvian experiment.

Another possible hypothesis which would tend to explain the Peruvian managers failure to perceive change is related to the nature of the Peruvian workers. Perhaps the perspectives and values of the workers associated with their role and behavior with respect to the organization which employed them had not yet changed enough to result in effective worker participation within the changed formal authority structure. Also, it was possible that the structural changes implied by the Industrial Community Law involved insufficient real participation for the workers to enable any change in the goals hierarchy to occur.

The data related to Hypotheses IV and V provided additional information pointing to greater similarity among the Peruvian managers' rankings of goals than those of the Yugoslav managers. The Peruvian managers' rankings were more consistent between large and small firms and between industries than were the Yugoslav managers. This result may be related, in part, to differences in the degree of socio-cultural homogeneity among the managers in Peru and that found among the managers in Yugoslavia. Although it appears that the socio-cultural heterogeneity of all employees in the Peruvian firms was greater than that in the Yugoslav firms, the socio-cultural characteristics of the managers interviewed in the Peruvian firms appears to have been more homogeneous than those of the Yugoslav managers.

Another surprising feature of the comparative data is that Yugoslavia, with a longer history under a power equalization system and a comparatively more stable political system, yielded managers with perceptions of greater change in the organization goal hierarchies of their firms over the past five year period than did Peru. This result is difficult to explain.

Table 7

RANK ORDER CORRELATION COEFFICIENTS BETWEEN THE RELATIVE FREQUENCY DISTRIBUTIONS OF THE REPORTED ORGANIZATIONAL GOAL HIERARCHIES BY INDUSTRY AND SIZE OF FIRMS—MAY, 1975

	Industrial Sectors Association Between Plastics & Textiles Firms		*Size of the Firm: First and Fourth Quartile Associations*	
	Peru	*Yugoslavia*	*Peru*	*Yugoslavia*
Spearman Rank Correlation Coefficient	.7408	.1662	.6029	.1900
(Level of Significance)	(.001)	(.166)	(.001)	(.133)
Kendall Correlation Coefficient	.5993	.1993	.5388	.1607
(Level of Significance)	(.001)	(.116)	(.001)	(.084)

Perceptions of change are relative phenomena and are, to a considerable extent, subjective phenomena. The extent of perceived change in one dimension of life or activity may be formulated from a context of comparison with degrees of perceived change in other dimensions, rather than from objective measurement of appropriate indicators of the magnitude of change applied in isolation. Organizations, and decision-makers within them, require some degree of perceived order in the societal systems in which they exist if they are to function effectively. The threat of massive change can generate subjective perceptions of less change than an objective analysis of the facts would warrant. Perhaps the Peruvian managers perceived changes in the goals hierarchy in the comparative context.

In comparison with the instabilities they perceived in other dimensions of the societal system, the change in the goal hierarchy of their firms may have appeared minimal. The managers' perceptions of what the goal hierarchy had been five years before may have been adjusted to reflect greater historical continuity than actually occurred. This hypothesis receives some support from the finding that the Peruvian managers, on the average, ranked profitability fourth both when their firms were purely private enterprises (1970) and currently when some progress had been made toward co-determination. The Yugoslav managers, in contrast, could gauge changes in their firms' goal hierarchies in a context of relatively high political, social, and economic stability.

An alternative hypothesis would be that the Peruvian managers did not expect that the movement toward power equalization would be effective in shifting the fundamental authority structure or that the movement would be temporary, as stated earlier. The concept of minimal dislocation responses by organizations to an external disturbance and concepts associated with legitimacy dynamics may have some explanatory power in this situation. The Yugoslav efforts toward organizational change had become highly institutionalized within the Yugoslav economic, political, and socio-cultural systems by the 1970s. The Peruvian experiment, however, was tentative, and only the initial steps had been taken to make it an integral part of the total societal system. Under these circumstances, the potential changes perceived by the Yugoslav managers would be much less threatening to them, and accommodation to the requirements of change circumstances much more appropriate than the potential changes in the societal system would be to the Peruvian managers. The Yugoslav managers had attained their positions by career progress within a system which had widespread legitimacy within the society and which they largely accepted. The Peruvian managers had acquired their positions largely through responsiveness to boards of directors representing family owners of private enterprises, and the extent of legitimacy with which the power equalization movement had across the Peruvian society was less than it was in Yugoslavia.

The Yugoslav managers might, then, be more predisposed to perceive change in the goal hierarchies of their firms than the Peruvian managers. The average rankings of the Yugoslav managers indicated more perceived change but much less aggregate consensus about the nature of the changes.

The findings and tentative interpretations presented here do not conflict with the proposition that both socio-cultural differences and externally mandated organizational structures influence the configuration of the goal hierarchies of the organizations. The extent to which the interpretations are speculative and tentative is consistent with the proposition that analysis and understanding of cross-cultural matters important to management science are in their early stages of development.

REFERENCES

Adizes, Ichak. *Industrial Democracy Yugoslav-Style*. New York: The Free Press.
1971

Bernstein, Harry. "Democracy on the Job: Grand Goal in Sweden." *Los Angeles Times*.
1974 November 9:1, 21, 25.

Bernstein, Paul. "Necessary Elements for Effective Worker Participation in Decision-
1976 Making." *Journal of Economic Issues*. 10:490–522.

Etzioni, Amitai. "Two Approaches to Organizational Analysis: A Critique and a
1960 Suggestion." *Administrative Science Quarterly*. 5:257–278.

Fine, Keitha S. "Workers' Participation in Israel." In Gerry Hunnius, *et al.* (eds.), *Worker's*
1973 *Control: A Reader on Labor and Social Change*: 226–267. New York: Vintage.

Flaes, Robert M. B. "Yugoslavian Experience of Workers' Self-Management." In
1973 *International Sociological Conference on participation and Self-Management*: 113–122. Zagreb: Institute for Social Research.

Glueck, William F., and Kavran, Dragol. "The Yugoslav Management System." In Donald
1973 S. Hanley (ed.), *International Business*. Michigan: Michigan State University Press.

Karlsson, Lars Erik. "Experiments in Industrial Democracy in Sweden." In *International*
1973 *Sociological Conference on Participation and Self-Management 3*: 71–102. Zagreb: Institute for Social Research.

Kuhne, R. J. "Codetermination: A Statutory Restructuring of the Organization."
1976 *Columbia Journal of World Business*. 11:17–25.

Mumford, E. "Towards the Democratic Design of Work Systems." *Personnel*
1976 *Management*. September: 32–35.

Parsons, Talcott. *Structure and Process in Modern Societies*. New York: The Free Press.
1963

Perrow, Charles. "The Analysis of Goals in Complex Organizations." *American*
1961 *Sociological Review*. 26:854–865.

Sills, David L. "The Succession of Goals." *The Volunteers*. New York: The Free Press.
1958 253–268, 270.

Simon, Herbert A. "On the Concept of Organizational Goal." *Administrative Science*
1964 *Quarterly*. 9:1–22.

Thompson, James D. *Organizations in Action*. New York: McGraw-Hill, Inc.
1967

Thompson, James D., and William J. McEwan. "Organizational Goals and
1958 Environment." *American Sociological Review*. 23:23–31.

Vanek, Jaroslav. *The Participatory Economy*. Ithaca: Cornell University Press.
1974

Zimblist, Andrew. "The Dynamic Worker Participation: An Interpretive Essay on the
1975 Chilean and Other Experiences." *Administration and Society*. 7:43–54.

Zimblist, Andrew. "Worker Management of Chilean Industry 1970–1933: An Empirical
1976 Investigation." *Journal of Economic Issues*. 10:476–488.

Managerial Responses and Organizational Adaptation to Environmental Uncertainty in Denmark and the U.S.

WARREN B. BROWN
University of Oregen
JAMES S. BLANDIN
Naval Postgraduate School

Organization theorists and management practitioners alike are devoting increasing attention to examining the interrelationships between environmental uncertainty, managerial behavior and organization structure. The reason is simple: environmental uncertainties are associated with growing economic, technological, and socio-political changes in the industrial world. Hence, the study of these interrelationships represents a fruitful area for management research. This paper reports the results of a comparative study of these interrelationships carried out in the U.S. and Denmark. Specifically, the study was designed to test a series of hypotheses involving the effects of uncertainty on the information search behavior of managers, the organization's degree of differentiation, and its use of a variety of integration methods.

ENVIRONMENTAL UNCERTAINTY: CONCEPTUAL BACKGROUND

Environmental uncertainty has been conceptualized and operationalized in a variety of ways in the management literature. Dill (1958) and Thompson (1967) conceptualize uncertainty in terms of two dimensions of task environments. Their homogeneous-heterogeneous dimension represents the degree to which entities in an organization's task environment are similar to one another. Their stable—shifting dimension represents the degree to which the contingencies posed by these entities remain basically the same over time or are in a continual process of change. They argue that organizations facing heterogeneous and shifting environments will experience the greatest amount of uncertainty in planning and decision making with respect to environmental constraints, contingencies and opportunities.

Lawrence and Lorsch (1969) define and measure uncertainty as a function of a manager's subjective perceptions along the following dimensions: (1) clarity of environment related information; (2) degree of certainty of cause and effect relationships in the environment; and, (3) time required before definitive feedback from the environment is received by the organization. Unfortunately, however, there is no widely accepted standard method of measuring environmental uncertainty. Objective measures are difficult to obtain, especially for comparative purposes, and perceptual measures may reflect personal biases. The Lawrence and Lorsch method (1969) involves perceptions, and despite some limitations (Tosi *et al*., 1973) it was chosen for use in this study. This method of measuring uncertainty appears to be supported by Duncan (1972), who has shown that the level of perceived uncertainty for a manager is directly related to the homogeneous-heterogeneous and stable-shifting dimensions of an organization's environment. Managers in heterogeneous-shifting environments perceive the greatest amount of uncertainty while managers in homogeneous-stable environments experience the least.

Although this earlier research provided important insights into the conceptual relationship between the environment and perceived uncertainty, Downey and Slocum (1975) recently suggested that potential sources of uncertainty which are separate from environmental attributes might also be considered. They suggest that uncertainty can be conceptualized as a psychological state, and that, in addition to environmental attributes, perceived uncertainty may vary as a function of individual cognitive processes, individual experience and social expectations. To date these issues remain unresolved, especially from an empirical standpoint. It should be noted that our research project did not focus on this related question of how perceived uncertainty is effected by individual differences. This aspect of uncertainty measurement remains an open area for future research.

UNCERTAINTY AND ORGANIZATIONS

An expanding literature is beginning to develop which analyzes uncertainty as a key variable affecting organization design and decision-making behavior. Many of the conceptual arguments presented in these articles have been similar. Dill's (1958) study of two Norwegian firms was one of the first efforts to conceptualize and examined the impact of environmental differences on organization structure and behavior. He found that firms which faced a relatively heterogeneous and unstable task environment tended to have more autonomous work relationships among the management groups than those which faced a relatively homogeneous and stable environment.

Thompson (1967) later argued that all types of organizational task environments can be located simultaneously along a homogeneous-heterogeneous continuum and a stable-shifting continuum. In combination, these dimensions present varying degrees of environmental uncertainty for the organization—uncertainty which the organization attempts to manage in order to achieve greater rationality in its decision making. According to Thompson, the fundamental problem facing complex organizations involves coping with and managing this uncertainty. To this end, he proposes that organizations will vary systematically in structure and behavior to reflect the amount of uncertainty inherent in their environments. Specifically, he assumes that with a more heterogeneous and shifting task environment, an organization will: (1) exhibit greater structural differentiation at the organizational boundary for better surveillance and adaptation; (2) devote more attention to environmental monitoring activities; and, (3) rely more on forecasting in order to anticipate the environmental shifts.

Following the same type of logic, Lawrence and Lorsch (1969) also contend that environmental uncertainty is a key variable affecting the structure and behavior of organizations. In their study, they found that organizations operating in uncertain environments tend to be more highly differentiated and develop more elaborate mechanisms for achieving integration than organizations operating in more certain environments.

In line with these concepts, the following hypotheses were developed for testing in this study; they are directly related to the work of Thompson (1967), Lawrence and Lorsch (1969), and Kefalas and Schoderbek (1973).

(1) The more uncertain the environment a firm faces, the more frequently its management will consult informal sources of information.
(2) The more uncertain the environment a firm faces, the more frequently its management will consult formal sources of information.
(3) The more uncertain the environment a firm faces, the more frequently its management will consult all sources of information (formal and informal).
(4) The more uncertain tho environment a firm faces, the more time its management will allocate to environment-related information gathering activity.

These hypotheses are also related to the assumption that information plays a crucial role in the process of uncertainty reduction (Cyert and March, 1963). It is expected that the resources an organization devotes to gathering information about the environment will vary directly with the amount of environmental uncertainty that is perceived to exist. In addition, it is expected that an organization operating in a complex and dynamic environment will strive to reduce uncertainty by using a wide variety of forecasting techniques, encompassing more specialized methods than organizations operating in relatively static environments. Thus we have the following hypothesis:

(5) Organizations operating in relatively uncertain environments will employ a wider variety of forecasting techniques than organizations operating in relatively stable environments.

Again extending the basic thesis, it was felt that environmental uncertainty would affect the integration and differentiation of organizational subunits. Environments characterized by rapid rates of change and general uncertainty would logically create a demand for greater differentiation of boundary spanning units, and also a wider variety of methods to integrate the organizational subunits. This reasoning leads to the last two hypotheses:

(6) Organizations operating is relatively uncertain environments will exhibit greater structural differentiation of the boundary spanning

units than will organizations operating in relatively stable environments.

(7) Organizations operating in relatively uncertain environments will employ interdepartmental committees, specific integrators, task force teams, and managers operating outside official channels to a greater extent to achieve integration than firms operating in relatively stable environments.

SOME DANISH-U.S. DIFFERENCES

The above reasoning and hypotheses were expected to hold for industrial companies in both the U.S. and in Denmark. Nonetheless, the second part of our research project was to explore the possibility of differences in the results between the two countries, differences which might be caused by cultural factors. Although both countries in question belong to the group of industralized, relatively rich, "Western World" nations, there are definite dissimilarities.

One of the most apparent differences is that the scale of operations and corporation size in the U.S. is far larger than that in Denmark. In the Scandinavian country, a typical firm is quite moderate in size by U.S. standards, employing perhaps 100 workers; few Danish corporations employ more than 500 people. This size factor results in a good deal of specialization by firms, and the existence of many cooperative associations for firms in similar industries. We suspect that the cooperative associations absorb some of the environmental uncertainties which would otherwise impinge directly on the individual companies. The managers of these moderate-sized operations use the cooperative associations to aid in interpreting the broader environment and for much of their long-range planning.

The other very apparent factor creating possible differences is the more socialized and controlled economy found in Denmark. There is a great deal of national planning in Denmark, and the results affect the activities of every businessman. Such national planning is evident in many areas, such as the economy, national agreements on wage scales, land use planning, education, and policies concerning the funding of research and development.

We believe that these two factors, in particular, might be associated with differences in the organizational responses between the two countries; such an examination would provide us with some initial data in this cross-country comparison.

SAMPLE

For both the U.S. and Denmark we estimated that for statistical purposes we would need a total of 70 questionnaire responses from top level managers in eight medium-sized firms; four from an industry which was thought to have a relatively stable environment, and four from firms in a relatively more uncertain environment. The firms were medium-sized by U.S. standards, large by Danish standards. In the U.S., the two industries selected were electronics and wood products, with electronics firms presumably facing more dynamic environmental conditions. Two of the U.S. electronics firms were involved with the development and production of electronic instrumentation, and two were engaged in the development of radar and guidance systems. All four U.S. electronics firms engaged in basic as well as applied R & D. The four U.S. wood products firms were involved with the milling and distribution of a variety of wood products. Although to a lesser degree than the electronics firms, all four wood products companies engaged in some applied R & D, primarily in the areas of new products and reforestation. The U.S. response to the questionnaire was very satisfactory, providing all the needed data.

In the Danish part of the study the electronics industry was again chosen, but the original choice for a comparative industry, the meat-packers, had to be discarded. After introductory discussions with the industry representatives they declined to participate, apparently due to time pressures and competition. This created some difficulty, since the size and structure of Danish industry precludes a wide selection of appropriate industries. After some consultation with Danes knowledgeable about the structure of Danish industry, a group of capital intensive, process industry companies were chosen. All four of these were large enough to have the required potential for organizational complexity. We anticipated that they would have organizational characteristics similar to the wood products firms in the U.S. because of their relatively large investments in plant and equipment and other process industry features.

After some discussion with our colleagues at the Dansk Management Center, it was decided to translate the questionnaires to Danish (although many Danish executives speak English rather well), and to contact the electronics firms *via* a seminar at the Center due to their common membership in the Danish Confederation of Electronic Manufacturers. The contacts with the process industry companies would be done individually, *via* personal visits to the firms in question.

The eight Danish firms in our sample cooperated in varying degrees, providing us with about two-thirds of the information which was originally desired for statistical analysis. These companies were not randomly selected with each of the industries because of practical considerations, but within each company the executives who participated in this research were random choices, so long as they fitted the "upper and top management" category. Consequently, we acknowledge that our statistical conclusions allow inferences only to the sampled companies; however, as these companies are presumed to be representative of their respective industries we have in our discussion referred simply to our results as organizational and management characteristics of those industries overall.

THE QUESTIONNAIRE

The questionnaire we designed was a modification of that used by Lawrence and Lorsch (1969). The first section of the questionnaire was designed to measure the independent variable, perceived uncertainty. A five-point scale was used to record responses along the following three dimensions:

1. The degree to which the manager felt informed about developments in the firm's environment (1 = fully informed; 5 = uninformed).

2. The manager's perception of the degree of certainty of cause and effect relationships between developments in the environment and their impact on the organization (1 = very certain; 5 = very uncertain).
3. The typical length of time before the manager receives definitive feedback concerning actions taken by the organization and their impact on the environment (1 = one month or less; 5 = more than one year).

It should be noted that the scale we used, scoring responses from 1 (low) to 5 (high), is arbitrary. Other scales, such as from 0 to 1, or 10 to 100, could have been used. Such other scales would naturally modify the absolute values of the raw data, but presumably the relative responses would remain essentially the same.

In the Danish case, item No. 2 of the uncertainty measure had to be dropped due to persistent translation difficulties which surfaced in the pretests. The item itself seemed to have face validity, however, based on the executives' comments in follow-up interviews. Hence the uncertainty scores in Denmark were averaged over two dimensions, rather than three which was the case in the U.S.

Reactions to these three dimensions (or two, in Denmark) were measured for each of five environmental sectors: (1) Market Sector; (2) Government; (3) External Technological; (4) Internal Technological; and, (5) Other. The uncertainty scores for each firm were then calculated by finding first, the average uncertainty score for each sector; and second, averaging the scores across all five sectors to get an overall uncertainty score for each firm.

The next part of the questionnaire was designed to obtain data on the information sources and the frequency of their use as managers employ them to monitor the environment; the design of this section benefitted from the work of Aquilar (1967) and Kefalas and Schoderbek (1973). Each manager was asked to indicate which source from the following list he considered to be his most important source *vis-a-vis* monitoring the environment, and the frequency of use for the source (daily, weekly, monthly, semi-annually, annually).

1. Internal Formal Source—To include organization reports, department memos, formally scheduled meetings.
2. Internal Informal Source—To include professional journals, trade magazines, technical publications, government and consulting reports, professional and trade association meetings.
3. External Informal Source—To include informal conversations with customers, suppliers, competitors and governmental officials.

In addition, estimates were gathered on the number of hours per week managers in each firm devoted to environment-related information gathering activities. The last sections of the questionnaire briefly examined the use of possible forecasting techniques and the types of methods used to facilitate both the integration process and organizational differentiation *via* the boundary-spanning units. In each of these cases the manager could simply indicate from a list of possible choices, those characteristics which were appropriate for his firm. These responses were the basis for "percentage-of-use" calculations, which were then to be compared.

RESULTS

The summary data are presented in Tables 1–6, and a summary of the results from the tests of the hypotheses is shown in Table 7. As shown in Table 1, U.S. managers in both electronics and wood products organizations perceived higher levels of uncertainty than their Danish counterparts aggregated over all sectors of the environment. However, it can be seen that the average Danish uncertainty scores were not appreciably different between the electronic companies and those in the process industries. In particular the electronics scores appear low, both in terms of the scale (1 = low uncertainty; 5 = high uncertainty) and relative to the U.S. results. Possible reasons for this may be: (1) the greater overall economic controls associated with the smaller, socialized economies of Western Europe; and, (2) a relatively greater emphasis on both basic and applied research in the U.S., stimulating increased technological uncertainty. This can be seen in the data presented in Table 2. These results suggest that the greatest sources of uncertainty for the firms in the study were the external and internal technological sectors for U.S. electronics firms and the government sector for Danish electronics companies.

With regard to the use of informal and formal sources of information there appears to be little if any difference in the Danish data between the electronics sector and the process industries (Table 3). Here, and in the following tables, we find that the responses of the Danish managers are not significantly different, regardless of whether they are from managers in the electronics sector or in the process industry When the information measures are combined to obtain an "all sources" score (also in Table 3), the lack of differentiation in the Danish data is again evident. This can be contrasted with the results from the American study (Table 3), which indicate significant contrasts. Apparently, executives in a socialized economy, operating small to medium-sized firms by U.S. standards, share far more managerial-behavioral characteristics across industries than is expected from U.S. experience. One might speculate that the well-known homogeneity in a Scandinavian nation gives rise to this development, overriding the expected environmental differences facing various kinds of industries.

When examining the results concerning executive time spent on information gathering activity, the Danish data are again quite blended. One aspect of interest is that in the electronics industry Danish executives appear to spend

Table 1

AVERAGE UNCERTAINTY SCORES BY INDUSTRY

Industry	*Score**	*Range*	*No. of Responses*
U. S. Electronics	3.0	2.6–3.6	35
U. S. Wood Products	2.6	2.3–2.8	35
DK Electronics	2.5	2.2–2.8	20
DK Process	2.3	2.1–2.7	28

*Measure: 1 (low) to 5 (high uncertainty)

Table 2

AVERAGE UNCERTAINTY SCORES BY INDUSTRY AND SECTOR OF THE ENVIRONMENT (TOP 10)

Industry	*Sector*	*Average Score*	*Range*
U. S. Electronics	External Technology	3.5	2.9–4.0
DK Electronics	Government	3.3	2.4–3.9
U. S. Electronics	Internal Technology	3.2	2.8–3.6
U. S. Electronics	Market	3.1	2.6–3.5
U. S. Electronics	Government	2.9	2.2–3.8
DK Electronics	External Technology	2.8	2.6–2.9
DK Process	External Technology	2.8	2.4–3.1
U. S. Wood Products	Government	2.7	2.5–3.0
U. S. Wood Products	Internal Technology	2.5	2.1–2.6
DK Process	Government	2.5	2.2–2.9

far *less time* on gathering information related to environmental developments than do their American counterparts. Perhaps the immediacy of widespread competition as well as a greater emphasis on R & D in this industry in the U.S. is the reason for the higher U.S. figures. By contrast, Danish electronics executives often work through their Confederation of Electronic Manufacturers for external information.

Turning to Table 4, we again see a blended group of Danish data, with little contrast between industries. However, there is a sharp contrast with the U.S. firms where a much wider variety of forecasting techniques is commonly employed. This would seem to reinforce the apparent pattern mentioned in the above results, i.e., that U.S. firms are more concerned with, and respond more actively to, environmental uncertainty. The explanation for the difference might lie partly in the traditional American emphasis on using modern management techniques. Alternatively, the Danish managers may perceive less uncertainty due to greater governmental regulation, greater use of information from associations, and therefore see less need (relatively) for using a variety of forecasting techniques.

The data on organizational differentiation *via* boundary-spanning units (Table 5) once again provides us with the same pattern: undifferentiated Danish data; U.S. data providing a contrast; and some Danish-U.S. data differences indicating a greater organizational responsiveness in the U.S., presumably due to greater uncertainty.

This pattern reappears for the measures of integration (Table 6). The use of traditional methods, i.e., formal communications through the management hierarchy and routine control procedures, were used equally frequently between Danish firms in the electronics industry and those in process industries. However, the American electronics companies significantly preferred non-traditional methods for organizational integration, as contrasted with both the U.S. wood products firms and the Danish electronics companies. This leads to

Table 3

AVERAGE NUMBER OF DAYS IN A WORK-YEAR (260 DAYS) THAT THIS SOURCE IS CONSULTED (WHERE LISTED AS "MOST IMPORTANT")

Firm	*Informal Source*		*Formal Source*		*All Sources*		*Information Gathering Activity (Environment-Related Information) Average Hours/Week*	
	DK	*US*	*DK*	*US*	*DK*	*US*	*DK*	*US*
DK U.S.								
Process/Wood Products								
1	102	160	145	53	247	213	14.5	15.4
2	67	114	37	64	104	178	7.6	9.9
3	83	100	76	61	159	161	11.4	9.2
4	45	70	75	75	120	145	11.4	9.1
Electronics:								
E–1	78	158	59	91	137	249	11.0	16.4
E–2	81	142	53	95	134	237	12.0	16.7
E–3	55	123	40	93	95	216	9.0	10.0
E–4	178	108	26	79	204	187	12.6	14.1

Table 4

UNCERTAINTY AND THE USE OF VARIOUS FORECASTING METHODS

Danish Firms	*Forecasting-Use Score (per cent)*	*U. S. Firms*	*Forecasting-Use Score (per cent)**
E–1	37	E–1	87
E–2	54	E–2	88
E–3	38	E–3	83
E–4	42	E–4	83
P–1	54	W–1	86
P–2	30	W–2	81
P–3	53	W–3	77
P–4	41	W–4	80

*This score represents the percentage of responses in each firm who indicated that any given forecasting technique was used. Six major types of forecasting were used in the questionnaire: Statistical Trend Extrapolation; Published Industry Forecasts; Formal Executive Surveys; Personal Evaluation; Polling of Customers and Suppliers; and Computer Modelling. This, if each manager in the U. S. E–1 firm indicated that he used all six types of forecasting, the forecasting-use score for the U. S. E–1 firm would = 100 %.

Table 5

DIFFERENTIATION VIA BOUNDARY-SPANNING UNITS*
(11 POSSIBLE UNITS LISTED ON QUESTIONNAIRE)

Denmark		*U.S.*	
Electronics Industry:		Electronics Industry:	
E–1	18	E–1	92
E–2	64	E–2	96
E–3	59	E–3	88
E–4	70	E–4	75
Average:	53 %	Average:	88 %
Process Industry:		Wood Industry:	
P–1	61	W–1	76
P–2	47	W–2	69
P–3	71	W–3	77
P–4	66	W–4	74
Average:	61 %	Average:	74 %

* Differentiation scores were based on the percentage of responses in each firm which indicated that departments, staff groups or primary individual functions existed as separate entities from the following list: Policy Planning; Market Research; Applied R & D; Basic R & D; Public Relations; Legal; Customer Relations; Advertising; Labor Relations; Manpower Planning; and Government Relations.

Table 6

TYPES OF METHODS RANKED AS MOST IMPORTANT IN FACILITATING THE INTEGRATION PROCESS*

	"More Traditional"					*"Less Traditional"*								
	Formal Communications through Management Hierarchy %		Routine Control Procedures %			Inter-departmental Committees %		Specific Integrating Individuals %		Managers Acting Outside Office Channels %		Special Task Force/Project Management Teams %		
	DK	US	DK	US	Total	DK	US	DK	US	DK	US	DK	US	Total
Electronics	22		11		33 %DK	28		6		0		33		67 %DK
Industry		6		0	6 %US		47		6		18		23	94 %US
Process Industry (DK) and	29		4		33 %DK	29		19		0		19		67 %DK
Wood Products (US)		23		6	29 %US		28		11		32		0	71 %US

*For example, 22% of DK electronics managers in the sample indicated that Formal Communications through the Management Hierarchy represented their most important method of facilitating integration/coordination.

the interesting result that Danish managers appear to be more traditional than their counterparts in the U.S. regarding methods of organizational integration.

The explanation may lie in a somewhat simple relationship: a more socialized economy leads to a more stable environment for individual business firms, which in turn leads to less organizational differentiation and a greater reliance on traditional forms of integration. The homogeneity of a Scandinavian nation with its relatively stable social structure and moderate-sized firms may accent this relationship. In addition we believe that the U.S. electronics industry would be widely regarded as a world leader, and would therefore quite likely be associated with organizational as well as technological innovation.

CONCLUSIONS

In Table 7 the Danish and U.S. data are combined in order to focus on the impact of environmental uncertainty independent of national differences. Overall, the results give solid substantiation to most of the hypotheses. These findings are consistent both with the conceptual literature dealing with the role of information in uncertainty reduction (Cyert and March, 1963; Thompson, 1967), and with several empirical investigations focusing on information search behavior at the institutional level of the organization (Aquilar 1967; Kefalas and Schoderbek, 1973).

Briefly, the data show that variations in search for external information depends on the type of environment an organization faces; and the managers in more dynamic task environments make more intensive (frequent) use of all information sources (both internal/external and formal/informal).

In addition, the data indicate that a firm's propensity to use a variety of forecasting techniques was correlated with the degree of environmental uncertainty faced by the firm. Finally, with regard to organizational differentiation and integration, the data clearly showed that firms operating in relatively uncertain environments exhibit significantly greater differentiation of boundary-spanning units, and that the U.S. firms use a wider variety of integration methods; that is, managers in these firms placed much less reliance on formal communication and routine control procedures as integrative devices than did managers in more stable environments.

However, when the Danish data was viewed separately, it often showed some variations in the general pattern just described. It appears that the combination of a socialistic economy, a high degree of homogeneity in the population, and little emphasis on being a world leader in research (especially basic research), has created an overall situation wherein Danish business managers: (1) often do not perceive as much environmental uncertainty as their U.S. counterparts; (2) perceive "government" as a relatively major factor affecting their overall operations; (3) are less affected by the uniqueness of a particular industrial sector; (4) use fewer modern management techniques; and (5) are more traditional in their methods of organizational integration.

Do such differences reflect cultural variations between two "Western World" nations? The answer is not clear from this study. The measures used here did not attempt to examine cultural factors directly. Further, even moderate variations in the size of the organizations used in our sample could create

Table 7

SUMMARY RESULTS

			Combined Danish—U.S. Data	
Hypothesis	*Variables*	*Hypothesized Relationship*	r_s *Value*	*Significance*
1.	Environmental uncertainty and use of informal information sources	Positive	.51[a]	$p<.05$
2.	Environmental uncertainty and use of formal information sources	Positive	.25[a]	Non-significant
3.	Environmental uncertainty and use of all information sources	Positive	.51[a]	$p<.05$
4.	Environmental uncertainty and managers' time allocation to information gathering activity	Positive	.41[a]	Non-significant
5.	Environmental uncertainty and use of forecasting	Positive	.74[a]	$p<.01$
6.	Environmental uncertainty and differentiation of boundary-spanning units	Positive	.50[a]	$p<.05$
7.	Environmental uncertainty and use of special integration methods	Positive	.66[a]	$p<.01$

[a] Spearman rank correlation coefficients.

confounding effects. Thus the Danish-U.S. differences—such as they are—can more appropriately be said to be based in cross-national factors, rather than cross-cultural dimensions.

Overall, the results the need for managers to assess the relative uncertainty of their environment, and to make appropriate adjustments regarding information acquisition, organizational integration and differentiation. Especially when facing a relatively uncertain environment, managers need sufficient time to consult both formal and informal information sources from the outside, e.g., professional and trade association publications and contacts. Further, due to the importance of informal communications, it is clear that interpersonal relations skills are particularly important for those in the boundary-spanning roles. These people may be helped by management training and job rotation.

The latter part of the study indicates that increased organizational specialization is a concomitant of increased environmental uncertainty. Consequently we find that special boundary spanning units evolve to handle the uncertainty, along with integrative methods such as project management groups, special integrators, interdepartmental committees, and allowing managers the freedom to occasionally act outside of official channels.

In closing we want to mention an intriguing extension of the logic used here. Sasaki (1977) has suggested that the effects of environmental uncertainty on managerial behavior and methods of organizational adaptation may not be symmetrical. By this he means that in the context of a growing economy, high degrees of uncertainty may indeed give rise to greater structural differentiation and more delegation of authority, such as we found in this study. However, growing uncertainty in a declining economy may cause management to act in the opposite way: to tighten controls through recentralization of authority and to turn to greater use of formal methods of integration. A longitudinal study is clearly needed; it is one of the future challenges for research in this area.

REFERENCES

Aquilar, F. J. *Scanning the Business Environment*. New York: MacMillan.
1967

Cyert, R. M. and J. G. March. *A Behavioral Theory of the Firm*. Englewood Cliffs, N.J.:
1963 Prentice Hall.

Dill, W. R. "Environment as an Influence on Managerial Autonomy." *Administrative*
1958 *Science Quarterly*. 2:409–443.

Downey, H. K. and J. W. Slocum. "Uncertainty: Measures, Research, and Sources of
1975 Variation." *Academy of Management Journal*. 18:562–578.

Duncan, R. B. "Characteristics of Organizational Environments and Perceived
1972 Uncertainty." *Administrative Science Quarterly*. 17:313–327.

Kefalos, A. and P. Schoderbek. "Scanning the Business Environment—Some Empirical
1973 Results." *Decision Sciences*. 4:63–74.

Lawrence, P. and J. Lorsch. *Organization and Environment*. Homewood, Ill.: Irwin.
1969

Sasaki, N. Correspondence with the authors.
1977

Thompson, J. D. *Organizations in Action*. New York: McGraw-Hill.
1967

Tosi, H., R. Aldag and R. Storey. "On the Measurement of the Environment: An
1973 Assessment of the Lawrence and Lorsch Environmental Uncertainty Questionnaire." *Administrative Science Quarterly*. 18:27–36.

Paradigm Differences and their Relation to Management, with reference to South-East Asia*

S. G. REDDING
University of Hong Kong
T. A. MARTYN-JOHNS
University of Hong Kong

The degree to which culture affects managerial behavior has recently been examined again in the light of the effects of corporate size (Hickson *et. al.*, 1974), but the culture-free thesis has been refuted by Child and Keiser (1976) who point out after research in the United Kingdom and Germany that "at every point in the causal chain posited by culture-free contingency analysis, other influences, mostly cultural in origin, are likely to interpose." The large scale empirical research on which both these arguments have been based has been entirely Western in context, and Hickson *et. al.* themselves note that

> The weakness of this position is that it stands on data from three Anglo-Saxon societies only, and cannot command confidence until tested on reliable data from a much wider spectrum of societies in which levels of industrialization are varied (1974:74)

Recent research on managerial attitudes in Asia (Redding and Casey, 1976), has suggested that a much wider discrepancy exists between Asian managerial attitudes and those in Western countries than exists between countries within the Western group. It is worthwhile to pursue the understanding of the Asian variations in an attempt to throw more light on the culture-free controversy.

It is proposed to deal with what seems a fundamental issue in comparative management and one which is rarely examined. It is summed up in the commonest of the phrases used by the Western practising manager dealing with his Asian equivalents—"They think differently". What I want to examine are the

* Thanks are due to the following companies who kindly contributed towards the costs of fieldwork for the initial empirical data collection: Cathay Pacific Airway, ICI (China) Ltd., Hongkong and Shanghai Bank, Chase Manhattan Bank, Gilman & Co., British American Tobacco Co., Esso Standard Oil, Hang Seng Bank, Dodwells Ltd., Hutchison International Ltd., IBM, Royal Interocean Lines and Hilton International.

ways in which they think differently and the possible effects on managerial behavior and organization.

We begin with a problem of definition. What is a paradigm? After some compromise solution to that problem, we proceed to examine what might otherwise be termed cognitive structures or ways of thinking and look at their effects on managerial behavior. The aim is to indicate cross-cultural differences in ways of seeing reality and the inevitable differences in behavior which result. The thinking which has led to this paper *follows from* a large-scale empirical survey of managerial beliefs in South East Asia and the ideas are thus hypotheses indicating future research directions rather than ideas already tested. Nevertheless some empirical support for them is indicated.

THE COGNITIVE PROCESS

A starting point is the notion that to understand organizational behavior, and to build organization theory, one must eventually come to terms with the way each individual attaches himself to the system being studied. As Silverman (1970:120) points out "Without reference to human motivation it is arguable that one cannot explain why social life has the characteristics that it does." More specifically, referring to the comparative study of organizations (and in the process, advocating the investigation of non-Western examples to throw the Western ones into relief), he indicates five issues as being of particular importance for research.

1. The nature of the predominant meaning-structure and associated system in different organizations and the extent to which it relies on varying degrees of coercion or consent.
2. The characteristic pattern of involvement of the actors; differing attachment to rules and definitions of their situation.
3. The typical strategies used by actors to attain their ends.
4. The relative ability of different actors to impose their definition of the situation upon others. The nature and sources of the symbolic 'sticks' (resources) available to the actors; their relative effectiveness.
5. The origin and pattern of change of meaning-structures (institutionalization and de-institutionalization of meanings) in different organizations." (Silverman, 1970:171).

It is clear that "meaning-structures" and individual "definitions of the situation" take a central place in this view and before examining the point further, it is necessary to acknowledge that the need for research to move in that direction appears to have been accepted. The emergence of ethnomethodology (Garfinkel 1967, Cicourel 1972) the use of the Action Frame of Reference (Silverman 1970, Harré and Secord 1972) indicate an increasing concentration on the individual's perception of the situation he is working in, as the fundamental unit of analysis. Much of the force of this movement has been provided by the realization that the open systems approach to organizational analysis contains a degree of reification which is not sufficiently acknowledged.

If then, one is to move towards an acceptance of the individual's definition of the situation, and to make a contribution to the understanding of why this varies across cultures, it is necessary to clarify what area of the elaborate

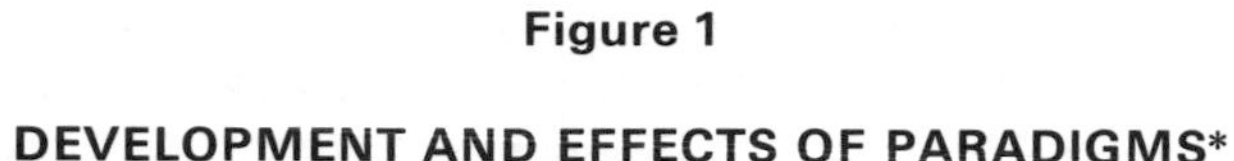

Figure 1

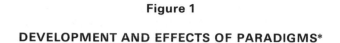

DEVELOPMENT AND EFFECTS OF PARADIGMS*

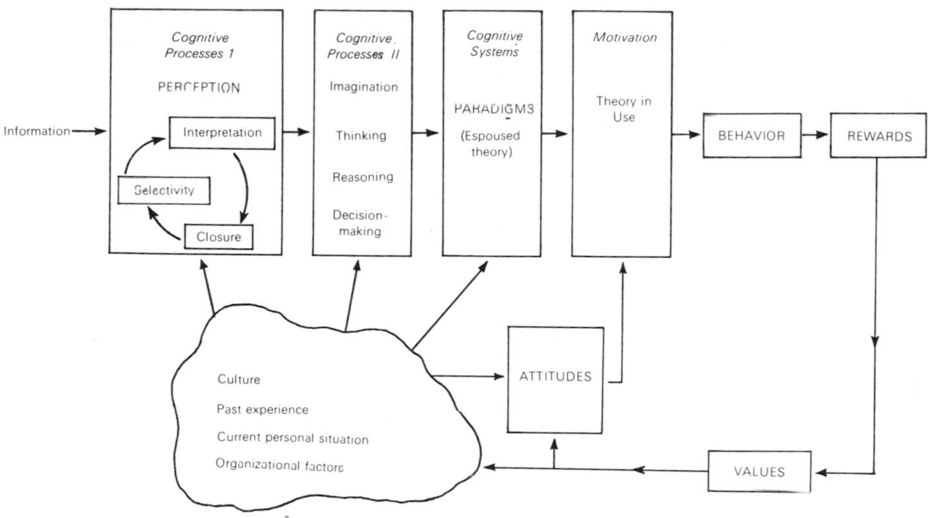

* The view of the perception process is partly derived from Litterer (1965)

cognitive process is to be considered, and how it relates to organizations.

Figure 1 proposes a general view of the process of paradigm development and acts as an introduction to the definition of paradigms. Three mental states are envisaged between the impinging of information on the person and the eventual motivation to behave. First, the process of perception which acts *via* selectivity, interpretation and closure to take information and transmit it in an amplified, distorted, filtered or relatively "pure" form. This information is then worked on in the stage 2 cognitive processes of imagination, thinking, reasoning and decision-making and is then processed into a way of seeing reality. This latter stage is seen as a set of cognitive systems, or paradigms, which are relatively stable over time. They are the "maps by which we steer" (Armstrong 1973:4), the systems of both belief and understanding, whether articulated or subconscious, which become the main guides to behavior.

At this point, we have reached the level of what Argyris (1976) would call "espoused theory", and it may be valuable to use the same distinction which he proposes between "espoused theory" and "theory-in-use". His definitions are:

> Espoused theories of action are those that people report as a basis for actions.
> Theories-in-use are the theories of action inferred from how people actually behave (Argyris 1976b:367).

The implication is that action itself is not *directly* explicable in terms of the espoused theory contained in the cognitive system, but an intervening variable occurs. This latter "theory-in-use is affected by attitudes and brings into play the "feeling" element which is separate from "thinking". The model proposes that "theory-in-use" be seen as synonymous with motivation, and that this is influenced by both cognitive (paradigms) and affective (attitudes) systems, each of these in turn being influenced by a series of external factors.

It is necessary also to acknowledge that rewards, or valued outcomes from behavior, must be associated with patterns of cognition. People develop ideas about what is valuable to them, which then serve as guidelines for future behavior. This allows the idea of culture to contain an element of direction whereby the organizing of social activity is based on meanings and values which make it worth doing things one way rather than another. This values element is incorporated into the model as a feedback link between rewards and attitudes, also feeding back into the general set of background factors affecting paradigms.

PARADIGMS AND THE PROBLEM OF DEFINITION

Sturtevant (1964) has proposed the following definition of a paradigm.

> A paradigm is a set of segregates which can be partitioned by features of meaning, i.e., a set some members of which share features not shared by other segregates in the same set.

It is necessary to amplify this further by seeing it in the context of what Sturtevant was discussing, which was ethnoscience. Ethnoscience itself

> . . . refers to the 'reduction of chaos' achieved by a particular culture . . . a culture itself amounts to the sum of a given society's folk classifications, all of that society's ethnoscience, its particular ways of classifying its material and social universe.

The paradigm thus becomes both the end product of the attempts to make sense of the world until now and the set of guidelines for its interpretation in the future. It is the grid of references which controls and guides the process of cognition. As Maruyama (1974:137) puts it, it is "the structure of reasoning", and paradigmatology is

> a science of structures of reasoning which vary from discipline to discipline, from profession to profession, from culture to culture, and sometimes even from individual to individual.

It would be improper to conclude an attempt to define a paradigm without some reference to Thomas Kuhn's use of the word in his examination of the processes of science (Kuhn 1962). In this respect Masterman's (1970) questioning of Kuhn's definition (or, rather, lack of definition) of the concept is valuable. She points out that Kuhn uses the word in at least twenty-one different senses and then proposes the following three principal categories:

Metaparadigms. Paradigms of a philosophical sort equated with a set of beliefs, a myth, an organizing principle governing perception itself, a map, and something determining a large area of reality;

Sociological. Paradigms seen sociologically as scientific achievements, political institutions or accepted judicial decisions; and

Construct Paradigms. Artefact-type paradigms in the form of textbooks, tools, instruments, grammars or analogies.

This serves to clarify my meaning somewhat and it is proposed that Masterman's "metaparadigm" is what has been defined earlier. The sociological and construct paradigms may be seen as manifestations of the deeper underlying structure of the cognitive process in the metaparadigm. It is proposed therefore that the study of the linkage between culture and organization take into account the metaparadigm of that culture and that it be defined as:

> The set of guidelines used in the process of understanding reality. A societal aggregate of the individual ways of cognition which serve to classify and to structure information. The underlying source of patterns of understanding which provide the reasons for action.

It is also an important assumption that this metaparadigm is heavily influenced by culture, and that reality is very largely a social construct (Berger and Luckmann, 1966).

The cross-cultural study of cognition processes has been reviewed by Berry and Dasen (1974) who indicate the consistency of major research themes and classify them as: (a) studying *qualitative* differences in the method of cognition; (b) studying *quantitative* differences, an area which easily becomes ethnocentric and value-laden; and (c) studying the comparative *growth* of cognition. The research reported here is relevant to category (a), qualitative differences.

In considering methodology, Berry and Dasen (1974:14) indicate three usual goals of comparative cognitive psychology, namely: (1) transporting hypotheses and laws (from the West) and testing their generalizability; (2) exploring other cultures to find cognitive variations; and (3) comparing old and new understandings to generate more universal laws, and hypotheses. The method of this research is relevant to category 2 and attempts to look at cognitive variations displayed in South East Asia.

DIVIDING UP THE METAPARADIGM

It is impossible to construct a set of categories both mutually exclusive and exhaustive, which will represent the metaparadigm of a culture. Our present state of knowledge of the processes is too rudimentary and, in any case, the basis of the categorizing will usually be some question of a specific nature. The question we are faced with can be stated as "What are the effects on organizations, of different paradigms?" This allows us to narrow the field but still leaves it uncomfortably wide.

Taking the functions of management, such as planning, organizing, etc., and working back to the kind of mental constructs which could underlie them, five major categories can be constructed. These will be called Causality, Probability, Time, Self, and Morality, and the reasons for their inclusion follow.

Causality

The structuring of organizations and the imposition of control systems onto the structure, imply a view of cause and effect relationships and some form of abstraction. To say that somebody must be in charge of marketing and that there must be a department with that role, implies the acceptance of a concept called marketing which is different from other concepts like personnel or finance. It also implies that connections are seen between the various parts of the abstracted picture. This same principle applies at a more micro level in an organization, down to the categories used by a secretary for filing, or the procedures instituted by an office manager for progressing work. It may seem surprising that the view of causality together with a tendency to think in abstract concepts may vary across cultures but it would appear that it does and this becomes the first category.

Probability

Organizational decision-making, and hence much managerial effort, is directed towards predicting some future event, such as sales to be achieved, what competitors will do, the likelihood of plant breakdown, the success of an advertisement, etc. It could be argued that a sensitivity in viewing future events could be critical to the managerial role and certainly much effort has been directed towards making such processes more accurate through decision theory and the use of mathematical modelling. If probability is seen differently, then this will materially effect the process of management thinking and in turn it will effect management action.

Time

An essential part of any sophisticated approach to management is planning. This is predicated on a particular view of time. The view of time not only dictates the kind of conceptual framework in which any future thinking is made, but will also effect the sense of urgency with which activities are pursued, and the manifestations of this in management control systems.

Self

Two aspects may be distinguished in regard to the self, firstly, at the psychological level, the way the individual sees himself and secondly, at the interpersonal level, the way the individual sees his relations with others. Both are important for understanding the behavior people exhibit in organizations. The internal view of the self will affect patterns of motivation and the external view of the self will affect interpersonal relations and much social behavior.

Morality

Here again, two aspects are distinguishable. There is a base of moral beliefs which people in a society share and there is the process whereby influence to conform presses upon the person. The base usually consists across cultures of variations on the same themes and it is not proposed to examine it. The latter process, that of ways of influencing conformity, is of great interest when understanding behavior and becomes important in the organizational context. The principal dichotomy is that between "shame" cultures and "guilt" cultures and this will be examined for effects on interpersonal behavior.

In order to summarize the way in which these different paradigms (i.e., parts of the metaparadigm) impinge on the functioning of organizations a matrix is given in Figure 2. Following the precedents of Farmer and Richman (1965) and

Figure 2

MANAGEMENT FUNCTIONS AS AFFECTED BY PARADIGMS

	Causality	Probability	Time	Self	Morality
Planning		✓	✓		
Organizing	✓				
Staffing	✓			✓	
Directing & Leading				✓	✓
Control	✓		✓		

Negandhi and Estafen (1969), the cultural factors are related to the principal functions of management as normally treated in the literature (e.g., Koontz and O'Donnell, 1976).

EMPIRICAL SUPPORT

Each of these interconnections will now be examined and, where possible, in the light of supporting evidence. It is fairly safe to say that no major empirical study has been carried out specifically to investigate all such connections, and certainly not in South East Asia, but some relevant data exist, and will be used. These data fall into the following categories:

(a) Results of an 800n. survey of managerial beliefs and attitudes in S.E. Asia, using the Haire, Ghiselli and Porter (1966) instrument. (Redding and Casey, 1976)[1].

(b) A survey of probabilistic thinking, cross-culturally, carried out by the Decision Analysis Unit of Brunel University, (Wright *et. al.*, 1977) partly in co-operation with the University of Hong Kong.

(c) Various individual pieces of post-graduate research carried out at the University of Hong Kong.

(d) Related findings reported in a varied literature in sociology, anthropology, management and psychology.

CAUSALITY

Maruyama (1974) has drawn a distinction between what he terms the "unidirectional causal paradigm" and the "mutual causal paradigm", and has argued that the former is typical of Western thinking and the latter of Oriental thinking. A selection of the respective paradigm characteristics which he proposes is given in Table 1.

[1] Despite criticism of this instrument, it was felt necessary for this exploratory research to be able to relate to a large body of comparative data from other parts of the world and this was the principal reason for its use.

Table 1

TWO IDEAL-TYPE PARADIGMS (AFTER MARUYAMA)

	Unidirectional Causal Paradigm	*Mutual Causal Paradigm*
Science	Traditional "cause and effect" model	Post-Shannon information theory
Cosmology	Predetermined universe	Self-generating and self-organizing universe
Ideology	Authoritarian	Co-operative
Philosophy	Universalism	Network
Ethics	Competitive	Symbiotic
Religion	Monotheism	Polytheistic, harmonic
Decision Process	Dictatorship, majority rule or consensus	Elimination of hardship on any single person
Logic	Deductive axiomatic	Complementary
Perception	Categorical	Contextual
Knowledge	Believe in one truth. If people are informed, they will agree	Polyocular. Must learn and consider different views
Analysis	Pre-set categories used for all situations	Changeable categories depending on the situations

It is worth noting that, in spite of the variety of paradigm dimensions, the titles given to them derive from the view of causality. The mental picture of the process of cause and effect is fundamental to understanding all other thinking and hence we have the primary split between "unidirectional" causal thinking and "mutual" causal thinking.

Of the former, Maruyama argues that it is related to "hierarchical, classificational, anthropocentric, quantitative, homogenistic and competitive social organization and perception." For instance the notion of God as creator and prime mover and of only one God, is hierarchical, as is the tendency to think in terms of rank. The Westerner's tendency to think in categories, the high status of abstract ideas, and the logic of deduction, all conspired to forbid circular reasoning. The world is perceived in layers of categories and there is a strong tendency towards closure of concepts. In non-religious terms there is an assumption of *one* truth, *one* logic, *one* right way of doing things, and the ethnocentrism which can result derives from the kind of homogenistic thinking which sees no alternatives.

Of the mutual causal paradigm, Maruyama argues that it is "related to non hierarchical, heterogenistic, symbiotic, harmonistic, contextual, relational, polyocular and process-oriented social organization and perception." Many societies display patterns of interaction which do not depend on superior-subordinate status, and which concentrate on harmony and concern for the individual. Perception is related to context and logic is not based on abstraction *via* a material metaphor. Concern with the process, rather than substance, of life leads to the acceptance of uncertainty and to the fatalism so typical of many oriental cultures.

Much of this is reminiscent of the discussion in cognitive psychology of the global-articulated dimension of thinking (Witkin, 1967), which is operationalized through field-dependence tests. This has been shown to be influenced by culture and indicates variations in contextual thinking, but this approach has tended to see the continuum as underdeveloped-developed and is therefore asking different questions.

Support for the idea of the processes of cognition in Oriental cultures, as falling within the mutual causal paradigm, is strong in the literature which has looked specifically at oriental thinking (e.g., Nakamura, 1964, Maruyama, 1971). Northrop (1946) argues that societies developed away from a form of perception which he terms naïve realism and which he saw as a sort of primitive natural history. In the West, there developed (largely as a result of Greek philosophy) a form he terms logical realism and this is the basis of modern science. In this, knowledge is built up of tested but abstract theories of relationships between sensed observations. It is held together by a relational and sequential logic.

He further argues that such a transition was not made in Asia, which moved instead in the direction of "radical empiricism". This is held to be an equally consistent theory of knowledge but with different foundations. Here, existence depends on the perception of it and there is no reality outside the sensing of it. The properties of objects depend on the perceiver and the situation. Logic is not derived by intellection and does not exist in an abstract framework. What the oriental mind perceives is the "undifferentiated aesthetic continuum." Things include their context and cannot really be thought of without it. The explanation of an event must incorporate all surrounding elements and is therefore impossible to simplify. In a view of reality where things are inextricably mingled, immediate sense perception and the "now" become all important. Nakamura's description of the Chinese way of thinking is relevant here, and he lays particular emphasis on the way in which the language structure results in: (a) concreteness of expression related to sense perception and the "picturing" of things; (b) a lack of abstracts and universals; and (c) contextual thinking and a sensitivity to complex relationships (Nakamura, 1964).

That such an epistemology can still produce rational behavior is due to pragmatism, and the lack of an abstract logic is no barrier to an appropriate coming to terms with reality. As Weber points out, of Confucianism

> Confucianism is extremely rationalistic since it is bereft of any form of metaphysics. . . . At the same time it is more realistic than any other system . . . in the sense that it lacks and excludes all measures which are not utilitarian. (Weber, 1951)

This approach is capable of throwing light on a number of well known phenomena such as the intense pragmatism of the Chinese, their aptitude as students for subjects such as mathematics, chemistry, physics which do not use broad abstract concepts; and, conversely, their avoidance of sociology, philosophy and the more concept-oriented disciplines. This different form of perception is indicated in the semantic differential data from a survey of 800 managers in eight South East Asian countries.

In their large survey of managerial attitudes, Haire, Ghiselli and Porter (1966) reported results of a semantic differential testing of basic cognitive dimensions or qualities of meaning which underlay fifteen concepts relating to

Table 2

LOADINGS OF NINE SCALES ON FIVE FACTORS *

	Factors				
Scales	*Prestige*	*Scope*	*Activity*	*Firmness*	*Difficulty*
Important	.88	.16	.20	.14	.10
Profound	.73	.26	.26	.28	.17
Active	.33	.12	.87	.15	.12
Wide	.27	.91	.15	.13	.08
Difficult	.17	.09	.13	.11	.96
Good	.33	.36	.32	.61	.22
Stable	.17	.04	.09	.92	.04
Interesting	.54	.37	.37	.33	.19
Strong	.22	.34	.53	.53	.17

* Haire, Ghiselli and Porter (1966:291).

Table 3

LOADINGS OF NINE SCALES ON THREE FACTORS, FOR S.E. ASIAN DATA

	Factors		
Scales	*Prestige Scope Activity*	*Firmness*	*Difficulty*
Important	.91	.35	.15
Profound	.89	.36	.20
Active	.88	.30	.30
Wide	.90	.33	.25
Difficult	.28	.22	.93
Good	.66	.68	.27
Stable	.30	.93	.18
Interesting	.90	.28	.30
Strong	.71	.59	.32

management on nine bipolar scales. They reported the existence of five factors as explaining 85 per cent of the common variance, and their factor loadings are given in Table 2. The results of recent research using the same instrument, administered to managers in eight South East Asian countries (n = 800) are given in Table 3.

The Haire, Ghiselli and Porter data come from countries which are primarily Western or Westernized, the list of countries being Denmark, Germany, Norway, Sweden, Belgium, France, Italy, Spain, England, U.S., Argentina, Chile, India and Japan. The other data reported comes from a group of Asian countries, namely Hong Kong, Singapore, Japan, Philippines, Malaysia, Thailand, Vietnam, Indonesia. It is clear that the degree of Westernization in the latter group is distinctly lower than in the former, and that the two groups may reasonably be termed Western and Oriental.

It is noticeable that the factors which emerge from the Asian data indicate a marked decrease in differentiation. There is one major factor which accounts for 83 per cent of the variance (see Table 4), which compares with three factors in the Haire, Ghiselli and Porter data. In fact, what appears to be indicated is that while the Western group differentiates in cognitive space between Prestige, Scope and Activity, this does not occur in the Oriental group and the three elements combine into one factor. Firmness and Difficulty remain differentiated and in the same sequence, but account for only small parts of the variance.

It has been argued earlier that the Causality paradigm of many Oriental cultures operates with a less differentiated view of reality and that abstraction into conceptual categories does not take place so strongly as in the West, and here is evidence of a marked divergence from the Western mode of thinking. Prestige, Scope and Activity are somehow more closely bound together for the Oriental mind. The mutual causal paradigm, with its all-embracing, non-linear, cause and effect linkages, may be what is being expressed.

The implications of this paradigm for management are largely bound up with the way a person would look at an organization. The rationality of the modern large-scale organization is founded on a basis of linear logic and abstracted concepts. This applies both to the relatively static areas of organization structuring and to the more dynamic areas of management control. The difficulty in transferring these forms to many Oriental contexts may have deeper causes that the ones of motivation usually considered, and may result from different cognitive structures.

Table 4
VARIANCE PERCENTAGES BY FACTOR BEFORE ROTATION (ASIAN DATA)

Factor	*Eigenvalue*	*% of Variance*	*Cum. %*
1	7.47	83.0	83.0
2	.70	7.8	90.8
3	.61	6.8	97.5
4	.10	1.1	98.7

It is possible that people do not "get organized" because the process of thinking in abstract terms about the elements of organizations does not come naturally. It is very noticeable in Oriental cultures that businesses tend to be small scale (Japan is an exception). Recent research in Hong Kong (Lau, 1977) has indicated that most Chinese businesses operate without any organized planning system, with very little formalized information, and with very little clear allocation of responsibilities. Such things have been explained in the past in sociological terms, as results of the reliance on family obligations and networks, but there may also be a more fundamental cognitive tendency not to see an alternative.

Figure 3

CALIBRATION CURVES*

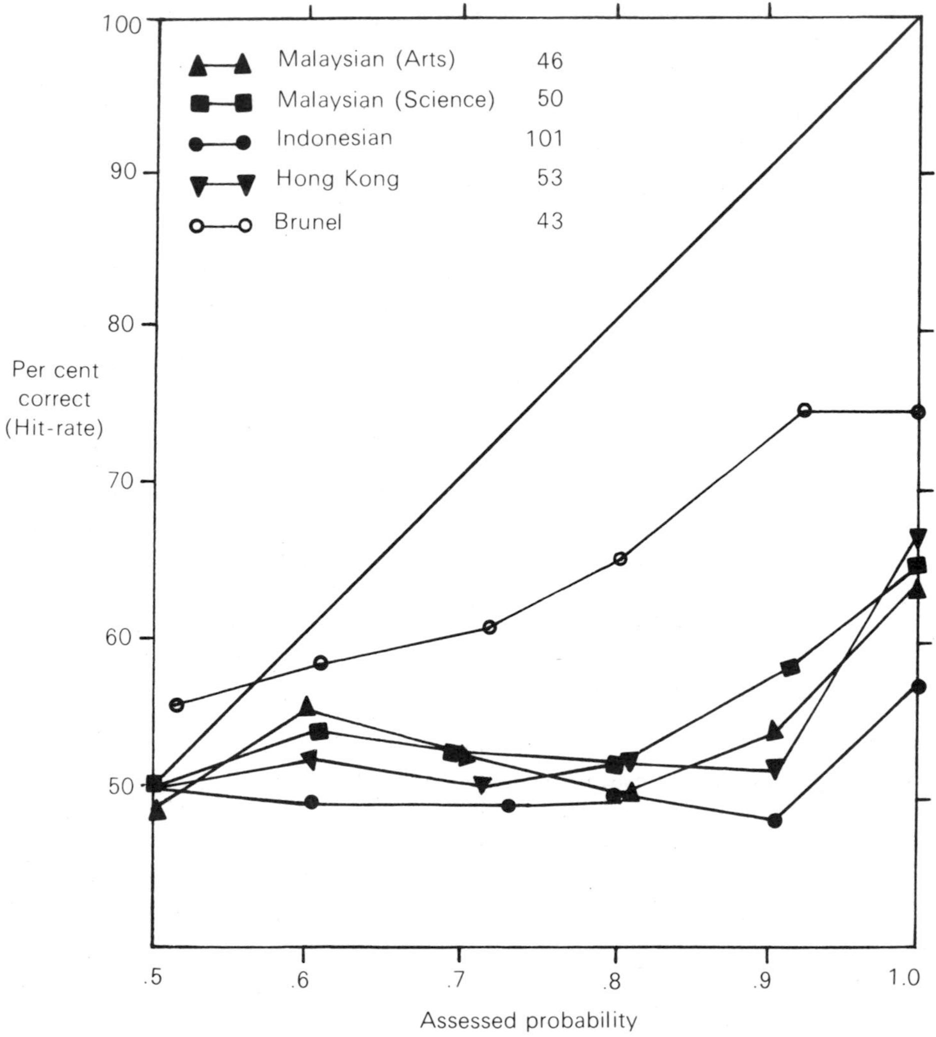

* After Wright, *et. al.*

PROBABILITY

Many descriptions exist of Oriental "fatalism" and the tendency to see a close relationship between man and nature. An inexorable cycle of events is taking place and the inevitability of things becomes an important factor in constructing explanations. This paradigm is by no means restricted to the Orient, and the West has its own version in proverbs like "What will be, will be." But it appears to have become particularly pervasive in Oriental cultures, and has important implications for cognitive processes.

The view of probability can be taken as a manifestation of this tendency and, among the few psychological studies carried out in South East Asian cultures, this aspect has recently been examined by the Decision Analysis Unit of Brunel University (Wright *et. al.*, 1977). In this research, interest was focused upon the comparison, within a group from one country, of accuracy of response to straightforward questions, and estimations by the subjects of the probability of being right. The questions were of such a general nature that there was no sharp distinction between the English and Asian groups in the overall proportion of items answered correctly. There was however a sharp distinction in terms of the estimated accuracy, i.e., probability, of being right. English students were better "calibrated" or more realistic in their assessments. Figure 3 indicates the differences, and shows that the Asian groups in Malaysia, Indonesia and Hong Kong were right in only 50 per cent of the cases when they were assessing the accuracy of their responses at 90 per cent. The English group's accuracy rate was 75 per cent when they were 90 per cent sure they were right.

Although pointing to the need for "purer" methods of measurement, Wright *et. al.*, do draw two implications from their work. First, the technology of decision analysis must be treated with caution in Asian cultures because of the different forms of subjective probability which appear to exist. Second, the communication of uncertainty across cultures must be handled with caution. Both of these have clear implications for practising management and for organization theory.

TIME

In an investigation of time perception in a non-Western culture, Cole, Gay and Glick (1968) pointed to the paucity of experimental research on the topic, and the amount of potential conflict which can occur if the Western sense of punctuality is violated, a point similarly made by Hall (1959). The normal description of the Western manner of "seeing" time is of an unending continuum (usually in the mind as going from left to right), which can be subdivided into precise units forming part of an interlocking logical system. The following is a description of the Asian equivalent.

> Time in Asia does not have a beginning. While the West thinks in terms of the space-time continuum, and perhaps views history as a continuous process having a beginning and progressing toward an end, Asians see time as phases rather circular in form. One season follows the next, one life leads into another, one king's reign is followed by another's, one dynasty moves into

> the next, one calendar decade divided into 12 parts, each named after an animal, moves into the next. Hence while time and punctuality are of cardinal importance in the West, Asians do not take time seriously. (Sithi-Amnuai, 1968:82)

Such observations can be supported by a large volume of anecdotal information, (and by unstructured data on the topic collected on training courses by the University of Hong Kong) and studies of nontechnological peoples in other areas of the world, bear out the difference (e.g. Hallowell, 1955; Doob, 1960).

What is important is the likely effects of such a construct on organizational functioning and here it is possible to point to two problem areas: (a) a lower sense of urgency is likely among people who "do not take time seriously"; and (b) a cyclical view of time may be related to the "fatalism" already noted when discussing probability and may produce a view of the future in which planning and forecasting do not easily fit, at least if they are transferred straight from a western planning model as occurs with corporate strategy and budgeting systems.

Hall has described a major distinction between "monochronic" time and "polychronic" time, and the way in which such systems of time perception affect organizational behavior (Hall, 1976). His argument is that monochronic time perception creates a system in which scheduling and keeping to dates is given high priority, and this allows for co-ordination of complex processes and decentralized systems. Polychronic time perception leads to more of a stress on general accountability for end-results, but not in a time-frame, and this leads to centralized control and smaller organizations as co-ordination is hindered.

SELF

We have argued that perception in Oriental cultures is highly contextual, that the tendency to differentiate reality and abstract concepts out of it is less than in Western cultures. The argument now extends to the view of the person and considers implications for the idea of personality, if the individual is seen as less differentiated from society.

Hsu (1971) has argued that personality is a Western concept rooted in individualism, which does not transfer easily to Oriental cultures. In the latter, a more appropriate concept is "jen".

> This is the Chinese word meaning 'man', and if we must have an English equivalent for it we may roughly designate it as *personage*. I suggest the term *jen* advisedly because the Chinese conception of man (also shared by the Japanese but pronounced *jin*) is based on the individual's transactions with his fellow human beings. (Hsu, 1971:29)

If the person is seen as inextricably bound up with a social context, then it is not surprising that individualism is less relevant. If the self is not perceived in the same way, then self-actualization will not be the same process. Maruyama (1974) has also pointed to the ethnocentrism of Maslow's hierarchy and questioned its validity in oriental cultures. Empirical support was provided for such questioning in a replication of the research of Haire *et. al.*, on managerial needs (Redding, 1977).

These data (given in an Appendix as graphs) also indicate a distinct shift in managerial beliefs in Asia towards the "autocratic" end of the continuum, but paradoxically combined with a greater expressed respect for subordinates than is found in the West. This finding may be accounted for by the view of the self as closely connected with surrounding others, the heightened interpersonal sensitivity and thereby greater awareness and respect for subordinates as people (a separate dimension perhaps from subordinates as hierarchical inferiors). The operation of this factor is noted by Hall (1976) is his distinction between high context and low context societies.

Much of Western management theory and the techniques which derive from it, such as management by objectives, job enrichment, participative decision-making, is based on the universality of the psychological maturing process which ends with the fulfillment of esteem and self-actualization needs. What is now needed is a deeper understanding of the implications for work of the Oriental paradigm of the self, and by extension, a cross-cultural theory of motivation.

MORALITY

Under this heading we will not discuss morality *per se*, but the difference in the "mechanics" of its operation, and in particular the difference between "shame" and "guilt" cultures. This distinction was first made widely understood by Benedict (1946) in her study of Japanese society, and her description of its operation is as follows:

> A society that inculcates absolute standards of morality and relies on men's developing a conscience is a guilt culture by definition. . . . True shame cultures rely on external sanctions for good behavior, not, as true guilt cultures do, on an internalized conviction of sin. Shame is a reaction to other people's criticism. . . . Shame has the same place of authority in Japanese ethics that 'a clear conscience', 'being right with God', and the avoidance of sin have in Western ethics. (Benedict, 1946:222)

This produces a radical difference in the process of socialization, the implications of which have recently been discussed by Ng (1977). The conformity to socially acceptable behavior in the West is achieved through morality based on guilt, the pain of which is well known. In the Chinese case the same end product of acceptable behavior is achieved through

> The adoption of a lofty model prescribed in traditional terms and the meticulous and unsparing efforts to try to attain it. The better to pursue it, the individual trains himself or is trained to have a sensitive pride, which reminds him with a painful sense of shame or wounded pride whenever he falls short of it. (Ng, 1977:35)

A manifestation of this in social behavior is "face" and its powerful effect on interpersonal relations is something which cannot be ignored in the cross-cultural study of organizational behavior. In particular, it is necessary to examine the assumptions built into systems of management control and to take into account the difference in the mechanics of influence. In shame cultures, the person aligns himself towards the verdict of others and thereby acts with them in mind. This can only produce a relatively greater restraint on at least interpersonal behavior (and perhaps other behavior also). The individual socialized by guilt is to a greater extent accountable to himself and the means of influencing his behavior must take that into account. The overlap of these considerations with those discussed under the self paradigm are inevitable as the two paradigms are closely related.

SUMMARY AND HYPOTHESES

In order to pull together the strands of the argument, the diagram originally given in Figure 2 is now filled out (Figure 4) and it summarizes the information in terms of focuses of potential problems. From this a number of hypotheses may be proposed.

Figure 4

AREAS OR FOCUSES OF POTENTIAL PROBLEMS IN APPLYING WESTERN MANAGEMENT PRINCIPLES TO ASIAN CULTURES

	PARADIGMS				
FUNCTION	Causality	Probability	Time	Self	Morality
Planning		Subjective probability. Sensitivity. Fatalism.	Sequencing. Long term planning.		
Organizing	Definition of necess-ary func-tions. Co-ordin-ation				
Staffing	Understanding of influence processes. Training. Selection.			Subjective assessment. Team con-sciousness	
Directing & Leading				Motivation. Leadership behavior. Social Responsib-ility	Interpersonal relations. Business ethics
Control	Management information systems. Feedback. Budgeting.		Sense of urgency. Use of time.		

HYPOTHESES FOR FUTURE RESEARCH

Planning

In Oriental[2] cultures, the fatalistic view of probability will result in a lower sensitivity in the calculation of future events. Processes of extrapolation will be carried out with less conviction if they are carried out at all. The view of time, which we have simplified as circular in the Oriental paradigm as opposed to linear in the Western, will also affect the process of planning. The most radical effect will be that planning as such may not take place in any identifiable way and companies will be run more on an *ad hoc* basis. These two influences come together in having the same effect and this may be represented in the following hypothesis:

Hypothesis 1: Oriental companies will use either less formal planning systems, and/or planning systems with fewer variables than equivalent Western companies.

Organizing

It has been suggested earlier that the perception of reality in Oriental cultures is more immediate and less given to the use of abstracts than in the West. Many of the ideas of organization employed in the West are founded on an abstract view of the firm, and its divisions begin with what are basically theoretical constructs such as marketing or personnel administration. Similarly, ideas such as control and co-ordination are abstracts. If these concepts are seen less clearly or not seen at all, then the firm will find alternative forms of organization such as reliance on interpersonal networks and obligations, or will simply operate in a less organized manner. This leads to the second hypothesis.

Hypothesis 2: In Oriental companies the degree of formal organization (in terms of defined differentiation of functions, integrating control mechanisms and co-ordinating processes) will be less than in an equivalent Western company.

Staffing

The staffing function, as treated by Koontz and O'Donnell (1976) is defined as "manning the organization structure through proper and effective selection, appraisal, and development of personnel to fill the roles designed into the structure." It is seen as a key managerial function and not something which can be assigned to a personnel department. The heart of the matter is guiding the growth of managerial skill and capacity among subordinates. The kind of thinking in which the idea of management development fits is sequential and

[2] For the sake of simplicity the word "Oriental" is used as an umbrella phrase for the context which is being studied here. It is meant to embrace Hong Kong, Singapore, Malaysia, Indonesia, Thailand, the Philippines (and originally, South Vietnam). Japan is omitted from the list because of its special cultural nature and because of the degree of Westernization which has taken place there, but some of the ideas are still held to apply there.

has a linear logic. If manager A is sent to this department for six months, then sent on X training course, then given two years on the road, he will be ready to take manager B's job in three years time.

It is proposed that this form of linear thinking is not natural to many Oriental minds with their mutual causal paradigm, and that consequently the related behavior is not found. What is found instead is a "let's wait and see what happens", "something will emerge", type of approach. This is not to say that no preparation is made but it tends to be one of general education such as that given to sons due to take over the business, and the more precise analysis of training and development effects does not take place. This leads to the third hypothesis.

Hypothesis 3: In Oriental companies the staffing function will be less programmed and will contain less formal training than in equivalent Western companies.

A further factor when considering staffing is the view of the self. The person (i.e. the manager) is seen as being more closely bound up with others and this may well extend to subordinates who may be due for promotion, thus lowering the objectivity of any assessment. This is a difficult hypothesis to propose and test, but at least one formulation could be

Hypothesis 4: Oriental managers make promotion decisions using less objective data than equivalent Western managers.

Directing and Leading

In Koontz and O'Donnell's terms this is "the interpersonal aspect of managing" and, as such, the paradigm of the person in relation to others takes on particular significance. It has been suggested that individualism is part of the Western metaparadigm and that it is not so strongly represented in Asia, where the view of the person is of a being much more closely enmeshed in surrounding society. This is likely to have an effect on the attitudes and behavior of people in a leadership position although the precise effects are still problematic. It could for instance mean a general softness in leadership style or alternatively it could be related to a greater hierarchical sensitivity and norms sanctioning authoritarian behavior (which might be the societal responses to maintaining control). It is even possible for softness, in the sense of unwillingness to deal with interpersonal confrontation, to be combined with hardness in the sense of authoritarian decisions.

Research on such topics is virtually non-existent (except in Japan) and any hypotheses will reflect this, but let us propose

Hypothesis 5: The style of leadership employed by Oriental managers will rely less on interpersonal confrontations with subordinates than would be the case with Western managers, and in order to compensate, different social structures and norms will operate to facilitate control.

In pointing to the contrast between guilt cultures and shame cultures, it was noted that social manifestations of the shame mechanism, such as "face" would operate in the management context and these are seen as particularly relevant to the leadership function. Much behavior is carried out in the light of its effect on others both up and down the hierarchy and between equals. This leads to

Hypothesis 6: Managerial decisions in Oriental companies will take greater account of effects on the relative status of other people, than in Western companies.

It is tempting, while discussing the effects of the morality process, to add a hypothesis about the relative effects of shame and guilt on business ethics, but as this needs to take corruption into account it becomes virtually impossible to research and is thus omitted.

Control

Management control is making sure that plans are adhered to and it usually rests on a system of performance measurement and feedback. This presupposes the breaking down of a general aim into more specific contributory aims and the monitoring of progress towards these. The entire edifice is based on a linear cause-and-effect logic and thus belongs firmly within the Western paradigm. Its extension to Asia is doubtful and thus we have

Hypothesis 7: The control of performance in Oriental companies will be less formal, using less information and a shorter time span of discretion than the Western equivalent.

The principal effect of a different view of time is on a sense of urgency. A culture which sees time as constantly recurring in cycles will tend to think in terms of another opportunity coming round rather than of time being lost for ever and therefore precious. This leads to

Hypothesis 8: Oriental managers will display less precision and less urgency in matters of time such as timekeeping, scheduling, and completion of programs than Western equivalents.

These hypotheses beg questions about comparability which there is not space to deal with here and the extraneous factors which would also need to be considered have not been openly acknowledge, but they are presented as indicators of possible underlying causes of difference which are fundamental to comparative analysis. They are obviously only part of the story.

Another important warning is that considerable liberties have been taken in discussing groupings of countries and the differences between them. Like all ideal types, the paradigms referred to are constructs, and the intention in using them is to indicate ranges of possibilities. It may be more accurate to think of them as the poles of a continuum rather than discrete categories, and to acknowledge that the location of a particular culture along the continuum is still a matter for further research in most respects.

Finally, a number of more general points must be made. This paper is exploratory and largely hypothetical. As stated earlier, it followed from a large research project on managerial thinking and its conceptual framework, has not yet been put to empirical test.

Study of the cognitive process remains bedevilled with problems of definition and with inevitably ethnocentric models. Some time ago Gladwin (1964) pointed to the problem in discussing the culture-bound nature of psychology and said,

> Their starting point is our familiar symbolic logic and relational abstract thinking. They do not have before them a range of other possible basic approaches to thinking, learning and problem-solving. . . . In this vital area we make no cross-cultural comparisons, and indeed have no theoretical framework within which to make them.

Research and theory building in comparative management have ignored for too long the area of cognition, and have at the same time been relatively unsuccessful this past decade in breaking new ground in understanding. The comprehension of organization must eventually come to terms with the nature of meaning-structures. To start with an understanding of how the individual sees the world around him is to allow some progress towards understanding how he sees the organization and his attachment to it.

REFERENCES

Argyris, C. *Increasing Leadership Effectiveness*, New York: Wiley.
1976

————. "Single-loop and double-loop models in research on decision-making."
1976b *Administrative Science Quarterly*. Vol. 21, 3:363–375.

Armstrong, D. M. *Belief, Truth and Knowledge*. Cambridge: Cambridge University Press.
1973

Benedict, R. *The Chrysanthemum and the Sword*. New York: Meridian.
1946

Berger, P. L., and T. Luckmann. *The Social Construction of Reality*. London: Penguin.
1966

Berry, J. W., and P. R. Dasen (eds.). *Culture and Cognition: Readings in Cross-Cultural*
1974 *Psychology*. London: Methuen.

Child, J., and A. Kieser. "Organizational and Managerial Roles in British and Western
1976 German Companies—an Examination of the Culture-Free Thesis." Paper presented at the Third International Conference of the International Association of Cross-Cultural Psychologists, Tilburg.

Cicourel, A. V. *Cognitive Sociology: Language and Meaning in Social Interaction*.
1972 London: Penguin.

Cole, M., J. Gay, and J. Glick. "Some Experimental Studies of Kpelle Quantitative
1968 Behavior." In J. W. Berry and P. R. Dasen (eds.). *Culture and Cognition: Readings in Cross-Cultural Psychology:* London: Methuen.

Doob, L. W. *Becoming More Civilized: A Psychological Exploration*. New Haven: Yale
1960 University Press.

Farmer, R. N., and B. M. Richman. *Comparative management and Economic Progress.*
1965 Homewood, Ill.: Irwin.

Garfinkel, H. *Studies in Ethnomethodology.* Englewood Cliffs: Prentice Hall.
1967

Gladwin, T. "Culture and Logical Process." In W. H. Goodenough (ed.), *Explorations in*
1964 *Cultural Anthropology*: 167–177.

Haire, M., E. E. Ghiselli, and L. W. Porter. *Managerial Thinking An International Study*.
1966 New York: Wiley.

Hall, E. T. *The Silent Language.* New York: Doubleday.
1959

Hall, E. T., *Beyond Culture*, New York: Doubleday.
1976

Hallowell, A. I. *Culture and Experience*. Philadelphia: University of Philadelphia Press.
1955

Harré, R., and P. F. Secord. *The Explanation of Social Behaviour*. Oxford: Blackwell.
1972

Hickson, D. J., C. R. Hinings, C. J. McMillan, and J. P. Schwitter. "The Culture-Free Context of Organization Structure." *Sociology*. 8:59–80.

Hsu, F. L. K. "Psychosocial Homeostasis and Jen: Conceptual Tools for Advancing
1971 Psychological Anthropology." *American Anthropologist*. 73:23–43.

Koontz, H. and C. O'Donnell. *Management: A Systems and Contingency Analysis of*
1976 *Managerial Functions*. 6th edn. London: McGraw-Hill.

Kuhn, T. *The Structure of Scientific Revolutions*. Chicago: Chicago University Press.
1962

Lau, S. "Managerial Style of Traditional Chinese Firms." Unpublished dissertation.
1977 University of Hong Kong.

Maruyama, M. "Paradigmatology and Its Application to Cross-Disciplinary, Cross-
1974 Professional and Cross-Cultural Communication." *Dialectica*. 28, 3–4: 135–196.

Masterman, M. "The Nature of a Paradigm." In I. Lakatos and A. Musgrave (eds.),
1970 *Criticism and the Growth of Knowledge*: 59–89. Cambridge: Cambridge University Press.

Maruyama, M. "Preconditional Theory of Asian Management." *Jimbun Kiyo*, 3:30–60
1971 Tokyo: Chiba University.

Nakamura, H. *Ways of Thinking of Eastern Peoples*. Honolulu: East-West Center Press.
1964

Negandhi, A. R., and B. D. Estafen. "A Model for Analysing Organizations in Cross-
1969 Cultural Settings: a Conceptual Scheme and some Research Findings." *Comparative Administration and Research Conference*. Kent, Ohio: Kent State University.

Ng, M. "A Critical Study of Freud's Theory of Guilt in Society." Working Paper, Center of
1977 Asian Studies, University of Hong Kong.

Northrop, F. S. C. *The Meeting of East and West*. New York: Macmillan.
1946

Redding, S. G. "Some Perceptions of Psychological Needs among Managers in South
1977 East Asia." In Y. H. Poortinga (ed.), *Basic Problems in Cross-Cultural Psychology*. Amsterdam: Swets and Zeitlinger.

Redding, S. G., and T. W. Casey. "Managerial Beliefs among Asian Managers." In
1976 R. L. Taylor *et. al.* (eds.), *Proceedings Academy of Management 36th Annual Meeting*: 351–355. Kansas City: Academy of Management.

Silverman, D. *The Theory of organizations*. London: Heinemann.
1970

Sithi-Amnuai, P. "The Asian Mind." *Asia*. Spring: 78–91.
1968

Sturtevant, W. C. "Studies in Ethnoscience." In J. W. Berry and P. R. Dasen (eds.)
1964 *Culture and Cognition: Readings in Cross-Cultural Psychology*. London: Methuen.

Weber, M. *The Religion of China: Confucianism and Taoism*. New York: Free Press.
1951

Witkin, H. A. "Cognitive Styles Across Cultures." In J. W. Berry and P. R. Dasen (eds.),
1967 *Culture and Cognition: Readings in Cross-Cultural Psychology*. London: Methuen.

Wright, G. N. *et. al. Cultural Differences in Probabilistic Thinking: an Extension into*
1977 *South East Asia*. Technical Report 77–1. Decision Analysis Unit, Brunel University.

Appendix

Figure 1

ATTITUDES TO MANAGEMENT PRACTICES—RAW SCORES

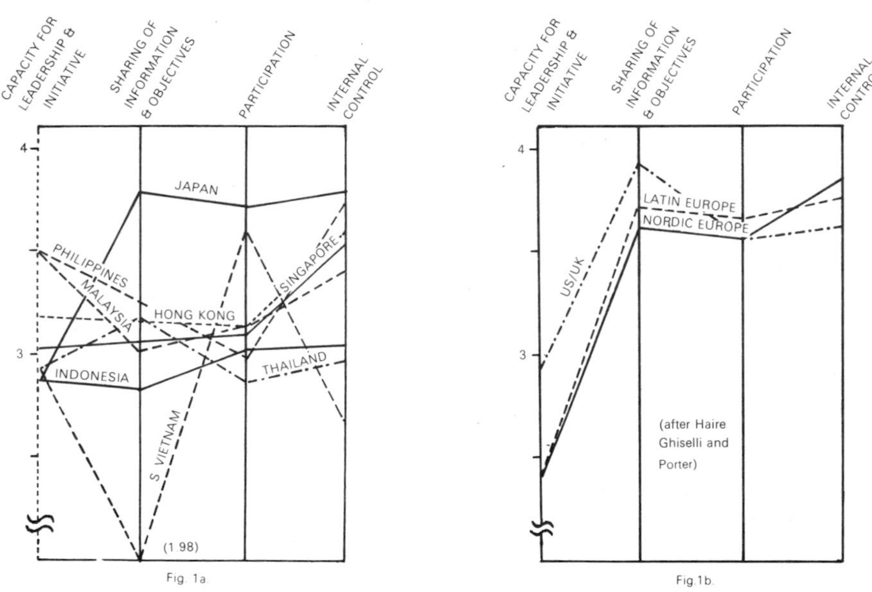

Fig. 1a. Fig. 1b.

Figure 2

NEED FULFILMENT—RAW SCORES

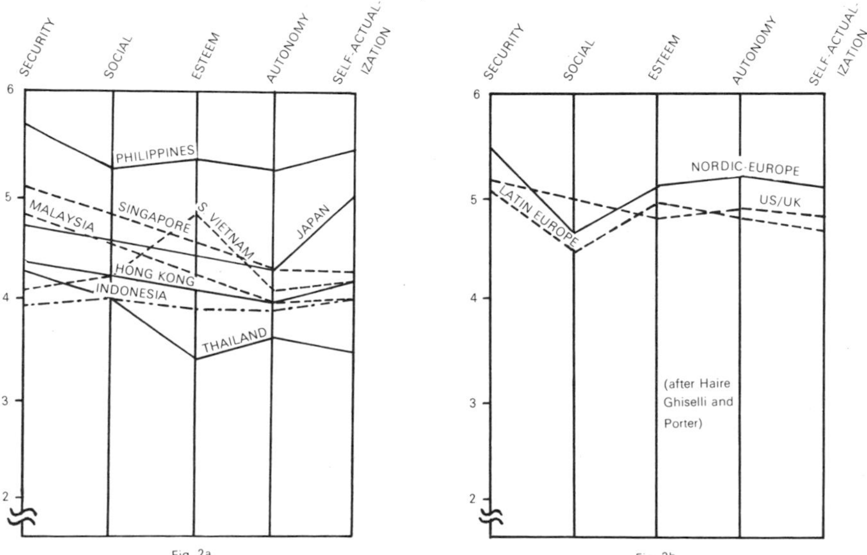

Fig. 2a. Fig. 2b.

Figure 3

NEED SATISFACTION—RAW SCORES

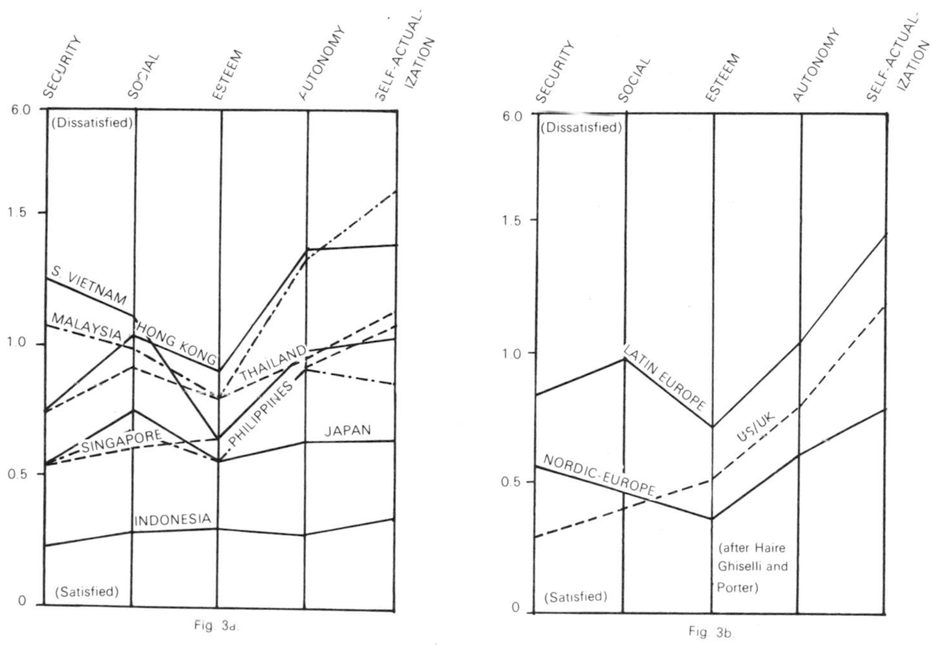

Fig. 3a. Fig. 3b.

Figure 4

NEED IMPORTANCE—RAW SCORES

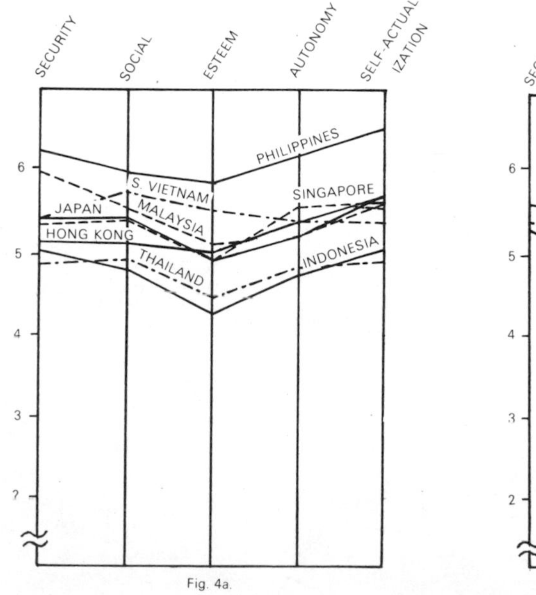

Fig. 4a.

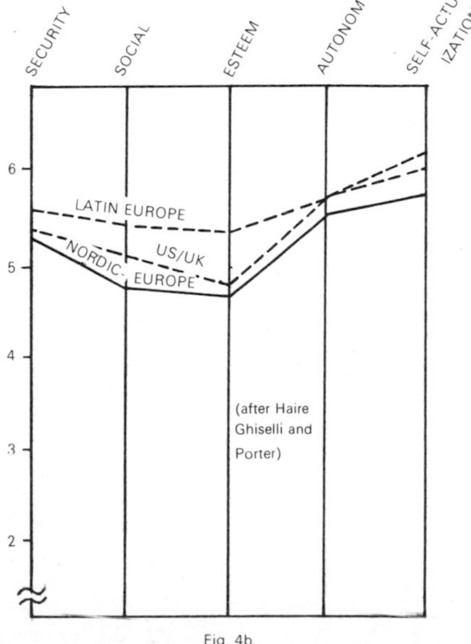

Fig. 4b.

Studies on Values, Goals, and Decision-Making: A Critical Evaluation

Editorial Note:

In this chapter and Chapters 11 and 15, we have attempted to provide a critical evaluation of research studies presented in Section I. The commentators were asked to critically evaluate the specific studies and those comments were fed back to the authors to enable them to undertake revision of their papers wherever feasible. The comments that appear in the following pages are based on the revised papers of the authors. In reproducing these comments, the editors have used, sometimes rather heavily, their editorial prerogatives to ensure continuity and reduce redundance. Those commenting on the preceding studies are:

(1) James Miller, Georgia State University
(2) Keith Davis, Arizona State University
(3) Wolfgang H. Staehle, Technical University Darmstadt
(4) Naoto Sasaki, Sophia University
(5) J. Faison, University of Hawaii

Comments on Whitely's Paper

METHODOLOGICAL PROBLEM—*James R. Miller*

Although the author's methodology shows logic and clarity of thought, the problem lies in the two survey techniques used by the author: mail-in questionnaires in Australia and personal interviews in India. This could lead to questionnaire respondent bias in Australia and interviewer bias in India. However, it is understood why this may have had to be done; and it would appear that the results of the study have not been affected dramatically.

The results of the study do appear to make significant contributions to the literature. The work of England (1975) is supported with the added assistance of making his model more explicit. It was found that the value systems of the four groups of managers are very different, and the within-country differences are relevant. There appears to be considerable confirmation that value orientation is a moderator of value in systems-behavior relationships.

The joint effect of value orientation on both value systems and relationships is interesting; but the statement that "now these are properties of subsystems of values rather than individual values" needs more explanation.

The comparisons between the managers from the two countries is interesting also, and bears out limited personal observations by this author. Further, this author would concur that the types of ownership should have a significant effect, just as size and type of business has on managers in the U.S. In addition, the type of industry, its structure, conduct, and performance, and the level of technology in the firms should affect managerial values and experience.

The conclusions drawn by Whitely are logical and illuminating. His suggestions for areas of needed research should prove helpful for those who follow this area of interest.

Comments on Heller and Wilpert's Paper

EQUIFINALITY MODEL NEEDED—*Keith Davis*

The paper by Heller and Wilpert concerns a major research effort involving research associates in a number of nations. It is large-scale, detailed research of the kind that often leads to useful results in comparative management. The size of the research project is indicated by the fact that this paper reports data on 625 matched dyads of senior and subordinate managers in seven countries. Even though the paper reports only a part of the total research project, the amount of data covered is substantial, so there is a sound basis for making some tentative conclusions.

Conceptually, the paper focuses on factors that influence decision-making and power-sharing among two levels of senior management in successful corporations. This is useful information in comparative management. We need to understand how senior managers make decisions in different environments. How do they share their power with the next levels of management? In what ways do they develop participation? Do national and cultural differences influence these decision patterns; and, if so, how much and in what ways? We need information about contingencies in decision-making, and this research proposes to secure it from senior management dyads in different nations.

This type of research, however, does have its limitations. As the authors recognize, they are studying decision-making as it is currently practiced, not how it should be practiced for more effective results. Emphasis is on the *status quo*, accepting whatever value premises and decision sophistication that the participants have. The researchers have somewhat overcome this limitation by studying organizations that they label "successful". Presumably, these organizations are better than some of their competitors, so the results reported here should represent some of the better quality decision-making currently practiced. However, there should be no implication that the results reported here represent the most desirable or best patterns of decision-making. We should be cautious to insure that less sophisticated readers do not interpret these results as telling how decisions *should* be made for maximum results. No prescriptive theories of decision-making are implied.

On the other hand, certain prescriptive approaches to decision-making may develop indirectly from the research results. For example, one significant finding of this research is that subordinate skill is significantly related to decision-making. As the authors state, "where skill resources are great, participative decision-making is significantly more prevalent than in circumstances where skill resources are low or seen to be low." In other words, more skilled subordinates, or those that are thought to be skilled, have more opportunity to participate in decision-making. A type of prescriptive approach that may derive from this research conclusion is that *if* managers or subordinates wish to increase participation in decision-making, *then* increasing skills is a probable way to increase participation. This "if-then" relationship is the essence of a contingency approach to decision-making. It explains the contingency relationship in a situation so that if management wants to accomplish a certain result, then it knows what practices have a higher probability of helping it reach that result. This is the kind of research information that management can use.

The authors' conclusion on the relationship of skill and participation is what might be expected. That is, the greater the subordinate's skill, the more likely the superior manager will share decision-making with that subordinate. From what we know of human behavior, it seems probable that managers will have stronger drives to share decisions with those in whom they have confidence and trust. However, it is helpful to have these intuitive thoughts supported by research. We have often discovered that what seemed to be correct, intuitively, has not been supported by research results.

The authors' comments about authentic participation and non-authentic participation are especially appropriate. Their research seems to imply that authentic participation occurs when there is genuine use of subordinates' skills and capabilities. On the other hand, non-authentic participation is based on ideas of going through the motions of participation, such as consultation, but without any real intention of using the ideas, skills, and capabilities of employees. This kind of participation is likely to have both ethical and operative negative consequences, making it worse than no participation at all. The authors suggests, therefore, that training packages designed merely to encourage people to use the procedures of participation are not likely to be successful, because they probably will not lead to authentic participation. This is a useful conclusion that many operating managers need to consider.

An important limitation of the research is that it explains only a small amount of the variance of decision-making. The results, therefore, indicate only moderately probable relationships, rather than certain relationships. For example, national differences appeared to account for only 10–15 per cent of the variance, according to the authors. This figure seems to be rather small in terms of what one might expect and what some observers have suggested. For example, the research failed to support findings of Haire, Ghiselli, and Porter (1966) that managerial attitudes appear to fall into recognizable clusters of countries. It also failed to support the marked differences between German and Anglo-Saxon managerial systems that a number of authors have reported.

With regard to technology, some 5–10 per cent of the variance was explained by technology. This gives some support for the research of Woodward (1958) and others concerning technology's effect on management, but it also implies that there are many other significant variables in the managerial decision-making situation. We may conclude from this discussion that one of the most useful results of this research is that it gives new evidence that either supports or fails to support earlier research in comparative management. In this way we move one small step closer to understanding the significant variables in comparative management. The complex nature of management means that progress will be slow, and it will be many years before we develop a mature understanding in comparative management.

One of the areas of strongest argument in comparative management is that of cultural convergence compared with divergence in management practice. The research by Heller and Wilpert does not seem to give strong support to either point of view. Rather, their research indicates that there are a multitude of variables influencing management practice in different environments, and national differences account for only a small amount of the variance. We are beginning to identify some of the other variables, such as technology, but there are many more that we probably do not even recognize. There are so many variables, and management situations are so fluid, that what we have is a condition of *equifinality* in which there are many different combinations of decision making and management practice that will lead to optimum results for an organization. In other words, there are many ways to practice effective management. All of them may produce approximately equal optimum final results, but their intermediate routes toward these results may be different. There is no one *best* way.

This condition of equifinality appears to be the situation with comparative management at the present time. We can identify a multitude of variables, and we can relate them in combinations with some predictive probability; however, there is no one best way. A number of different combinations appear to have approximately equal success, as in the different practices in Japan, Germany and the U.S. Perhaps an appropriate academic term for this concept is the *equifinal model of comparative management*. It clearly implies that there is no one best way to managerial effectiveness. Rather there are a number of different routes that may have different intermediate effects, but all will reach the top, which is defined as optimum organizational effectiveness.

Comments on Hoover, Troub, Whitehead and Flores' Paper

OTHER METHODS NEEDED TO "EXPLAIN" CULTURAL DIFFERENCES—

Wolfgang H. Staehle

This cross-cultural study aims at discovering, identifying, comparing, and explaining change or stability of the perception of the hierarchy of goals of their firms by chief executive officers operating under the Peruvian co-determination system and their counterparts in the Yugoslavian self-determination system. The major *a priori* hypothesis of this study is that power equalization efforts in both countries (defined as any attempt to broaden the distribution of decision-making power in an organization by modifying the structure of authority in the management system) are resulting in a major change in the perception of the goal hierarchy in the new Peruvian system and less change in perception in the older Yugoslavian system. However, data of an empirical study in these countries did not support these and related hypotheses (see summary of the five hypotheses in Figure 1).

Figure 1

SUMMARY OF FINDINGS IN TERMS OF HYPOTHESES

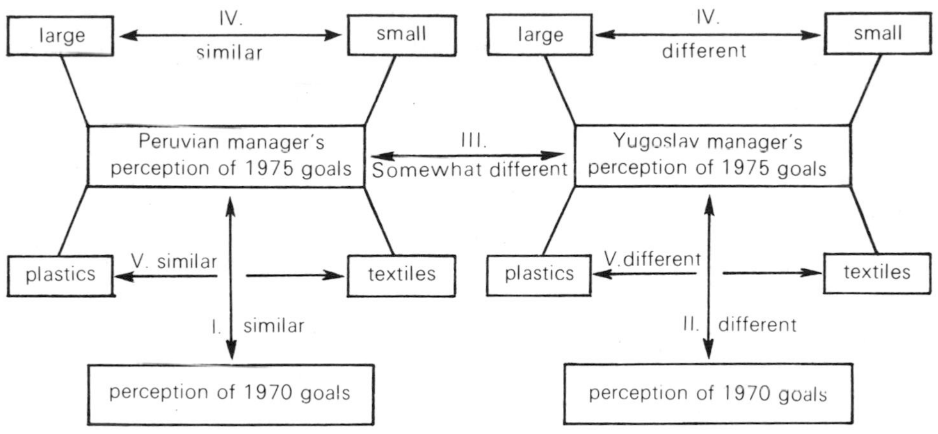

Later in the paper, the authors offer a set of possible explanations for these surprising results.

Problems. As long as the authors discover, identify, and compare similarities and differences, their methods and procedures seem adequate. But when they start explaining their findings, the weaknesses and limitations of their comparative approach become evident. Cross-cultural studies, as presented here, serve in the first place to discover and identify problems. For explanation and understanding we need other types of methods and other theoretical approaches. It is not sufficient to analyze the consequences or the impact of isolated structural variables on behavior by collecting individual data on a micro-level. We need concepts from social psychology, political science, and organization theory (especially contingency theory) to explain such phenomena as changes in the environment and their consequences for changes in the perception of individuals. It is doubtful that data collected from individual managers can explain the impact of such structural changes. The change in perception of the hierarchy of goals can only be partly understood by interviewing a group of individuals who might show some reactions on structural change, i.e., the modification of the authority structure in government and management systems.

Attempts of power equalization by participation are relevant to different levels (individual, group, organizational, and societal), and have important implications for the organization-environment interface. These relations have been changed in Yugoslavia far more intensively than in Peru, which might give attention to the differences in the perceptions of goal hierarchies between Peru and Yugoslavia.

Another major problem in the research paper seems to be the lack of a clear distinction between *objective facts* on real change and personal, *subjective prejudices,* and wishful thinking on perceived change. Since we only have information about the latter, it is very difficult to interpret the findings, e.g., when the authors describe the Yugoslavian systems as a self-determination model where "workers determine production and investment programs, price products, and set the compensation for their productive contributions". This has nothing to do with reality. In spite of self-determination since 1950, we find that: power distribution in Yugoslavian companies is autocratic; and a power elite of managers and specialists is responsible for the greatest number of proposals accepted later in the workers' council.

Obradovic (1972) reported that these top managers represent an average of only 8.21 per cent of the company's work force, but dominate up to 70.4 per cent of the discussions, bring up 78.6 per cent of all problems, formulate 72.9 per cent of all proposals, and present 67.6 per cent of the accepted proposals. This and similar research carried out on Yugoslavian councils confirm Mulder's central hypothesis on participation and power equalization: "When there are relatively large differences in the expert power of members of a system, an increase in participation will increase the power differences between members" (Mulder, 1971:34).

One central problem of any attempt to power equalization or participation is the lack of motivation and the low level of information on the part of the workers. Due to the lack of adequate training, it is very difficult for them to analyze economic decisions and their consequences in the appropriate context. Therefore, workers tend to reduce their areas of influence to personal and social problems (as found in Germany) or lose their inclination to participate completely because they experienced no effective change as a result of their efforts.

In essence the low skills and training of workers to participate, the perceived low power to participate, and the low motivation of workers to participate results in a power vacuum which is filled by those who were already possessing the power. Although in both countries there are large differences in the expert power of the organizational members, there are still important distinctions. Contrary to the Peruvian experiment:

1. the Yugoslavian structural changes, starting in 1950, were an absolute "must" since the country was confronted with an economic disaster (the Russians stopped all economic aid at that time);
2. self-determination was not completely new for the Yugoslavian worker, since he experienced participation a long time ago in rural cooperatives (called Zadruga), and in 1948, 75 per cent earned their living from agriculture;
3. the Yugoslavian manager finds himself in a role conflict, since he has to fulfil different functions, i.e. as manager, preparing and executing the decisions of the work council, and political official (97 per cent of the managing directors are members of the communist party);
4. there are tremendous differences in personal income for comparable jobs (see Table 1), which have consequences for the manager's perception of goal hierarchies; and
5. in Yugoslavia there is no such goal as "profitability" (improvement in

Table 1

HIGHEST AND LOWEST PERSONAL INCOMES FOR COMPARABLE JOBS IN BELGRAD, 1967*

Type of Job	*Personal Income* max.	min.	*Difference* in %
Managing Director	4987	1055	472
Managing Engineer	3569	975	366
Controller	3779	800	472
Administrative Director	3278	882	371
Accountant	2761	413	668
Engineer	2565	705	364
Highly Qualified Worker	1959	703	279
Qualified Worker	1421	474	300
Semiqualified Worker	1203	391	308
Unqualified Worker	1024	306	335
Cleaning Lady	1275	330	386
Messenger	1093	322	339

* Šefer (1968:434)

the rate of ROI). As comprehensive research on the Yugoslavian experiment indicates, the major organizational goal is "maximization of net income per capita". This goal has some negative consequences, e.g., increase in sales price, investment of earnings in the same company (which might be detrimental from a macro-economic viewpoint), and no interest on the part of the collective to hire additional labor (which in 1974 resulted in an unemployment rate of 9 per cent and 900,000 Yugoslavs working outside of Yugoslavia.

This additional information might be helpful to interpret and explain the differences and similarities found in the study between the perceptions of goal hierarchies in Peru and Yugoslavia. However, these are only small pieces of the mosiac. Without a conceptual framework, which was asked for earlier, we are left with the outcome of comparative research alone and do not know what to do with it and how to explain it.

Comments on the Brown-Blandin Paper

METHODOLOGICAL PROBLEMS—*Naoto Sasaki*

The Brown-Blandin paper aims to apply the Lawrence-Lorsch method to a comparative study of interrelationships between environmental uncertainty, managerial behavior and organizational structure in the U.S. and Denmark.

It seems that some vague methodological procedures and conceptualization of Lawrence and Lorsch's work are apparent in Brown and Blandin's paper. For example, the paper enumerates two "cultural" factors differentiating the firms in the U.S. and Denmark, which are the size of the firm and the fact that the Danish economy is much more socialized and controlled than that of the U.S. Brown and Blandin "believe that these two factors, in particular, might be associated with differences in the organizational responses between the two countries."

Keeping aside the question of whether it is reasonable to consider these two factors as cultural ones, the treatment of their findings and the logic or the reason of them still remains obscure. They chose, for example, eight "medium-sized firms" in each country which were "medium-sized by U.S. standards, large by Danish standards." This research setting seems to give us eight firms of the same size. Is this aimed at eliminating the effect of the "cultural" variable, namely, "size of the firm"? This is contradictory to the logical setting of their research.

In many other countries in the free world some industries are publicly regulated; the extent of such regulations is dependent upon the changes of governmental policies. To call this factor "cultural" in an international comparison, is not logically sound. If an industry in the U.S. under an equivalent regulation by the government to that in Denmark had been chosen, a better comparison could have been made.

Moreover, the relation between uncertainty and organizations in the paper seems to be not very convincing. Four electronics firms are chosen from each country because they have a more dynamic and uncertain environment, and four wood products firms of the U.S. and four process firms of Denmark are chosen because they have a relatively stable environment. But Table 1 in their paper does not seem to convince us of this uncertainty difference.

Brown and Blandin claim that this socialized economy and the homogeneity in a Scandinavian nation give rise to the lower score of uncertainty. According to Table 4 (in their paper) "U.S. firms are more concerned with, and respond more actively to, environmental uncertainty", "the Danish managers may perceive less uncertainty due to greater governmental regulation, and therefore see less need for using a variety of forecasting techniques" and this leads to "formal communication" and "routine control procedure" in the Danish firms.

Thus, uncertainty differences between industries does not play such a role as that of the difference between nations. To describe simply, the formula is socialized economy—stable environment—formal and traditional. However, in the paper we find that "Denmark is heavily dependent on maintaining a strong export position." This usually means that Danish firms are selling their products to very competitive foreign markets which have much uncertainty. As a matter of fact the Danish economy seems to be very fragile internationally. Can this be compatible with the "less uncertainty the Danish managers perceive"?

The next question is again about size. Concerning Table 6, the authors state the "Danish managers appear to be more traditional than their counterparts in the U.S. regarding methods of organizational integration." If we look at the behavior of an organization from the viewpoint of its size, it is generally believed that the larger organizations show more "formal communications" and more "routine control procedures", which are, according to the paper, traditional methods. Do Brown and Blandin mean relative size, that is, medium-size by U.S. standards and large-size by Danish standards.

In my opinion, the effect of uncertainty upon an organization does not seem to be symmetrical. Growing uncertainty in a growing economy, which guarantees at least absolutely growing profits to the firm, may give rise to more authority delegation and greater structural differentiation in the organization of the firm. But growing uncertainty in a declining economy, which may result in losses to the firm, more likely brings a tighter control in the firm. If the study by Brown and Blandin gives us a clue to this asymmetrical effect of uncertainty upon organizations, it would make a profound contribution to our understanding of them.

Comments on the Redding and Martyn-Johns Paper

REVIEW—*Edward Faison*

The paper by Redding and Martyn-Johns develops a series of testable hypotheses of how Western and Eastern managers are likely to differ in their execution of management functions as a result of differing perceptions of causality, probability, time, self, and mortality.

I do not take issue with this basic point and look forward to subsequent studies being conducted to test these hypotheses. The principal criticism of the paper is the rather inadequate linkage with an underlying theoretical structure which is called cognitive paradigms. No one who savors the sounds and subtleties of western language can swallow the concept of "paradigmatology". A preferable and more popular term in use in the U.S. is "model". The authors describe a rough cognitive process model which utilizes information as an input and behavior as an output. Before information is converted to behavior it passes through four stages: perception; higher order cognitive processes such as thinking; cognitive systems (espoused theory paradigms); and motivation. All of these steps are influenced by experience and environment.

While this may be an accurate model of the inner world, there are many alternate models. Who is to say, based on current evidence, whether motivation occurs before or after perception? The basic point is that it makes no difference as far as the Redding and Martyn-Johns hypotheses are concerned. They can be supported or rejected wholly apart from this theoretical posturing. What is important to management theory is the generation of hypotheses. These hypotheses should be explored in depth without being mired in questionable and perhaps unmeasurable theory which does not aid in hypothesis generation.

As a last point, the authors cite factor analytic data based on semantic differential scales administered in separate studies in the east and west and conclude that there is a "marked decrease in differentiation" from the Asian data. These data have been so twisted and turned that one would be hard pressed to accept the conclusion that they support the view that the "causality paradigm of many Oriental cultures operates . . . [so that] . . . abstraction into conceptual categories does not take place so strongly as in the west." Based on my own experience it can be argued that the eastern mentality, if anything, is more likely to utilize abstract conceptions while the westerner is more likely to take a pragmatic approach.

Despite these minor points, the authors have developed worthy hypotheses which deserve to be tested on a broad scale.

REFERENCES

Haire, M., E. E. Ghiselli, and L. W. Porter. *Managerial Thinking: An International Study.*
1966 New York: Wiley.

Henning, B. "Die wirtschaftspolitischen Prinzipien des jugoslawischen Silbstvert-
1975 waltungssystems und deren konkrete sozio-ökonomische Ausgestaltung zwischen Anspruch und Realität." Diss. Gie en.

Mulder, B. "Power Equalization through Participation?" *Administrative Science*
1971 *Quarterly.* 1:31–38.

Obradović, J. "Distribution of Participation in the Process of Decision-Making on
1972 Problems related to the Economic Activity of the Company." In *First International Conference on Participation and Self-Management, Vol. II:* 137–164. Dubrovnik.

Šefer, B. "Rasponi ličnih dohodaka njihovo fromiranje i tendencije." In *Obračhun i*
1968 *raspodjeli osobnih dohodaka u radnim organizacijama, Teil I:* 421–438. Symposium im März 1968 in Opatija.

Woodward, Joan.
1958

Section II

TECHNOLOGICAL VERSUS CULTURAL IMPERATIVES

Explaining Cultural Differences in the Perceived Role of Work: An Intranational Cross-Cultural Study

MARY ELIZABETH BERES, O. P.
JAMES D. PORTWOOD
Temple University

A great deal of interest in culture as a contributory factor influencing human attitudes and behavior has been evident in recent organizational and management research (e.g., Whyte and Williams, 1963; Whitehall, 1964; Haire *et. al.*, 1966; Heller, 1973; Peck, 1975; Burger and Doktor, 1976). However, despite the large number of studies involving culture, this is still a relatively new field. Several reviews of the "cross-cultural" literature (Roberts, 1970; Negandhi, 1973; Moore, 1974; Evan, 1975) clearly demonstrate that most work has not evolved past the descriptive empirical and case study stage. Such studies have been characterized as primarily atheoretical and of limited scope (Goodman and Moore, 1972), thus leading to problems in comparability and generalizability of results.

Some theorists are now suggesting (Roberts, 1972; Negandhi, 1973) that sufficient descriptive information has been accumulated to support meaningful conceptual development and a movement toward hypothesis testing in research. With this suggestion in mind, the purpose of this paper is to propose a tentative model of the cultural influence process and report some preliminary research findings related to one critical link in this framework. Recognizing that disciplines other than organization theory and management have had considerably more experience with culture as a focus of study, the authors have drawn ideas from both anthropology and sociology in generating the proposed cultural influence model. Taking the anthropological approach, culture has been explained in ecological, historical terms; that is, culture is a frame of reference which members of a group have found beneficial for survival in dealing with their particular common environment, and have, therefore, retained and transmitted to successive generations. Thus, culture may be viewed as that portion of a person's beliefs, values and behaviors which may be directly attributable to contact with the beliefs, values and behaviors of preceding generations. Based on this definition, a model is offered which assumes that:

(a) individuals are the link between culture and its social consequences; and (b) culture changes over time through a nonevolutionary process in which societies continually attempt to cope with an ever-changing environment.

The empirical portion of this paper consists of two separate, secondary analyses of existing data sets. The first analysis is undertaken to operationalize the definition of culture expressed above. Since no direct measurement of previous generations' attitudes or behaviors is possible, the values of cultural ancestors have been identified from an analysis of writings, recorded activities, and reported studies of societies originating in Europe, Africa, and North America. This approach differs from much of the previous research which has treated measures of contemporary attitudes as representing cultural values.

The second phase of the empirical research utilizes data from a representative sample of the United States male and female working population (N>10,000) to test hypothesized differences in the perceived role of work across groups with identifiable differences in ancestry. While this analysis is by no means a test of the model, it provides valuable information on several methodological and conceptual issues critical to an understanding of the cultural influence process. First, the data set used is designed to be representative at a societal level. One criticism of much current research (Roberts, 1970) has been that it compares a relatively small number of individuals or groups drawn from one or a few organizations. It is important that a variable as complex and global as culture be analyzed in a sample reflecting the complete composition of any relevant society.

Other advantages lie in the "intranational" nature of the data set. Having a reasonably comparable current environment across the sample provides an opportunity to concentrate on the impact of the diversity in ancestral backgrounds within the population. Also, it allows a test of the assumption that meaningful cultural distinctions can be made on grounds other than current national location (Hesseling, 1973).

On a conceptual level, the testing of a model of the scope proposed here will be difficult, time consuming and expensive. However, the current research is able to consider the least studied link in the "culture→attitude→individual behavior→organizational functioning" chain; namely, the link between culture and individual attitudes. Specifically, the study examines the relationship between ancestral value systems and current perceptions of the role of work. Results generally indicate that, controlling for current environmental and personal characteristics, individuals' present values tend to reflect values associated with their predecessors. This analysis is especially interesting in that presumptions about individuals' perceived role of work are central to many organization and management theories.

AN ECOLOGICAL, FEEDBACK MODEL OF CULTURAL INFLUENCE

The study of culture has been the special province of anthropologists, among whom the prevailing conceptualizations have two properties (see Kroeber and Kluckholn, 1952, for a review). First, culture consists of beliefs, values, feelings and practices of a group of people. This property implies that individuals in a cultural group have similar mind-sets (cognitive frames of reference), and they act according to a commonly understood pattern of behavior. Second, anthropologists believe that culture is acquired through training in the group, i.e., individuals must learn the appropriate beliefs, values, feelings and practices through other group members. According to this property, culture is passed from one generation of group members to the next generation in a continuing process. Thus, the mind-sets and practices are shared not only among contemporary individuals, but also among ancestors and descendents. Both of these properties of culture are emphasized in the definition which is the basis for the proposed model, i.e., *culture is a cognitive frame of reference and a pattern of behavior transmitted to members of a group from previous generations of the group.*

From the way in which culture is defined, it is apparent that cultural processes involve several dimensions of behavior: (a) a psychological dimension in the learning and use of a mind-set; (b) a social dimension in the interactions among group members; and (c) an historical dimension in the transmission of mind-sets and practices across generations of a group. In order to represent each of these dimensions, theories from several social science disciplines have been used to develop the model. These theories and their major assumptions will be described briefly before the model itself is presented.

Theoretical Foundations of the Model

Since culture and cultural processes involve human behavior, the primary assumptions in this study are the ones concerning the nature of human action. In this area, the first premise is that individuals are dependent on their environment for physical, social and intellectual life (Murphy, 1947). On the one hand, the environment presents certain constraints which must be overcome if the individual is to survive. On the other hand, the environment provides the resources which individuals use for life and growth. This relationship is basic to the model and leads to the ecological assumption described later.

The second assumption is that individuals are cognitive beings (Murphy, 1947; Heider, 1958). As such, they become aware of their environment through a process of perception, which involves experiencing the environment through the senses, and then interpreting the experiences, using a frame of reference. Because it is a frame of reference, culture is central in the process of perception.

With respect to cognitive processes, two areas of psychological theory are especially relevant: (a) theories explaining how individuals acquire a cognitive frame of reference; and (b) theories explaining how a cognitive frame of reference is related to behavior. According to Heider (1958), each person develops a mind-set from experiences. This view is important because it implies that individuals are not born with culture. Rather, it must be acquired through a learning process. For Heider, an understanding of how the environment works is an important part of this learning process. To survive, the individual must learn which elements of the environment can be dangerous, which can be helpful, and how to influence events so that they will have beneficial results. This understanding of causal relationships is translated into behavior through the individual's decision-making processes (see March and Simon, 1958). Thus, an individual's cultural heritage develops from socialization experiences and leads to behavior.

The third basic assumption of the study is that individuals are social beings, able to interact in ways that increase their understanding of the environment and their ability to make use of it. Two interaction processes, communication and socialization, are essential to the existence of culture as it has been defined. Through communication, individuals share their mind-sets with one another, at least to some extent. This sharing is necessary if individuals are to have a common frame of reference and commonly understood practices. In small groups the required interaction can take place directly between all members. A common understanding can develop in large groups as long as each individual interacts with some other members and every interacting group of members is linked to other groups.

Socialization is a special process of communication by which the frame of reference of one generation of individuals is transmitted to another. In the process, a "new" individual gains an understanding of the environment by means of others' experiences, either through formal training or through the ways previous generations have altered the environment (Inkeles and Levinson, 1969). Without the processes of communication and socialization, individuals would develop unique mind-sets, rather than culture.

The dependence of individuals on the environment and the way in which they learn about it through perception increases the importance of the social processes leading to culture. Because individuals learn from experience, they are always in a situation of having to act without a full understanding. This leaves individuals uncertain about the results of their actions. To reduce uncertainty, people tend to share information and build together a causal frame of reference (Festinger, 1954). This development of a common frame of reference and common practices is the first stage in the development of culture; and, since it takes place continually among groups of individuals, culture is always in the process of formation.

Three assumptions underlie the historical dimension of the proposed model. First, the development of culture is considered to be an ecological process. The beliefs, values, feelings and practices which are shared by group members center around the survival problems presented by the environment. This assumption is the social extension of the premise that individuals are dependent on the environment. Group members share in order to make better decisions about how to cope in the environment. The mind-sets and practices which prove effective are kept by the group, and they are communicated to the next members to help them survive.

Since groups use their understanding to influence environmental processes, culture leads to changes in the environment of the group. These changes include modifications of the physical environment and the development of a potentially complex social environment. Consequently, the development and influence of culture are feedback processes. The second historical assumption of the study is that this feedback process is multilinear. A typical systems feedback model is circular in form, i.e., when a change occurs in a system, there is a reaction which returns the system to its original state. In the case of culture, however, the changes introduced by a group's response to the environment create new conditions which require new forms of coping which lead to new environmental conditions, and so on, as the generations of individuals follow one another. In addition, changes take place within the physical and social environments which are separate from the culturally induced changes, so that several change processes interact through time. Thus, feedback from the environment to culture to the environment is a temporal process taking place at multiple levels.

In assuming that cultural development is a temporal process, it may seem that the proposed model is evolutionary. This is not the case. In relatively short periods of time, while the environment remains stable, groups may successively improve their coping with the problems of survival and, in this sense, evolve. On the other hand, groups could choose to maintain their culture until it is threatened by some new problem. Over the long term, however, the environment changes due to its own processes and the actions of various groups. These changes create new survival problems which require new ways of coping. The cultural response of the group may sometimes be an advance over the previous adjustment, but at other times the adjustment may take the group in a new direction or represent a regression from the past. The assumption in this study is that the historical process is nonevolutionary and follows a type of "rise and fall" pattern of change (Appelbaum, 1970).

Together, the theoretical foundations of this study imply a process of cultural development. This process serves as a summary of the main assumptions of the study and helps to clarify the definition of culture. The ecological assumptions imply that culture begins with environmental conditions. The conditions are interpreted by interacting individuals, who develop a common frame of reference and pattern of behavior. Because of the complexity of the environment, the outcomes of the interpretation process are problematic, depending on perceptual skills, the sequence of events, and the methods used (Jones *et. al.*, 1965). In addition, there are a variety of ways to

Figure 1

THE DEVELOPMENT OF CULTURE

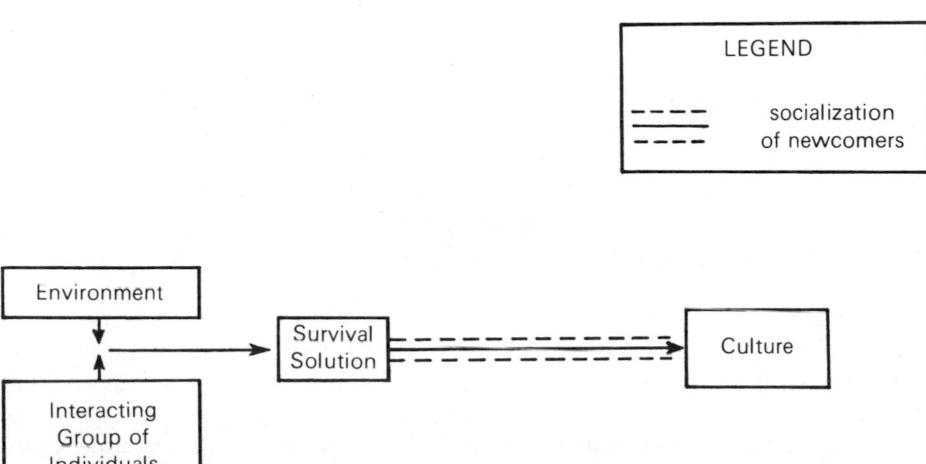

successfully cope with a given environment. Consequently, the survival solutions of any one group of people, are likely to be different from the survival solutions of another group. Hence, culture develops from an interaction between the environment, which presents particular problems, and a group of people, who develop solutions by interacting. Finally, the solutions which appear effective in coping with the environment are transmitted to the next generation of group members. This process of cultural development is represented in Figure 1.

In the next section, the model will be described at a general level applicable to all aspects of the cultural influence process. Due to the constraints imposed by using an existing data set, specific justification and operationalization of variables included in the empirical study will be reserved until after the data set has been described in the empirical methodology section.

The Process of Cultural Influence

The specific concern of the proposed model is the way in which culture influences the structure and effectiveness of organizations. According to the theoretical assumptions just outlined, the influence of culture is through its effects on individuals who are members of the organization and on individuals who interact with members. Negandhi (1973) has suggested that a model based on this premise should include an explanation of: (a) how the culture of a group affects an individual member's frame of reference; (b) how an individual's frame of reference relates to behavior; and (c) how individual behaviors affect an organization. March and Simon's (1958) theory provides an integrative, organizational framework for these three stages of influence which is consistent with the theoretical basis of the study.

The model will be presented in order of the stages of influence leading from culture to organization structure. Because a primary objective of this study is the explication of a logically complete model of cultural influence, a discussion of the full model is included. This is done even though only the first stage can be empirically studied with the available data set. Support for this first stage provides the justification for further pursuit of the model.

The Influence of Culture on Individuals

The first phase of cultural influence involves the development of individuals' beliefs, values, feelings and practices. These mind-sets and behavior patterns are the cumulative result of three interacting processes. So far, attention has been given to the contribution of culture, which occurs through socialization by predecessors. The effects of socialization are limited, however, by communication and personal experiences of the environment. These factors contribute unique, contemporary dimensions to each individual's frame of reference.

Because of the distortions that occur in communication, each individual develops a personal version of the cultural frame of reference. In addition, the experiences of each contemporary generation of individuals depend on current environmental conditions. While individuals use their existing frame of reference to interpret experiences, direct interactions with the environment also present special survival issues. These survival concerns may arise from a number of different characteristics of the environmental context. At an ecological level, such factors as climate, soil fertility, and availability of water present physical survival problems. Population distribution and other demographic properties present constraints and opportunities relating to social interaction patterns. In responding to environmental conditions, individuals build social structures, including organizations, which, in turn, create new survival situations. Finally, general environmental characteristics affect individuals through the circumstances of their personal situations. Together, contemporary aspects of the environment shape the conditions with which a current generation must cope.

The conditions presented to individuals by their immediate environment lead to new causal insights and innovative survival solutions. These new perspectives modify cultural heritages. Hence, at any point in time, socialization, communication and personal experience jointly affect the individual's frame of reference. These processes constitute the first stage of the cultural influence process and are represented by the relationships summarized in Proposition 1. The Time 0 section in Figure 2 illustrates this proposition.

PROPOSITION 1: Culture, the ecological/demographic environment, the social/organizational environment, and personal circumstances each influence an individual's frame of reference and pattern of behavior.

Figure 2

A PROCESS MODEL OF CULTURAL INFLUENCE

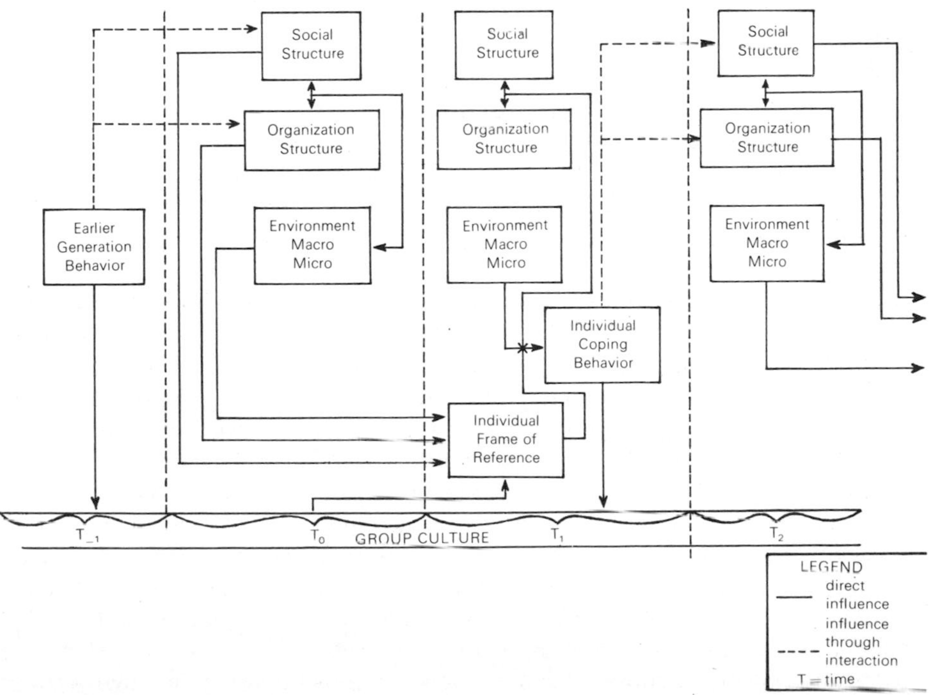

The Relationship between Frames of Reference and Behavior

The second stage of cultural influence includes the processes through which an individual's mind-set leads to action. According to March and Simon (1958) decisions about how to act are a result of interactions between: (a) a cognitive frame of reference; and (b) conditions in the environment. Unless the existing practices are expected to be ineffective, these decisions involve the selection of some established pattern of response. In describing decision-making, March and Simon explain the first step leading to action without considering the relationship between decisions and behavior. This relationship is important, however, since decisions result from the perceived environment, but behavior takes place within the "objective" environment. Unrecognized circumstances and inadequate estimates of personal ability cause discrepancies between a decision and the resulting behavior. Thus, behavior results from a two step process of interaction between the environment and the individual. First, individuals interpret environmental stimuli in the light of their cognitive and behavioral frame of reference. Second, individuals implement action decisions within actually existing environmental constraints. Proposition 2 summarizes this second stage of the influence process.

PROPOSITION 2: The behavior of an organization member results from interactions between: (a) the cognitive/behavioral frame of reference of the individual; (b) the environment as perceived; and (c) the objectively existing environment.

Stage two of the model is illustrated in the Time 1 section of Figure 2 presented earlier. This stage begins with an individual's cognitive frame of reference, as shaped by environmental influences in Time 0, and ends with the behavior resulting from interactions with the environmental conditions existing in the current time period.

The Impact of Individual Behavior on an Organization

The final stage of the model provides an explanation of how, through individual actions, culture influences the characteristics of organizations. The key assumption at this stage is that any one organization member's behaviors affect an organization as a contributing part of the aggregate behaviors of all members.

According to March and Simon (1958), each member examines what is expected and what is offered by the organization and then decides how to perform. Since these decisions occur simultaneously, it is possible for one member's actions to be offset by the actions of others. In such a case, an isolated decision will not be evidenced in the structure or effectiveness of the organization. On the other hand, if an individual is singularly ciritical in the organization, that person's decisions may directly affect organizational performance. The latter situation is illustrated by managerial decisions concerning organizational strategy and procedures. Even in this case, however, the cooperation of other members is required for implementation. Finally, when members' decisions are consistent with one another, their actions collectively shape the organization. What they do constitutes the characteristics of the organization. Since culture results in shared dispositions, a collective form of influence is likely to occur when the members of an organization have the same cultural background.

In each of the situations described, the influence of any one individual on an organization depends on that individual's relationship to other members. The details of the interactive process have been described elsewhere (Beres and Schmidt, 1977). For present purposes it is sufficient to note that the impact of individual behavior on an organization will be a function of: (a) the action taken; (b) the singularity of the actor's role; and (c) the response of others to such actions. Thus, in the third stage of the model, culture's influence on the behavior of individuals at Time 1 leads through interactions to the structure and effectiveness of the organization at Time 2 (See Figure 2). Proposition three represents this final stage of the cultural influence model:

PROPOSITION 3: An individual's behavior has an impact on an organization to the extent that: (a) it is a singular contribution to the organization structure or output; and/or (b) it produces changes in the behavior of other organization members; and/or (c) it contributes to the collective impact of consistent behavior patterns.

In summary, the proposed model identifies culture as having a direct influence on the cognitive frame of reference and patterns of behavior of individuals. Through this influence, it affects individual's actions, and, in an interactive process, the structure and effectiveness of organizations. The process is complex, in that culture's influence is mingled with the effects of the contemporary ecological and social environment. In addition, cultural influence is a temporal process. The survival solutions of one generation are transmitted to another. The transmitted solutions lead, subsequently, to specific actions; and the actions of one period become institutionalized as the organizational structure of later periods. While the diagram of the model shows only one time sequence, each previous generation has impacts on a given group through similar transmission processes. The amount of influence from a given generation depends on the nature of the intervening survival problems. Hence, the culture of a group consists of components derived from various preceding generations and integrated during the process of transmission.

The model offered in this study makes explicit many of the assumptions about culture that have previously been implied but not stated in earlier research. Therefore, the model is not a radical departure from current approaches but it provides an opportunity to more clearly operationalize and test these assumptions empirically. It is also hoped that this framework will stimulate further model building.

EMPIRICAL METHODOLOGY AND SPECIFICATION OF THE MODEL

Any empirical study of the full model requires: (a) a representative sample of current cultural groups; (b) data on the values, beliefs, practices of current individuals, and on current ecological, social and organizational environments; and (c) data on the survival solutions of previous generations of the cultural groups. The present project, however, evaluates only the first stage of the model—the influence of culture on individual dispositions. This limits the data requirements to information on the values, beliefs, and environment of current individuals and the survival solutions of their predecessors. Data available on the subject population contains measures of current attitudes, but information only on the geographic origins of subjects' ancestors. This limitation necessitates a two phase empirical study.

Phase one involves identifying (through an analysis of period writings, recorded actions, and previous culture studies) the value systems which predominated in the various regions inhabited by subjects' forebears. These values systems provide predictions about subjects' current attitudes, which form the basis for phase two. The second step in the study is an empirical evaluation of the cultural influence process as it relates to individual work attitudes.

Data Sources

Data describing the current population comes from responses and information gathered as part of the National Longitudinal Survey (NLS) conducted by the Ohio State University Center for Human Resources Research under contract with the U.S. Department of Labor. Having begun in 1966, the NLS is a ten year longitudinal study of the work experience of four sex-age cohorts in the population: men, age 45 to 59; women, age 30 to 44; young men, age 14 to 24; and young women, age 14 to 24, at the time of the initial interview. Subjects were chosen with the idea of providing an accurate national sample of the working age population in the U.S.

For this study only the male and female adult cohorts were used. The sample was further reduced by including only those non-farm individuals employed at the time of data collection. For the men, this reduced the original cohorts sample from 5024 to 4524 (approximately 10 per cent). For the women the reduction was more drastic, from 5083 to 2525 (50 per cent). Virtually all of this drop was due to the large number of women voluntarily out of the labor force. Small additional losses were incurred during the various data analysis procedures due to missing data on one or a combination of the variables under study.

Lack of access to all the data has been one problem encountered by the researchers in this study. Other limitations are also inherent in this data set. As a beginning point it should be noted that the current project is a secondary study, since the data base was not created specifically for the type of analysis now being undertaken. This fact puts severe restrictions on what can be done with the analysis. Many potentially interesting variables are not part of the data set and cannot be created. In other cases the variables are not measured or recorded in the most desirable form. The dependent variable in this study, perceived role of work, is a dichotomous variable, thus, eliminating many potential data analysis techniques due to inadequate variance. In spite of these problems, there are sufficient data available for a preliminary evaluation of the first stage of the proposed model.

The data source for the characteristics of a group's ancestors depends, of course, on the groups involved. Based on the identification included in the NLS survey, this study draws from anthropological and sociological studies of past European and African societies for ancestral data. Since the historical backgrounds of respondents can be identified only in terms of broad geographical areas, their cultures must be described in terms of properties common to the ancestral groups from the given regions. For the purpose of this study, Max Weber's (1968) analysis of the work-related values of Protestant and Catholic societies in Europe and Obenhaus' (1965) study of the economic bases of Hebrew and Christian religions are sources for identifying the relevant cultural characteristics of the different European groups. Lomax' (1972) taxonomic study of world cultural differences (based on Murdock, 1967) and Forde's (1960) study of environmentally induced adaptations in West African cultures form the basis for the description of the Afro-American cultures. From these sources, inferences are made to the underlying cognitive sets of prior generations. This provides information for the measurement of the cultural dimension of respondents' work-related values and constitutes the first phase of the empirical study.

The Measurement of Culture

According to the proposed definition, culture is a cognitive and behavioral frame of reference developed within an interacting group of ancestors and transmitted to contemporary descendents. Hence, a first step in operationalizing group culture is identification of the ancestral "roots" of respondents. Two measures of ancestry are available in the NLS data (1) ethnicity; and (2) race. The ethnicity variable represents the region of origin of the respondent's parents or, if the parents were born in the U.S., the respondent's grandparents. The regions which are sufficiently represented for analysis are: United States and Canada; north and west Europe; central and east Europe; and south Europe. For the countries included in each of the European regions, see Figure 3.

Evidence regarding ecological characteristics, religions and economic systems suggests that there is greater cultural homogeneity within these regions than between. South Europe's climate differs from the other areas due to latitude and sea coasts. North and west Europe is the area in which both Protestantism and industrialization were adopted the earliest. On these grounds, the three regions are considered distinct cultural areas, in spite of intra-regional differences.

The race variable separates respondents into Black, Caucasion, Oriental and native American groups. Too few subjects in the latter two groups participated in the survey to be included in this study. Cross-tabulation of the race and ethnicity variables indicates that black respondents are at least third-generation Americans. This fact makes it reasonably certain that these subjects' forebears were brought to this country as slaves. Figure 4 (*The World of Africans and Afro-Americans*, 1971) shows the area of Africa from which most slaves were taken. As the figure shows, cultural groups in Africa are numerous and varied. Lomax's (1972) taxonomic study, however, aggregates the groups into two cultural types: (a) African gatherers and (b) black Africans, the gardners and herders. Based on the region of their origin, most Afro-Americans are descended from black African cultures. Hence, this study focuses on the shared properties of black African tribes.

Once ancestral origins are identified, measures of the previous generations' values are obtained from descriptions of their lifestyles and socio-economic systems in the secondary analysis identified as phase one of the empirical study.

Sources used in this phase discuss how previous generations solved the problems of survival and indicate the value systems they were likely to have transmitted. Of particular interest in this study are data concerning the role of work in individuals' lives. Since they are likely to affect an individual's decisions to participate and to perform, work values are expected to be a significant vehicle for cultural influence in organizations.

In this study, culture is measured in terms of the cognitive orientations and behavior of subjects' ancestors. This procedure differs from the usual practice, but is more consistent with a definition that emphasizes a transmission process. The approach used here also avoids the tautological problems that arise when culture is measured from the attitudes of contemporary individuals and then

Figure 3

CULTURAL REGIONS OF EUROPE

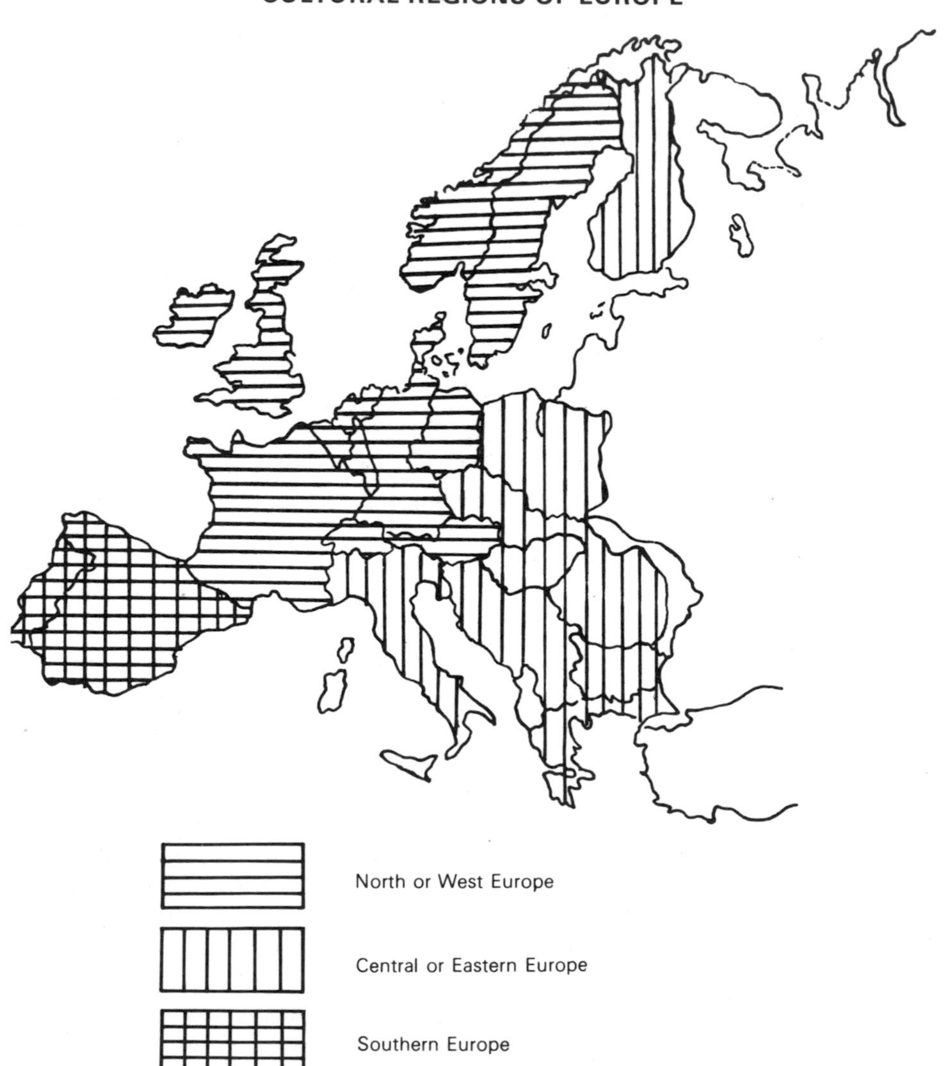

Figure 4

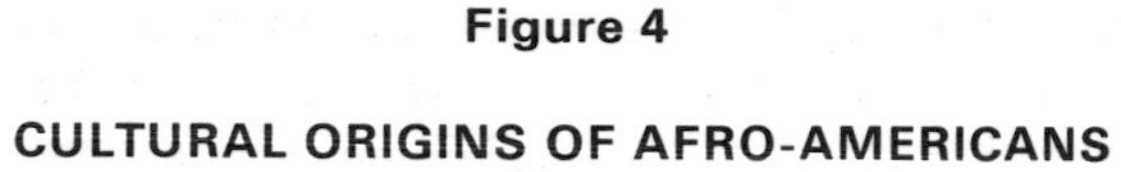

CULTURAL ORIGINS OF AFRO-AMERICANS

used as an independent variable explaining these same attitudes. Finally, identification of cultural values through independent data makes it possible to distinguish cultural and contemporary components of respondents' value systems.

Alternative Influences on Work Values

The main focus of the empirical study is Proposition 1 of the influence model:

> Culture, the ecological/demographic environment, the social/organizational environment, and personal circumstances each influence an individual's frame of reference and pattern of behavior.

This proposition lists several influences on attitudes, in addition to culture. Each of these influences is actually a multivariate dimension composed of several, relatively independent variables. The following descriptions identify the variables from the NLS data which operationalize the dimensions, and the measures by which they are represented.

Ecological/Demographic Environment and Personal Circumstances

The environment can be viewed at the macro level of general physical and population characteristics and at the micro level of the individual's personal situation. In addition, the environments of the past and of the on-going context contribute to an individual's immediate frame of reference or value system. The NLS data includes information on each of these components of the environment. For the purpose of this study, only the variables which represent conditions related to the importance of work are included.

At the macro environmental level, climate and urbanization are potential influences on the role of work. Climate variations indicate the relative benevolence of the physical environment. The less threatening the environment, the more likely that individuals will have time for activities other than work, and the perceived role of work is expected to vary accordingly. In the NLS data, the regional locations of respondents are identified in terms of census tracts. The southern, south Atlantic, south central and Pacific tracts are grouped as the more benevolent environments. The New England, middle Atlantic, north central and mountain tracts are grouped as the less benevolent. This distinction is made primarily on the basis of temperature variations.

Although there is evidence that city workers may be more alienated than town workers, the potential impact of urbanization on work values is unclear. Since different ethnic groups are differentially distributed between cities, towns, and rural areas, however, relationships between ethnicity and individual values could be the spurious result of location. Urbanization is included to control for this possibility. The measure of urbanization is the size of the local labor force as indexed by the Department of Labor.

The respondents' past demographic environments are represented by their responses to a question concerning the type of location in which they were living at age 15. The alternatives range from rural areas to large metropolitan centers. The relative size of the population is the measure of the urbanization of the respondents' past environment.

Past personal environments of respondents are represented by two variables: (a) family structure at age 15 and (b) social status of family at age 15. These measures represent the practical importance which work had during the respondent's formative years, and the impact of class variations in cultural socialization. Family structure is measured in terms of the presence or absence of a father or step-father. The social status of the family unit is measured by the job status of the head of the household as reflected in the Duncan Index. In view of the interview format of the survey, both of these measures are dependent on the respondent's recollections of the past, and, consequently, subject to memory errors.

From the characteristics of the individual's ongoing personal situation, five have been selected which represent potential demands on the extrinsic outcomes of work. In particular, this dimension of the environment is represented by variables which could make wages a more critical concern of the worker. These include: the number of dependents; marital status; the sharing of wage earning responsibility, age; health; and job tenure. The number of dependents, marital status and wage earning responsibility represent the demand for and supply of wages. Number of dependents is the number of individuals supported by the respondent. Marital status is divided into two categories: (a) married, spouse present and (b) other. Wage earning responsibility is considered to be shared if the spouse of the respondent is earning at least $1000 at the time of the survey. Age, health, and job tenure represent aspects of the personal history which may present particular types of work related problems to individuals and, hence, may affect their work values. Age and job tenure are measured in years. Health status is divided into the categories of: (a) affecting or (b) not affecting work.

Social Structure

The societal structure surrounding a person is another environmental source of influence on the perceived role of work. An individual's position within this structure is represented by his or her socio-economic status. The economic aspect of a status has immediate impact on the relative need for wages. The social component of status operationalizes class differences in work values. When societies are stratified, the members of one class interact more with one another than with members of other classes. The stratified groups are also presented with different types of problems. These conditions lead to class differences in the solutions to survival problems. Such differences are as much a part of the socialization of individuals as are general cultural differences. Because the NLS data does not indicate the class of a respondent's ancestors, class differentials in culture cannot be examined in this study. Only the stratification effects of an individual's immediate environment can be examined using the survey. Three measures of current socio-economic status are available: (a) level of education, (b) job status, (c) level of income. Education is measured by the number of years of formal schooling. Job status is estimated from the Duncan Index for the respondent's current or last job. A measure of income level is constructed by summing earnings from the respondent's and the respondent's spouse's wages and business activities. This measure excludes special sources of income, but it correlates .92 with a measure of net family income. The latter measure is available from the NLS tapes but is not used in this study because of the large number of missing respondents.

Organization Structure

Because the National Longitudinal Survey was concerned with the labor market behavior of individuals and not with organizations, the data provides no indication of the conditions existing in the organization in which a respondent works. Consequently, the contribution of organization structure to an individual's work values cannot be estimated in this study. The absence of this type of data also prevents use of the NLS data for any study of the third stage in the cultural influence process.

Individual Work Values

Individuals' cognitive frames of reference are the dependent variable in the

Table 1

SUMMARY OF VARIABLES

Variables	*Operational Definition*	*Measures*
Group Culture	Bounded sets of individuals who share experiences	Race, Ethnicity
Work Values	Perceived role of work	Wages–Work item
Ecological/Demographic Environment	Climate, Population distribution	Region of the country; Size of labor market;
Past Environment	Population, distribution Family structure and class	Size of residence area; Presence of father at age 15; Head of household's Duncan
Personal Environment	Individual differences in personal situation	Marriage status; Job tenure; Age; Health; Number of dependents; Wage earner responsibility
Social Structure	The strata of a society in which an individual is located	Education level; Job status; Income level

first stage of the cultural influence process. As indicated earlier, work values are the component of a frame of reference focussed on in this study. Of the few attitudinal measures in the NLS data, one falls in this area, namely, the respondent's answer to the question:

> What would you say is the more important thing about any job—good wages or liking the kind of work you are doing (NLS, 1966 interview schedule)?

An individual's response to this question is interpreted as an indication of the meaning which work has for the person. The response "good wages" identifies work as a means to an end. The alternative, "liking the work itself" implies that some intrinsic value is attached to work. In the first case, work functions as a means, and, in the latter instance, it is seen as an end. These differences in the perceived role of work operationalize the individual work values element of the influence model.

The measures of culture, alternative influences on attitudes, and individual values, which have been described above, are summarized in Table 1. Evidence obtained in this study and the conclusions drawn are a function of these variables and their measures.

Statistical Methods

Because the dependent variable—perceived role of work—is measured by a dichotomous choice, standard regression methods could not be used in this study. Instead, linear discriminant analysis has been employed. According to Kerlinger (1973) and Klecka (1975), canonical correlation and standardized discriminant coefficients in a linear discriminant function can be interpreted analogously to the multiple correlation and standardized beta weights of a multiple regression. Such an analogy is followed in analyzing the results.

Two assumptions must be met for discriminant analysis to be meaningful: (a) predictor variables must be linearly related and (b) group variances should be similar. In a few cases where non-linear relationships existed, dummy variable transformations have been made. These produced the best fit for the data. There are some problems with the homogeneity of variances when the total sample is included in the analysis. A systematic partitioning of the sample reduces the differences in variances. Since the results from the partitioning are essentially the same as for the aggregate, only the aggregate coefficients are reported here. Multicollinearity is another potential problem in discriminant analysis. Of the independent variables in this study, only the measures of social environment are highly correlated with each other. Since these variables represent the same dimension in the model, the intercorrelations don't threaten the interpretability of the discriminant coefficients.

EMPIRICAL RESULTS

The results of the empirical study are presented in four sections. First, the anthropological and sociological evidence concerning the nature of American ancestral groups is presented. This evidence indicates the work values of the generations preceding the current population. Since they provide predictions of current values, this part of the study is critical to the remaining analyses. The second and third sections present results relating to the first proposition from the cultural influence model in a comparison of: (a) blacks and whites and (b) groups whose ancestors are from North or West Europe, Central or East Europe, and South Europe. In the concluding section, a work values "map" of the United States is presented which describes the population in terms of the diversity of ethnic origins and work values. This "map" is a response to the suggestion of Evan (1975) that the general culture of a country must be identified in order to be able to determine the representativeness of a given organizational sample.

Work Values in European and African Cultures

This study relies on Weber's (1968, 1958) analysis of the Protestant ethic and his comparison between Protestant and Catholic values as a source for identifying the work values of the ancestors to American, white ethnic groups. According to Weber, the ascetic Protestant emphasis on the principle of predestination was translated into a concern for engaging in good works. These works were the sign to individuals that they were among the chosen. So that:

> however useless good works might be as a means of attaining salvation, for even the elect remain beings of the flesh, and everything they do falls infinitely short of divine standards, nevertheless, they are indispensable as a sign of election (Weber, 1958:115).

This view transformed ascetism into activity in the world and one's success in the world became the test of faith. According to this doctrine, wealth was to be valued only in so far as it reflected an individual's performance of duty. The major emphasis was on a life of good works. Weber concludes that these religious forces were decisive in the formation of the national character which supported the development of a spirit of capitalism.

From Weber's analysis, an emphasis on work as a measure of the value of a person can be easily inferred. The ancestral groups which appeared the most accepting of this view were the Protestant societies in north Europe and the Puritan groups. Consequently, it is the northern European and early American groups which were most likely to transmit to their descendents an emphasis on work as an activity to be valued in itself.

In his comparison of Catholicism and Protestantism, Weber (1968) suggests that the transcendental aspect of the former belief system led to less emphasis on the performance of good works. Unlike Protestantism, which tends to equate work with salvation, the Catholic value system treats economic pursuits as subordinate to salvation (Obenhaus, 1965). Work is subject to the rules of morality and should not be allowed to interfere with the real focus of life, which is sanctification. Just as Weber associates Protestantism with industrialization, Obenhaus draws a connection between Catholicism and the feudal economies of the Middle Ages. As practical affairs should be subject to the supernatural order, so the peasant is subject to the lord of the manor. In a Catholic, peasant-oriented society, there would be more emphasis on how one works than on the spiritual significance of work. In the absence of a special stress on the meaning of work, members of the society would be more likely to have a variety of perceptions. Since Catholicism and a slower rate of industrialization are characteristic of much of central, east and south Europe, it is expected that groups in these areas would transmit to descendents a less work centered value system than groups in the Protestant north and west Europe.

African cultures are the second major grouping from which respondents in the study have come. In Lomax's (1972) evolutionary model, the relatively differentiated black African groups appear just prior to the European agricultural cultures. These groups raised large animals and grains and practiced land inheritance. In some instances, they maintained herds as symbols of wealth. Although these characteristics indicate a somewhat production-oriented economic system, the emphasis was in no way comparable to the production orientation of the Protestant, European cultures. In general, the African groups lived in harmony with their environment, working it for what they needed. Work was integrated into a value system that placed emphasis on communal relationships of the family and tribe (see also, Obenhaus, 1965; Forde, 1960). This suggests that work would be more likely to be seen as a means, rather than an all-consuming basis of self-definition. Consequently, it is expected that black African groups would transmit a utilitarian meaning of work.

It could be argued that the slavery experience intervening between black African generations and the present black population in the United States may have altered the transmitted work values. This is not expected, however, for two reasons. First, during the slavery period, the isolation of blacks from the surrounding white groups resulted in limited transmission of values between the

Table 2

WORK VALUES OF ANCESTORS OF U.S. RESPONDENTS

Location of the Ancestral Group	Perceived Role of Work	
	Men	*Women*
North Europe Early America	Work Itself	Wages
South Europe	Work Itself	
Central and Eastern Europe	Mixed	Wages
Black African Regions	Wages	Same as Men (Wages)

two groups. Second, the work experienced by the slaves was of a manual service nature, and not likely to generate intrinsic values in itself. These two conditions would appear to limit the likelihood that the slavery experience offered any survival solutions which would lead to a change in work values. Hence, the slave generations would also be likely to transmit an extrinsic attitude toward work, which would be reflected in an emphasis on wages.

Lomax (1972) also examines the relationships between men and women with regard to the role of work. Among black Africans the women were a central part of the production activity. They worked the fields while men herded. Apparently, the benevolence of the environment allowed the women to care for children without interrupting their routine. As a result, they tended to dominate the cultures. By contrast, the women in the European countries faced a harsh environment in which they had to focus primary attention on the protection of the children. In these situations the men dominated the economic order. In this latter situation, work was seen as appropriate for men, but as an activity to be engaged in by women only under extreme necessity. From Lomax's analysis two inferences can be drawn: first, that similar work values would be transmitted to black women and black men and, second, that extrinsic work values would be transmitted to white women.

The conclusions drawn from the work of Weber and Lomax provide measures of the work values of ancestors to the current survey population. Table 2 summarizes the results of this first step in the empirical analysis. From these measures, the work values of descendents are predicted. The correspondence between the predicted values and those obtained in the survey are presented in the next two sections of the results.

Black-White Differences in Work Values

To test the predicted impact of African and European cultures, the work values of current United States respondents are compared with expected work values. In the first analysis, all of the European cultures and the early American

Table 3

CROSS TABULATIONS OF PERCEIVED ROLE OF WORK BY RACE

MEN				WOMEN			
Perceived Role of Work	White (%)	Black (%)	Total	Perceived Role of Work	White (%)	Black (%)	Total
Good Wages	607 (19.1)	616 (51.6)	1223 (28.0)	Good Wages	335 (20.4)	365 (44.0)	700 (28.3)
Work Itself	2563 (80.9)	577 (48.4)	3140 (72.0)	Work Itself	1307 (79.6)	465 (56.0)	1772 (71.7)
Totals	3170 (72.7)	1193 (27.3)	4363 (100.0)	Totals	1642 (66.4)	830 (33.6)	2472 (100.0)

$X_2 = 451.8$ Sig. = 0 $X_2 = 149.8$ Sig. = 0

cultures are grouped together. Since these groups are expected to have relatively similar values, this first comparison examines the differences between white, western cultures and the black African culture. Cross tabulations indicating how representative samples of individuals perceive the role of work are presented in Table 3.

These results indicate, first of all, that there are very significant differences between the role of work as perceived by blacks and whites. For the men the differences are consistent with the predictions, i.e., white men are likely to see work as intrinsically valuable. Black men are slightly more likely to perceive a job in terms of wages. This latter finding is not as strong as expected from the cultural analysis but does indicate a considerable contrast between the value distributions of whites and blacks.

Although black women see work in intrinsic terms by a slight majority, the prediction that they will have similar perceptions to black men is supported. On the other hand, the differences expected between white men and white women do not appear. Apparently among working white women the perceived role of work is the same as that among white men. Because the NLS data provides a measure of perceived role of work only for women in wage earning jobs, however, a definitive rejection of the hypothesis is not possible. According to the argument supporting the prediction, the emphasis in European cultures on the home-maker, child-rearer role would lead women to view their own participation in the labor force as a means rather than an end. Since women in this role were not asked the work values question and they represent over half of the sample, their absence could be producing spurious results. Absence of respondents may also be distorting the distribution of responses among black women. However, in their case, over half of the sample are included in the working population.

The second part of the analysis of black-white differences examines the relative influences of culture, the ecological/demographic environment and the social environment. For this purpose, measures of the variables representing each multivariate dimension have been entered into a discriminant analysis. As Table 4 indicates, the discriminating power of the combined set is highly significant. On first examination, however, it might seem that the amount of explained variance is small. When it is remembered that several thousand respondents have been selected to be representative of millions of Americans, the amount of explained variance appears in another light. If fifteen variables, some of which have been measured by gross indicators, could explain much more than 15 per cent of the variance in the population of the United States, one could begin to question either theories of individual differences or the representativeness of the sample.

The standardized discriminant coefficients for each of the contributors to the perceived role of work are reported in Table 5. The differences in sign between the men's and women's coefficients are a function of the matrix manipulations of the data. The direction of discrimination between wages and work is the same for both groups in the case of every predictor with the exception of job tenure. In the case of tenure, men who have been at their jobs longer are more likely to value the work itself; women who have been at their jobs longer are more likely to value wages.

The significance levels reported in Table 5 indicate how much a given variable adds to the discriminating power of the linear function when it is entered in the order indicated. These levels show that past experience contributes little or nothing to the individual's perceived role of work. For women the personal environment also has no discriminating influence on individual work values. Among the men, job tenure, health, the presence of three

Table 4

RACE AS A PREDICTOR OF PERCEIVED ROLE OF WORK—DISCRIMINANT ANALYSIS

	MEN	*WOMEN*
Canonical Correlation	.396	.322
Centroids		
Grp 1—Wages	−.690	−.545
Grp 2—Work	.270	−.213
% Correctly Predicted		
Grp 1—Wages	62.9	55.3
Grp 2—Work	79.8	75.8
Total	76.6	73.2
X_2 of Prediction	986.6	496.1
(Significance)	(0)	(0)
N	3484	2295

Table 5

DETERMINANTS OF PERCEIVED ROLE OF WORK–BLACK-WHITE DIFFERENCES

	MEN			WOMEN		
		Significance*			Significance*	
Independent Variables	*Standardized Discriminant Coefficient*	*Race Entered Last*	*Race Entered First*	*Standardized Discriminant Coefficient*	*Race Entered Last*	*Race Entered First*
SOCIAL CLASS		(1)**	(3)		(1)	(3)
Education	.492	0	0	−.476	0	.000
Job Status	.175	.000	.000	−.234	.000	.003
Family Income	.057	.013	.115	−.108	.001	.087
ENVIRONMENT		(3)	(3)		(3)	(3)
Climate	−.079	.000	.092	.004	.075	.864
Urbanization	−.070	.006	.091	.030	.057	.613
PAST EXPERIENCE		(4)	(2)		(4)	(2)
Family Structure	−.068	.690	.575	.050	.761	.484
Head of Household's Job Status	−.093	.451	.039	***		
Urbanization	−.045	.438	.000	.110	.042	.000
PERSONAL ENVIRONMENT		(2)	(4)		(2)	(4)
Age	−.000	.909	NE	−.084	.173	.183
Job Tenure	.105	.022	.010	.100	.031	.153
Health	−.154	.000	.000	.104	.029	.071
Marital Status	.028	.109	.503	−.050	.285	.497
1 or 2 children	−.068	.072	.150	−.036	.444	.740
3 or more children	−.125	.000	.020	−.023	.819	.791
Sole Wage Earner	−.093	.016	.012	−.008	.257	NE
RACE	−.594	0(5)	0(1)	.557	.000(5)	0(1)
		N = 3484			N = 2295	

* Significance of the change in Rao's V when variable enters the discriminant function

or more dependents, and responsibility as the sole wage earner affect values. With the exception of job tenure, the more these environmental factors increase the need of money, the greater the likelihood that the individual will value work for the wages it earns. Finally, both men and women who are in higher socio-economic classes are more likely to value a job for the work itself. This is understandable since wages are less critical to survival when individuals have adequate income.

Since macro environmental variables are significant or approach significance only when they enter the function before race, this apparent relationship must be due to the differential distribution of the races through the regions of the country and between rural and city locations. As would be expected from the time lag property of the influence model, past environment discriminates significantly only when it enters before contemporary environmental variables. This suggests that the past environment has its effects on perceived role of work by influencing the individual in the direction of a particular contemporary environment.

Since race has highly significant discriminating power whether entered into the function first or last, this variable is directly related to the work values of individuals. The same is true for measures of social class (The low coefficient for income level is due to the high inter-correlations between the social status variables). Environmental variables appear to be more important for men than for women. In summary, the first proposition of the cultural influence model is generally supported by the NLS data. Each multi-variate dimension, i.e., culture, environment, and social structure, has an influence on the individual's perceived role of work, with the exception that the environment has no significant relationship to the work values of working women.

European Regional Differences in Work Values

The analyses reported in this section are parallel to that just presented. Instead of examining black-white differences, however, the focus is on

Table 6

CROSS TABULATIONS OF PERCEIVED ROLE OF WORK BY EUROPEAN REGIONS

	MEN				*WOMEN*			
Perceived Role of Work	*North or West (%)*	*Central or East (%)*	*South (%)*	*Total*	*North or West (%)*	*Central or East (%)*	*South (%)*	*Total*
Good Wages	142 (14.6)	75 (23.1)	53 (23.7)	270 (17.8)	55 (15.2)	30 (27.3)	26 (24.5)	111 (19.2)
Work Itself	829 (85.4)	250 (76.9)	171 (76.3)	1250 (82.2)	308 (84.8)	80 (72.7)	80 (75.5)	468 (80.8)
Totals	971 (63.9)	325 (21.4)	224 (14.7)	1520 (100.0)	363 (62.7)	110 (19.0)	106 (18.3)	579 (100.0)

differences between descendents of various European groups. For many Americans, of course, Europe was at one time the location of ancestors. Only those respondents who are first, second or third generation American are of concern here. The responses of these individuals to the question of the perceived role of work are presented in Table 6.

The prediction that northern Europeans would be more work-oriented than wage-oriented is fully supported. Western Europeans are included with this group because of the way in which the information has been coded on NLS tapes. The hypothesis that central, eastern and southern Europeans would be less work-oriented is also supported. As in the previous analysis, the differences predicted between white men and white women are not found. Although the variation in distribution between individuals from different European cultural regions are not great, they are significant at the .001 level. When it is considered that many of these individuals have lived and worked in the American environment, which is numerically dominated by work-oriented individuals, the findings of the predicted differences are even more meaningful.

The first stage of the cultural influence model has been evaluated relative to European cultural groups in the same way as it was evaluated relative to blacks and whites. Tables 7 and 8 present the results of the discriminant analysis.

The differences between the north/west European group and the central/east European group are the major ethnic contribution to the significant canonical correlations. The correlations indicate that only 4 to 5 per cent of the variance among European groups is explained by the analysis. It is interesting to note that the predictor variables appear stronger for the women than for the men. This may indicate that the men have been more integrated into the surrounding society than the women, possibly through their participation in the labor force. Such a suggestion is worth pursuing in future research as it may help to explain

Table 7

EUROPEAN REGION AS A PREDICTOR OF PERCEIVED ROLE OF WORK—DISCRIMINANT ANALYSIS

	MEN	*WOMEN*
Canonical Correlation	.195	.232
Centroids		
Grp 1—Wages	—.423	—.491
Grp 2—Work	.093	.115
% Correctly Predicted		
Grp 1—Wages	34.1	25.0
Grp 2—Work	84.6	81.1
Total	77.4	80.6
X_2 of Prediction	356.2	199.8
(Significance)	0	0
N	1186	532

Table 8

REGION DIFFERENCES DETERMINANTS OF PERCEIVED ROLE OF WORK—EUROPEAN

	MEN			WOMEN		
		Significance*			Significance*	
Independent Variables	*Standardized Discriminant Coefficient*	*Region Entered Last*	*Region Entered First*	*Standardized Discriminant Coefficient*	*Region Entered Last*	*Region Entered First*
SOCIAL CLASS		(1)**	(3)		(1)	(3)
Education	.332	.061	.143	.550	.000	.001
Job Status	.329	.000	.001	.096	.458	.569
Family Income	.081	.594	.546	.176	.817	.796
ENVIRONMENT		(3)	(3)		(3)	(3)
Climate	.168	.245	.264	.065	.629	.641
Urbanization	—.008	.691	NE	—.021	.501	.825
PAST EXPERIENCE		(4)	(2)		(4)	(2)
Family Structure	.138	.382	.285	.288	.130	.045
Head of Household's Job Status	.048	.661	.050	***		
Urbanization	—.025	.883	.654	.031	.720	.677
PERSONAL ENVIRONMENT					(2)	(4)
Age	.173	.110	.168	—.098	.598	.610
Job Tenure	—.071	.618	.651	—.151	.507	.444
Health	—.222	.065	.112	NE	NE	NE
Marital Status	.413	.013	.022	.269	.435	.482
1 or 2 children	—.445	.018	.013	—.258	.175	.315

Table 8 *(Contd.)*

Independent Variables	*MEN*			*WOMEN*		
		*Significance**			*Significance**	
	Standardized Discriminant Coefficient	*Region Entered Last*	*Region Entered First*	*Standardized Discriminant Coefficient*	*Region Entered Last*	*Region Entered First*
3 or more children	—.143	.471	.406	—.148	.518	.571
Sole Wage Earner	—.114	.334	.425	.308	.489	.602
REGION Compared to		(5)	(1)		(5)	(1)
North or West						
Central or East	—.351	.043	.020	—.514	.017	.010
South	—.169	.286	.044	—.245	.210	.040

* Refers to change in Rao's V upon entering function
** Order of entry
*** Not available in women's data
NE Too little discriminating power to enter

differences between the roles of men and women in the society and it could shed additional light on the relationship between culture and societal influences.

The results of the discriminant function analysis (See Table 8) indicate that only the central/east European ethnicity discriminates after the influences of other variables have been considered. Among both men and women, southern European ethnicity discriminates only when it is entered into the analysis at the beginning, and then it predicts weakly. Although this result is insignificant, the difference between southern European and north/west European is in the direction predicted.

As in the analysis of racial differences, the social structure variables are the only ones which strongly discriminate, other than ethnicity. For the men some of the personal environment measures are also significant, but none of these variables appear relevant to the work values of the women. In this analysis, neither macro environmental nor past environment measures predict work values. Thus, among the European regional groups the culture and social structure variables are the only ones which give evidence of being related to work values. Other environmental variables are unrelated. This data partially supports proposition one of the cultural influence model.

The results presented are of particular interest in two respects. First, the significant differences between groups descended from different areas of Europe and the differences shown between blacks and whites in the U.S. demonstrate the cultural heterogenity of this country. This finding lends support to the reviewers who have cautioned against assuming cultural uniformity within national boundaries. Second, the findings of predicted cultural differences within a shared American context suggest that stronger differences should be obtained if European descendents of past European generations were to be studied. The support shown for the predicted work values is an argument for their use in the design of cultural studies of current European and African populations.

A Work Values Map of the U.S. Population

The final empirical analysis is an examination of the work values currently characterizing American Society. The results of this analysis are represented in a "map" of the work values (See Table 9). The cultural diversity of the population is amply illustrated. Because the black population of the U.S. was over-sampled in the NLS study, the cross tabulations in Table 9 are slightly distorted. When corrections are made, the proportion of the sample which has Afro-American ancestry is only 10 per cent. This adjustment shifts the overall distribution between those favoring wages *versus* work form 28 per cent *versus* 72 per cent to 21 per cent *versus* 79 per cent. The differences between ethnic groups continue to be significant with the adjusted data. One of the most important consequences of the cultural differences indicated in the map is the indication that any organizational samples which over represent a particular ethnic group will provide a non-representative reflection of the U.S. population. If this has happened in U.S. sampling for cross-cultural studies, then the differences obtained may reflect the impacts of past non-U.S. cultures rather the current value orientations of Americans.

Given the definition of culture suggested in this study, the "map"

Table 9

CROSS TABULATIONS OF PERCEIVED ROLE OF WORK–AMERICAN NATIONAL SAMPLE

			MEN			
Perceived Role of Work	*Afro-American*	*U.S. OR Canada*	*North/West Europe*	*Central East Europe*	*South Europe*	Total
Good Wages	616 (51.6)	232 (17.8)	142 (14.6)	75 (23.1)	53 (23.7)	1118 (27.8)
Work Itself	577 (48.4)	1074 (82.2)	829 (85.4)	250 (76.9)	171 (76.3)	2901 (72.2)
	1193 (29.7)	1306 (32.5)	971 (24.2)	325 (8.1)	224 (5.6)	4019 (100.0)

			WOMEN			
Perceived Role of Work	*Afro-American*	*U.S. or Canada*	*North/West Europe*	*Central East Europe*	*South Europe*	Total
Good Wages	365 (44.0)	162 (15.7)	55 (15.2)	30 (27.3)	26 (24.5)	638 (26.2)
Work Itself	465 (56.0)	867 (84.3)	308 (84.8)	80 (72.7)	80 (75.5)	1800 (73.8)
	830 (34.0)	1029 (42.2)	363 (14.9)	110 (4.5)	106 (4.3)	2438 (100.0)

Table 10

THE PREDICTION OF PERCEIVED ROLE OF WORK–AMERICAN NATIONAL SAMPLE

	MEN	*WOMEN*
Canonical Correlation	.291	.268
Centroids		
Grp 1–Wages	−.580	.511
Grp 2–Work	.158	−.152
% Correctly Predicted		
Grp 1–Wages	55.7	50.6
Grp 2–Work	81.2	78.6
Total	79.4	77.2
X_2 of Prediction	3425.4	2244.7
(Significance)	0	0
N	*9910	*7603

*The number of respondents in the weighted sample is a function of the weighting factor.

Table 11

DETERMINANTS OF PERCEIVED ROLE OF WORK–AMERICAN NATIONAL SAMPLE

	MEN			*WOMEN*		
		*Significance**			*Significance**	
Independent Variables	*Standardized Discriminant Coefficient*	*Ethnicity Entered Last*	*Ethnicity Entered First*	*Standardized Discriminant Coefficient*	*Ethnicity Entered Last*	*Ethnicity Entered First*
SOCIAL CLASS		(1)**	(3)		(1)	(3)
Education	.414	0	0	—.468	0	0
Job Status	.246	.000	.000	—.229	.000	.000
Family Income	.048	.025	.060	—.136	.000	.011
ENVIRONMENT		(3)	(3)		(3)	(3)
Climate	—.023	.003	.559	—.000	.022	.862
Urbanization	.015	.009	.579	.105	.000	.012
PAST EXPERIENCE		(4)	(2)		(4)	(2)
Family Structure	—.002	.057	.168	—.116	.000	.000
Head of Household's Job Status	—.032	.847	.000	***		
Urbanization	—.023	.575	.001	.152	.000	.000
PERSONAL ENVIRONMENT		(2)	(4)		(2)	(4)
Age	.046	.057	.210	—.156	.000	.000
Job Tenure	.062	.137	.045	.060	.051	.138
Health	—.149	.000	.000	.124	.001	.002
Marital Status	.141	.000	.000	—.090	.010	.304
1 or 2 children	—.119	.000	.001	NE	NE	.648
3 or more children	—.147	.000	.001	—.029	.887	.502
Sole Wage Earner	—.097	.004	.008	—.084	.089	.249

Table 11 (*Contd.*)

	MEN			*WOMEN*		
	Standardized Discriminant Coefficient	*Significance**		*Standardized Discriminant Coefficient*	*Significance**	
Independent Variables		*Ethnicity Entered last*	*Ethnicity Entered First*		*Ethnicity Entered Last*	*Ethnicity Entered First*
ETHNICITY COMPARED						
TO US/CANADA		(5)	(1)		(5)	(1)
Afro-American	−.590	0	0	.473	0	0
North/West Europe	.066	.040	.000	−.137	.000	.000
Central/East Europe	−.129	.000	.005	.182	.000	.000
South Europe	−.029	.436	.139	.093	.032	.023

* Refers to change in Rao's V upon entering function
** Order of entry
*** Not available in women's data
NE Too little discriminating power to enter

represented by Table 9 is not actually a cultural map. Rather it reflects the current U.S. social value system. This set of values is a mixture of past cultural values and newly evolving values, and it represents the potential cultural influence of current Americans on successive generations.

Since all of the analyses to this point have been conducted on the actual respondents to the National Longitudinal Survey, corrections which make the sample representative of the population may eliminate the discriminating power of the cultural and social variables. A discriminant analysis, comparing all groups to those of white American ancestry, was conducted with properly weighted data in order to assess this possibility. The results are presented in Tables 10 and 11. Canonical correlations are slightly reduced for both men and women, indicating that somewhat less variance is explained in the weighted sample than in the unweighted sample. The correlations continue to be significant, however.

Once the sample is weighted, nearly all of the predictors—cultural, social, and environmental—are significantly related to perceived role of work. This change is due to the large increase in the "Number" of respondents. In the weighted sample, the only ethnic difference which does not discriminate is the difference between southern European men and the U.S./Canadian respondents. Respondents with ancestors from north or west Europe show the north/west European descendents to be significantly more oriented to work as a value than are the U.S./Canadians.

If the pattern of coefficients is compared with the patterns in Tables 5 and 8, a similar relationship between environmental influences and work values is shown. Culture and social structure have the greatest discriminating power. For the men, personal environmental variables are next. One difference is that in the weighted sample past experience appears to discriminate among women's values.

Because of the limited amount of attitudinal data in the NLS study, the "map" presented here deals with only one aspect of individuals' work value system. This leaves much further work to be done in response to the recommendations of the reviewers of cross-cultural studies. The work value relationships illustrated here, however, suggest that such research is feasible and necessary. The final section of this paper will summarize the conclusions and implications which are suggested by the combined conceptual and empirical approach taken in this study.

DISCUSSION AND IMPLICATIONS

The current research was undertaken with three general objectives in mind:

1. To present a complete conceptual model of the processes by which culture influences organizations.
2. To make a preliminary evaluation of the first stage in the model, which relates culture and environmental influences to individual values, focusing on perceived role of work.
3. To assess the validity of certain methodological criticisms that have been raised about existing cross-cultural research.

Recent reviews have identified the atheoretical nature of much cross-cultural research as one of the weaknesses in this area. By drawing upon the micro and macro levels of social science, as well as management theory, this study has presented a definition of culture and a conceptual model of its influence. This model leads to several significant conclusions concerning the nature of culture and its potential impact on both the study and practice of management. First, implicit in the definition of culture as a frame of reference passed down across generations, is the inference that culture (and therefore its influence) is relatively stable within a given generation. At the organizational level this means that efforts to change culturally-based work values or attitudes to conform to rigid organizational stereotypes are likely to meet with considerable employee resistance. A more feasible solution might well be to design management techniques and structures to be responsive to the inherited values of the existing work force.

Empirical results of the current study suggest that the problem of organizational responsiveness is compounded by the fact that organizations may face multiple diverse cultures even within a single country or geographic area. Further, various cultural value sets may be added or removed from the organizational environment as the participants in the organization change.

From these findings, it is clear that no single management style or organizational framework is likely to accommodate such diversity in the long term. Rather it would seem that organizations must be designed to allow for complex dynamic responses to diverse shifting cultural environments.

Another conclusion involving the study of culture is that such research should, at least, be carried out with awareness of existing work across the disciplines of psychology, sociology, and anthropology, as well as management. Optimally, research teams should be cross disciplinary in composition so that the various views and findings from these fields could be incorporated into a more completely integrated picture of the cultural influence process. The authors have taken a first step in this direction with the current study but much more remains to be done in the future.

Testing of the conceptual model was limited to the first stage of the cultural influence process (culture to individual attitudes); however, this is an important link, since evidence of links between attitudes and behavior and between individual behaviors and organizational effectiveness have been well established in the existing literature. Results were generally supportive of this first step in the model and suggest that individuals are influenced by the experiences of preceding generations.

A more specific implication of these results is that practitioners will likely be faced with work forces having no common perception about the meaning of work. Since motivation theorists such as Maslow (1954), Vroom (1964), and Lawler (1973) have all suggested that individuals are motivated only by the prospect of outcomes they desire and, since the current findings suggest wide disparity across cultures as to why they work (money or the work itself), it is evident that practitioners will need some understanding of the cultural composition of the work force in order to tailor motivational efforts to the needs of employees. Other aspects of individual organization interaction, such as authority relationships and aptitude for independent action may also be culturally influenced; however, this remains to be determined by further research.

Earlier in this paper the authors reviewed several methodological criticisms of past cross-cultural research. The most basic questions raised about cross-cultural studies involved the assumption of intra-national cultural homogeneity and the relative value of results based on atheoretical comparisons of differences. The findings in this study suggest, first, that there are identifiable subcultures within a society as complex as the United States, and that these differences can be shown to be predictably related to reported work attitudes. These findings suggest that researchers can no longer assume in sample selection that all people or all organizations are alike simply because they are located within a single nation. More credence will have to be given to Evan's (1975) conclusion that any cross-cultural, cross-national study must have representative samples of both organizations and individuals (both within organizations and in the larger societal culture). This, he suggests, is necessary to measure "organizational subculture" as well as societal culture (p. 12).

As for the second problem, Roberts (1970) rested her argument against atheoretical research on the fact that spurious and/or misleading results could be accepted as fact in the absence of a conceptual framework against which to evaluate and clarify the results. Current findings show clearly that Roberts' fears were justified.

Tests of predictions concerning the role of work among black and white males and females show mixed results compared to what was predicted from their cultural heritage. However, if this study had merely sought differences between blacks and whites, highly significant results would have been obtained. This would likely have led to the questionable conclusion that there is a large cultural effect operative. This outcome emphasizes the need to be able to suggest, *a priori*, a direction of influence based on previously identified differences in culture—rather than simply finding differences and making the assumption that culture is a causal factor.

The current study also hoped to test the viability of a conceptual model of the cultural influence process. Following the lead of Moore (1974), the cultural influence process was conceived of as a complex multidimensional process in which culture interacts with a number of other environmental variables to influence individuals' frames of reference. It was hypothesized that, while other factors such as social status, personal environment, ecology, and past conditions may have some influence on personal frames of reference, culture would also prove to have a significant, predictable, independent effect. In general, this proposition was supported. Importantly, other variables (social class, education, etc.) which have not been considered in most previous cultural studies also showed significant impacts. This suggests the great likelihood of biased results for studies which merely seek differences across cultural lines, without considering alternative explanations for any observed differences.

In addition to the implications flowing from the purposes of this study, certain other potentially beneficial outcomes and insights have resulted. Evan (1975) suggests that accumulation of baseline cultural data from individual countries is an important prerequisite for both cross-cultural and intra-cultural research. This study will hopefully provide a first step in the direction of elaborating the multi-cultural, multi-dimensional nature of the American society.

Another implication which may be derived from a realization of the multi-dimensional character of the society is that this information will fuel the arguments of those theorists like Fiedler (1965) and Heller (1973) who have suggested the need for a contingency approach to management. They emphasize the need for flexibility so important in dealing with a diverse or turbulent environment.

Further research will be necessary to test the second and third stages of the conceptual model proposed in this study. Other significant environmental variables will also likely be found and added to the model, but this study has served as a beginning point and, hopefully, will make the succeeding steps in the elaboration of the culture construct less difficult and more fruitful.

REFERENCES

Appelbaum, R. P. *Theories of Social Change*. Chicago: Markham Publ. Co. 1970

Beres, M. E., and S. M. Schmidt. "A Model of Organizational Conflict," Paper 1977 presented at the Fall, 1977 American Institute of Decision Sciences meeting, Chicago, Ill.

Burger, P. C., and R. Doktor. "Cross-Cultural Analysis of the Stucture of Self 1976 Perceptions and Attitudes Among Managers From India, Italy, West Germany, and the Netherlands." *Management International Review*. 16:71–78.

Evan, W. M. "Culture and Organizational Systems." *Organization and Administrative* 1975 *Science*. 4:1–16.

Festinger, L. "A Theory of Social Comparison Processes." *Human Relations*. 7:117–140. 1954

Fiedler, F. D. "The Contingency Model: A Theory of Leadership Effectiveness." In 1965 H. Proshansky and B. Seidenberg (eds.), *Basic Studies In Social Psychology*. New York: Holt.

Forde, D. "The Cultural Map of West Africa: Successive Adaptations to Tropical Forests 1960 and Grasslands." In S. Ottenberg and P. Ottenberg (eds.), *Cultures and Societies of Africa*: 116–138. New York: Random House.

Goodman, P. S., and B. E. Moore. "Critical Issues of Cross-Cultural Management 1972 Research." *Human Organization*. 31:39–45.

Haire, M., E. E. Ghiselli, and L. W. Porter. *Managerial Thinking: An International Study*. 1966 New York: Wiley.

Heider, F. *The Psychology of Interpersonal Relations*. New York: Wiley. 1958

Heller, W. "A Symposium: Cross National Organizational Research." *Industrial* 1973 *Relations*. 12(2):137–247.

Hesseling, B. "Studies in Cross-Cultural Organization." *Columbia Journal of World* 1973 *Business*. December: 120–134.

Inkeles, A., and D. J. Levinson. "National Character: The Study of Model Personality and 1969 Sociocultural Systems." In G. Lindzey and E. Aronson (eds.), *The Handbook of Social Psychology*, 2nd edition. 4:418–505. Reading, Mass.: Addison and Wesley.

Jones, E. E. *et. al.* "Some Conditions Affecting the Use of Ingratiation to Influence 1965 Performance Evaluation." *Journal of Personality and Social Psychology*. 1:613–625.

Kerlinger, F. N. *Foundations of Behavioral Research*. New York: Holt, Rhinehart and
1973 Winston.

Klecka, C. *The Measurement of Children's Masculinity and Feminity*. Dissertation,
1975 Northwestern University.

Kroeber, A. L., and C. Kluckhohn. *Culture: A Critical Review of Concepts and*
1952 *Definitions*. Cambridge, Mass: Peabody Museum of American Archaeology and Ethnology, Harvard University.

Lawler, E. E. *Motivation in Work Organizations*. Monterey, Calif: Wadsworth
1973 Publishing Co.

Lomax, A., and N. Berkowitz. "The Evolutionary Taxonomy of Culture." *Science*.
1972 177:228–239.

March, J. G., and H. A. Simon. *Organizations*. New York: Wiley.
1958

Maslow, A. H. *Motivation and Personality*. New York: Harper and Row.
1954

Moore, R. "Cross-Cultural Study of Organizational Behavior." *Human Organi-*
1974 *zation*. 33(1): 37–45.

Murdock, G. P. *Ethnographic Atlas*. Pittsburgh, Pa.: Univ. of Pittsburgh Press.
1967

Murphy, G. *Personality: A Biosocial Approach to Origins and Structure*. New York:
1947 Harper.

Neghandi, A. R. "Cross-Cultural Studies: Too Many Conclusions, Not Enough
1973 Conceptualization." In A. R. Negandhi (ed.), *Modern Organizational Theory:* 313–316. Kent, Ohio: Kent State University Press.

Obenhaus, V. *Ethics for an Industrial Age*. Conn.: Greenwood Press.
1965

Peck, R. F. "Distinctive National Patterns of Career Motivation." *International*
1975 *Journal of Psychology*. 10:125–134.

Roberts, K. H. "On Looking as an Elephant: An Evaluation of Cross-Cultural
1970 Research Related to Organizations." *Psychological Bulletin*. 74:327–50.

———. "Interorganizational Research: Comparative Studies of Organizations in
1972 Different Environments." In W. K. Graham and K. Roberts (eds.), *Comparative Studies in Organizational Behavior*. New York: Holt, Rinehart and Winston.

The National Longitudinal Surveys' Handbook. Columbus, Ohio: Ohio State University
1973 Center for Human Resource Research.

The School District of Philadelphia. *The World of Africans and Afro-Americans*.
1971 Philadelphia: Instructional Services.

Vroom, V. H. *Work and Motivation*. New York: Wiley.
1964

Weber. M. *The Protestant Ethic and the Spirit of Capitalism*. New York: Charles
1958 Scribner's Sons.

Weber, M. *Economy and Society*, 3. Vol. New York: Bedminster Press.
1968

Whitehall, A. M. "Cultural Values and Employee Attitudes: United States
1964 and Japan." Journal of Applied Psychology. 48:69–72.

Whiting, J. W. M. "Methods and Problems in Cross-Cultural Research." In G. Lindzey
1968 and E. Aranson (eds.), *Handbook of Social Psychology*, Vol. 2 (2nd ed.), Reading, Mass.: Addison Wesley.

Whyte, W. F, and L. K. Williams. "Supervisory Leadership: An International Com-
1968 parison." *Proceedings of the International Council for* Scientific Management, Thirtieth International Management Congress 26:481–488.

National Contexts and Technology as Determinants of Employee's Perceptions[1]

GEORGE W. ENGLAND
University of Minnesota
International Institute of Management, Berlin

ANANT R. NEGANDHI
Kent State University, Kent, Ohio
International Institute of Management, Berlin

The controversy between those who support and those who deny an "industrial convergence" model of organizational functioning remains with us today much as was the case twenty-five years ago. Two of the pioneers in cross-cultural organizational studies, Harbison and Myers, argued that "organization building has its logic . . . which rests upon the development of management . . . and . . . there is a general logic of management development which has applicability both to advanced and industrializing countries in the modern world" (Harbison and Myers, 1959).

One aspect of this viewpoint is that technological factors play an important role in shaping the industrial organization, its structure, its effectiveness, and the human behavior that occurs within the organization. Support for this contention has come from theorists, such as Perrow (1973) and Woodward (1965), who have pointed out the considerable impact of technology on organizational functioning. Other theorists have argued that comprehensive understanding of organizational functioning requires knowledge about energy transfers not only within an organization but, perhaps more importantly, between the organization and its external environment. Such argument is evident from the studies of Emery and Trist (1965), Thompson (1967), Dill (1958), and Lawrence and Lorsch (1969), to name a few, as well as in a number of studies included in this volume. For many who are interested in cross-cultural organizational functioning, Oberg's view which was expressed more than a decade ago, is still shared: "If the ground rules under which the manager operates are different in different cultures and/or countries, then it would be fruitless to search for a common set of strategies of management . . . cultural differences from one country to another are more significant than many writers appear to recognize . . . A (universalist claim) is hardly warranted by either evidence or intuition at this stage in the development of management theory" (Oberg, 1963:141–143). In one form or another, some argue for the primacy of technological and structural determinants of organizational functioning, while others argue that national and/or cultural determinants are of prime importance.

PURPOSE OF THIS PAPER

The purpose of this paper is to show the extent of actual national differences in the employee's perceptions. In more specific terms, we have attempted to examine national differences between India and the U.S.A. in perceptions about the following issues:

1. Employee concern about various societal issues and problems, such as crime and delinquency, the country's economy, health-care, youth, preventing war and achieving peace, the educational system, pollution, development of science and technology, housing, and cultural life.
2. Importance of job-content areas, such as security, good pay, a safe and healthy work place, opportunity to get promoted, chance to develop abilities, responsibilities, variety, and independence.
3. Nature of management styles (autocratic *versus* democratic), and preference and willingness to participate in decision-making.

ABOUT THE STUDY: SAMPLE AND DATA-COLLECTION PROCEDURE

The study reported in this paper represents a small part of a large-scale study undertaken in nine countries. It involved workers in the steel industry, and sought to evaluate the impact of technology and socio-economic systems upon work attitudes and behavior. This paper only examines the data collected from two countries, namely India and the U.S.A. Samples of workers in both countries were drawn to represent relatively high and relatively low levels of technologies as utilized in the steel industry in the respective country. All work places or major job types in the selected plants were sampled. None of the samples can be said to be representative of all steel workers within the country, but the samples were, to a large extent, comparable in terms of the design for the nine nations' steel study.

The data collection instruments (interview guides and questionnaires) were identical and the data collection procedures were similar in the two countries.[1]

USE OF REFERENCE GROUP

To highlight the extent of national *versus* industrial (technology) differences, we utilized a reference group of employees in the American auto

[1] For a detailed description on methodology of this nine-country study, see Spray, S.O., Adamek, R., and Negandhi, A., *United States National Report: Technology and Steelworkers* (mimeographed report), Kent State University, 1976.

industry.[2] Both the instruments and the procedures for data collection were very similar for the auto industry in the U.S., as well as the steel industry in the U.S. and India. The logic of our analysis and of using a reference group (in at least one country) is both simple and straightforward: (1) In the domain of content with which we are dealing, the differences must be relatively large in magnitude before they are viewed as possible significant country differences; (2) We need to be concerned with both the level of responses, and the pattern of responses in identifying significant country differences; and (3) Country differences in employee responses within the same industry must be *considerably greater* than differences in responses of employees in different industries within a country—before we have identified important national differences.

We are interested in examining, then, only relatively large differences in employee perceptions where there is reference group support for the assertion

Table 1

CHARACTERISTICS OF THE SAMPLES

	U.S. Auto (*N*=205) %	*U.S. Steel* (N=193) %	*Indian Steel* (N=141) %
Age			
18–28	20	27	17
29–43	32	32	68
44–50	32	20	9
Over 50	16	21	5
Education			
Grade School	12	2	49
Some high school	20	21	41
Completed high school	49	54	04
Some college	19	23	05
Job Tenure			
1 year or less	11	16	6
2 to 10 years	53	61	61
Over 10 years	36	20	33
Job Type			
Supervisor	9	3	0
Maintenance	21	17	9
Set-up	16	0	20
Operators	37	52	36
Other	17	28	35

[2] For a fuller description of the U.S. automobile sutyd, see: Jacob, Betty M., England, G. W., Jacob, P. E., Pratt, R. C., Whitehill, A. M., and Ahn, C. *The Automobile Worker: A Multinational Perspective Report of the United States Research Team* (mimeographed report), University of Hawaii, 1975.

that this appears to be an area of significant country difference. It is only these differences that merit the painstaking effort required to show that they are "culturally or environmentally determined" differences and to trace those elements of culture and/or environment that seem to produce them.

Table 1 shows selected characteristics of the three samples. As can be noted, the samples are roughly similar to each other in terms of these characteristics with two exceptions. The Indian steel sample is particularly heavily represented in the middle-range (29–43 years), and less heavily represented in the young- and in the old-age range. The Indian sample has a lower educational level than the two U.S. samples.

ANALYSIS OF RESEARCH RESULTS

Concern about Public Issues

Figure 1 presents data for the three worker-samples on the extent of their personal concern about ten public issues. Not surprisingly, this is a content area where real national differences seem to exist. The difference in level of concern about each of the ten issues between the United States steel workers and Indian steel workers is large (both in a statistical and in a practical sense), and the pattern of responses for the two groups is quite different. The Indian sample indicates a high level of concern with only two issues: the country's economic problems and housing problems. Both issues may well reflect important and

Figure 1

MEAN LEVEL OF CONCERN WITH PUBLIC ISSUES

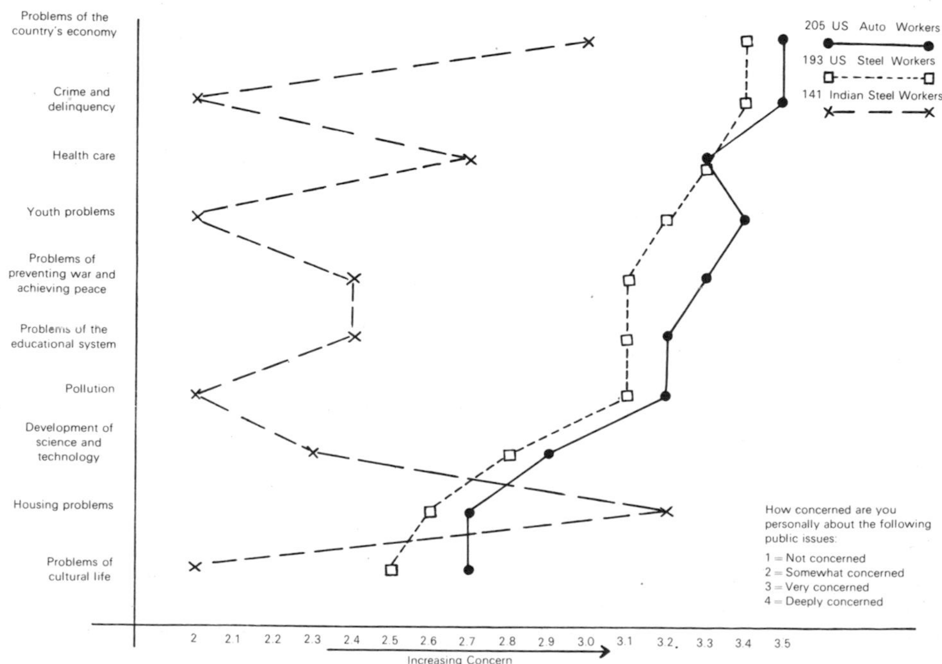

elemental needs for basic survival. In contrast, American steel workers indicate a high level of concern with a much wider range of issues. These include elemental needs as well as more collectively oriented concerns, such as youth problems, problems of war and peace, and pollution.

The contention that these are real national differences, is strengthened by the fact that the two U.S. samples show very similar levels of concern with each individual issue and almost identical patterns of concerns. In short, the differences between countries in level and pattern of response are large, while the intra-country differences are small.[3]

THE EMPLOYEE'S COMMITMENT TO INDUSTRIAL LIFE

Since the 1950's, cross-cultural management scholars and those interested in the economic development process in the third world have devoted considerable attention to probing the needs, preferences and values of industrial workers in those countries. In the main, arguments have been advanced to suggest that industrial workers in developing countries are not committed to industrial work and/or to an urban life as compared to workers in the industrialized countries. It has been argued (without much evidence) that workers in the former countries are not able to adapt to rational bureaucratic organizations, regular time-keeping, and career patterns which the industrial firms demand (Slotkin, 1960; Myers, 1958; Moore, 1965; Moore and Feldman, 1960; McClelland, 1961).

Turning specifically to an Indian case, Ornati, in his study of an Indian factory system observed:

> Indian workers are not interested in factory work; they resist adjustment to the type of life which goes with industrial employment. In the value scheme of the majority of Indians, factory labor does not offer any avenue for the expression of their individual personalities; wage increase and promotion do not operate as stimulants to greater exertion, nor does greater exertion lead to changes in status. (Orrati, 1965:55)

OUR FINDINGS

Figure 2 compares the three samples of workers in terms of the relative importance of the workers' jobs, providing or containing eight major job areas. Indian steel workers attach greater importance to all eight job facets than do U.S. steel workers, significantly so on six of the eight items. The establishment of these differences in "work values" as representing real national differences, is severely questioned by the fact that intra-country differences between the two U.S. samples are as large or larger than the inter-country differences on four of the eight items. Additionally, the very similar patterns of responses (relative ranking of the eight items) among the steel workers in the two countries mitigate

[3] A relatively similar difference in concerns was found between national samples of the two countries twenty-five years ago in the pioneering work of Hadley Cantril, as reported: *The Pattern of Human Concerns*, New Brunswick, New Jersey: Rutgers University Press, 1965, Chapters 4 and 5.

Figure 2

PERCENTAGE OF EACH GROUP INDICATING THE ITEM IS VERY IMPORTANT

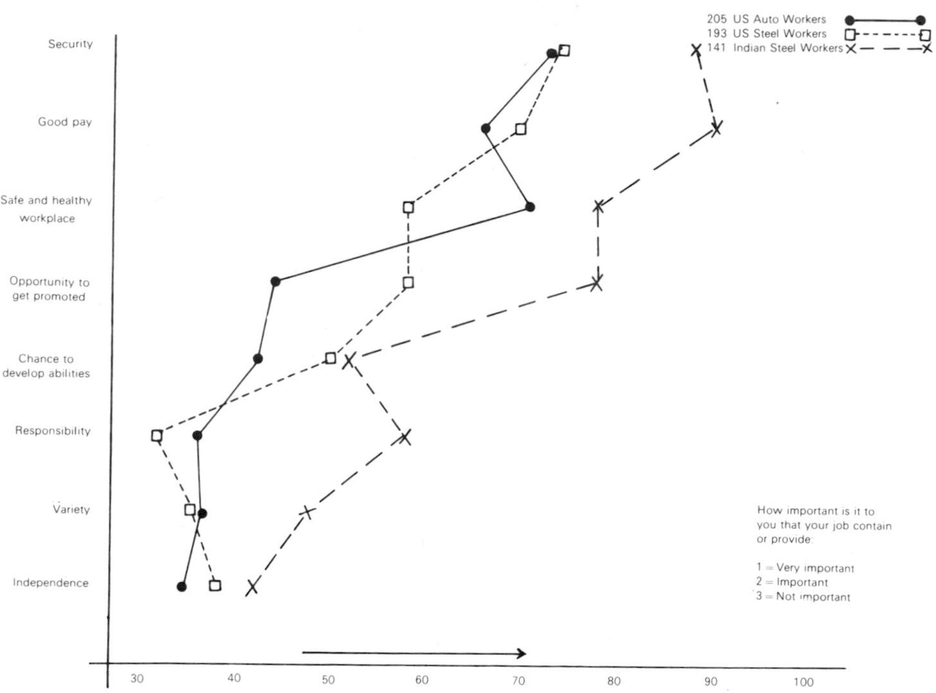

against the conclusion that large and meaningful country differences exist in work values across the two countries.

The question of whether or not there are major national differences in terms of the extent to which the presence of various job facets "explains" or predicts the level of overall or general job satisfaction, has recently attracted considerable attention (Hofstede, *et. al.*, 1975). The real question centers around the issue of whether there is some small subset of job facets whose presence or absence is crucial in determining one's satisfaction with his work situation, or conversely, is the determination of work satisfaction largely idiosyncratic at the level of individuals and nations. Figure 3 presents the correlations between the perceived presence of twenty-seven job facets and an independent measure of overall job satisfaction for the three worker samples. It is clearly evident that the level of correlations and the pattern of correlations are more similar within the same industry (steel) but across the two countries, rather than across the industries (steel and auto) but within one country (U.S.A.). These results, then, do not support the notion that there are large and meaningful differences between Indian and American workers about what "explains" or "produces" general job satisfaction; indeed, the intra-country differences are more impressive than the inter-country differences. The real question posed by this data is: why are the U.S. automobile workers so different from both groups of

Figure 3

CORRELATIONS BETWEEN PERCEIVED PRESENCE OF JOB FACET AND OVERALL JOB SATISFACTION

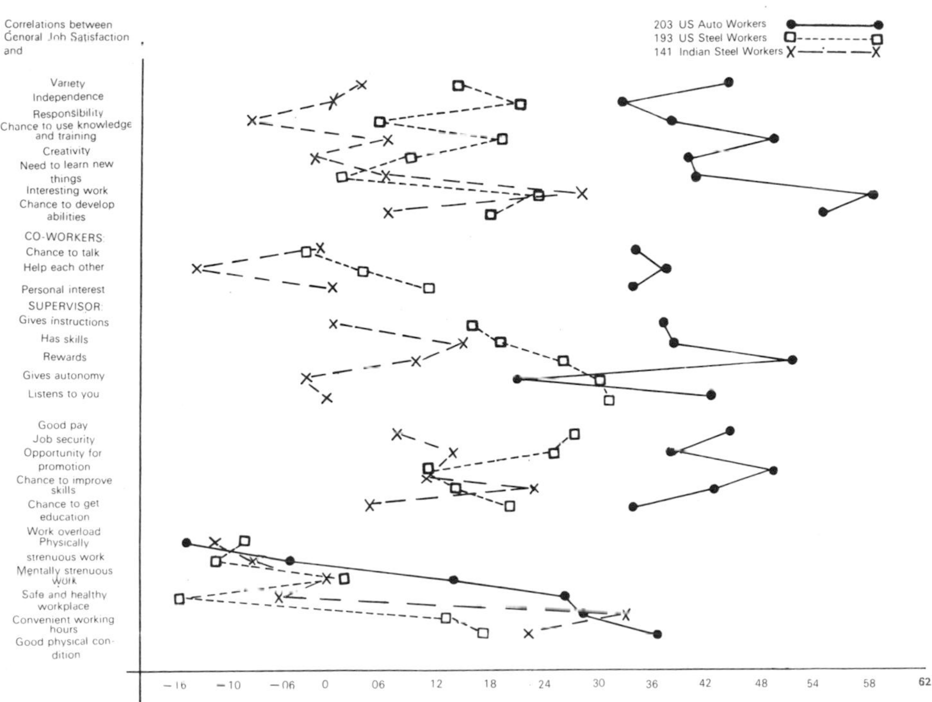

steel workers in terms of these relationships? An interesting question, but thus far we have not probed it further.

A lack of meaningful national differences can also be observed when one examines the workers' perceptions about the factors influencing promotion. Figure 4 shows the relatively perceived importance of five factors in obtaining a promotion for the three samples. While it is clear that the level of importance attached to each of the five factors is somewhat lower for Indian workers than for either of the American samples, the pattern similarities and the fact that intra-country differences are about as large as inter-country differences cautions against viewing these findings as supporting the establishment of meaningful country differences. The evidence is ambiguous at best, and to a large extent, reflects the harsh realities of economic (but not cultural) life in India.

With reference to worker satisfaction, Figure 5 shows the measured satisfaction for each of the three samples in terms of three independently measured forms of worker satisfaction (a single item measure), satisfaction with management and company (a five item measure), and overall satisfaction with the union (a single item measure). There are rather large differences (both in a statistical and a practical sense) between Indian and American steel workers on all three measures of work-satisfaction. One would certainly be tempted to view this as an area where real national differences exist. However, when one views

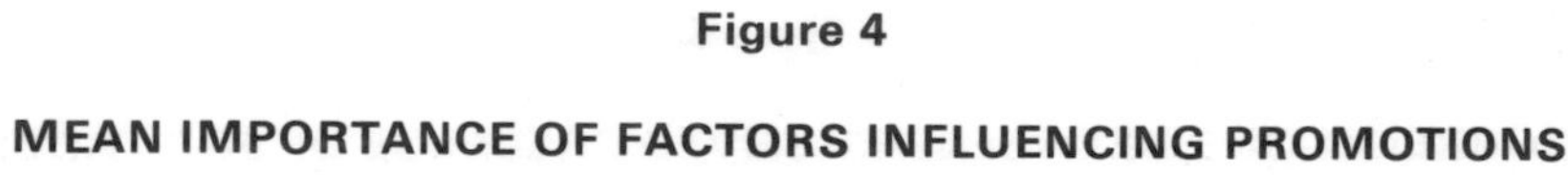

Figure 4

MEAN IMPORTANCE OF FACTORS INFLUENCING PROMOTIONS

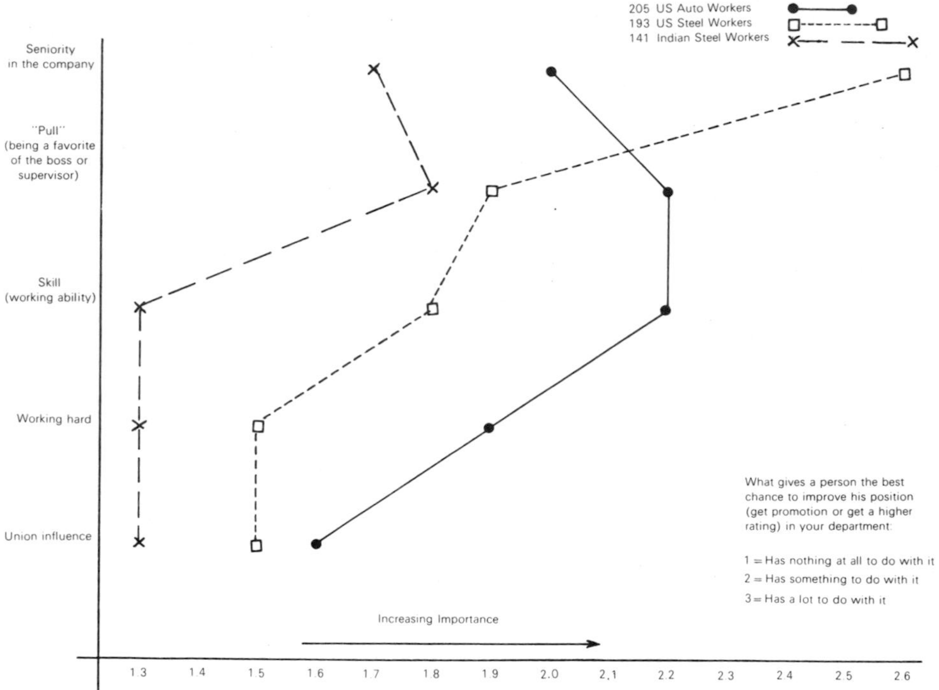

the reference group results of American automobile workers, it is apparent that the within-country differences in satisfaction measures are approximately as large as the between-country differences. Thus, our reference-group analysis, as well as the pattern similarity, cautions against clear interpretation of the observed country differences as indicating meaningful national level differences.

Obviously, we are in the minority among cross-cultural management researchers in down-playing the importance of national differences in employees' commitments, aspirations, and desires. It is interesting to note, however, that several of the well documented studies undertaken in India and other developing countries seem to support our contention. For example, Gangulli found in his study of factory workers in India, that:

> The four most important things that the workers want are sufficient and adequate income, a sense of security, an opportunity for promotion and advancement, and finally, the opportunity to learn more [a] interesting trade. . . . In these and also in their aspirations and expectations, there does not seem to be any fundamental difference between this group and other groups of factory employees in other countries. (Gangulli 1954:10)

Desai (1958), in his study of blue-collar and white-collar employees in India, found that both groups prefer higher wages, better fringe benefits, profit-

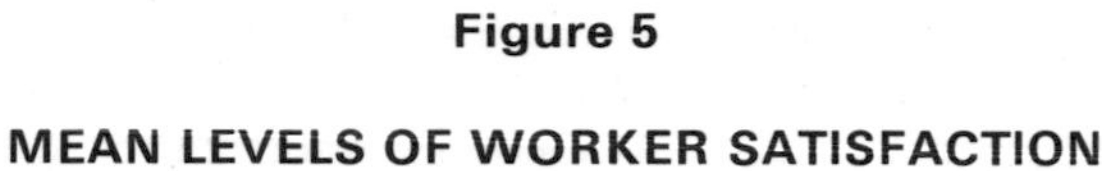

Figure 5

MEAN LEVELS OF WORKER SATISFACTION

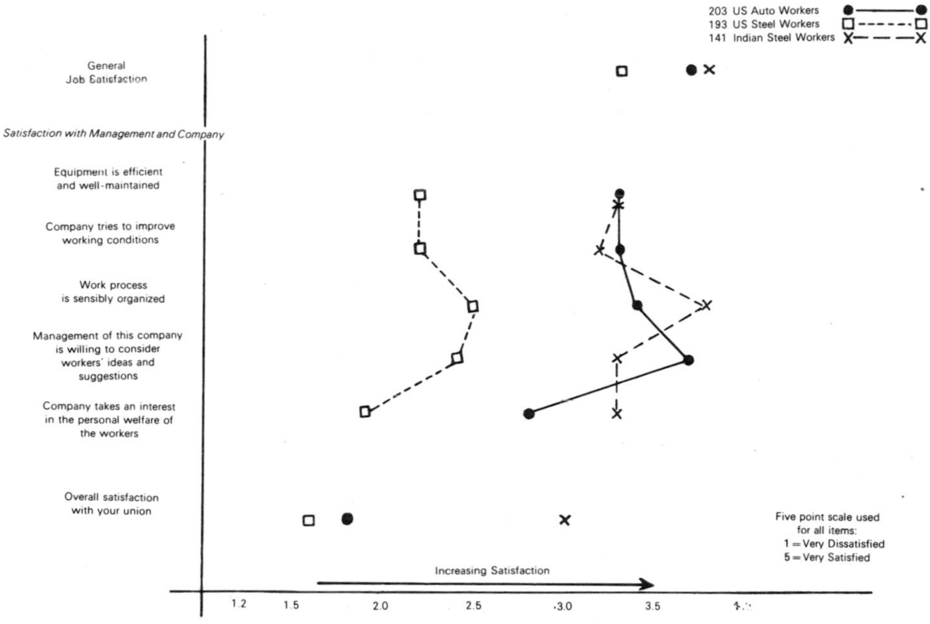

sharing plans, and impartial policies in promotion and reward systems.

Morris, in his studies of industrial workers in Bombay and Jamshedpur, found that:

> The evidence from Bombay and Jamshedpur suggests that the creation of [a] disciplined industrial labor force in a newly-developing society is not particularly difficult. . . . The difference in worker stability cannot be accounted for by any substantial differences in the psychology of the raw labor recruited. Nor can it be attributed to dissimilarities in the traditional environment from which the workers came. If there were differences in work-force behavior, these flowed from employer policy. (Morris, 1965:4)

In a more recent study entitled *South Indian Factory Workers*, Holmström (1976) inquired as to how factory workers see their jobs. His findings are:

> . . . (workers) see factory work as a citadel of security and relative prosperity, which it is; it offers regular work and promotion and predictable rewards, as against the chaos of terrifying dangers of life outside. For every one inside the citadel, there is a regiment outside trying to scale the walls. Even educated Brahmans will take unskilled, casual factory work in the hope of permanent jobs. (Holmström, 1976:137)

In criticizing the socio-cultural explanation, Holmström goes on, saying that:

> The argument that Indian factory workers keep up a minimum standard of performance because they think of a job as something like the right to perform a customary service in the village *jajmaani* system may have been

> true in the past or in other places—not in Bangalore now. The evidence used to support that view can be explained as the result of management practices and/or the logic of the worker's situation inside the citadel, but with obligations to a number of people outside it. The factory worker is not quite an economic man minimizing risk, but much of his behavior can be explained as the pursuit of a limited number of economic and other goals, and informants can often say specifically what they are: security, higher pay, easier or more interesting work, freedom from close supervision, a pleasant atmosphere at work, respectability, a better chance for one's children, socialism, work well done as religious duty and so on. (Holmström, 1976:139–40)

Similarly, Mandelbaum, a social anthropologist, warns us that it is a misguided notion that there are inherent contradictions between established customs and modern industrial life. Drawing from his comprehensive anthropological study of Indian villages, he states:

> . . . there has been considerable cultural continuity along with the modern social change. . . . One of the ways of maintaining both persistence and change is through compartmentalization, the traditional mode of separating the standards of the work sphere from those of the domestic sphere. (Mandelbaum, 1970:645)

Referring to Milton Singer's (1968) study of leading industrialists in Madras, India, Mandelbaum states:

> In their household behavior, members of these families tend to observe spiritual standards much more closely than they do in their activities outside the house. These industrialists separate the two spheres of action more sharply than was done in their boyhood homes. . . . This device is not restricted to the industrial elite. Even the men who pull rickshaws in the streets of Lucknow (a city in India) similarly separate their standards for conduct in their work domain from those followed in their homes. (Mandelbaum, 1970:645)

Turning to other developing countries, Fillol, in his study in Argentina, found:

> There is no reason to believe that Argentina workers have basically different attitudes toward their jobs from workers anywhere else in industrialized Western countries. . . . Industrialists in general do not seem to have given any thought to the fact that the productivity, motivation, and cooperation of labor are primarily determined by the management which employs it and not by the more or less enlightened social and economic policies of government. (Fillol, 1963:76)

Finally, in their comprehensive study of twenty-five countries (industrially developed and underdeveloped), Sirota and Greenwood (1971) raise considerable doubts about the prevailing thesis of the impact of socio-cultural variables on employee commitment and motivation. They found that the most important goal of workers everywhere is to have an opportunity for individual achievement. In criticizing the cultural thesis, they have argued that such generalizations, although interesting, are

> . . . based mostly on the subjective impressionistic experiences of

> observers . . . acceptance of these conclusions must therefore depend largely on faith faith both in the observer's objectivity, and in the representativeness of the anecdotal evidence he usually presents as proof of his case. (Sirota and Greenwood, 1971:53)

MANAGEMENT STYLES AND DECISION-MAKING

Much has been written on management style and decision-making in different countries (Harbison and Myers, 1959; Haire, Ghiselli and Porter, 1966; Heller, 1971). There seems to be a consensus, among cross-cultural management researchers, that the managerial styles in developing countries are relatively more authoritarian than in the industrially developed countries, although there are substantial differences among the latter countries themselves (Heller, 1971; Wilpert, 1977).

Observations of Davis, in Mexico, reflect the views of many other cross-cultural researchers (Lauter, 1969; Lauterbach, 1966; Fillol, 1963; Flores, 1967; Whyte, 1963; Jain, 1968). With respect to Mexico, Davis states:

> The most characteristic feature of the authority system is its centralization. In more traditional Mexican firms, it is the centralization of all power in the one top man who is simultaneously organizer, owner, manager, and the sole decision-maker. Here, management is a person, not a position, concept or function. Authority, likewise, resides in this person and is not spread throughout a managerial organization for, indeed, no such organization exists. . . . The Mexican manager (says Davis's interviewee) . . . would delegate work but not authority. (Davis, 1971:174)

To "explain" authoritarianism in developing countries, scholars have probed into the psychological characteristics of people in developing countries, and arrived at conclusions such as: "The people in developing nations are more authority-prone than those in industrially-developed countries." For example, Zurcher *et. al.*, (1965), using the Stouffer-Toby Role Conflict Scale among 230 bank employees in Mexico and the U.S.A., found that Mexicans are significantly more particularistic than Anglo-Americans.

Administering the Thematic Apperception Test (TAT) to subjects (students) from industrially developed and less developed countries, Josh (1965) found that subjects from the former countries were more insecure, non-conforming, experimental, and progressive, while those from the latter countries were more secure, conforming, tradition-bound, conventional, and resistant to change. With respect to India, Sharma (1969) found that Indian students were less dominant (hence more dependent on authority) than were the Caucasian Americans. Similarly, Narain (1971) has argued that Indian men are more passive and submissive to authority.

OUR RESULTS

To test some of the above generalizations, we examined three related issues on decision-making among the auto and steel workers in the U.S.A., and the steel workers in India. Figure 6 provides data concerning the perceived possibilities of participation in various decisions, which include such items as

Figure 6

PERCEIVED PARTICIPATION POSSIBILITIES

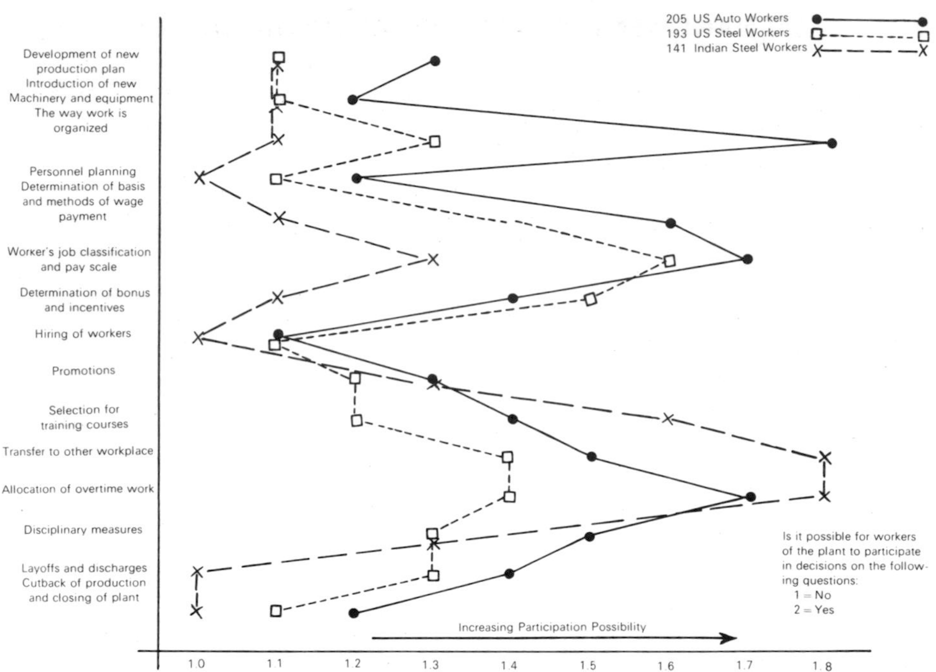

development of a new plant, introduction of new machinery, organization of work, personnel planning, hiring, promotion, and lay off of workers. Our results, as shown in Figure 6, clearly indicate that intra-country differences are of similar or greater magnitude than the inter-country differences on thirteen of the seventeen participation items. The pattern of response is also quite similar for all three groups.

A similar trend was observed when we examined data concerning the opportunities and willingness of workers to participate in decision-making. These data are reported in Figure 7.

In our estimate, data reported in Figures 6 and 7 do not support any contention of big and meaningful differences between the two countries (U.S.A. and India) in terms of participation in decision-making; rather, they would question such generalization.

SUMMARY AND IMPLICATIONS

This paper assessed the extent of national differences in workers' perceptions on the following issues:

1. Employees' concern about various societal issues, such as crime and pollution.
2. Importance of job content areas, such as security and good pay.

Figure 7

PARTICIPATION OPPORTUNITIES AND WILLINGNESS

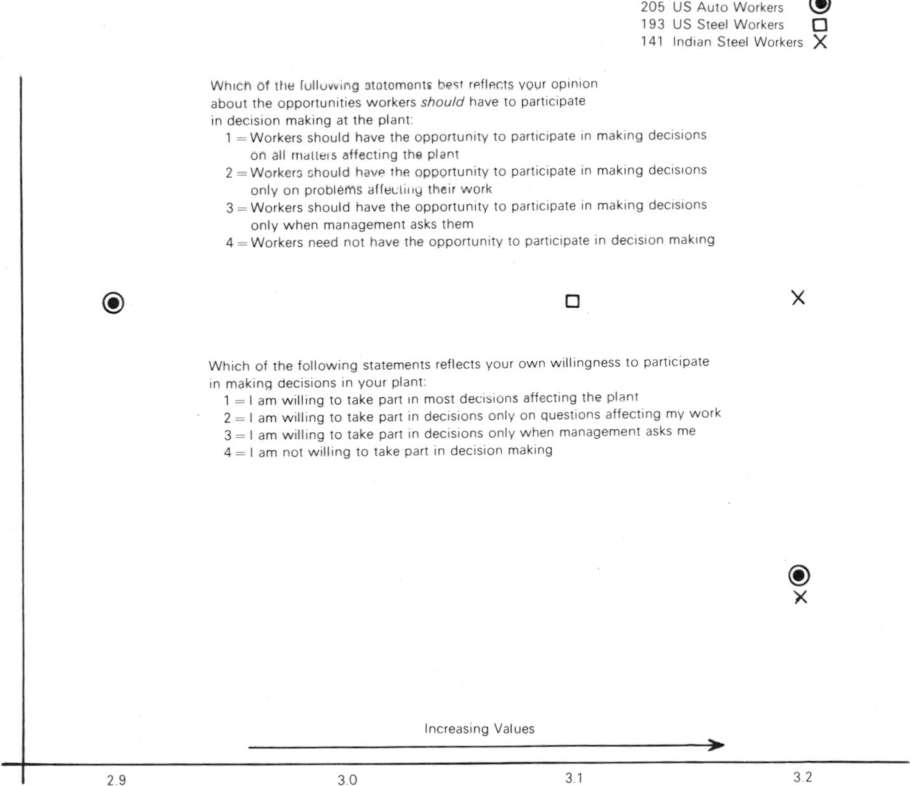

205 US Auto Workers
193 US Steel Workers
141 Indian Steel Workers
Which of the following statements best reflects your opinion about the opportunities workers *should* have to participate in decision making at the plant:
1 = Workers should have the opportunity to participate in making decisions on all matters affecting the plant
2 = Workers should have the opportunity to participate in making decisions only on problems affecting their work
3 = Workers should have the opportunity to participate in making decisions only when management asks them
4 = Workers need not have the opportunity to participate in decision making
Which of the following statements reflects your own willingness to participate in making decisions in your plant:
1 = I am willing to take part in most decisions affecting the plant
2 = I am willing to take part in decisions only on questions affecting my work
3 = I am willing to take part in decisions only when management asks me
4 = I am not willing to take part in decision making
Increasing Values
2.9
3.0
3.1
3.2

3. Nature of management styles, preferences, and willingness to participate in decision-making.

The sample of the study consisted of steel workers in the U.S.A. and India. To discern national differences *versus* differences resulting from the use of different technologies, we utilized a reference group of workers from the auto industry in the U.S.A.

Our findings indicate that national differences in worker perceptions existed only on such global issues as pollution, national economy and housing problems, while national differences with respect to job content areas, factors influencing promotions and employees satisfaction, preferences and willingness to participate in decision-making, were marginal at best. In other words, intra-country differences in employees' perceptions were as large or larger than the inter-country differences.

In our judgment, the literature purporting to show real national and cultural differences in employee-attitudes, behavior, and commitment are highly exaggerated. From the massive data generated during the last two decades or so, one can easily be convinced that the attitudes, beliefs, values, and need hierarchies, are vastly different in different societies. They are even different among different subgroups (ethnic and/or occupational) within a given society. We believe that many of the culture-related concepts are ill-defined, and their operational measures are poorly conceived. For example, as Ajiferuke and Boddewyn have stated: "Culture is one of those terms that defy a single all-purpose definition, and there are almost as many meanings of culture as people using the term" (1970:154). It also appears that culture, although used as an independent variable in most cross-cultural management studies, has an obscure identity and often is used as a residual variable. As comparative researchers, we would argue that one should not get overly excited about observed national differences, unless they are rather large in magnitude, in an *absolute sense* and in a *relative sense*, when compared to observed differences within a given country. It is only when national differences are large in both an absolute and a relative sense, that it seems worthwhile to pursue the very difficult issues surrounding the reasons (cultural and other)—why such differences exist, and what the consequences of such differences could be. Suggestions of this type are not popular among social and behavioral scientists, who view null-hypothesis testing as the major function of their research, or for the less sophisticated "difference detectors." Nevertheless, we believe that this moral has considerable merit.

REFERENCES

Ajiferuke, M., and J. Boddewyn. "Culture and Other 'Explanatory' Variables in 1970 Comparative Management Studies." *Academy of Management Journal.* 13:153–163.

Caplow, T. "Organizational Size." *Administrative Science Quarterly.* 1:484–505. 1957

Child, J. "Organization Structure and Strategies of Control: A Replication of the Aston 1972 Study." *Administrative Science Quarterly.* 17:163–177.

Davis, St. M. *Comparative Management: Organizational and Cultural Perspectives.* 1971 Englewood Cliffs, N.J.: Prentice Hall.

Desai, K. G. "A Comparative Study of Motivation of Blue-Collar and White-Collar 1958 Workers." *Indian Journal of Social Work.* 28:380–87.

Dill, W. R. "Environment as an Influence of Managerial Autonomy." *Administrative* 1958 *Science Quarterly.* 2:409–443.

Emery, F. E., and E. L. Trist. "Socio-Technical Systems." In *Systems Thinking.* 1969 Harmondsworth, England: Penguin Books. pp.

Fillol, Th. R. *Social Factors in Economic Development: The Argentine Case.* Cambridge, 1963 Mass.: MIT Press.

Flores, F. C., Jr. *Applicability of American Management Know-How to Developing* 1967 *Countries: The Case of the Philippines.* Unpub. doctoral dissertation. Graduate School of Business Administration, University of California at Los Angeles.

Gangulli, H. C. "An Enquiry into Incentives of Workers in an Engineering Factory." 1954 *Indian Journal of Social Work.*:10.

Haire, M. D. E. Ghiselli, and L. W. Porter. *Managerial Thinking: An International Study.* 1966 New York: Wiley.

Harbison, F., and C. Myers. *Management in the Industrial World.* New York: McGraw-1959 Hill.

Harvey, E. "Technology and the Structure of Organizations." *American Sociological*
1968 *Review*. 33:247–259.

Heller, F. A. *Managerial Decision-Making: A Comparative Study of American and British*
1971 *Managers*. New York: Harper and Row.

Hofstede, G., A. I. Kraut, and S. H. Simonetti. "The Development of a Core Attitude
1976 Survey Questionnaire for Internal Use." Working Paper 76–17. European Institute for Advanced Studies, Brussels.

Holmström, M. *South Indian Factory Workers—Their life and Their World*. Cambridge.
1976 Cambridge University Press.

Indik, B. P. "Some Effects of Organization Size on Member Attitudes and Behavior."
1963 *Human Relations*. 16:369–384.

Jain, S. "Old Style of Management." In S. B. Prasad and A. R. Negandhi (eds.),
1968 *Managerialism for Economic Development*: 8–19. The Hague: Martinus Nijhoff.

Josh, V. "Personality Profiles in Industrial and Pre-industrial Cultures: A TAT Study."
1965 *Journal of Social Psychology*. 66:101–11.

Lauter, P. G. "Sociological-Cultural and Legal Factors Impeding Decentralization of
1969 Authority in Developing Countries." *Academy of Management Journal*. 12:367–78.

Lauterbach, A. *Enterprise in Latin America*. Ithaca, N.Y.: Cornell Univ. Press.
1966

Lawrence, P. R., and Jay W. Lorsch. *Organization and Environment*. Homewood, Ill.:
1969 Richard D. Irwin.

Mandelbaum, D. G. *Society in India: Change and Continuity*, II. Berkeley: University of
1970 California Press.

McClelland, D. C. "The Achievement Motive in Economic Growth." In B. F. Hoselitz
1963 and W. E. Moore (eds.), *Industrialization and Society*: 74–96. Atlantic Highlands, N.J.: Humanities Press.

Moore, W. E. *Industrialization and Labor*. New York: Russell & Russell.
1965

Moore, W. E., and A. S. Feldmann. *Labor Commitment and Social Change in*
1960 *Developing Areas*. Midwood, N.Y.: Kraus Reprint.

Morris, M. D. *The Emergence of an Industrial Labor Force in India: A Study of the*
1965 *Bombay Cotton Mills, 1859–1947*. Berkeley: University of California.

Myers, C. A. *Labor Problems in the Industrialization of India*. Cambridge, Mass.: Harvard
1958 University Press.

Narain, D.

Negandhi, A. R. *Organization Theory in an Open System: A Study of Transferring*
1976 *Advanced Management Practices to Developing Nations*. New York. Dunellen Publishing Company.

Oberg, W. "Cross-Cultural Perspectives on Management Principles." *Academy of*
1963 *Management Journal*. 6:129:143.

Ornati, O. A. *Jobs and Workers in India*. Ithaca, N.Y.: Cornell University Press.
1955

Perrow, C. "A Framework for the Comparative Analysis of Organizations." *American*
1967 *Sociological Review*. 32:192–208.

Sharma, K. L. "Dominance-Deference: A Cross-Cultural Study." *Journal of Social*
1969 *Psychology*. 79:265–66.

Singer, M. "Indian Joint Family in Modern Industry." In Milton Singer and Bernard
1968 S. Cohn (eds.), *Structure and Change in Indian Society*: 423–52. Chicago: Aldine Publishing Company.

Sirota, D., and J. M. Greenwood. "Understand your Overseas Work Force." *Harvard*
1971 *Business Review*: 49: 53–60.

Slotkin, J. S. *From Field to Factory*. Glencoe, Ill.: The Free Press.
1960

Stogdill, R. M. *Managers, Employees, Organizations*. Columbus, Ohio.: The Ohio State
1965 University Bureau of Business Research.

Thompson, J. D. *Organizations in Action.* New York: McGraw-Hill.
1967

Whyte, W. F. "Culture, Industrial Relations, and Economic Development: The Case of
1963 Peru." *Industrial and Labor Relations Review*: 6:107.

Wilpert, B. *Führung in deutschen Unternehmen.* Berlin: Walter de Gruyter.
1977

Woodward, J. *Industrial Organization: Theory and Practice.* London: Oxford University
1965 Press.

Zurcher, L. A. *et. al.* "Value Orientation, Role Conflict, and Alienation from Work: A
1965 Cross-Cultural Study." *American Sociological Review*: 30:539–48.

[1] Data for U.S. and Indian Steel industry were supported by the Ford Foundation Grant at Kent State University. Professors S. Lee Spray and Raymond J. Adamek of Sociology Dept at Kent State are collaborators in this project. The U.S. Auto industry project collaborators are Professors Phil and Betty Jacobs and Art Whitehill of University of Hawaii. We are thankful to our collaborators for the use of data for this paper.

Are Organization Structures Culture-Free? The Case of Hospital Innovation in the U.S. and France*

JEAN de KERVASDOUE
Escole Polytechnique, Paris

JOHN R. KIMBERLY
Yale University

This paper is a status report. It is one product of an ongoing effort by the authors to use organization theory to explain and predict variability in patterns of adoption of innovation in French and U.S. hospitals. The point of departure for this paper is a study originally designed to test a series of hypotheses about the relationships between organizational structure and innovation. This study was a venture in the comparative analysis of organizations, an undertaking which was in the mainstream of developing research and theory in organizational sociology in the late 1960's and early 1970's. During the course of the study, and particularly its extension to France, we became increasingly aware of the limitations—both theoretical and empirical—of the paradigm within which we were operating, and of the need to develop an amended or alternative framework.

This paper is designed to trace the evolution of our dissatisfaction with the structural perspective in organization theory and of the directions in which our work and thinking is moving. We begin with a description of the original study of hospital innovation in the U.S., and then outline some of the methodological problems encountered in replicating the study in French hospitals and how the problems led us to begin to question our approach. In the third and fourth sections, we present the results of the comparative cross-national study, holding reservations aside. Our second thoughts are fully outlined in part five, and in the final section we sketch the beginnings of an amended approach to using organization theory to explain and predict hospital innovation cross-nationally. The flow of the paper, therefore, roughly corresponds to stages in the

* The French part of this research was supported in part by contracts from the C.O.R.D.E.S., the D.G.R.S.T. and the I.N.S.E.R.M. The authors are indebted to William H. Money for his helpful comments on an earlier draft of this paper.

progress of our research and reflection, and in a sense constitutes as much of a venture in the sociology of knowledge as in the sociology of organizations.

THE STARTING POINT: A STUDY OF HOSPITAL ADOPTION OF INNOVATION

In 1967, a group of researchers at Cornell University initiated a major study of organizational innovation. As originally conceived, the study was designed to examine the extent to which variability in rates of adoption of innovations in medical technology in a national sample of American hospitals could be accounted for by variations in their structure. The study was deliberately designed to permit testing of a number of hypotheses in the sociology of organizations and particularly those derived from the "entrepreneurial theory" of Becker and Gordon (1966). The study represented, at the same time, an attempt to examine the adoption of innovation at the organizational level. Previous adoption research had focused on individual persons as the unit of analysis, and there was a great deal of interest in moving beyond the individual to the organization. The health-care/hospital literature was extensively reviewed, as was that in organization theory (Gordon and Fisher, 1975; Zaltman, Duncan and Holbeck, 1973).

Both the theoretical foundations and the design and methodology of the Cornell study emanated from the comparative structuralist paradigm. Implicit in this paradigm are the notions that: (1) the formal structural attributes of organizations are intrinsically important and theoretically interesting; and (2) simultaneous analysis of the structural attributes of many organizations is the most efficacious way to build and test theory. Although these notions are being increasingly questioned, it is still accurate to say that this paradigm is dominant in the field of organizational sociology.

The Cornell study was based on a sample of nearly one thousand hospitals and relied on both primary and secondary data sources. The dependent variable—adoption of innovations—was based on hospital documentation of the purchase, rental, lease, or, in the case of surgical procedures, use, of a number of innovations in the diagnosis, treatment or prevention of respiratory disease. Respiratory disease was chosen for examination because it was not feasible to study innovations in all disease areas potentially served by a hospital. A strong case can be made, however, that hospital response to innovations in respiratory disease technology is likely to be reasonably representative of response to innovation in medical technology in general because many illnesses which require surgery and therefore the services of an anesthesiologist require respiratory disease technology for anesthesiology and post-operative care. Furthermore, many illnesses carry or can carry respiratory complications which in turn require that the hospital have respiratory disease diagnostic and/or therapeutic capacities. Thus, it was felt that problems of generalizability would be minimized by focusing on innovations in this area.

Data on the twelve innovations selected for the study, with the cooperation of naturally-known experts in the field of pulmonary medicine, were collected from the hospital by means of a mailed questionnaire. Available evidence indicates that the data were both valid and reliable, particularly when compared to studies of innovation based on recall, (Gordon *et. al.,* 1974; 1975).

The independent variables included measures of size, structure of decision-making, range of services, technological complexity, type of ownership, research activity and economic status. Data on these variables came from questionnaires mailed to the Hospital Administration and Chief of Medicine or Chief of Staff in each hospital and from the American Hospital Association's annual survey of member hospitals. Analyses indicated satisfactory reliability and validity for the independent measures as well (Gordon *et. al.*, 1975). The final sample used for analysis consists of those 489 hospitals from which both questionnaires were received. These 489 hospitals are roughly representative of the population of American hospitals in terms of the distribution of number of beds and geographic location. Government federal hospitals are somewhat over-represented proportionally and proprietary hospitals are somewhat under-represented in the sample.

The Cornell study was carried out between 1968 and 1970. The French co-author of this paper was a member of the Cornell research team who, when he completed his doctoral work in the United States, was interested in pursuing the study of hospital innovation in France. Upon his return to France, he was able to obtain funding for a study which was in part an extension and in part a replication of the U.S. study. It was an extension in that innovations in the diagnosis, treatment and prevention of cancer were included in the design, and a replication in that an effort was made to collect comparable data from the French organizations. The basic objective of the study was to examine the extent to which the adoption of innovation in French and American hospitals could be accounted for by similar variables. The epistemological rationale for this approach was solidly grounded in the dominant paradigm exemplified by the work of, for example, Blau and his colleagues in the U.S. and the Aston group in England.

INITIAL QUALMS: A METHODOLOGICAL ANOMALY

The procedures followed to identify innovations in the French component of the study were identical to those followed in the U.S. component. The data collection strategy, however, was slightly different. Because the number of organizations to be studied in France was smaller and because of reservations about the likelihood of receiving useful information from French hospital administrators and doctors *via* a mailed questionnaire, it was decided that interviews would be used to collect data in each organization. It was felt that the presence of an interviewer would also permit the collection of more detailed information about the innovations and the conditions under which they had been adopted. At least one, and sometimes two, interviewers, armed with an interview schedule containing questions comparable to those used in the U.S. study, visited each of the 137 organizations in the sample.

However, the interviewing process initially resulted in feelings of bewilderment, subsequently feelings of frustration, and ultimately, in a reassessment of the design, assumptions and theoretical underpinnings of the entire study. The initial qualms were occasioned by the difficulty respondents had in answering some questions and the content of their responses to certain others. The questions which were difficult for them to answer had to do with decision-making authority. In the U.S. component of the study, a series of questions had been developed to analyze the centralization of authority. These questions asked the respondent to indicate who or what body in the hospital had the authority to make a number of different kinds of decisions ranging from the hiring of certain categories of personnel to the purchase of certain kinds of equipment. The French respondents often seemed puzzled by these questions. As we later learned, this was because the questions were not applicable in the French context. On the other hand, there were a number of questions about travel to professional meetings at hospital expense, about the use of outside speakers in the hospital, and about hospital sponsorship of research which all respondents answered in roughly the same way; in the negative. Both kinds of responses were at variance with experiences in the U.S. study. These differences were initially regarded as annoying, but trivial, methodological problems. Subsequently, they helped shed new light on the comparative study.

FORGING AHEAD: AN EMPIRICAL COMPARISON OF HOSPITAL ADOPTION OF INNOVATION IN FRANCE AND THE UNITED STATES

The French component was completed in spite of the difficulties encountered, and a data set permitting the comparative analysis that had been envisioned was developed. At this point, although we had some reservations, we were primarily concerned with cross-national analysis based on contemporary theory. The theoretical framework utilized for the purpose of developing a testable model is based on the work of Lawrence and Lorsch (1967). They demonstrated that, to be effective, organizations must develop structures appropriate for their milieu. Particularly important structural characteristics are levels of differentiation and integration. High levels of differentiation are appropriate when the external milieu is complex and rapidly changing. Specialized units, whose purpose is to make contact with the external milieu, are needed to interface with the environment. As internal differentiation increases, however, there are needs for integration which mirror the diversity of the external milieu. As Lawrence and Lorsch argued:

> . . . we have found that the state of differentiation in the effective organization was consistent with the diversity of the parts of the environment, while the state of integration achieved was consistent with the environmental demand for interdependence. But our findings have also indicated that the states of differentiation and integration was inversely related. The more differentiated an organization, the more difficult it is to achieve integration. To overcome this problem, the effective organization has integrating devices consistent with the diversity of the environment. The more diverse the environment, and the more differentiated the organization, the more elaborate the integrating devices. (1967:157).

The external milieu of the hospital is, according to their definition, complex and turbulent. Inputs are heterogeneous, as sick people can have a variety of illnesses with a correspondingly large variety of appropriate interventions by the hospital. Because of this heterogeneity, the treatment of patients cannot be

Figure 1
RELATIONSHIPS AMONG DIFFERENTIATION, INTEGRATION, SIZE, SPECIALTY IMPORTANCE AND INNOVATION

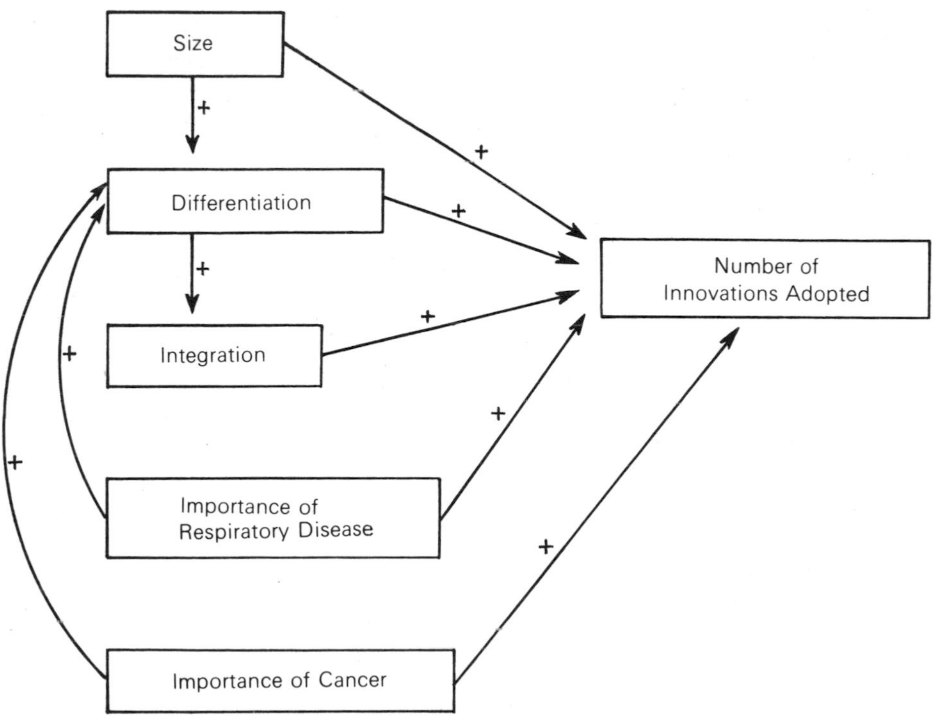

preprogrammed or, in Perrow's (1967) terminology, the technology has to be non-routine. In addition, the technology available to hospitals has evolved at an enormously rapid pace, particularly in the past 25 years and is continuing to evolve with the concomitant expansion of medical specialties. A "good" hospital, one that is well-adapted to these environmental conditions, must therefore be highly differentiated; that is, it must have many departments representing many medical specialties. At the same time, however, it must be well-integrated, with numerous committees coordinating the work of the various specialities.

The criteria for a "good" or effective hospital are less readily apparent than for an industrial firm. In the case of industrial organizations one can say that a "good" or effective firm is one that makes a profit, and there are widely accepted ways for determining levels of profitability. In the case of hospitals, one can say that a "good" hospital is one that gives high quality care. Although quality of care is itself difficult to measure, a necessary condition for high quality is availability of appropriate diagnostic and therapeutic capabilities. We would argue that this, in turn, means that the hospital must have medical innovations which have been judged by experts to be useful. Thus, applying the theoretical perspective of Lawrence and Lorsch to the analysis of hospitals, one should expect to find positive relationships among differentiation, integration and adoption of innovation.

The fact that hospitals vary in size must also be taken into account. As size—measured by the number of beds—increases, the number of cases in which innovations can be applied increases and the relative cost decreases. Thus, the probability that an innovation will be needed and hence adopted increases with the size of the hospital. In the same vein, increasing size makes the creation of specialized services easier, so one might expect a positive relationship between size and differentiation. Since we were predicting adoption of innovation in specific medical fields (respiratory disease in the U.S. and respiratory disease and cancer in France), it was also necessary to control for the importance of these specialties in the subject hospitals. This reasoning led us to develop the following model:

Measures

Size was measured by the number of beds in the hospital. Differentiation was measured by the number of different medical facilities and services in the hospital. Integration was operationalized as the number of times per year a number of different hospital committees met. The importance of the medical specialties of respiratory disease and, cancer, in France, to the hospital was a perceptual measure based on the chief medical officer's response to a question about the role of that specialty to the hospital (See Appendix I). The innovation score for each hospital is based on the number of medical innovations adopted. A Guttman scale analysis of the innovation data resulted in a coefficient of reproducibility of .92, thus justifying treatment of the individual innovations in an additive fashion (Gordon *et. al.*, 1975; Moch, 1976).

The model and measures are intentionally simple. Although committee meetings, for example, are obviously only one structural vehicle for integrating an organization, they are commonly used. Certainly no attempt to measure integration would be complete without taking meetings into account. Hospital structure is complex, and we do not pretend to have mapped this complexity in the same way that other researchers such as Camstock and Scott (1977) have. Rather, our strategy was to build a model which reflected some basic theoretical cornerstones of the structuralist paradigm, and to examine the explanatory power of the model both in the context of hospital innovation and in the context of cross-national comparisons.

Results

The first analysis performed examined the intercorrelations among the variables for the two samples as a whole. If the patterns of correlations were in the predicted direction and comparable for the two samples (taking the differences in sample size into account) then we would have found support for the argument made most forcefully by the Aston group (Hickson *et. al.*, 1974) that organization structures are culture free, as well as for the predictive validity of the Lawrence and Lorsch contingency perspective cross-nationally. If the pattern were different, it might be argued that cultural differences were involved. The results of the first analysis are presented in Table 1.

These results generally support the Lawrence and Lorsch perspective for

Table 1

CORRELATIONS AMONG DIFFERENTIATION, INTEGRATION AND SIZE IN FRENCH AND AMERICAN HOSPITALS

	French Hospitals					
	1	2	3	4	5	
1. Innovation	—					
2. Integration	−.38**	—				
3. Differentiation	.29**	−.15	—			
4. Size	.10	−.01	.84**	—		
5. Importance of Respiratory Disease	.34**	−.17	.42**	.35**	—	
6. Importance of Cancer	−.08	.22	−.16	−.18	.16	n = 137
	U.S. Hospitals					
	1	2	3	4		
1. Innovation	—					
2. Integration	.23**	—				
3. Differentation	.68**	.22**	—			
4. Size	.21**	.08	.24**	—		
5. Importance of Respiratory Disease	.36**	.09	.31**	.15		n = 489

** p<.001

U.S. hospitals. The relationship among all variables are significant and positive, as predicted, with the exception of that between size and integration. The French data, however, do not support the perspective. The only relationship that was significant and in the predicted direction was that between size and differentiation. The relationship between integration and innovation was significant but in the opposite direction to that predicted. All other relationships were non-significant and in the opposite direction to that predicted.

The correlations by themselves do not enable us to determine the explanatory power of the model as a whole. To examine the amount of variance in innovation adoption accounted for by the independent variables in the model, multiple regression analysis was used. The results for the two samples are presented in Table 2.

The data in Table 2 indicate that the model's explanatory power is greater for U.S. hospitals than for French hospitals, although even for the U.S. hospitals it is unable to account for half of the variance in innovation adoption. What is most interesting is the fact that the variables in the model behave roughly as predicted in the case of the U.S. hospitals—at least all of the beta weights are positive—whereas in the case of the French hospitals they do not. Integration has a significant but negative effect on innovation adoption, as does size, the reverse of what was predicted. Thus the plausibility of the model is severely questioned by the French data, and therefore, so, is the culture free context of organization thesis.

Table 2

REGRESSION RESULTS FOR FRENCH AND U.S. HOSPITALS

	French Hospitals		U.S. Hospitals	
	B	*Beta*	*B*	*Beta*
Differentiation	.50	.46*	.47	.56*
Integration	−.10	−.29*	.02	.05
Importance of Respiratory Disease	1.37	.23*	.66	.18*
Importance of Cancer	−.00	.07	—	—
Size	.45	−.35*	.00	.01
R^2	.29		.44	

*p<.05
**p<.01

RECOGNIZING DIVERSITY: SUB-SAMPLE ANALYSES

Based on our experiences with data collection in France and in light of our growing familiarity with the French system of health care, the regression results did not come as a total surprise. In an effort to clarify these results, we elected to carry out a number of sub-sample analyses. It was possible that by including all French hospitals in the same sample we were confounding the analysis. There is a distinction in France between "hôpitaux" and "cliniques" with the former being public institutions and the latter private. With only one exception, all of the 27 "hôpitaux" were larger than any of the 103 "cliniques." This could be responsible for some sign reversal in the regression. The French government controlled and regulated the former to a much greater extent than the latter. Because the "cliniques" are "for profit" institutions, it would not be unreasonable to expect that they might have evolved different configurations of differentiation, integration and size to meet their own needs. For this reason, we felt that it would be appropriate to examine each group of organizations separately. In the case of the U.S. hospitals the distinctions were less clear, but there were potentially important differences among them. We reasoned that Vetern's Administration hospitals, owned and operated by an agency of the federal government, might be analogous to the French "hôpitaux" whereas proprietary hospitals—private, for profit institutions—might be analogous to the French "cliniques." It was possible, in other words, that differences in the nature of ownership and control were confounding relationships among size, differentiation, integration and innovation and that once they were controlled for, the patterns of relationships among variables would be similar. Thus, it was decided to compare V.A. hospitals with French "hôpitaux" and proprietary hospitals with French "cliniques." A third group of U.S. hospitals, community general hospitals, for which there was no French counterpart, would

Table 3

SUB-SAMPLE ANALYSIS

	French Hôpitaux					
	1	2	3	4	5	
1. Innovation	—					
2. Integration	−.24	—				
3. Differentiation	.19	.04	—			
4. Size	−.13	.20	.83**	—		
5. Importance of Respiratory Disease	.18	.17	.09	.18	—	
6. Importance of Cancer	−.35*	.35*	.10	−.13	.15	n = 27 R^2 = .49
	U.S.V.A. Hospitals					
	1	2	3	4		
1. Innovation	—					
2. Integration	.10	—				
3. Differentiation	.24	.23	—			
4. Size	.49*	.21	.12	—		
5. Importance of Respiratory Disease	.41*	−.36*	−.10	.52*		n = 15 R^2 = .33
	French Cliniques					
	1	2	3	4	5	
1. Innovation	—					
2. Integration	−.44**	—				
3. Differentiation	.21	−.38**	—			
4. Size	.13	−.12	.45**	—		
5. Importance of Respiratory Disease	.42**	−.27*	.08	.01	—	
6. Importance of Cancer	.11	.06	.09	.01	.33	n = 103 R^2 = .30
	U.S. Proprietary Hospitals					
	1	2	3	4		
1. Innovation	—					
2. Integration	.07	—				
3. Differentiation	.46*	.19	—			
4. Size	.56**	.19	.58**	—		
5. Importance of Respiratory Disease	.30*	−.04	.37*	.26		n = 28 R^2 = .46

* $p < .05$
** $p < .01$

be analyzed separately. The results of these analyses are presented in Table 3.

The results of the sub-sample analyses led us to draw a number of conclusions. First, the hypothesis that French hôpitaux and American V.A. hospitals would exhibit similar patterns of intercorrelation among size, differentiation, integration and innovations as a consequence of similar ownership and control was not supported, nor was a similar hypothesis regarding French cliniques and American proprietary hospitals. Furthermore, the total amounts of variance explained by the model differed considerably from one to the other. This led us to conclude that comparison of hospitals in the U.S. and France using the theory and methods of one of the dominant paradigms in organizational sociology was problematic. The only consistent relationships were those between differentiation and size and, to a lesser extent, between differentiation and innovation. In the case of the French organizations, the relationship between differentiation and innovation was true by definition (a legal requirement). One hardly needs the sociology of organizations to explain it.

A second conclusion was that the prototypical hospital—as defined by the tenets of contingency theory—is the U.S. community general hospital. The subsample analyses revealed that the original model was supported by the data from community general hospitals. Large, highly differentiated, highly integrated community general hospitals are most effective. More than half of the variance in innovation adoption was accounted for by the model.

This second conclusion led to a third: it is dangerous to accept a nominal definition of organizational type and expect that all organizations included within that definition will exhibit similar patterns of structure and/or behavior. This observation is not new. It has been made with respect both to rehabilitation organizations by Kimberly (1975), and in more general terms (Kimberly, 1976; McKelvey, 1975). It is sharply reinforced by the data presented here. French "hôpitaux" are different from French "cliniques" and American V.A. hospitals are different from American proprietary hospitals which, in turn, are different from American community general hospitals. To include them all in the same sample without controlling for this difference is to assume that it doesn't matter.

So far our comments have been aimed at analysing and interpreting the results of the statistical analysis of our model as if we were on solid ground both with the model and the operationalization of the study variables. We have presented these comments as if we believed in what we wrote. We would have three years ago. We don't today. Why then did we bother to go through this presentation? We felt it was necessary to make every possible effort to give a fair test to the model, to find identical and good operationalization across the two cultures. As explained in the introduction, these large studies were made by researchers who participated in both the French and the American data collection and analysis, who knew the two cultures, and were committed to be as rigorous as possible in this cross-cultural comparison. It failed, not as a research endeavor, but as an attempt to test the general validity of the model, and we believe that the different stages of our thinking should be presented. It is doubtful that research proceeds as shown in journal articles, whereas in 99 per cent of the cases, we see success stories.

A measure of integration which would be a close operationalization of the concept and was identical in the two cultures was the goal of this research. The only common mechanism of integration found was that of committee meetings at the hospital level. In both countries these meetings have some integrating functions but they are not always aimed at coordinating the activities of the different departments. This is even truer in France than it is in the United States, where committees meet because it is a legal requirement and where little is done during these meeting to effectively integrate the multiple functions of the organization. However, this is the only formal mechanism that does exist.

The differentiation of hospitals was also measured by computing the number of different medical facilities and services present in each of them. We are aware that this could be called complexity and not differentiation, and, in the case of public hospitals in France, that this is not a response to local demand, but rather depends on special authorization from the Health Ministry at the rational level.

It was also assumed that the number of new respiratory disease items was a measure of organizational innovation. It has since been discovered, in the French study, that the number of innovations adopted in the field of respiratory diseases are almost unrelated to the number of innovations in the field of cancer treatment. This raises a basic question to most of the studies on diffusion of innovation in organizations where identical assumptions are made and never tested. We think that these limitations may go further than the model presented here.

Finally, in order to understand hospital innovation in the U.S. and France it is necessary to move beyond the comparative structuralist paradigm and perhaps ask somewhat different questions. Lammers (1977), Van Doorn (1977) and Brossard and Maurice (1975), among others, would introduce socio-political, historical and cultural factors into the analysis of organizations. We should also question some of the basic assumptions of organizational research. The remainder of this paper sketches the nature of these concerns and some directions to be taken.

REASSESSING THE ORIGINAL DESIGN: SECOND THOUGHTS ABOUT BASIC ASSUMPTIONS

The original design for the cross-national study was based on a theoretical and empirical perspective of Anglo-Saxon origin. As one looks at the results obtained by working within the paradigm, it becomes clear that it was no accident that the community general hospitals in the U.S. most closely approximated the model. Underlying the comparative structuralist perspective, and in the sociology of organizations in general, are two key assumptions.

The organization is itself an appropriate level of analysis for understanding the adoption of innovation. Organizational structure is the most important constraint on effectiveness. By changing structure, management can improve effectiveness. For this assumption to be valid one has also to assume that the organization is autonomous, that it has the capacity to make decisions about structure and outcomes. Although this assumption appears to be valid to some extent with respect to the French "cliniques" and American proprietary and community general hospitals, it is highly questionable in the case of the French "hôpitaux" and the American V.A. hospitals. The problem of autonomy and decisional discretion was pointed out by Argyris (1972) in his critique of Blau and Schoenherr's (1971) study of employment agencies. A strong case could be made that the employment agencies studied were not free-standing organizations but were rather branches of a central organization and thus had limited decisional discretion and structure mandated by the central authority rather than deliberately chosen at the local level. And of course the capacity to make decisions does not guarantee that they will be made. Structure does not evolve solely in response to managerial imperatives to improve efficiency. It is also the legacy of struggles for power unfolding over time. Organizations do not develop in a social vacuum. The issue cuts deeper. For some types of questions, it is more useful to seek answers outside organizations and to view organizations as representing instruments in struggles for power and influence in particular societies. This is not to say that the effects of organizations are negligible or that the organizational level of analysis is inappropriate for all questions. Rather it is to say that the comparative structuralist perspective is limited in its explanatory power. The organizational level may or may not be the limiting factor, depending on the issue involved.

A second assumption that has to be questioned is the notion that one organization equals another. This notion flows directly from the preceding one, because if one accepts the premise that the organization is an appropriate level of analysis, this means that organizations have special qualities or intrinsic characteristics, which distinguish them from other social aggregates and which make them more like each other than like any other collectivity. The dimensions which describe them should then be the same from one organization to the next, and the ways in which they are measured should be identical. This assumption is most clearly articulated in the work of Blau and his colleagues, although the work of Haas, Hall and Johnson (1963) should perhaps have been a signal that its tenability was questionable. Organizations in this view are governed by universal laws, applicable, under certain conditions, to all organizations no matter what their culture. Our research, however, strongly suggested that in these two samples of organizations, both of which shared the goal of patient care, one organization did not equal another one; it is not obvious that these are animals of the same species; and this fact has implications for understanding patterns of innovation adoption in medical technology.

Once these assumptions are made explicit, the dominant paradigm can be critically examined more easily. In this case, it was only after experiencing some problems in data collection and then pursuing their implications that questions were raised. In a sense, then, the results of this research have as much relevance for the sociology of knowledge as for the sociology of organizations in that they illustrate some of the constraints influencing the research process and the production of new knowledge.

SHIFTING THE ANALYTIC FRAME: THE SOCIO-POLITICAL CONTEXT OF ORGANIZATIONS

The results of this research and reflections on it have led to a shift in the analytical frame of reference and indicates a need for much greater emphasis on the socio-political context within which organizations function. In the remainder of the paper, the conceptual foundations of the approach will be discussed and illustrated by reconsidering the adoption of innovations in French hospitals.

An organization is not an empty shell in which hierarchical structure and departmentalization determine the satisfaction of organizational members, the utilization of resources, and its survival. An organization is also a place where struggle between those who dominate and those who are dominated unfolds; where conflict between those who have technical knowledge and those who have legal, commercial, or administrative knowledge is commonplace; where a sort of equilibrium among opposing forces is established over time and through history. Rationality is not only limited by information systems, it is also produced by certain groups as a consequence of knowledge, ownership rights and belonging to certain social classes. Organizations, therefore, change with groups and the legitimation of their power. Organizations are also instruments which are designed to solidify power or to facilitate the strategies of different social groups. This is why organizations having identical functions, such as hospitals, are different from one country to another. Technological determination exists to a much lesser extent than organizational sociologists of today would admit because technical rationality is only one rationality among several.

The organization is thus, at the same time, a point of contact between groups and an issue for these same groups and for others. The analogy which makes the most sense is neither that of a machine nor that of a living organism, but that of a battlefield. On this field are several armies fighting for several positions. This battlefield is part of a larger war. What takes place on the battlefield cannot be understood without taking more global strategies into account. For this reason behaviors which seem abberent in the immediate context in which they take place can become understood in the context of the more general situation. In the long run social groups can change the geography by changing the rules of the game. The terrain is not fixed. The contesting groups make up rules which are not eternal, even if they evolve slowly in some cases. To pursue this military image one step further, a comparison can be made to the progress in war machines such as planes, tanks, and other missles, which have, in a certain sense, changed the terrain by making strategies change their conceptions of war. A kilometer is not the same thing for a wagon and a supersonic airplane.

Rejecting the organization as a unique level of explanation does not mean that the organization does not exist or that its effects are negligible. It simply means that it is not sufficient if one wants to understand what organizations do. Other units of analysis from the society need to be introduced. The term "social groups" may appear vague, and in effect it is, because a union, an association, or even a group of individuals having comparable status and training, such as engineers, are all examples of social groups. The power of these groups depends, in part, on their formal existence. Therefore, we are especially interested in social units having a charter or some legal status, and whose goal is the defense of certain interests ("interests" being defined either in the narrow sense of monetary benefits, or in the broader sense of an ethical concept). For example, associations which fight laws against abortion are interest groups which advocate a concept and not a monetary benefit.

Groups have, at any given point, a *logique d'action*, a rationale for their behavior. As Karpik (1972) says, *logiques d'action* are the principles by virtue of which individuals and groups organize their behavior. However, we do not believe that *logiques d'action* are a faction which is sufficiently stable to serve as a central focus of analysis. Groups change their behavior because the situation and the power balances have shifted and their old rationale is no longer adapted to defense of their interests. But if the *logiques d'action* cannot serve as the focus of analysis, they are nonetheless important. It is essential to know the relationship between ideology and action in order to understand the evolution of the social system, even if we do not expect to find parallel between ideology and social organization. Thus, to understand the functioning of organizations, an important part of our analysis has to be devoted to formal groups for which these organizations are an issue, either because the members of these groups work there or because these organizations are an important resource in their strategy. As a consequence, our analysis cannot take place outside the historical and social context. Also the social groups which are involved will vary according to the problem studied. For example, as will be shown later, the medical fraternity in France is united and monolithic for certain problems, but divided for others; and the degree of unity or division of the profession depends on the problems being studied. There is no sociology without ethnology.

This way of approaching organizational analysis will be viewed by some as unscientific, and it is true that we are far from searching for universal laws, even if we believed that the process of control and domination between groups didn't take on an infinity of forms. We are also far from certain statistical models which attempt to determine causal relationships. It is evident that the phenomena studied are over determined, that is, there are a few cases and many explanatory variables.

THE CASE OF HEALTH CARE IN FRANCE

The earlier analyses suggested that "hôpitaux" and "cliniques" in France are different and that these differences had consequences for their adoption behavior. To know that they are different in a statistical sense is not necessarily to understand why. These institutions have a history and a set of origins which are different. The indicators of these historical differences are their size, the number of activities which take place within them, the kind of services they offer and the kinds of innovations that are found are rather than the evolution of technology or the quality of their management.

Without going back to the origins of these institutions and to the strategy of the medical profession one can note that there is a discontinuity between the size of the hospitals and the clinics. The smallest hospital in the sample has more beds than the largest clinic with one exception. Moreover, at the national level, according to statistics from 1973, the average size of a clinique is 38 beds while that of a hospital is 240 beds if one only counts the short term beds and 389 if one counts long term and psychiatric beds as well. This discontinuity should sensitize the researcher to the fact that there might be differences in the basic nature of these establishments. The number of beds in a hospital, whether it is public or private, has historical origins, and these origins can be traced to the conception of the establishments and to the utilization which different pressure groups have made of them over time.

In analyzing the health system in the U.S., Friedson (1971) spoke of the dominance of the medical profession. The adjective "dominant" does not fit the French situation. "Independent control" and "monopoly of means of production" capture the effects of the strategy pursued by the medical profession in France. Of course, this strategy did not develop in a vacuum. The medical profession used the institutional terrains in a different fashion. Also the advantages furnished by the technical evolution of care have not been utilized in the same way in clinics and hospitals.

A clinic above all else, was conceived as a *means* which permitted one or more doctors to practise their art. It is not chance alone that determined that these doctors were most often surgeons or obstetrician-gynecologists. In the case of these specialties the patients have to undergo certain kinds of interventions and must be carefully watched during the days which follow the intervention. Therefore, it is necessary to have an institution with operating rooms, surgical personnel, and so on. (This necessarily is less pressing in the case of doctors if they choose a special clientele such as patients with chronic illnesses, or geriatric patients.) This explains why in such private clinics, surgical and ob-gyn beds represent 75 per cent of the total (the figure is 33 per cent in the case of hospitals). The clinics were thus created to permit certain doctors to practice their art.

The ideal for these doctors was to financially control the institutions. The type of ownership of the 105 clinics studied is instructive. Five are owned by a single doctor; nine are owned entirely by the doctors who work in the establishment, that is, the only stockholders are doctors who are working directly for the clinic (this number may be greater in reality because very often it is close relatives who are stockholders). Thus in 13 per cent of the cases the institution is totally controlled by the physicians who work there.

In other cases, however, the physicians or their families were not able to generate the necessary funds. Therefore, they either worked for charitable institutions or found private funds. In many cases one sees a form of organization in which there is ownership of the building and the materials by a corporation which offers not only financial advantages to the owners, but which also assures the medical staff complete freedom; the only charge being to pay rent to the corporation that owns the building. The reason for this independence is that the interests of the doctors working in the clinic and those of the person or persons who have advanced the funds are more or less the same.

The private clinics, therefore, have legal forms which are analogous to those found in other sectors of the economy. However, it should not be concluded that they are organizations like any other. In only about 38 per cent of the cases does at least one physician in the clinic have his actual office within the clinic's walls, and in only 10 per cent of the cases are his office personnel paid by the clinic. We are thus faced with a form of organization where the expenses associated with principal personnel are not paid by the organization. It is as though the salary of the office personnel for a chief executive officer of a business firm was paid directly by the chief executive officer and not by the firm. Unlike the physician, the chief executive officer is a wage earner but this is not a sufficient reason to explain this phenomonon which, moreover, has some exceptions.

This phenomenon, which may seem somewhat trivial, is very characteristic of the conception that physicians, surgeons, and gynecologists have of the clinics in which they work. It is a means to an end. They do not think of their practice as being formally organized. Thus, they often pay even their office staff as though they were in private practice.

Another fact which sheds some light on the basic thesis is that 62 out of 99 clinics do not have any sort of medical committee whatsoever. Thus, there is absolutely no formal coordination mechanism between the different individuals who practice in the clinics. Although these establishments are relatively small, size does not explain the absence of medical committees. Hospitals of similar size in other countries have such committees. Furthermore, in services of comparable size in public hospitals there are frequent meetings of the medical staff to discuss difficult cases. Such is not the case in the clinics, where the patients are not defined as patients of the establishment or of the particular service, but rather of a particular physician. The patients are the responsibility of particular doctors who, in many cases, have been especially sought out by the patients. Medical staff have complete autonomy, both *vis a vis* the rest of society and other physicians practicing in the clinic. Internal controls are at an absolute minimum. When the physician does not own the clinic, his only constraint is to keep patients coming in to ensure profitable operations. But is this really a constraint? It would certainly appear that it is in the physician's own best interests to have many patients.

The history is not the same for the hospitals in France. In the beginning it was not a question of creating a means of production for professionals in the sense that it was for the clinics, but rather of constructing asylums where the poor and the disinherited could be lodged and, perhaps, eventually cured. Hospitals initially were a form of hostel. Size was primarily a function of the number of indigent people in the catchment area. One or more physicians were attached to each asylum and came there to practice a form of collective charitable medicine, but it was not the central location of medical practice. Only recently has the evolution of technological progress led the medical profession to consider this institution essential. Starting out as a form of institution for the poor, the hospital became the place where the means necessary to practice modern medicine were concentrated. In fact, the means themselves became so important and so expensive that only the state could regulate them. (When we speak of hospitals, we are not talking about university based hospitals. For two centuries they have played a central but special role, well described by Foucault (1963) and Steudler (1972), in which the tactic of the medical profession was not exactly the same. However, even there the success was total because 100 per cent of the teachers on the medical faculties are doctors, whereas this monopoly does not exist in any other country in the world.)

The non-university hospitals were transformed from poorhouses to prestigious centers of medical practice for contemporary medicine. This evolution took place very rapidly, which explains why these institutions still have a number of their old functions existing side by side with modern medical services and sophisticated emergency surgery in intensive care and reanimation. The current trend is toward eliminating all of the old functions and retaining only the technical role. This evolution is, of course, favorable to the group in control, i.e., the medical profession.

In the context of this evolution one can ask how the medical profession could maintain its independence in the face of increasing governmental intervention. The interests of the state, after all, might well be different from those of the medical profession. The solution was to create services, in the same fashion as in the university hospitals, where the chief of service was the absolute master and to multiply these services following the development of modern medicine. This strategy was not without problems. However, only this solution allowed the independence of the physicians in their particular service, a large number of positions for physicians wanting to practice in these institutions, and the use of modern and specialized equipment which is a source of prestige, all at the same time. A different solution emerged in the United States. The difference is in large measure a function of the control that the medical profession exercises and its desire for absolute independence even within its own ranks.

The absence of any significant correlation between the size of a French hospital and the number of times that medical committees meet is not surprising, given this pattern of historical development. In contrast to the U.S., there are no utilization committees, tissue committees, etc., at the level of the hospital itself in France. There are, of course, certain medical committees which function in a consultation capacity, but their role is usually limited to the management of the hospital and they do not deal in a direct way with medical affairs. Each physician, therefore, reigns supreme over his barony which is called the service, the only control being medical ethics.

On these different terrains we find elements of a similar strategy. Familiarity with this strategy provides explanatory leverage which is lacking in technological or structural determinism. For example, we are able to understand why hospitals in the U.S. and France have evolved different structural configurations even though they may currently have similar objectives, technologies and size; and why coordination mechanisms do not exist in French cliniques, although contemporary organization theory would predict their existence.

Structural configurations are the product of strategy not only at the organizational level (Chandler, 1962; Child, 1972) but also at the level of groups which transcend the organization. When these groups are different there is no reason to expect that structural configurations of the organizations they develop should be identical or should have similar effects on a given outcome, such as the adoption of innovations. This is not to say that structure is irrelevant for the adoption of innovation, only that, by themselves, structural explanations are incomplete.

CONCLUSION

In this paper we have explored organizations in the context of a cross-national study of hospital innovations. In the course of our efforts to understand innovation, we have been constrained to reflect critically on contemporary Anglo-Saxon organization theory and have found it wanting in several dimensions. These results are both illustrative of some of the weaknesses of contemporary theory and suggestive of new approaches.

The results of both the quantitative and qualitative analyses show that the culture-free context of organization structures hypothesis is open to serious question. Relationships among indices of structure were different in U.S. and French hospitals. and historical analysis of the development of the medical profession and hospitals in France suggests that cultural differences help explain why the relationships are different. Such explanations may hold true for other kinds of organizations, however. It may be, for example, that relatively new organizations based on relatively new technologies, located in different countries, do not reflect cultural differences to such an extent. The process of rapid technology transfer may lead to structural comparability across national boundaries. This is certainly an area where more research needs to be done.

Our enthusiasm for contemporary organization theory as a vehicle for predicting organizational adoption of innovation has been somewhat tempered by this analysis. Contemporary theory and research tends to take an atomistic view of organizations. An expanded perspective, in which greater attention is paid to social, historical and political factors as they bear upon the question of who stands to gain and who stands to lose as innovations are developed and diffuse in a population of potential adopters, would be beneficial. In other words, greater attention has to be paid to the environmental context of innovation (Kimberly, 1978). Attributes of organizational structure are by no means the sole determinant of innovation adoption. Innovation adoption can play multiple roles in the strategies of groups who control organizations or who dominate the possibilities for the creation of new organizations. Innovation can be a weapon as well as a problem-focused solution. This means that research on innovation adoption needs to be, at the same, more clinical and more institutional. Researchers need to be less constrained by narrow conceptions of scientific research and more concerned with depth of understanding. This paper may serve both as an indicator of some possibilities and as an example of how much remains to be done.

REFERENCES

Argyris, Chris. *The Applicability of Organizational Sociology*. New York: Cambridge
1972 University Press.

Becker, Selwyn W., and Gerald Gordon. "An Entrepreneurial Theory of Formal
1966 Organizations, Part I: Patterns of Formal Organization." *Administrative Science Quarterly*. 11:315–344.

Blau, Peter M., and Richard Schoenherr *The Structure of Organizations*. New York: Basic
1971 Books.

Brossard, Michel, and Marc Maurice. "Existe-il un model universel des organizations?"
1974 *Sociologie du Travail*. 6:188–197.

Chandler, Alfred D., Jr. *Strategy and Structure*. Cambridge, Mass.: M.I.T. Press.
1962

Child, John. "Organization Structure, Environment and Performance: The Role of
1972 Strategic Choice." *Sociology*. 6:1–22.

Comstock, Donald E., and W. Richard Scott. "Technology and the Structure of Subunits:
1977 Distinguishing Individual and Work Group Effects." *Administrative Science Quarterly*. 22:177–202.

Foucault, Michel. *La naissance de la Clinique*. Paris: Presses Universitaires de France.
1963

Friedson, Eliot. *Professional Dominance.* New York: Dodd-Mead.
1971

Gordon, Gerald, E. Morse, S. Gordon, J. de Kervasdoue, J. Kimberly, M. Moch, and
1974 D. Swartz. "Organizational Structure, Environmental Diversity, and Hospital Adoption of Medical Innovations." In A. Kaluzny, J. Gentry and J. Veney (eds.), *Innovation in Health Care Organizations*: 75–89. Chapel Hill: University of North Carolina Department of Health Administration.

Gordon, Gerald, John R. Kimberly, and Ann MacEachron "Some Considerations in the
1975 Design of Problem-Solving Research on the Diffusion of Medical Technology." In W. J. Abernathy, A. Sheldon and C. K. Prahalad (eds.), *The Management of Health Care*: 29–61. Cambridge, Mass.: Ballinger.

Gordon, Gerald, and Lawrence Fisher. *Diffusion of Innovations in Medicine.* Cambridge,
1975 Mass.: Ballinger.

Hass, Eugene, Richard H. Hall, and Norman J. Johnson. "The Size of the Supportive
1963 Component in Organizations: A Multi-Organizational Analysis." *Social Forces.* 42:9–17.

Hickson, David J., C. R. Hinings, C. J. McMillan, and A. R. Schwitter. "The Culture-
1974 Free Context of Organizational Structure: A Tri-national Comparison." *Sociology.* 8:1–14.

Karpik, Lucien. "Organisations et Logiques d'Action." *Sociologie du Travail.* 4:38–56.
1972

Kimberly, John R. "Classification and Organizational Analysis: The Case of
1975 Rehabilitation Organizations." *Western Sociological Review.* 6:47–60.

———. "Organizational Size and the Structuralist Perspective: A Review, Critique,
1976 and Proposal." *Administrative Science Quarterly.* 21:571–597.

———. "Managerial Innovation." In P. C. Nystrom and W. H. Strabuck (eds.),
1978 *Handbook of Organizational Design, Vol. I.* New York: Elsevier/North Holland.

Lammers, Cornelius J. "Organizational Sociology: Past, Present, and Future." In
1977 C. J. Lammers and D. J. Hickson (eds.), *Toward a Comparative Sociology of Organizations.* Amsterdam: Elsevier.

Lawrence, Paul R., and Jay W. Lorsch. *Organization and Environment.* Boston: Harvard
1967 Graduate School of Business Administration.

McKelvey, Bill. "Guidelines for the Empirical Classification of Organizations."
1975 *Administrative Science Quarterly.* 20:509–525.

Moch, Michael. "Structure and Organizational Resource Allocation." *Administrative*
1976 *Science Quarterly.* 21:661–674.

Perrow, Charles. "A Framework for the Comparative Analysis of Organizations."
1967 *American Sociological Review.* 32:194–208.

Steudler, Francois. *L'Hospital en Observation.* Paris: Seuil.
1972

Van Doorn, Jacques. "Organizations and the Social Order: A Pluralist Approach." In
1977 C. J. Lammers and D. J. Hickson (eds.), *Toward a Comparative Sociology of Organizations.* Amsterdam: Elsevier.

Zaltman, Gerald, Robert Duncan, and Jony Holbek. *Innovations and Organizations.*
1973 New York: Wiley.

Technological *Versus* Cultural Imperatives: A Critical Evaluation

Continuing our previously established pattern, we provide, in this Chapter, a critical evaluation of the papers presented in Section II. The commentators are:

(1) John B. Miner, Georgia State University
(2) Pjotr Hesseling, Erasmus University
(3) William H. Money, Kent State University

Comments on Beres and Portwood's Paper

PROBLEM OF RESEARCH IN CROSS-CULTURAL RESEARCH—
John B. Miner

This paper describes an attempt to test a single proposition: culture, the ecological/demographic environment, the social/organizational environment, and personal circumstances each influence an individual's frame of reference and pattern of behavior. This is a causal statement. Implicit in it is the view that past studies which merely contrast two or more nations or cultures on certain dependent variables may well over-estimate the effects of culture by attributing to it the confounded influences of differences in ecological/demographic and social/organizational variables. Furthermore, the authors consider cultural and national boundaries to be separate and distinct; in particular, they are concerned regarding cultural heterogeneity within national boundaries and the implications it may have for the interpretation of multi-nation comparative research.

Conceptual and Methodological Problems. The research suffers from a number of limitations, many of which the authors fully acknowledge. Most pronounced among these is the fact that the data derive from a national survey which was carried out for purposes quite independent of those inherent in the current research. Reliance on these data forced the authors to omit testing the roles of "organizational environment" as an independent variable and "pattern of behavior" as a dependent variable, as stated in their basic proposition. Their only dependent variable is a single item, dichotomized index of extrinsic *versus* intrinsic work motivation of unknown but probably low reliability. The alternatives appear to provide relatively good fits for the Protestant cultures of Europe (intrinsic) and the black cultures of Africa (extrinsic), but do not appear to permit as adequate a test of hypotheses related to the Catholic cultures of Europe.

Another difficulty of indeterminate significance relates to the fact that the male and female samples are entirely non-overlapping in age. The men are age 45–59 and the women are age 30–44. Given that longitudinal analyses were not carried out, it is impossible to determine whether these age differences might have contributed to what are interpreted as sex differences—the differential relationships involving tenure for instance.

The basic proposition is stated in causal terms. Do the data permit causal inference? The answer has to be that they are consistent with such an interpretation and that the hypothesized causal chain is an entirely possible explanation, but that is really all one can say. The documentation of the values and motives of past generations in Europe and Africa is of variable quality. It would have been desirable to have had hard data rather than interpretations of anthropological observations and artifactual evidence. The difficulties inherent in these sources appear to be particularly manifest with regard to the perceived role of work among the European women of past generations (Lomax and Berkowitz, 1972; Weber, 1904, 1922).

Finally, and this is not a major point, the authors appear to view culture and individual differences as distinct sources of variance in dependent variables such as intrinsic-extrinsic work motivation. An alternative position utilizes the reductionist argument and views the two as merely representing different levels of conceptualization and measurement (sociological and psychological) and thus as broadly overlapping (Wanous, 1974).

The Contributions of the Research. In spite of its limitations the research does demonstrate that wide intra-national cultural variations may well have their origins in the earlier cultures of Europe and Africa. This latter interpretation is strongly reinforced by the parallel study conducted by Kelley and Reeser (1973) who found considerable evidence that traditional Japanese values related to managerial behavior and organizational processes persist in Hawaiian branch bank managers of Japanese ancestry. Sizable differences in the hypothesized direction were found in comparisons with Caucasion managers in the same banks. Subsequent research by Kelley and Worthley (1974) involving samples of Japanese managers, offers additional support. Whether cultural variations as large as those found in the United States can be anticipated within other nations is of course an empirical question, but in many cases it seems unlikely.

The research also makes a strong case for the view that past research may often have over-estimated the effects of culture by failing to control for ecological/demographic and social/organizational differences among samples. This argument appears to be most applicable to studies that utilize a broad range of individuals spread widely throughout the societies. It is less applicable to research, such as that focused directly on business managers, which reduces, if it does not entirely hold constant, the influences of such factors as social class, education, organizational context, and the like. Thus, studies such as those by Haire, Ghiselli, and Porter (1966), England (1974) and Hofstede (1976) would appear to be relatively free of contaminating influences. It is interesting to note, however, that as in these studies, when extraneous factors are eliminated, cultural differences, although present, are often much smaller than might have been anticipated.

Data from a Study of Management Consultants. A particularly striking demonstration of what clearly appears to be culture-based differences is provided by a study done some years ago, which is not widely known to students of international management. The findings are contained in Table 1. This research utilized samples of management consultants employed by the same firm (Miner, 1971). On the evidence the samples are matched in terms of occupation, organization, sex (all are male), age (there is a 2-year difference favoring the non-U.S. group), education, and probably in a number of other aspects as well, including social class. The U.S. consultants are all citizens of the United States and work out of six different offices scattered across the country. The non-U.S. consultants work out of six offices also, but five of these are located in European countries—Great Britain, France, Germany, The Netherlands, and Switzerland; 2 of the 30 are employed in an office in Australia. None of the group are U.S. citizens and 87 per cent are citizens of European countries, predominantly those in which the firm's offices are located. The remainder are all citizens of countries whose cultures historically have been under a strong European influence.

The consultants were all administered the Tomkins-Horn Picture Arrangement Test (Tomkins and Miner, 1957) shortly after hiring. This test provides a number of different measures of work and social motivation and those which yielded statistically significant correlations with success criteria in one or both samples are noted in Table 1.

The success measures were obtained from a year-and-a-half to two-and-a-half years after hiring. The criteria used were: (1) an overall rating of effectiveness as a consultant; (2) a rating of potential for advancement into partnership in the firm (both were made by present partners located almost exclusively in the country of employment); (3) total compensation at the time of follow-up; (4) the rate of change in compensation since hiring; and (5) the *per diem* charge to clients made for the consultants' services. These five measures were all significantly intercorrelated in both samples with the majority of the coefficients falling in the .60's and some rising into the .90's.

The success measures reflect the highly pragmatic and adaptive values of the firm (Miner, 1974). A consultant is viewed as effective if he convinces clients he is effective. The *per diem* charge is raised as rapidly as client confidence will permit. Compensation increases are closely tied to client relationships. Thus, what is reflected in the success criteria is largely the perception of what constitutes good consulting services held by top level managers in U.S. and non-U.S. (predominantly European) companies respectively. The adaptive strategy has yielded handsome returns for the consulting firm as a whole both in the United States and in Europe; the firm is one of the most successful in the world.

However, it is apparent from Table 1 that adapting means something quite different in the U.S. than it does in Europe. In the U.S. social motivation is important, although not with peers, and working too hard, doing too much, perhaps attempting to implement recommendations too forcefully, yields

Table 1

HIGH SIGNIFICANT CORRELATIONS WITH A SUCCESS CRITERION MEASURE IN U.S. (N=51) AND NON-U.S.(N=30) SAMPLES OF MANAGEMENT CONSULTANTS FOR INDEXES OF WORK AND SOCIAL MOTIVATION

Motivational Indexes	*U.S. Consultants*		*Non-U.S. Consultants*	
	r	*p*	*r*	*p*
Work Motivation				
Desire to work when it is easy to do nothing	−.35	<.01	.42	<.05
Desire to work when doing nothing is made difficult	−.37	<.01	None significant	
Desire to work when challenged by problems in the work	−.31	<.05	None significant	
Desire to work when distracting temptations are present	−.42	<.01	.39	<.05
Desire to seek out work	−.31	<.05	.43	<.05
Desire to avoid work	.30	<.05	−.40	<.05
Overall work motivation	−.39	<.01	.37	<.05
Social Motivation				
Desire for social interaction in nonwork situations	.33	<.05	None significant	
Desire for social interaction with authority figures	.38	<.01	None significant	
Desire for group interaction with peers	−.28	<.05	None significant	
Desire for social interaction involving emotional support	.30	<.05	−.36	<.05
Desire to avoid social interaction	−.27	<.05	.37	<.05
Overall social motivation	.32	<.05	None significant	

negative results. It appears to be the consultant who likes to spend time with clients, but in a strictly planning and advisory role, who meets the expectations of the U.S. business culture. In contrast, in Europe, this type of social interaction is, if anything, viewed negatively. Furthermore, it is the active doer, the implementer, who is considered the best consultant. Clearly business values as regards the role of the consultant differ sharply in the two cultural contexts.

Conclusions. It is becoming increasingly evident that the study of culture and its effects can make a useful contribution to our understanding of organizations and their functioning. The explanatory power of cultural variables is probably under-estimated in the Beres and Portwood study due to the questionable nature of variance estimates from canonical correlations and the probable unreliability of the single item dependent variable. Nevertheless, the research does present convincing evidence of the key role of cultural variation. Future research in this area might well benefit from using designs that emphasize success criteria that are embedded in the values of the culture, as in the management consultant study. This approach should prove particularly effective in teasing out cultural variance.

Comments on England & Negandhi's Paper:

THE EXPLANATION OF CULTURE THROUGH USE OF REFERENCE GROUPS—*Pjotr Hesseling*

England and Negandhi present in their paper impressive arguments that culture is often a residual variable and that interfirm differences might be as much, if not more so, functions of such contextual variables as size, technology, location, and market conditions as they are of sociocultural variables. Since the 1950's we have been continuously plagued by the ambivalence of culture as an explaining factor. Prior to that culture was the domain of anthropologists studying tribes and national stereotypes, and management and organizational theorists stressed rationality in decision making for effective performance. Culture was all but ignored.

1. *European studies.* The transfer of American management and technology to Western European countries during the post war recovery (Marshall plan) stimulated reflections on inter-European variation in organizational functioning. Many of the European study teams visiting the U.S.A. tried to identify an appropriate European or national style in adopting management practices in industrialization. The inter-European evaluation of American know-how and practice has been a valuable contribution to European patterns of organization (Hofstede and Kassem, 1976).

2. *Developing countries.* The second trend, after the European recovery, was the transfer of Western technology and management to the so called third world. In this situation many of the European countries were heavily involved as former colonial masters and an impressive amount of data on language, history and local administration has been collected. Many of these studies were observed from some supposedly superior standpoint and referred to native or local habits (Williams, 1976). The re-interpretation of 'colonial' knowledge for autonomous development in each independent nation-state is in full operation and has not yet led to clearly identifiable new patterns of say Indonesian, Nigerian or Sudanese management. Political independence cannot be easily translated into an appropriate fit between aboriginal and imported sources of management and administration, as in the European case. The translation needs a long period of selective absorption and an autonomous research tradition within each nation state. It can be understood that the first period of independence in most cases thinly spread available imported knowledge and know-how through formal education and particularly through many new universities. An empirical research tradition did not exist and data were collected by visiting scholars with local assistance. The Haire studies and the various national studies in Harbison and Myers project on Industrialism and Industrial Man are good examples. It seems fair to locate England's and Negandhi's studies in this perspective.

3. Japanese studies. Parallel with the selective European absorption of management know-how and the Western impact on the third world, Japan's phenomenal growth impressed the research community. Many of us became intrigued by Japanese patterns of organization and management. After a more stereotypical approach, as exemplified by studies of R. Benedict (1967), and Abegglen (1973), many observers continue to probe for a detailed analysis and trying to capitalize on Japanese sources. Recently the European association for Japanese studies and many other national associations for Japanese studies have intensified the search for a more 'authentic' comparative approach (S.O.A.S. conference on modern Japan, April, 1977 and Uppsala conference in May 1977 are good examples). By 'authentic' here is meant that there is equal participation from the Japanese and European sides in concept development design and data in explaining Japanese phenomena.

THE IMPORTANCE OF REFERENCE GROUPS

This brief survey of three trends in cross-cultural studies of organizational functioning stresses the importance of reference groups. I welcome England's and Negandhi's suggestion for analyzing intra-national data along technological lines. Their paper indicates an important lesson for cross-cultural studies. The main question seems to be: what are relevant reference groups and how do we collect data to guarantee functional equivalence? It seems naive (by coincidence the English fifteenth century adjective 'naif' has the same root as 'native' and 'nation' and relates to the universal phenomenon of the importance of the place in which one is born) to start from research data as designed and collected by national researchers in each case, but I would defend such a claim for the future. The data on the workers in the steel industry represent the perceptions of people 'within the citadel' of an imported technology. In the Indian case it seems a fair judgment that work in the steel industry "offers regular work and promotion and predictable rewards, as against the chaos and terrifying dangers of life outside". In this case it seems legitimate to conclude that contextual variables explain more of workers' perceptions than sociocultural variables. But assume that we compare data on perceptions of officials within public administration e.g. in the department of social affairs in an advanced country, such as Holland, and a developing nation, such as Indonesia. In this case the legalistic tradition might be similar, but the interpretation of e.g. the poverty line as explained by president Suharto on 16 August 1977 and by the new Dutch cabinet in 1977, will be completely different. The sociocultural condition of each country is likely to explain more of the perceptions than technological or other contextual variables. Indeed, empirical data are lacking to prove this expectation. Also in a comparative study of workers' perception within the ministry of social affairs in various countries I accept the need of comparable reference groups e.g. in other ministries and I agree with the proposal of comparing firstly intra-national differences before one concludes differences as the impact of culture. As a general label 'culture' is inappropriate for comparative studies. It needs to be broken down into operational variables, and here methodology assumes prime importance.

SOME METHODOLOGICAL OBSERVATIONS

The quality of data depends on the methodology used to identify social reality. Interviews and questionnaires are the main vehicles in transforming social reality into research data. Particularly in developing countries, questionnaires and surveys seem to offer a quick and safe road towards data. Participation and direct observation studies are rare. Nevertheless the development of organization studies in the Western world seems to have started from practitioners and participant observers before data were corroborated and extended by questionnaires, surveys and more structured approaches. Many developing countries organization and administrative studies are undertaken by graduates from Western universities without prior experience in the practice of management or without participant observation. It can be expected that these graduates try to build a platform of data as rapidly as possible on borrowed methodology. There is no time for a careful test and retest of the labels used to describe 'work', 'decision', 'leader', 'motivation', or 'standard performance'. Moreover, the past presents an interrupted time series, where struggles for independence and revolutions prevent a longitudinal approach. The Biafra war in Nigeria and the so called Gestapu events in 1965 in Indonesia are good examples, where continuity in development and reconstruction is difficult. Comparative studies tend, therefore, to rely heavily on snap shot observations by questionnaires along specific dimensions.

Here again the Japanese case might offer some lessons. Japanese historical reflection is particularly strong and there seems no doubt that the adoption of Western knowledge and experience has been done very selectively over centuries. Many developing countries, however, have built centres for management and public administration upon very thin layers of authentic data.

THE FUTURE OF COMPARATIVE STUDIES

By way of confusion, I assume that comparative studies are in search for reference groups. There is no neutral set of data available to judge the performance, perceptions or values of a particular groups of workers, within an organization. For the moment England's and Negandhi's use of available data, in this case within the American context, is an imaginative and acceptable design for preventing the acceptance of a sociocultural explanation for organizational performance. I would welcome more observational and longitudinal data, but accept the proof. In each situation it seems better to start with contextual arguments, such as technology, size, salary and job requirements, and refer only to cultural arguments as a last resort. Cultural arguments can build easily a myth. I would emphasize the need for building empirical data on organizational functioning but starting from organizational phenomena in the third world and seeking one-to-one comparisons based upon functional equivalence. This will require the use of many reference groups. I hope that cross-cultural organization studies become more specific, apply a multi-method approach, start with understanding existing patterns of organization from within, and counterbalance the Western dominance.

Comments on Kervasdoue and Kimberly's Paper

PROBLEMS OF OPERATIONALIZING AND TESTING CROSS-NATIONAL PARADIGMS—*William H. Money*

This paper will review the paradigm provide by Kervasdoue and Kimberly and comment on the conclusion that ". . . there is no reason to expect that structural configurations of the organizations (in different groups) should be identical or should have similar effects on a given outcome such as the adoption of innovation." The authors reached this conclusion as a result of their attempts to predict hospital innovation cross-nationally. The authors have argued strongly that something (perhaps history and origin) is more important than structural configuration, technology, and management quality in influencing innovation adoption behavior and that structural configurations are products of group and organization level strategies.

The comments address three main questions. First, does the theory posed by Kervasdoue and Kimberly convincingly argue that U.S. and French hospitals should have similar or different structures and innovative adoption behavior? Alternatively, are there differences (which could be seen as cultural intervening or mediating variables) in either the U.S. or French hospital systems that suggest that the structural and innovation variables are or are not similarly related? Second, do these data (and their analyses) adequately test this structural paradigm? Finally, does the amended paradigm suggest a provocative starting point for the future comparison of hospitals or other organizations in a cross-national framework?

The Theory. The authors have sought to build a model that reflects "some basic theoretical cornerstones of the structuralists paradigm." However, their paper provides only a brief discussion of the theoretical definitions of their variables. It is difficult to determine if the same theory used to test these relationships is being used in each cultural setting. This conceptual problem is common in the structural literature in the United States. Analysis of the elements of the structuralist paradigm by Zald and Hair (1972) and Neuhauser and Anderson (1972) clearly point out that there is ". . . an enormous leap in the structural-comparative school between theoretical concepts and operational measures" (1972:108). These authors seem to imply relationships between their theory and their variables (as does the literature) rather than to clearly state their hypothesis. Hence, they too appear to be guilty of conceptual leaps that may limit their analyses before it has even begun.

A few examples of the relationships which require further clarification are presented below:

1. Why is the external milieu of the two different sets of hospitals assumed to be complex and turbulent. Although inputs are heterogeneous, hospitals regularly utilize statistical data (number of physicians, population demographics, previous history, etc.) to predict service utilization levels.
2. Why is the treatment of patients assumed to be non-routine in all institutions? Despite patients' demands (and frequent screams of

agony) routine procedures (and rules) are followed on many hospital admissions.

3. Must a "good" hospital be highly differentiated? Would data collected from many specialized hospitals support this assumption (i.e., children's, women's, rehabilitation, cancer treatment, burn, etc.)?

In summary, the theory (and structural paradigm) developed for this work is weak and requires more concise elaboration before the author's tests are conducted.

Operationalization of the Study Variables. The variables used in this study included innovative behavior (associated with "good" hospitals), integration (committees and meetings), size (measured by the number of beds), and differentiation (medical specialists). The brief discussion of the variables presented by the authors indicates that the methods used to operationalize each variable may have distorted the meaning of the concepts in the structural model. The authors' discussion of this issue does not demonstrate the severity of this problem in the research design. For example, a "good" hospital was assumed to be one with many departments representing many medical specialities (which should then be associated with innovation adoption behavior according to the implicit hypothesis). "Good" is a normative assumption in this research. A highly differentiated hospital (with many departments) may, in fact, be poorly managed, deliver a poor quality of care (and even have a *low* adoption rate for innovations). Similarly, well integrated hospitals should not be assumed to be represented by numerous committees (as the authors have done). Committees serve multiple purposes in U.S. hospitals, and perhaps very different ones in French institutions. For example, numerous committees are required by hospitals which wish to be accredited by the Joint Commission on Accreditation of Hospitals (1970), but the mere presence of a committee indicates little about the quality of the integrative efforts (Lorsch and Allen, 1973). Consider the numerous error sources in this variable. The number of meetings held may be high, but few physicians may attend. In fact, hospitals may even have physicians meet once, and count this as several committee meetings. The assumption that integration is represented by committees is not well supported for American or French hospitals by the authors. The dependent innovation measures of respiratory disease technology was assumed to be representative of response to innovation in general. This assumption is relatively weak, as the authors indicate, and should be explicitly examined. U.S. hospital purchasing decisions (for innovative equipment) are frequently made or not made because of budget constraints, or attempts to placate physicians who are unhappy with hospital resources in their specialty. Finally, size (as measured by number of beds) is a *notoriously* weak variable in the hospital literature. U.S. hospitals frequently report beds approved for use, but not equipped for service in many areas, or for which the hospital has insufficient staff. Previous research findings (Zald and Hair, 1972) illustrate this point. Extremely low correlations have been found between size (beds), and the number of medical specialties in hospitals.

In short, the operationalization of variables by these authors leads one to wonder what theoretical concept were actually being measured in the study in the U.S. hospitals. The authors' brief discussion of the comparability of the U.S. concepts to the French experience limits the ability of the reader to understand differences or similarities found in the data. According to available data (Roemer, 1976), the medical staff organization in France is quite different from that in the U.S. Specialists are seldom paid by patients, and usually receive only a small honorarium (part-time salary) while general payment is made to the hospital. Patients are generally cared for by physicians who are "on service" at the time in a hospital. The hospital staff may be described as being tightly closed with a sharp separation of general practitioners from the hospital. The average physician seldom uses the hospital as an extension of his private office practice (with private fees), and utilizes a separate system of "nursing homes" for a small class of high income patients. Would this hospital system have similar meaning associated with variables similar to those observed in the U.S.? One cannot be certain. For example, a high level of integration (committee meetings) may not be as necessary in a large closed French hospital as it would be in an American hospital of the same size. Part-time specialists may require more integrative activities than the closed staff. Integration may also be less necessary in clinics because of the similar activities performed by specialists in these institutions as Kervasdoue and Kimberly describe in the paper. A second variable, integration, as operationalized, could easily be an extremely expensive (perhaps unnecessary) service for the type of procedure provided in these clinics.

Paradigm Implications. The data analyzed[1] in this work and hypothesis tested have severe limitations because of the problems in determining which theoretical constructs were examined, and how they were operationalized. With this understanding, there can be little argument with the authors' conclusion that there are major differences between the hospitals in France and the U.S. on the variables presented in this study. These data do not warrant the authors' conclusion. Structure and innovation could still be related in a similar fashion in both cultures. Severe conceptual and operationalization problems may be the source for the dissimilarity in these data. However, Kervasdoue and Kimberly have emphasized that our *understanding of the meaning attached to the operationalization of a particular variable* may well be mediated by the culture, or occupational structure under examination. This does not present a new paradigm for the analyses of organizations. Instead, it emphasizes the inherent limitations of transferring any paradigm from one culture to another.

[1] The multivariate model developed early in the paper (see Figure 1) deserves a more complete test than the major use of correlation coefficients presented. A test for homogeneity of variance would indicate whether the differences in the coefficients (or lack of differences) can be attributed to sources other than those found in the paper. Finally, a Z test of difference between the correlation coefficients would be required to determine if there is a difference in the magnitude of the relationship for the two groups. For such a test to be conducted, the subjects (organizations in this case) must be randomly and independently selected, independent, have normal distributions for each variable, and have N's in both groups greater then twenty (see McCall, 1970). One cannot determine if such a test would be possible from the data presented because of the failure of the authors to include descriptive data on the variables in this study.

The authors have clearly highlighted the many assumptions about the meaning attached to certain supposedly "similar variables" that have been measured in a very specific fashion *within a culture*. Before conducting our research, we must ask if variables (such as size, differentiation, integration, etc.) can be compared directly across different cultures? The answer provided in this work is no. The implications drawn from these data are that we must interpret the variables to first assess their meaning in each culture. Perhaps our cross-cultural research project may then compare different meanings across common dimensions, or search for commality of meanings among different national (or other) groupings. In summary, it is very clear that researchers beginning a project in one culture must be aware of the risk to their findings of using well-developed hypotheses and operationalized variables in another situation (or culture) under the assumption that these data may have similar interpretations in both environments.

REFERENCES

Abegglen, J. C. *Management & Workest. The Japanese Solution.*
1973 Tokyo, Japan: Kodansha

Accreditation Manual for Hospitals. Chicago: Joint Commission on Accreditation of
1970 Hospitals.

Benedict, R. *Chrysanthemum & the Sword,* NAL.
1967.

Classification of Health Care Institutions. Chicago: American Hospital Association.
1974

England, G. W. *The Manager and His Values: An International Perspective.* Cambridge,
1975 Mass.: Ballinger.

Georgopoulos, Basil S. (ed.). *Organization Research on Health Care Institutions.* An
1972 Arbor, Mich.: Institute for Social Research.

Haire, M., E. E. Ghiselli, and L. W. Porter. *Managerial Thinking: An International Study.*
1966 New York: Wiley.

Hofstede, G. "Nationality and Espoused Values of Managers." *Journal of Applied*
1976 *Psychology.* 61:148–155.

Kelley, L., and C. Reeser. "The Persistence of Culture as a Determinant of Differentiated
1973 Attitudes on the Past of American Managers of Japanese Ancestry." *Academy of Management Journal.* 16:67–76.

Kelley, L., and R. Worthley. "Managerial Philosophy and Its Relation to Culture: An
1975 Empirical Study of Caucasian-American, Japanese-American and Japanese Managers." *Academy of Management Proceedings.* 243–245.

Kervasdoue, Jean de, and John R. Kimberly. "Are Organizations Culture-Free? The Case
1977 of Hospital Innovation in the U.S. and France." Paper presented at the Conference on Cross-Cultural Studies on Organizational Functioning, Honolulu, Hawaii.

Lomax, A., and N. Berkowitz. "The Evolutionary Taxonomy of Culture." *Science.*
1972 177:228–239.

Lorsch, Jay W., and Stephen A. Allen, III. *Managing Diversity and Independence.*
1973 Boston: Harvard University, Graduate School of Business Administration.

McCall, Robert B. *Fundamental Statistics for Psychology.* 2nd Edition. New York:
1970 Harcourt-Brace-Jovanovich, Inc.

Miner, J. B. "Personality Tests as Predictors of Consulting Success." *Personnel*
1971 *Psychology.* 24:191–204.

————. "The Cross-Cultural Perspective to Work Motivation." In S. K. Roy and
1974 A. Streekumar Menon (eds.), *Motivation and Organizational Effectiveness:* 29–42. Shri Ram Centre.

Neuhauser, D., and R. Andersen. "Structural-Comparative Studies of Hospitals." In
1972 Basil S. Georgoupolos (ed.), *Organization Research on Health Care Institutions*: 83–114. Ann Arbor, Mich.: Institute for Social Research.

Roemer, Milton I. *Health Care Systems in World Perspective.* Ann Arbor, Mich.: Health
1976 Administration Press.

Tomkins, S. S., and J. B. Miner. *The Tomkins-Horn Picture Arrangement Test.* New
1957 York: Springer.

Wanous, J. P. "Individual Differences and Reactions to Job Characteristics." *Journal of*
1974 *Applied Psychology.* 59:616–622.

Weber, M. *The Protestant Ethic and the Spirit of Capitalism*. Translated by Talcott
1904 Parsons. New York: Scribner.

————. *The Theory of Social and Economic Organization*. Translated by
1922 A. M. Henderson and Talcott Parsons. New York: Oxford.

Zalda, M. M., and F. D. Hair. "The Social Control of General Hospitals." In Basil
1972 S. Georgopolos (ed.), *Organization Research on Health Care Institutions*: 51–81. Ann Arbor, Mich.: Institute for Social Research.

Section III

INSTITUTIONAL GOALS AND ORGANIZATIONAL FUNCTIONING

Relations Between Organizational Goals and Structures: A Comparison of German and U.S. Police Organizations

GÜNTER ENDRUWEIT
Universität des Saarlandes

"There was once a man who aspired to be the author of the general theory of holes. When asked 'What kind of hole—holes dug by children in the sand for amusement, holes dug by gardners to plant lettuce seedlings, tank traps, holes made by roadmakers?' he would reply indignantly that he wished for a general theory that would explain all of these. He rejected *ab initio* the —as he saw it—pathetically common sense view that for the digging of different kinds of holes there are quite different explanations to be given. why then, he would ask, do we have the concept of a hole?" (MacIntyre, 1971:260). Under the obviously reasonable assumption that holes are not more complex than organizations we may extend the doubts about the feasibility of a general theory of holes to any general theory of organizations (Eldridge and Crombie, 1974:11)

Unfortunately, we need such a general theory of organizations in order to be able to make a cross-cultural analysis of organizations. General theory and comparative analysis of single phenomena are just the two sides of the same coin. When we realize difficulties in a comparative study they are mostly due to shortcomings in general theory. So we should come back to our analogy between holes and organizations because in a comparative analysis it is more difficult to ignore blanks in a theory.

Under these methodological threats it seems wise to restrict a comparison to holes that are dug by similar people for similar purposes, i.e. to organizations with similar instruments and goals.

THE THEORETICAL PROBLEM

We do not need the amusing observation of a widely traveled police researcher that patrolmen all over the world stand at the curb always with their hands on their back in order to make us infer that police organizations are quite similar to each other no matter the cultural context in which they are situated.

Although nobody knows how many police agencies exist in the United States—estimates are 40,000 (Gourley, 1970:2; Wilson; 1972:3)—it is said that each of them "is organized in roughly the same way under comparable, if not identical, legal codes, each of which performs similar functions" (Wilson, 1972:3; differently, Smith, 1960:21). These functions are described in a more detailed way by "their two major and interrelated purposes. . . : law enforcement and order maintenance. These purposes are usually elaborated into six functions. While some variations occur because of differing political and organizational arrangements, police generally (a) preserve the peace, (b) enforce laws, (c) protect life and property, (d) prevent crime, (e) arrest offenders and (f) recover property" (Earle, 1973:5). This is true, at least, for a "normal" police agency. It may not be fully valid for substitute police, like some sheriff's office in a remote area, university police or private protection services, which are created because a regular police is not necessary, not wanted or not effective.

German police laws have similar regulations for the tasks of police. Section 15 of the Police Law of the state of Nordrhein-Westfalen in its version of December 3, 1974 (GVBl, NW. S. 1504) may serve as an example for almost identically phrased sections in the other states: "Die Polizeibehörden haben die Aufgabe, Gefahren abzuwehren, durch die die öffentliche Sicherheit oder Ordnung bedroht wird . . . Daneben haben die Polizeibehörden die Aufgaben zu erfüllen, die ihnen durch Gesetz oder Rechtsverordnung übertragen sind. Sie sind insbesondere zuständig für die Verfolgung von Straftaten und Ordnungswidrigkeiten."[1] Historically different views of police work are more and more ironed out by present state legislation (Tschanett, 1975:236–238).

These coincidences notwithstanding, there may be some actual differences in goal perception and tracking which stem from differences in additional activities, policies of departments, national traditions, etc. Especially, some marginal conditions of police work may put a different emphasis on some goals. The existence of National Guards, for instance, relieves U.S. police from work that has to be done by their German colleagues. All these dissimilarities, though, are minor ones and do not affect the core of police work.

Thus we have found that police organizations in the United States and in Germany not only have similar, but even identical goals. It seems to be the same with the instruments of police activity. This applies certainly to the essentially unrestricted privilege of using force which Egon Bittner regards as the most characteristic universal property of police (Bittner, 1972:36–47), and also to the legal and technical paraphernalia of the police: their right to arrest, etc., has a similar shape all over the world (Sowle, 1969:37–73), and their chemical mace comes from the same factory. Finally, the organizational constraints, as seen in the relations of the organization with its societal environment, can more or less be regarded as not essentially different if not very much alike.

[1] "Police authorities have the task to protect against dangers which menace public security and order. . . . In addition to this, police authorities have to accomplish the functions which are assigned to them by law or government decree. They are in particular responsible for the enforcement of penal laws and of laws about misdemeanors."

This is the background for exploring the relationships between organizational goals, instruments and constraints on the one hand and organizational structures, functions and behaviors on the other hand.

In the first triad, goals and instruments are two variables which are mentioned by the vast majority of all organization theorists as essential criteria characterizing any type of organization (Albrow, 1973:401–406, 409; Azumi and Hage, 1972:414–417; Becker and Neuhauser, 1975:5; Blau, 1970:176, 1974:29; Champion, 1975:1, 97; Hall, 1972:9; Kosiol, 1959:22–26; Luhmann, 1964:31–32; Mayntz, 1963:36). There are only a few alternative approaches (e.g., Haas and Drabek, 1973:183; Luhmann, 1964:27, 38). The goal aspect is well established and highly developed although research on displacement, succession, etc., of instruments might be equally interesting. The constraint variable has only recently been expressly introduced as a regular definition element of organizations (Hill *et. al.*, 1976:17, 27, 369). It is a result of many attempts to determine the boundaries of a system. This becomes especially necessary when organizations are analyzed with an interactionist (Haas and Drabek, 1973:15–17) or a cybernetic approach (Beer, 1959:142–152; Hage, 1974:8–10; Levinson and Astrachan, 1976:219). From these viewpoints it was felt that goals and instruments were not sufficient to explain actual organizations, in particular, if the rest should not be left to anonymous societal influences. So it was said that constraints "stellen die relevanten Daten des Organisationsproblems dar: sie können im Rahmen des organisatorischen Gestaltungsprozesses weder manipuliert werden (wie die organisatorischen Instrumente) noch werden sie selbst angesteuert (wie die organisatorischen Ziele)" (Hill *et. al.*, 1974:12, 319).[2] One may illustrate this concept by imagining two companies in two countries which both produce a product with identical machinery, etc.: yet it still makes a difference for organization analysis if one has a monopoly or an oligopoly and the other works under competitive conditions (Krupp, 1961:60). This example shows that the border between organizational constraints and societal influences is difficult to draw. A general differentiation rule may be that constraints are part of the organization web or tissue, relatively persisting elements of the system, while social influences are stimuli which are deliberately and repeatedly directed to a specific organization, all organizations, or also non-organizations, but never integrated as elements of the organization. The sum of constraints is sometimes referred to as the organizational situation (Hill *et. al.*, 1976:320). Goals, instruments and constraints are regarded as the characterizing elements of each organization.[3]

The second triad does not mention specific elements of organizations. Structures, functions and behaviors can be found in all collective social subjects whether they are organizations or not.

[2] Constraints "are the relevant data of the organization problem: neither can they be manipulated in the course of the organizational development processes (as the organizational instruments) nor can they be something to be attained as such (as the organizational goals)".

[3] Additional elements, like normative order, authority ranks, communication systems, etc. (Hall, 1972:9), are often mentioned as general organization attributes but do, in fact, only characterize specific types (Pfeiffer, 1976:13) and are therefore an attempt to found a theory of holes just on a description of tank traps.

There is a basic belief about the relations between the two triads which is common to almost all organization theorists. It is indicated in Parsons' (1960:17) definition "Organizations are social units deliberately constructed and reconstructed to seek specific goals," a general sociological definition that has with good reason been adopted for organizational sociology by Amitai Etzioni (1964:3). Adding to this Charles Perrow's (1970:133) remark, "we must examine the end or goal if we are to analyze organizational behavior", and Hans Hoefert's (1976:27) rule, "Ziele müssen in Strukturen und Prozesse übersetzbar sein, um verhaltenswirksam sein zu können,"[4] we find the core of that tacitly shared belief about the nature of the relations between the different aspects of organization, mentioned above: goals, instruments and constraints are regarded as independent variables (see also Champion, 1975:98; Pugh *et. al.*, 1972:73), structures, functions and behaviors as dependent variables. These triads can be seen in a different connection, too. The first one contains the common elements of definitions of organization; they could, thus, be regarded as constitutional variables of an organization because their actual form and content determine the specific character of a particular organization. The second one comprises all those elements of an organization which have to be adapted in order to guarantee that the organization justifies its existence, i.e., that the program of the constitutional variables is run by these variables which might be called executive variables. In terms of a more cybernetics-influenced systems approach this would mean that the elements of the first triad are more input-oriented, the elements of the second triad more output-oriented. This seems to be a substantial parallel to the merely statistical distinction of the variables.

This configuration of variables suggests that either triad of variables can mutually be used as an explanation of the other triad of variables. Identical or similar goals, should generate identical or similar structures, and we should be entitled to infer identical or similar goals from the finding of identical or similar structures in a comparative analysis of organizations. If these suggestions were true we would not only have an immensely valuable methodological instrument for cross-cultural research but also a proof for the assumptions in our usual definitions of organization (see also Udy, 1964:162). We will try to test these suggestions by comparing some traits of police organization in Western Germany and in the United States.[5]

THE EMPIRICAL BASIS OF THE DATA

The data about Germany are taken from a research project on the police profession. This project was sponsored by the Conference of the Ministers and Senators of the Interior and it way conducted by a research team of the University of the Saar in 1972–76. Main sources of data were 6,059 classroom

[4] "Goals must be translatable into structures and processes in order to become relevant to behavior."

[5] This is an approach that differs from the method of Arnold S. Tannenbaum *et. al.*, who compared industrial plants in five countries, but subdivided them into capitalist and socialist goal orientation (Tannenbaum *et. al.*, 1974:XIX) while goals are here treated as a constant.

interviews[6] of a representative (5 per cent), disproportionate stratified sample out of all police officers of the German states.[7] Additional sources were two surveys of smaller samples, expert interviews, nonparticipant observations and evaluations of written material. The results have been reported to the sponsors in seven volumes of more than 1,600 pages. An abridged version is to be published in print.

During the pilot phase of the project mentioned above the author made a small-scale study on the organization and the training practices of police agencies in the United States. The data could not be collected in a methodologically comparable way, but had to be derived from expert interviews, observations in police departments and training institutions (e.g., FBI, Illinois State Police, Chicago and Evanston Police Departments)[8] as well as from the evaluation of documents, part of which have not yet been published. The study will be published in German.

As the data in both studies have not been compiled by the same methodology it would be in vain to make use of sophisticated statistical techniques of cross-cultural research.[9] Instead, the following data are more or less a comparative trend analysis of results of organizational developments. This seems appropriate because the decisive interest in this evaluation is not the relative difference between the single elements of police organization in either culture but their congruence or incongruence as such. Our focus is qualitative rather than quantitative because our research aims at problems of theoretical rather than applied organizational sociology. This can still comply with Peter M. Blau's (1970:175–6) widely shared exigencies for comparative study of organizations. If a study aims at finding the exact differences between concrete organizations and not just some evidence for the source of differences in general, it should collect primary data according to an elaborate set of variables as shown by Pugh *et al.* (1972:74)

FINDINGS ABOUT ORGANIZATIONAL DIFFERENCES

The comparison of American and German police organization yielded differences of quite unequal character and importance. These differences and

[6] The envisaged total of 6,630 interviewees included already an expected refusal rate of 10 per cent which was not even reached by this normative-coercive way (Galtung, 1970:147) of interviewing.

[7] These interviews had, though, but a minor impact on the following data because they were collected for other purposes.

[8] Therefore, I am very indebted to many officials and officers in America who readily gave me access to all kinds of information about police although I did not come on an official mission. As representative for all of them I just want to mention Carl F. Tucker, U.S. Department of Justice; Judge Angelo F. Pistilli, Joliet, Ill.; Supervisor John F. Burns, FBI, Washington; Special Agent John C. Noonan, FBI, Chicago; Superintendent Dwight E. Pitman and Major F. E. Piper, Illinois State Police; Director James T. McGuire, Chicago Police Academy; Superintendent James B. Conlisk, Chicago Police Department; Chief of Police William McHugh and Sergeant Larson, Evanston, Ill.

[9] For the same reason of heterogeneity of methods it is not useful to make general remarks about reliability and validity; data from official documents tend to have a high reliability while data from official expert interviews show more variation through time.

Table 1

SUMMARY OF ORGANIZATIONAL DIFFERENCES BETWEEN AMERICAN AND GERMAN POLICE

No.	Element	Germany	United States
1	System level	mainly state	mainly local
2	Organization size	high average, low variance	low average, low variance
3	Police density	high	low
4	Number of organizations	low	high
5	Budget autonomy	low	high
6	Hierarchy	high formal gradation, unclear functional differentiation	low formal gradation, clear functional differentiation
7	Age structure	relatively few young, many old officers	relatively many young, few old officers
8	Recruiting requirements	low minimum age	high minimum age
9	Educational requirements and realities	low	high
10	Selectivity	low	extremely high
11	Selection procedure	self-selection	self- and other- selection
12	Compulsory training	regularly 3 years minimum	between nothing and 11 weeks
13	Structure of training	system-oriented	situation-oriented
14	Place of training	5/6 "Bereitschaftspolizei", 1/6 police academy	mostly 1/1 police academy
15	Continuation training	very little	much

some attempts to find their causes can be listed as follows (a condensed information is given in Table 1).

Level of Organization

A very general difference is the fact that American police is mainly community police; German police is mainly state police. About 300,000 of the 358,000 police officers in the United States in 1965 were in local or county policy agencies (U.S. Bureau of the Census, 1965).

Local police organizations no longer exist in Germany[10] since even large cities like Munich can no longer afford the expenses for a modern police force and because the present discussion about optimal police organization tends to favor large agencies although there is a strong opposition against the endorsers of a "federalization" of police (see *Der Spiegel* No. 8/1977:44–47). In

[10] In 1974, only the states of Hessen (793 officers) and Bavaria (6,159 officers) still had community police agencies (Statistisches Bundesamt, Hrsg. Finanzen und Steuern. Reihe 4: Personal des öffentlichen Dienstes. Stuttgart: Kohlhammer, 1976:87).

comparison to about 20,000 federal police officers in the United States, the 22,000 officers of the Bundesgrenzschutz, about 900 agents of the Bundeskriminalamt[11] and the officers of the railroad police, taxes and customs investigation services and similar smaller institutions constitute a relatively strong centralized police power. Similarly, the 38,000 state police troopers in America cannot score up to the eleven German state police organizations counting about 147,000 officers in the Schutz- and Bereitschaftspolizei and 18,000 detectives (Stümper, 1975:367).

These are certainly no differences in goals or instruments, except may be in the constraints sets. There are more differences in the orientation system of the organization, and this justifies their treatment as an independent variable, influencing the dependent variables of structure, function and behavior.

Obviously, these differences have historical reasons. German police, as creatures of the regional rulers in the 18th and 19th century, were naturally organized on a state level, and local police was, without exception, an American import in the U.S. occupation zone after World War II and has almost entirely been abolished as dysfunctional in the existing system. American police, as successors to community self defense institutions, has its roots in the community while state police is, to a large extent, a by-product of highway construction.

These historical differences have subtle long-range bearings. A high ranking American police officer who helped rebuild German police in the late nineteen-forties argued that the self-image and the behavior of patrolmen in Germany and America are still shaped by their professional ancestors' roles as bailiff of the king or employees of an autonomous frontier community, respectively. One can imagine that these differences can create differences in the elements of actual behavior, like commitment to the population, loyalty to the employer, etc., with high importance for problems like impartial treatment, corruption, etc.

However, one can doubt that these phenomena are direct results of the historical facts rather than indirect functions because the historical structures may be preconditions for more general present structural differences which are the real causes for the behavior differences. While in Prussia it was a regular policy to station policemen from the West in the East and *vice versa*, a contemporary German policeman also has no guarantee that he will do his job in his residential, or even native, community. On the other hand, many American communities require their patrolmen to live within the city borders (Frost, 1959:176; Gourley, 1970:8). But police organization on state or community level is certainly an important factor for the police officer's behavior as one may guess from the well-established results of industrial sociology about different employee behavior under absentee ownership on one side and daily supervision by a critical employer on the other side.

Organization Size

A direct consequence of the just-mentioned differences is the size of police

[11] The figures for Germany refer to 1975; they were considerably lower in 1965 which is the year of U.S. data. The Bundeskriminalamt has, in addition to its police officers, about 2,000 administrative employees.

organizations as measured by their personnel. German police organizations range from 2,582 in Saarland to 30,344 in Nordrhein-Westfalen (1973)[12]. The variance is much higher in the United States. In just one county (Cook County, Illinois), there are five organizations with only part-time personnel, 23 organizations with 1 to 9 officers and the Chicago police department with about 18,000 policemen; the remainder agencies are inbetween (1971). Only the largest department in the States, New York, can equal Nordrhein-Westfalen.

The size of an organization is usually treated as one aspect of its structure with extremely important, though still heavily controversial, impacts on other elements of structure (see, among others, Caplow, 1964:25–28; Hall *et. al.*, 1967:903–905). For our purpose it is enough to state that these impacts which are certainly relevant to goal attainment have two different directions. A large sized organization is said to lead to, among other things, higher functional differentiation (Blau, 1970:204), greater chances of intraorganizational transfer and, hence, less desire to leave the organization (March and Simon, 1958:99), while a smaller size leads to fewer administrative functions (Haas and Drabek, 1973:271) and a better compatibility of organizational and other roles (March and Simon, 1958:98).

One can guess from these few examples that the functions of size should be calculated in their relation to the tasks of organization. We have not found this prior to a decision about size being made. Only recently has discussion in Germany emerged on this issue. But the final decision is, most probably, made according to legal and political standards which are far from the definition of goals for police organizations (see Stümper, 1975).

Police Density

If one compares how many inhabitants enjoy the protection of one policeman one finds that Germany has much more invested than the United States. Table 2 gives an impression of that. It shows that the three "city states" of Berlin, Bremen, and Hamburg have a higher police density than Chicago, and that even Evanston, an immediate northern suburb of Chicago, has a lower police density than the mainly rural state of Niedersachsen.

There can be no doubt that a relative increase of personnel enables an organization, all other factors kept constant, to get closer to goal attainment. There can also be no doubt that the United States could finance a higher police density if they wanted to. And there can be no doubt that the Germans could find alternative occasions on which to spend their money if they so desired. If there were no other criteria—in my impression, the U.S. police organizations make a fairly better use of their manpower—one might argue that the differences in police density are due to differences in societal emphasis on the need for police service.

Number of Organizations

We have already mentioned the high number of police organizations in America with about 40,000 agencies (Germann *et. al.*, 1966:153). Germany, on

[12] Organizational charts of different police organizations can be found in *Zeitschrift für Organisation* 44 (1975): 361–401, a special number devoted to police organization.

Table 2

POLICE DENSITY
Inhabitants per police officer (sworn personnel) in the U.S. (1971) and the FRG (1972)

Police Organization	*Ratio*
United States	
Chicago	1:270
Evanston	1:588
Wilmette	1:909
Germany	
Berlin	1:143
Bremen	1:246
Hamburg	1:252
Saarland	1:417
Bavaria	1:464
Schleswig-Holstein	1:469
Hessen	1:494
Nordrhein-Westfalen[a]	1:503
Niedersachsen[a, b]	1:512
Rhein land-Pfalz	1:575

[a] Police recruits included
[b] 1973

the contrary, has certainly not more than 30 organizations with police responsibility. This is obviously just the other side of average organization size.

Therefore, this structural feature also has no root in the set of independent variables. Under the aspect of police goals, the number of organizations must be judged in two directions. It is a general assumption that frictions and fissures tend to be more dangerous between organizations than within organizations. This would advocate a few big organizations if police goals are seen as general societal goals, to be reached through a sub-system. If police are expected, however, to react quickly to regional necessities it might be just the opposite. As organization leaders are more successful in implementing their strategies and the more they can steer their organizations independently (Hannan and Freeman, 1977:930) the greater the preference for smaller autonomous organizations. What type will prevail may be a function of the society's decision about the preferences for organization types: whether it should be a regularly working, though somewhat somnolent, administration, or a versatile, though not always reliable, security producer.

Budget Autonomy

Budgets are vital aspects of organizations. German police budgets are parts of the budget of the Ministry of the Interior of the state. Normally, police leaders take part in the preparation of proposals for the ministry's budget petition. However, their cooperation and even information usually ends when the petitions are discussed in the cabinet, combined with the government proposal and decided upon in the state parliament and its committees. They have only to adapt their expenses when they receive the final decision. This is the most frequent and the most important type of regular influence on police from other societal institutions (Wallat, 1975:376). Since only the procedure, as such, is institutionalized, but not the shape of the single event, this cannot be regarded as an organizational constraint. Many American chiefs of police, on the contrary, have uninterrupted close contact to the city council. Sometimes they present their proposal in the council meetings, and if the council wants to make cuts they may ask for a decision about what police activity should be affected by this cut. This seems to be an excellent base for well-grounded police-community relations although one must take into account that these "Grenzstellen" ("border-positions," see Luhmann, 1964:222f) introduce the danger of system disintegration.

Daily contact with practical cost-benefit calculations seems to create a special attitude toward the use of resources. America's police is economy conscious. The discussion of whether a squad car should be manned with two officers or one is accompanied by detailed figures about the cost of both alternatives (e.g., Larson, 1972:3; Wilson, Clowers, Piercy, Wynne and Governmental Research Institute in Chapman, 1970:181–244). Germany's police squad cars are usually manned by at least two officers, and there is not the least hint that this rationale is ever questioned on financial grounds. Their indirect relation to public resources makes them throw their hope on the Lord (Mt. 6:26). But from time to time one can see that this situation provokes other systemic reactions. Structural change under fixed budget conditions involves, almost invariably, a redistribution of resources across the sub-units and, thus, creates tensions within the organization (Hannan and Freeman, 1977:931). While expensive new anti-terror brigades are introduced in the uniformed police, 105 detectives in Cologne, one-fourth of the city's detective force, published an ad in June, 1977, in which they looked for jobs with a salary more adequate for their difficult work (*Saarbrücker Zeitung* of June 23, 1977, p. 9).

This process of keeping the balance between goal specification, function, and/or structure shaping is organized in a different manner which can be explained only by pointing to the differences in the political decision-making processes. Despite the close connection between police and council in an American city, the division between administration and politics seems to be much clearer than in Germany. Differences seem to be a product of general social structure and not of simple resource availabilities because in public finance all resources can be directed toward where they are needed.

Hierarchy

Ranks of American police are derived from the military. Above the patrolman we find corporals, sergeants, lieutenants, captains, majors and colonels. It depends on the size of the organization at which grade the top officer is placed. But this is only a rank order within a given organization. It does not allow a horizontal parallel between organizations: a captain in Evanston, Illinois commands 17 subordinates and earns $16,716 a year; his comrade in adjacent Chicago has more than 1,000 men and $28,000 (in 1972). In the same way, the functional differentiation between the grades is only a vertical order; but it exists in every case.

In Germany we find 16 grades between Wachtmeister and Leitender Direktor. Their labels are taken from civil service or they have special police titles. In either case they have their equivalent in the rank order of every type of public personnel activity; i.e., the police hierarchy is an exact blueprint of the hierarchies for soldiers, teachers, railroad employees, fiscal officers, prison wardens, and sanitary board doctors. It is easy to guess that this high degree of formalization is an obstacle to a branch-specific functional differentiation. Therefore, this does not exist in a clear way.

Reference group orientation is not a matter of intraorganizational variables, like goals and instruments, because the American police is less like the military than German police. Some indicators for this are: the difference between Police Academy and Bereitschaftspolizei as *loci* of first professional socialization; the different frequency in the application of classical infantry techniques; the existence of state National Guard in the U.S.; and the lack of waterguns in America and their abundance in Germany. An American author has argued that police staff thinking "was liberated (and somewhat modified) from the Army, and later added to by stealing from business" (Hansen, 1972:XI). We may confirm the first part for Germany too and change the last part insofar as business has to be replaced by general administration though its ideas were not stolen but were generously offered. When the Bundesgrenzschutz was converted by law from a semi-military border protection force into a federal police troop the first practical adaptation measure was the replacement of military ranks by police ranks. The police tries anxiously to keep in step with the development of general administration in Germany not only with respect to equal chances for promotion but also with respect to a similarly harmless image. I do not have comparable information about America. This would be a good field for detailed cross-cultural investigation because it is a "research problem involving variables whose values differ from one society to another but remain more or less constant in any given society" (Udy, 1964:162).

The above considerations about reference groups have already suggested that an explanation of hierarchy differences must refer to broader societal circumstances. This finds support in other peculiarities. The Illinois State Police confesses frankly that it "is a semi-military organization" (Illinois State Highway Police Academy, *Recruit Training Syllabus*, p. 80). German state and police officials have always tried to resist all attempts to introduce military components, that is, they did so verbally. But the German police unions have been, in every respect, opponents to military weapons, uniforms, ranks, and ways of conduct. The high degree of union membership is an argument for the thesis that societal and organizational orientation of police in Germany is strictly toward the general civil service.

That may explain why the hierarchical structures are copied from general administration. It cannot be explained from the police goals, etc. viz why the police of Nordrhein-Westfalen has more than twice as many ranks as a comparably manned department of New York. A high differentiation of ranks calls for a similarly high differentiation of functions, responsibilities, difficulties in tasks, etc. This can obviously not be presented in normal police work. Therefore, a major reason for the present unrest among German police officers is the fact that in many cases the same work is done by officers of three or four different ranks with equally different positions on the salary scale and equally different aspirations to leadership within the team (*Saarbrücker Zeitung* of June 23, 1977, p.9). Another property of high hierarchical differentiation is the trend to bigger organizations and, hence, to centralization. One general drawback of centralized structures, the relative difficulty in realizing mistakes and in correcting them (Ziegler, 1968:94), is clearly seen and expressively accepted (Wallat, 1975:37) because of the relative advantage which those structures offer when quick and fully coordinated reaction to new situations is in question (Mayntz, 1963:98). This is the view of police leaders while the rank and file officers are very sceptical of the existing hierarchy (Waldmann, 1977:75). In America, this topic seems to be in discussion only in connection with leadership techniques. But the structure, as such, is hardly questioned. Experts attribute this to the higher degree of compartmentalization of the American society into more or less self-sustaining units.

Age Structure

Age structures are difficult to compare because there are no general figures available. The data in Table 3 for the cities of Evanston and Des Plaines in Illinois and for the Saarland in Germany show a significant difference.

Their internal variances notwithstanding, the American data show a significant difference from the German age structure. American police officers are much younger than their German colleagues on the average, and officers over fifty years of age are quite rare. Informants said that these partial data are more or less typical for all police organizations in their country.

Three reasons can be given for the uncommon situation in the United States. First, police manpower has been enlarged in the last two decades; but that is true for Germany as well. Second, professionalization is, mostly since about 1955, a relatively new trend in the American police system which had been part of the patronage system with T.A.s (temporary appointees). Third,

Table 3

AVERAGE AGE OF POLICE OFFICERS (PER CENT)

Age Group	*Evanston*	*Des Plaines*	*Saarland*[a]
–30	42.9	48.1	22.0
30–40	35.2	23.4	22.5
40–50	16.4	24.7	33.6
50–	5.5	3.8	21.9
	100.0	100.0	100.0

[a] Source: Statistisches Amt des Saarlandes (Hrsg.). *Personalstrukturuntersuchung im Offentlichen Dienst 1968*. Saarbrücken: Statistisches Amt des Saarlandes, 1972.

many police departments in the U.S. have a minimum of only 15 years of service to qualify for pension, and they pay the pension at the age of 50, thus encouraging officers to leave the police service at that age.

These differences between the United States and Germany certainly have some influence upon the decision-making structure, communication within the police, and between police and certain groups of the public, the possibility of delegation, etc. The general argument that police work requires only young and able-bodied officers is incorrect. The differences must be related to general traits in the systems of civil service.

Recruiting Requirements

Both countries have almost identical requirements for recruits: citizenship, minimum height and physical fitness. Differences begin with age. German police recruits are hired at the age of 16, American officers normally not under 20. In Germany, more than two-thirds of the beginners in 1971 and 1972 were under 21 years of age. While personal reliability in Germany is in most cases only judged from documents and self-reports of the candidates, the New York Police Department has a Personnel Investigation Section of 74 officers who screen the applicants and their environments with ordinary police techniques, and thus excluded in January, 1967, about 45 per cent of the applications, transferred 31 per cent to an interview committee and accepted only 24 per cent immediately for further consideration (Arm, 1969:51f; Watson and Sterling, 1969:31f).

Certainly, the differences in age are due to the different length of general school attendance which is in Germany 8 or 9 years, in the U.S. 12 years, and depends on the different length of recruit training which should send only an adult officer into the streets. Nevertheless, German policemen, interviewed about their opinion on the minimum age for an active officer, answer with 62 per cent that it should not be under 22, and 35 per cent favored a minimum age of 26 years.

Educational Requirements and Realities

Minimum general education for a police recruit in Germany is the Hauptschule (9 years). American departments have different standards with a general trend to ask for at least a high school diploma (12 years) for everybody and 2 to 4 years of college for the higher echelons. Table 4 gives some data about the level of general education in three police organizations.

We have no information about how representative these data are for the police on the whole. Figures from the U.S. suggest that there is a remarkable fall from the West to the East, from the North to the South, and from Police to Sheriffs' departments (Saunders 1970:80). The German figures show a representative picture of the general increase of the educational level to which one must add that only 24 per cent (in 1973) of all police officers had no non-police professional education in addition to their general school attendance. Statements from American police officials indicated that about one-half of the recruits come to the police without any previous occupational experience.

As American policemen "are products of American schools, American

Table 4

GENERAL EDUCATION OF POLICE OFFICERS (PER CENT)

USA[a] *(Illinois 1971)*			*Germany*		
	Evanston	*Des Plaines*		*Baden-Würrttem-berg 1960–67*[b]	*6,059 Inter-viewees 1973*
High School not finished	3.9	—	Hauptschule (8 or 9 years) not finished	71	2
High School Diploma	52.3	79.5	Hauptschule		59
College, not finished	27.3	10.3	Other schools not finished	15	20
College 2 years	10.2	3.8	Realschule (10 years)	12	17
College, 4 years	5.5	6.4	Realschule (10 years)	12	17
Graduate	.8	—	Gymnasium (13 years)	2	2
	100.0	100.0		100	100

[a] These figures apply to officers in full service.
[b] These figures apply to recruits admitted to begin their police training (Source: Spiegelberg, 1971:111).

churches, and American cultural and social influences" (Chapman, 1970:10) and as German policemen are necessarily products of German schools, etc., the general level of schooling is an indicator for one important aspect of congruence between police organization and social environment. This may give an impression of who interacts with whom because the educational level is one regular aspect of stratification analysis. There is no rule that each organization should choose its personnel as an exact representation of the population. But it should be noted that discrepancies might cause trouble. In this respect it is interesting to compare the figures of Table 4 with the fact that of all pupils in Germany 18 per cent attended the Gymnasium, 11 per cent the Realschule and 71 per cent the Hauptschule (figures of 1973; Statistisches Bundesamt (Hrsg.), *Statistisches Jahrbuch 1975.*, Stuttgart: Kohlhammer, 1975:98) while in the United States 14 per cent of the enrolled students were in college, 17 per cent in high school and 59 per cent in elementary classes (again figures of 1973; U.S. Bureau of the Census. *Statistical Abstract of the United States: 1976*. Washington, D.C.: U.S. Government Printing Office). German police has an over representation of the middle strata, a slight underrepresentation of lower strata and a tremendous underrepresentation of higher strata, while the American police, as judged from these two departments, are far above the general level of education. Nevertheless, the fact that most agencies ask only for a high school diploma has often been criticized (Adam, 1974:246) although many city departments do in fact have more than 40 per cent of their officers with a higher level of education (Saunders, 1970:80). The U.S. President's Commission on Law Enforcement (1970:109) has already proposed to require, at least in the long run, each officer applicant to have a bachelor's degree as a minimum. The German police has had some pressure from their unions to raise the general level of education. But this should primarily be done within the police training system so that the U.S.-German differences in general socialization, selection chances, etc., would still continue. This may be due to a different societal view of the type of police officer and his functions; different police density, one or more men in a squad car, more or less training in military-like formation, etc.

Selectivity

The chances of American police organizations having a wide choice of applications for vacancies are enormously high. The FBI often had to choose from more than 100 candidates for one position. Illinois State Police offered 35 openings in 1973 and got 1,800 applications; the Chicago Police Department received the same number for 200 positions. In Germany, the Saarland police accepted one of five applicants for recruit training. This was in 1977, a year with high unemployment rates, but the newspapers concluded from this meager ratio that the police job has "obviously is in very great demand" (*Saarbrücker Zeitung*, of April 16/17, 1977, p. 18). Prior to the last three years the German police accepted 2 out of 5 applications.[13]

An explanation with reference to the job market seems to be more doubtful in this case than in others. This difference in the selection range, however, may offer an explanation for the different length of formal professional training which is described below. General sociological organization theory suggests that degree of selectivity and length and/or intensity of intra-organizational socialization and control processes are in inverse proportion to each other (see Etzioni, 1964:68–69). Nobody knows, though, whether there is a real causal relation between these phenomena insofar as these connections have deliberately been made in the organizations.

In every case, low selectivity has its disadvantages, like pressure to lower entrance standards, need of high efforts to compensate for these deficiencies during the subsequent occupational training, low fear of being fired, possible disciplinary problems, and, finally, a bad image of the whole job. If the same phenomena occurs as it sometimes seems in America, in a high-selectivity-setting, it is in spite of and not because of that high selectivity. But whatever is

[13] It may be interesting that the number of persons who asked for information about the conditions of a police job was much higher. The ratio of interested and definitely recruited persons was 12:1 in Hamburg, 10:1 in Niedersachsen, and 9:1 in Bremen. Half were lost between information and application.

done by an organization to improve its members who had been recruited under bad selection conditions, it is always a means of necessarily more organization-oriented socialization, i.e., for more organizational segregation from the environment.

Selection Process

Recruit selection in Germany is a procedure that is entirely run within the police organization. It is the same with the FBI. But other police organizations in the United States render only administrative service to the selection of recruits. The definite decision is made by civilian authorities like the State Merit Board in Illinois, the three members of which are appointed for 6 years by the governor, or the Civil Service Commission in Chicago, for which even the psychological testing of police applicants is done by private firms.

Differences in structure-constraint-relations of this type are certainly not self-explanatory. Nothing would hinder German authorities or the federal administration of the United States from institutionalizing civil recruitment boards for their police, and the Illinois and Chicago police organizations are certainly not incapable of selecting their recruits themselves. It seems to be a different view of the problems of self-selection or co-optation that makes the difference in procedures. It is more likely that organizations with a co-optation system may deviate from the organizational goal as a system serving subsystem goal by over emphasizing intra-organizational functions and goals. The other-selection system, on the other hand, may endanger the organizational goal as well, by making it subject to accidental extra-organizational goals or by creating the impression that it does so. This is an important part of the control panel by which the balance between internal and external organizational functions is kept.

Compulsory Formal Training

German police recruits have to pass a formal training, without exception. The states have still different regulations about content, sequence and length of the single periods of that training, and the overall duration varies depending on the general educational level of the recruit. The normal length of continuous formal training is not shorter than three years.

The American scene is extremely different. In 1968, there were only 31 states having legal provisions for police training (Saunders, 1970:147), only 17 of them making training compulsory for all officers. There are still police organizations who look for a guy "with big hands and a big voice," as the director of a police academy described it, and regard this as sufficient to preserve law and order. Many American movies show how this traditional sheriff, although mostly in small departments and hinterland counties, is a well-functioning counterpart to the remainders of cowboy capitalism. Even those states who believe that "there is no such thing as an instant cop" (Arm, 1969:41) have only minimal requirements compared with Germany. The Illinois Barber Law insists on 9 months with 1,872 hours of training for each barber; but the Illinois Police Training Act (approved Aug. 18, 1965; see Chapter 85, Section 508) leaves it to the community whether or not it adopts the standards of this law and gives an incentive by offering a 50 per cent state contribution to the costs of an officer's training. Formal training,[14] if it is established, is relatively short: mostly between 6 weeks (240 hours) and 11 weeks (400 hours). In Germany the total is between 4,000 and 5,000 hours.

One cannot explain these differences from any of the independent variables because police work has for many decades badly needed a thorough preparation of the officer, especially a kind of professional training which cannot be substituted by good general education although one must admit that changes are nowadays somewhat more rapid and drastic than before (Chapman, 1970:8). So the difference between both systems seems to be a function of the United States' late-coming in its reorganization of the civil service to the international standards of professionalism.

Structure of Formal Training

Curricula of American police academies generally differentiate course subjects according to a list that enumerates daily job situations. Subjects like defensive driving, stop and frisk, traffic regulation by hand, traffic accident investigation, officer as witness, etc., each get a certain amount of hours. The training is situation-oriented. Time tables in German police training institutions have a system-oriented approach. They list subjects like penal law, administrative law, criminology, technical instruction etc.

As the practical job does not show many differences between Germany and the U.S., the almost opposite approach in educational techniques seems to be due to more general cultural traits. Experts relate it to the prevalence of system thinking in Germany as opposed to the Anglo-Saxon predilection for pragmatic case solutions.

Place of Training

Formal training in Germany is divided between about 2 years 6 months of "Bereitschaftspolizei", a police troop for training and emergency purposes quartered in barracks and somewhat semi-military, and about 6 months of police academy.[15] The sequence of the periods varies from state to state. American departments sometimes have a trainee system (Gammage, 1963:265–276), but the regular institution is now more and more the police academy.

When asked about these differences, U.S. officers answered that their system had been judged the most appropriate one for the present-day needs. German officers referred to the traditionally good experience with their system.

Continuation Training

The above-mentioned differences in the basic training system suggest the opposite difference in continued training. Sixty per cent of the German police

[14] We disregard the manifold discriminations between training, schooling, apprenticeship, etc. (Caplow, 1964:172–178) and we call training all systematic education that is not only given by letting the recruit look over the shoulder of an officer on the job.

[15] The only exception is Hamburg where the training is in a police academy instead of the Bereitschaftspolizei.

officers said, in 1973, that they had not had even one continuation training course within the last three years, and only eight per cent had more than one month of training during that period. In the United States, continued training is very often part of the officer's duty. Officers in Los Angeles have to participate in brush-up courses of 40 to 80 hours in certain periods (Saunders, 1970:136). Evanston's police department throughout the year of 1972 always kept three or four of its 125 officers in courses. Many institutions, like universities, colleges, FBI, police academies and private enterprises, offer a wide variety of programs (Gammage, 1963:24f).

This situation cannot simply be regarded as a natural consequence of differences in basic training. Intensive basic training does not eliminate the need for continued training as the discontent of German police officers with their training practice shows. The old traditions of civil service are an obstacle, not only in the police branch, to stressing the needs of flexibility of personnel, of adopting new techniques of work, of proving continued workability, etc. The American attitudes and practices, on the other hand, are regarded, as a professor of criminal justice administration put it, as "just a formalized version of an old habit: to adopt the best that is available."

CONCLUSIONS

After the examination of 15 dependent, mostly structural, variables we found differences, the actual form of which could not be caused by similar differences in the independent variables of goals and instruments of American or German police organization, respectively, because the latter variables are alike. These variations in dependent variables also cannot be attributed to a specifically different constraint as that independent variable denotes "Komponenten der Organisationssituation", die "einerseits den . . . Eigenschaften der von den Systemmitgliedern zu erfüllenden Aufgaben, andererseits den . . . Eigenschaften der Systemmitglieder . . . zugeordnet werden" (Hill *et al.*, 1976:322).[16] Constraints are, therefore, organization-related boundary-setting influences from the society at large, but not all the regular or incidental stimuli from society that influence each organization and non-organization. One could tend to regard the differences in the selection procedure as a result of constraint differences. In fact, German police leaders are, even at the highest levels, career officers without the least political responsibility and power so that they have to serve every political direction. That might be a reason to entrust the whole procedure to them.

But in all the other cases we found no hint, neither from documents nor from the interpretation of experts, that the differences between German and American police organization were based on differences in goals, instruments or constraints. If we had made a *lege artis* hypotheses test and not just a "phenomenological" pilot investigation we would be compelled to confess that our attempt to explain all independent variables by relating them to dependent

[16] "Components of the organizational situation" which can "be related on one hand to . . . the properties of the tasks that are to be fulfilled by the system members, on the other hand to the properties of the system members."

variables has failed.[17] It was an experience similar to Stephen A. Richardson's (1956) who studied the hierarchy relations on American and British merchant ships under the expressed assumption that the independent variables in this setting were similarly identical as our police variables. He found, too, that there was no direct relation between the dependent and the independent variables so that the hierarchy differences had to be explained by a third variable, the difference of union activities, which he saw as part of the specific cultural environment. Ships, often seen as closed total institutions like mental hospitals, concentration camps, etc., had proven to be under important extra-systemic influences. One should expect this even more from the police which is regarded as "especially adapted to an analysis that stresses its relations with the organized environment" (Reiss and Bordua, 1967:25). One should expect, therefore, that there are a considerable number of studies on the influence of socio-cultural factors on police organization. The opposite is true, however. Exceptions occur mostly where obvious divergencies between the goals of the organization and the motivations and behaviors of its members are scrutinized (*e.g.*, Feest and Lautmann, 1971:39–62).

METHODOLOGICAL ASPECTS OF SOCIO-CULTURAL FACTORS IN ORGANIZATIONS

The negligence of socio-cultural factors in organizational analysis is no special feature of police sociology, it applies to organizational sociology in general. Researches have treated organizations for too long a time as closed systems (Champion, 1975:28–58; Haas and Drabek, 1973:18; Silverman, 1972:122; Terreberry, 1972:78). Glancing back for a moment at our introductory fable, we may characterize this as an attempt to formulate a theory of holes by just referring to nothing but holes and not to what is between the holes. We do not need an inverse analogy to Christian Morgenstern's poem "Der Lattenzaun" to make us realize that this is not feasible.

That is the reason why we find a number of statements in the literature on organizational sociology which put emphasis on the necessity of exploring the relations between organization and its environment, especially the socio-cultural factors which influence organizational functioning (Becker and Neuhauser, 1975:66–68; Child, 1973:92–94, 96–98; Haas and Drabek,

[17] Admittedly, one can find many dependent variables of police organization in either country that are identical and can be attributed to the identical independent variables. A striking example is the hierarchical pyramid. If we equal the captains to Germany's "höherer Dienst", lieutenants and sergeants to the "gehobener Dienst" and corporals and patrolmen to the "mittlerer Dienst" we get in five American departments a ratio of 1.54:13.46:85.00, and in the eleven German Länderpolizeien a ratio of 1.01:12.88:86.11 (unweighted means). This can be explained by pointing to the fact that the "instruments" of police require little vertical differentiation in the qualification of the officers. Positions for promotion stem, therefore, only from the internal administrative needs of the organization and are, consequently, not so numerous. One can also find different dependent variables that can be explained by different independent variables. But all these coincidences describe the, hopefully, regular aspects of organizations while we refer to the culture-based exceptions of organization construction.

1973:18; Luhmann, 1975:39; Thompson and McEwen, 1958:25; Wagenführ, 1973:12). But these arguments are mostly promises (Grunow and Hegner, 1972:211) and "few intensive analyses of organizational environments have been made to date" (Haas and Drabek, 1973:17). Peter M. Blau's (1970:186) statement is still valid: "The complaint often heard that we know virtually nothing about the impact of the social setting on organizations is quite justified."

One main cause seems to be that classical organizational theory, especially the one developed by economists, over-stressed the goal aspect and thus came to look at independent and dependent variables in a sense which was not adequate to the social nature of organizations. It is obviously a general shortcoming of our manoeuvering with independent and dependent variables that, for the sake of research simplicity and theory clearness, we tend to assume direct relations between the two sets of variables. We fail to realize, in these cases, that independent variables always influence dependent variables, but seldom do so in just one, exactly predictable way. In reality, an independent variable often has the choice between several dependent variables. Even if there is only one possible dependent variable to be influenced it is often still a question of what actual shape the influence will give to the dependent variable. The concrete form of causal relations between independent and dependent variables is determined by marginal conditions. There are two main groups of these marginal conditions: (1) internal conditions which, like the functional equivalents in structural-functional theory (Luhmann, 1964:109–110), open the opportunity of choice between principally equal ways of problem solution; and (2) external conditions which either prescribe the choice among the equivalents just mentioned or, at least, guide the choice into a certain direction.

The latter type of conditions is what we would like to call socio-cultural factors. Methodologically, they must be regarded as intervening variables, and that is what makes it so difficult to detect them. Their role in organization research has been described by Joseph A. Litterer (1973:259): "Culture places imperative demands on organizations. These demands seldom, if ever, require a specific structure; instead, set constraints or boundaries must prevail. Within these boundaries there are a variety of operations or structures possible to fill the irreducible minimum functional requirements."

As Litterer leaves it somehow open whether cultural variables open the choice between equivalent forms of independent variables so that the choice can be made according to intra-organizational criteria or whether it is the other way round, we would suggest that it seems to be a methodological prerequisite of general organizational theory to assume that there is basically, in every society, the opportunity to establish deliberately certain relations between independent and dependent variables of organizations, at least if formal organizations are concerned. In this context, socio-cultural factors work only as intervening variables. This configuration leads us to assume that the old controversy about the primacy of goals, etc., or structures, etc., has to be decided in favor of the goals. The doubts against this solution seem not to be well-founded as they are mainly based upon beliefs and assumptions. As an example, we will take Haas and Drabek (1973:183f) who qualify the primary orientation on goals as "somewhat simplistic and certainly incomplete." In proof of this, they quote Blau and Meyer who quote Novick (1965:97) who quotes Gilpatric. Blau and Meyer (1971:123) say: "as a high government official has remarked, goals were once determined by 'starting with a budget and sending it off in search of a program'. Funds were allocated for personnel costs . . . no attempt was made to link expenditures with objectives." This could really be interpreted as if the dependent variables of an organization were prior to those which we regarded as independent. But when we look closer at what former Deputy Secretary of Defense Roswell L. Gilpatric (1962:53) said, we find that "in the past, the Defense Department has often developed its force structure by starting with a budget and sending it off in search of program." This is now something quite different. It is not the founding of an organization, but some adjustments inside of an existing organization; nobody has ever questioned that in such cases, for instance during goal succession, structures can be prior to goals. And, we find that nothing is said about new goals, but only about new instruments which are another independent variable for new structures as dependent variables. Nevertheless, there is no reason to deny that, as in the case of goal succession or displacement, structures, etc., can be the causes for new goals, etc. A description of relations between variables in terms of a one-way road is usually not realistic in social sciences; a spiral model is more appropriate if it is part of a broader theory. But a narrow model of the priority of values to behavior seems still better than its opposite although Rodgers and Gardener (1969) and others have shown that under certain conditions a change of behavior can reformulate values.

Bringing back society into organization through an essentially sociological perspective is, then, a justified tendency (Grunow and Hegner, 1972:212). But it did not need the challenge of Marxist sociology which is said to have provoked the new orientation (Pfeiffer, 1976:128). It is a basic approach for all applied sociologies that they treat the influences of their specific object on society and the influences of society on their specific object. On this basis, we could sketch our view of the relation between goals, etc., structures, etc. and the social environment as in the following figure.[18]

This figure aims at combining, concreting and somewhat augmenting[19] what contemporary organizational sociologists have proposed as new scopes. Functional analysis paved the way to regard organizations as systems (Luhmann, 1964:24; 1975:9, 28) which force us to differentiate between inside and outside. A bunch of system theories (see Haas and Drabek, 1973:83–93; Grochla, 1977:10–13), like adaptation theory (Terreberry, 1972:85–90), closure-continuum-theory (Mott, 1972:1–16), ecological theory (Hannan and Freeman, 1977:929–933; Wagenführ, 1973:12, 14–15), cybernetic theory (Hage, 1974:8–10; Levinson and Astrachan, 1976:219), and contingency

[18] Ironically, organizational goals are on the input side of the organizational system because they are normally officially introduced into the organization by the societal super-system while social norms are on the side of the socio-cultural factors as intervening variables because they become mostly relevant through individual behaviors or value orientations of the organization members (if not imposed on the organization from outside). But this contradiction has already been treated since Emile Durkheim's "Suicide" (see Blau, 1974:78–79).

[19] See for this Figure 1 in Terreberry, 1972:86.

Figure 1

ORGANIZATION-ENVIRONMENT-RELATIONS

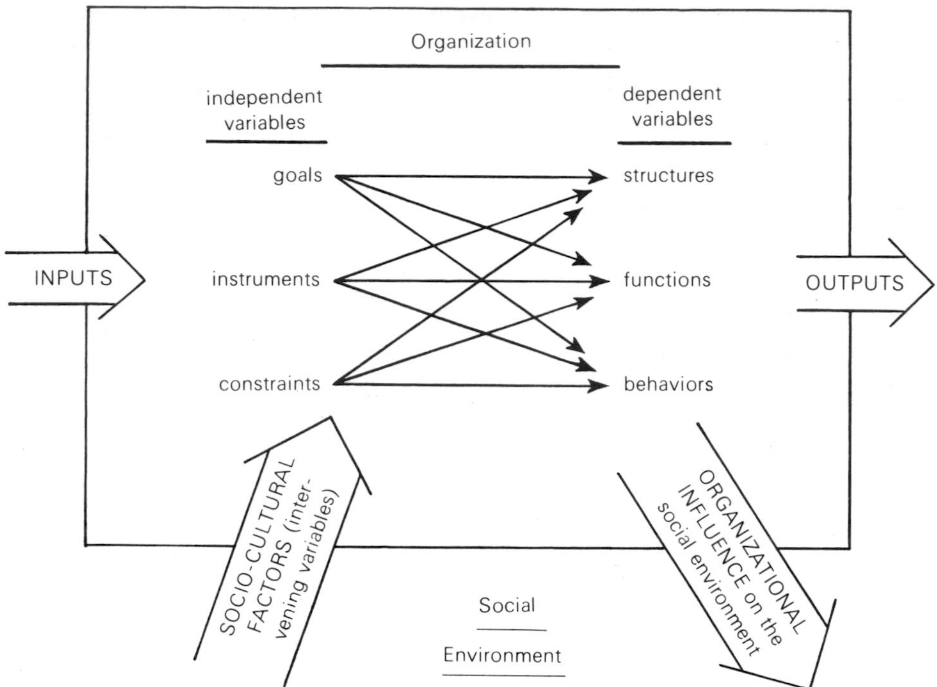

theory (Becker and Neuhauser, 1975:66–68; Lawrence and Lorsch, 1967:156–158, 185–210; Luhmann, 1975:39; Pfeiffer, 1976:120–123) discern between inputs, throughputs and outputs of an organization. But these are only those border-line relations that refer to the organization as a functionally specialized societal sub-system. The prejudices of structural-functional theory about the relations between systems and sub-systems make us forget that children grow up. Organizational power to "act on and modify their environments" (Haas and Drabek, 1973:18; similarly, (Mayntz, 1963:45–46) is not restricted to the narrow range of organizational functions. Empirical studies taught us that many aspects of organizations can only be understood by an analysis of the extra-functional activities of organization members (Porter, 1965:511–519; Presthus, 1974:149–150, 213–216) whose "competition, bargaining, co-optation, and coalition constitute procedures for gaining support from the organizational environment" (Thompson and McEwen, 1958:29). These procedures are traded for the societal influence on the basis of socio-cultural factors of organizational life.

In some details, this concept deviates from other approaches. Emery and Trist (1965:22) treat an aspect which they call L_{22} and which describes the interdependencies within the environment itself. Our view of organizational sociology must exclude this and transfer it to general sociology. Reiss and Bordua (1967:26) regard the legal system as one of the "basic environmental features." We would prefer to see it, at least in the case of a police organization, as one of the constraints because the legal position of the police is a basic part of its organizational web.

At the beginning of modern cross-cultural organizational analysis it was argued that our insight into the functioning of a single organization may profit from this approach because "the most extreme variations can be achieved by comparing organizations in different societies" (Udy, 1964:162). This paper tried to contribute to the methodological specification of that statement by showing that socio-cultural factors as intervening variables best come into a researcher's range of vision when he makes a cross-cultural study because a study of organizations within just one culture, even with a comparative approach, generally disregards socio-cultural factors. The organization-environment approach of the type outlined here allows for more clarification of intra-organizational processes and of exchange processes by determining the boundaries of the organization. Such a boundary "has a separating function" and "a transactional function" (Levinson and Astrachan, 1976:219). Police organizations would be an excellent field for detailed and methodologically sophisticated primary studies on these problems because, as Reiss and Bordua (1967:54) said ten years ago, "the police provide an unusual opportunity to develop and apply a transaction view of organizations, since, on the one hand, police departments have clearly defined boundaries, and yet on the other, they must continually engage in the management of highly contingent relationships that arise outside them."

REFERENCES

Adam, Robert. "Neue Bemühungen um Ausbildung der Polizeikräfte in den USA."
1974 *Deutsche Polizei*. 246–247.

Albrow, Martin. "The Study of Organizations-Objectivity or Bias?" In Graeme Salaman
1973 and Kenneth Thompson (eds.), *People and Organizations*: 396–413. London: Longman.

Arm, Walter. *The Policeman*. New York: E. P. Dutton.
1969

Azumi, Koya, and Jerald Hage (eds.). *Organizational Systems*. Lexington, Mass.:
1972 D. C. Heath.

Becker, Selwyn W. and Duncan Neuhauser. *The Efficient Organization*. New York:
1975 Elsevier.

Beer, Stafford. *Cybernetics and Management*. London: English Universities Press.
1959

Bittner, Egon. *The Functions of the Police in Modern Society*. DHEW Publication No.
1972 (HSM) 72–9103. Washington: U.S. Government Printing Office.

Blau, Peter M. "The Comparative Study of Organizations." In Oscar Grusky and George
1970a Miller (eds.), *The Sociology of Organizations*: 175–186. New York: Free Press.

———— "A Formal Theory of Differentiation in Organizations." *American*
1970b *Sociological Review*. 35:201–218.

———— *On the Nature of Organizations*. New York: John Wiley.
1974

Blau, Peter M., and Marshall W. Meyer. *Bureaucracy in Modern Society*. 2nd ed. New
1971 York: Random House.

Caplow, Theodore. *Principles of Organization*. New York: Harcourt, Brace & World.
1964

Champion, Dean J. *The Sociology of Organization*. New York: McGraw-Hill.
1975

Chapman, Samuel G. *Police Patrol Readings*. Springfield, Ill.: Charles C. Thomas.
1970

Child, John. "Organizational Structure, Environment, and Performance: The Role of
1973 Strategic Choice." In Graeme Salaman and Kenneth Thompson (eds.), *People and Organisations*: 91–107. London: Longman.

Earle, Howard H. *Police Recruit Training*. Springfield, Ill.: Charles C. Thomas.
1973

Eldridge, John E. T. and A. D. Crombie. *A Sociology of Organizations*. London: George
1974 Allen & Unwin.

Emery, F. E., and E. L. Trist. "Causal Texture of Organizational Environments." *Human*
1965 *Relations*. 18:21–32.

Etzioni, Amitai. *Modern Organizations*. Englewood Cliffs, N. J.: Prentice-Hall.
1964

Feest, Johannes, and Riidiger Lautmann (Hrsg.). *Die Polzei*. Opladen:
1971 Westdeutscher Verlag.

Frost, Thomas F. *A Forward Look in Police Education*. Springfield, Ill: Charles
1959 C. Thomas.

Galtung, Johan. *Theory and Methods of Social Research*. 3rd impression. London:
1970 George Allen & Unwin.

Gammage, Allen Z. *Police Training in the United States*. Springfield, Ill.:
1963 Charles C. Thomas.

Germann, A. C., Frank D. Day, and Robert R. J. Gallati. *Introduction to Law Enforce-*
1966 *ment*. Springfield, Ill.: Charles C. Thomas.

Gilpatric, Roswell L. "Defense—How Much Will It Cost?" *California Management*
1962 *Review*. V:53–58.

Gourley, G. Douglas. *Effective Municipal Police Organization*. Beverly Hills, Calif.:
1970 Glencoe Press.

Grochla, Erwin. "Entwicklungsstand und aktuelle Probleme der Organisationstheorie."
1977 *Sozialwissenschaftliche Annalen*. 1:1–26.

Grunow, Dieter, and Friedhart Hegner. "Überlegungen zur System-Umwelt-Problematik
1972 anhand der Analyse des Verhältnisses zwischen Organisation und Publikum." *Zeitschrift für Soziologie*. 209–224.

Haas, Eugene J., and Thomas E. Drabek. *Complex Organizations: A Sociological*
1973 *Perspective*. New York: Macmillan.

Hage, Jerald. *Communication and Organizational Control*. New York: John Wiley.
1974

Hall, Richard H. *Organizations: Structure and Process*. Englewood Cliffs, N. J.: Prentice-
1972 Hall.

Hall, Richard H., Norman J. Johnson, and J. Eugene Haas. *Organizational Size,*
1967 *Complexity, and Formalization*." *American Sociological Review*. 32:903–912.

Hannan, Michael T., and John Freeman. "The Population Ecology of Organizations."
1977 *American Journal of Sociology*. 82:929–964.

Hansen, David C. *An Analysis of Police Concepts and Programs*. Springfield, Ill.:
1972 Charles C. Thomas.

Hill, Wilhelm, Raymond Fehlbaum, and Peter Ulrich. "Konzeption einer modernen
1974 Organisationslehre." *Zeitschrift für Organisation*. 43:4–16.

Hill, Wilhelm, Raymond Fehlbaum, and Peter Ulrich. *Organisationslehre*. 2. Auflage,
1976 Bern/Stuttgart: Paul Haupt.

Hoefert, Hans Wolfgang. *Psychologische und soziologische Grundlagen der Organisation*. Giessen: Schmidt.
1976

Kosiol, Erich. *Grundlagen und Methoden der Organisationsforschung*. Berlin: Duncker & Humblot.
1959

Krupp, Sherman. *Patterns in Organizational Analysis*. New York: Holt, Rinehart & Winston.
1961

Larson, Richard C. *Urban Police Patrol Analysis*. Cambridge, Mass.: M.I.T. Press.
1972

Lawrence, Paul R., and Jay W. Lorsch. *Organization and Environment*. Boston: Harvard University Press.
1967

Levinson, Daniel, and Boris Astrachan. "Entry into the Mental Health Center: A Problem in Organizational Boundary-Regulation." In Eric J. Miller (ed.), *Task and Organization*: 217–234. London: John Wiley.
1976

Litterer, Joseph A. *The Analysis of Organizations*. 2nd ed. New York: John Wiley.
1973

Luhmann, Niklas. *Funktionen und Folgen formaler Organisation*. Berlin: Duncker & Humblot.
1964

———. *Soziologische Aufklärung 2*. Opladen: Westdeutscher Verlag.
1975

MacIntyre, Alasdair. "Is a Science of Comparative Politics Possible?" In *Against the Self-Images of the Age*. London: Duckworth.
1971

March, James G., and Herbert A. Simon. *Organizations*. New York: John Wiley.
1958

Mayntz, Renate. *Soziologie der Organisation*. Reinbek: Rowohlt.
1963

Mott, Paul E. *The Characteristics of Effective Organizations*. New York: Harper & Row.
1972

Novick, David (ed.). *Program Budgeting*. Cambridge, Mass.: Harvard University Press.
1965

Parsons, Talcott. *Structure and Process in Modern Society*. Glencoe, Ill.: Free Press.
1960

Perrow, Charles B. *Organizational Analysis: A Sociological View*. Belmont, Calif.: Brooks/Cole.
1970

Pfeiffer, Dietmar K. *Organisationssoziologie*. Stuttgart: Kohlhammer.
1976

Porter, John. *The Vertical Mosaic: An Analysis of Social Class and Power in Canada*. Toronto: University of Toronto Press.
1965

Presthus, Robert. *Elites in the Policy Process*. London: Cambridge University Press.
1974

Pugh, D. S., D. J. Hickson, C. R. Hinnings, and C. Turner. "The Context of Organization Structures." In Richard H. Hall (ed.), *The Formal Organization*: 73–110. New York: Basic Books.
1972

Reiss, Albert J., and David J. Bordua. "Environment and Organization: A Perspective on the Police." In David J. Bordua (ed.), *The Police*: 25–55. New York: John Wiley.
1967

Richardson, Stephen A. "Organizational Contrasts on British and American Ships." *Administrative Science Quarterly*. 1:168–206.
1956

Rodgers, William B., and Richard E. Gardener. "Linked Changes in Values and Behavior in the Out Island Bahamas." *American Anthropologist*. 71:21–35.
1969

Saunders, Charles B., Jr. *Upgrading the American Police*. Washington, D. C.: The Brookings Institution.
1970

Silverman, David. *Theorie der Organisationen*. Wien: Böhlau.
1972

Smith, Bruce. *Police Systems in the United States*. Rev. ed. New York: Harper & Bros.
1960

Sowle, Claude R. (ed.). *Police Power and Individual Freedom*. 4th printing. Chicago:
1969 Aldine.

Spiegelberg, Rüdiger. "Einige Daten zur Rekrutierung und ausbildung der Polizei." In
1971 Johannes Feest and Rüdiger Lautmann (Hrsg.), *Die Polizei*: 107–121. Opladen: Westdeutscher Verlag.

Stümper, Alfred. "Die Organisation der Polizei in der Bundesrepublik Deutschland."
1975 *Zeitschrift für Organisation*. 44: 367–374.

Tannenbaum, Arnold S., Bogdan Kavcic, Menachem Rosner, Mino Vianello, and Georg
1974 Wiesner. *Hierarchy in Organizations*. San Francisco: Jossey-Bass.

Terreberry, Shirley. "The Evolution of Organizational Environments." In Koya Azumi and
1972 Jerald Hage (eds.), *Organizational Systems*: 75–91. Lexington, Mass.: D. C. Heath.

Thompson, James D., and William J. McEwen. "Organizational Goals and Environment:
1958 Goal-Setting as an Interaction Process." *American Sociological Review*. 23:23–31.

Tschanett, Ernst. *Angleichungstendenzen im deutschen Länderpolizeirecht*. Jur. Diss.
1975 Würzburg.

Udy, Stanley H., Jr. "Cross-Cultural Analysis: A Case Study." In Phillip E. Hammond
1964 (ed.), *Sociologists at Work*: 161–183. New York: Basic Books.

U.S. President's Commission on Law Enforcement and Administration of Justice. *The*
1970 *Challenge of Crime in a Free Society*. Washington, D.C.: U.S. Government Printing Office.

Wagenführ, Horst. "Organisation und veranderte Umwelt." *Zeitschrift für Organisation*.
1973 42:12–16.

Waldmann, Peter. "Organisations- und Rollenkonflikte in der Polizei." *Monatsschrift für*
1977 *Kriminologie und Strafrechtsreform*. 60:65–82.

Wallat, Günter. "Organisation- und Führungsprobleme der Schutzpolizei." *Zeitschrift für*
1975 *Organisation*. 44:375–381.

Watson, Nelson A., and James W. Sterling. *Police and their Opinions*. Washington, D.C.:
1969 International Association of Chiefs of Police.

Wilson, James Q. *Varieties of Police Behavior*. New York: Atheneum.
1972

Ziegler, Rolf. *Kommunikationsstruktur und Leistung sozialer Systeme*. Meisenheim:
1968 Anton Hain.

An Exploration in Two Cultures of a Model of Political Behavior in Organizations

PETER J. FROST
DAVID C. HAYES
University of British Columbia

In the past few years, research interest in the concept of organizational politics has increased significantly. Early research by Dimock (1952) on conflict in bureaucracy, the writings of Burns (1961) on institutional change, March (1962) on political coalitions, and Wildavsky (1964) on the politics of the budgetary process, provide some of the historical antecedents to the current focus on the topic. More recently, Pettigrew (1973) has described, in a seminal book, a two-year study of politics and organizational decision-making in a retail organization. Pfeffer and Salancik (1974) studied the allocation of the university budget as a political process. Wergin (1976) outlines a political model for assessing organizational policy making. Efforts to conceptualize and define organizational politics can be found in the works of Burns (1961), Harvey and Mills (1970), MacMillan (1977), Mayes and Allen (1976), Pettigrew (1973), Porter (1976), and Robbins (1976). Pfeffer's (1977) discussion of power and resource allocation in organizations and Mechanic's (1962) views on sources of power of lower participants relate closely to the political domain of organizational behavior, without explicit development of a model of organizational politics. Despite some significant efforts to provide a theoretical understanding of organizational politics as a concept and a few pioneering ventures into its empirical examination, we feel that there is still no

[1] This research was generously supported in part by the Certified General Accountants' Association of British Columbia. We would like to thank the respondents to the interviews at the two institutions studied for their cooperation. We cannot name them individually due to the guarantee of anonymity provided. We also extend appreciation to our colleagues at U.B.C. for comments and their judgment activities: Merle Ace, Thad Barnowe, Izak Benbasat, Chris Fraser, Bob Gephart, Pat Larkey, Vance Mitchell, Larry Moore, Craig Pinder, Rick Pollay, Al Ponak, Jan Sweeney and Bob Zerbst. Other assistance and helpful comments were received from Linda Krefting, College of Business Economics, University of Kentucky, and Brian Little, MacMillan Bloedel, Ltd.

comprehensive definition of organizational politics and that there is ample room for extensive research into its antecedents and its consequences.

A Context for Defining Politics in Organizations

As our starting point in developing a conceptualization of organizational politics, we have taken the view of organizations as market places for the exchange of incentives by both individuals and groups or coalitions of individuals who are members of the organization (Georgiou, 1973). Organizational incentives are perhaps most readily defined in terms of resources available for allocation among organizational members. Likely resources include money, information, goals, policy commitments and so forth. Organizational members, in this view of organization, tend to coalesce around shared interests in order to better seek common organizational outcomes (Baldridge, 1971; March 1962; Cyert and March, 1963). We view these coalitions of individuals as including groups of organizational members formally designated, such as the "Production Department", the "Executive Team", and the "Bargaining Unit", as well as combinations or groupings of individuals with shared interests and commonly desired outcomes who are less formally or less permanently drawn together. These latter coalitions are sometimes recognized by labels such as "concerned workers", or "young Turks", or the "inner circle". Clearly, all such coalitions in an organization are not equal. Some coalitions of organizational members tend to dominate others through their ability to control important resources, and can be viewed as dominant coalitions in the organization (Child, 1972; Thompson, 1967).

We have, at this point, a perception of organizations which includes the notion of exchange of resources between and among individual organization members, coalitions of individual organizational members, coalitions of coalitions, and individuals and coalitions, where one or more coalition may be dominant relative to others in the organization.

The Distribution of Resources

The distribution of resources in an organization can be thought of as being accomplished through agreements and trade-offs among individuals and coalitions of individuals in their bids to obtain influence over decisions perceived to be of most importance to them (Barnard, 1938; Blau, 1964; March and Simon, 1958; Pondy, 1970; White, 1974). There appear to be two phases to this process of exchange of resources in the organization; one phase has to do with the negotiation of an exchange, the other with the enactment of the terms of the exchange once negotiated. The negotiation phase would seem to be best represented as one in which values, goals, and priorities are problematic, to be worked out rather than given (Peery, 1975). Concern is with trading-off or bargaining between two or more organizational members (individuals or coalitions). This is the organizational arena which we would term political (Dimitriou, 1973), in which conflict is institutionalized (Cyert and March, 1963; Pettigrew, 1973). The enactment phase, on the other hand, is perhaps best represented as one in which values, goals and priorities are given. Concern is with the implementation of an exchange between two or more organizational members. Examples include activities such as payment of salary in return for work produced, or with a dominant coalition providing scarce research dollars to other organizational members in return for their having agreed to pursue dominant coalition objectives. We would term this the rational or administrative arena in which consensus rather than conflict is institutionalized (Peery, 1975; Dimitriou, 1973).

The Role of the Contract

An important linkage between these two phases of an exchange is the contract between the organizational members party to the exchange. Such contracts vary in degree of explicitness and formality and are established through negotiation. The contract itself specifies actions and activities to be undertaken in the enactment or implementation phase. In the ongoing process of organization, contracts are both outcomes of exchanges and important inputs to subsequent exchanges. The content of a given contract may provide the basis of precedent or serve as a memory source for subsequent exchanges. It is possible, therefore, to depict both stable and changing aspects of the organization process. Cyert and March (1963) make a similar point in their treatment of mutual control systems such as budgets and function allocation, both of which can be represented by the contract concept.

An exchange contract should represent the content of what each party to the exchange will provide in terms of resources and what each party expects of themselves and the other party so as to fulfill the contract. In addition to the programmed steps incorporated in such a contract, there are two less obvious aspects. Such a contract specifies, or at least implies, a discretionary or nonroutine zone of behavior for each party to the contract, which can be deployed to fulfill the contract terms. This is akin to the "zone of indifference" concept of Barnard (1938), or the "zone of acceptance" concept of Simon (1976). There is an additional indifference area of behavior within such contracts, however. This behavior centers on the use of organizational resources by one party to an exchange with which the other parties have no interest or concern. Such behavior would be considered by the parties as incidental to, unrelated to, or not intruding on the exchange between the parties to that exchange.

To summarize thus far, we assume that organizational members engage in an exchange process to acquire or influence the development and deployment of resources available in the organizational marketplace. We assume also that the outcome of such an exchange is a contract which specifies (in varying degrees of explicitness) expected behavior from each party to the exchange toward its enactment, areas of discretion or nonroutine behavior relevant to enactment of the exchange, and areas of indifference in which each party to the exchange uses organizational resources in ways of no interest or concern to the other parties to the exchange. We perceive the negotiating phase of the exchange process to be the likely arena of organizational politics. We perceive the enactment phase of the exchange process to be the likely arena of administrative (programmed) behavior.[2] Discretionary (acceptable,

[2] It is interesting to note, in this context, the recent observation on exchange and organizational interdependency by Hall (1977.238), "Once an exchange agreement has

nonroutine) behavior is more difficult to locate within a single phase. It seems likely that discretionary behavior will be associated with both the negotiating and the enactment phases. It differs from political behavior in terms of acceptability and from administrative behavior in terms of routineness.

The Mechanism of Organizational Politics: The Role of Power

While the two primary phases involving a contract are concerned with negotiating or establishing a contract and its enactment, we perceive a number of subphases associated with the contract. Within the negotiation phase, attempts can be made to change the contract, unilaterally or multilaterally; efforts can also be made to resist change of the contract by one or more parties to the contract.

The resources available in the organizational marketplace derive from both the historical and current contributions which organizational members make to the marketplace. Members bring to an exchange the resources they have available to them. Such resources should provide the basis for participation in the exchange, and each such base can be conceptualized in terms of power (Dahl, 1957). Power is viewed here as the property of a social relationship (Emerson, 1962) and is defined after Dahl (1957), in the sense that A is powerful relative to B if A can get B to do something which B would not otherwise do. The probability that A will accomplish this is a function of B's dependence on A for the resources A has, as well as the degree of interest or need B has for the resources A offers (Emerson, 1962). The concept of coalitions of individuals allows a network view of power involving organizational members A and B with other members, so that dependencies among members are linked to availability and interest in the resources in the organizational marketplace. Power can be viewed as being both asymmetrical and reciprocal in a relationship between actors (Wrong, 1968). Thus, power may be balanced between or among actors to an exchange or it may be imbalanced, with power monopolized or centralized by one party. Wrong terms these intercursive and integral power respectively. Typically, exchanges involving a dominant coalition and other coalitions or individuals will be imbalanced in terms of relative power. A further important distinction introduced by Wrong is of alternating power differences. Actors in an exchange may alternate the roles of power holder and power subject (as in exchanges where a mix of professional (expert) and administrative resources are exchanged). Power differences may also be consistently reversed in given situations, one organizational member having greater power in one situation and the other member having greater power in another situation within the exchange. An example here is of union power in hiring and firing decisions and management power in long range technical planning. It is possible on this basis to view exchange and the establishment of contracts as dynamic processes in which the exercise of a power base by organizational members in an exchange

---

been reached, the nature of the interaction shifts. The interactions are more regularized and routine. The parties in the relationship give it less attention until a new exchange issue arises." Simon (1976) discussing "fact" and "value" in decision making and distinctions between policy and administration appears to be addressing the same issue.

relationship is characterized by degrees of symmetry, reciprocity and directionality. We have applied one further contribution from Wrong. He defines politics as "a struggle for power and a struggle to limit, resist and escape from power", (Wrong, 1968:675–6).

DEFINING POLITICAL BEHAVIOR IN ORGANIZATIONS

Integrating the various perspectives on power, we observe that Dahl's (1957) definition of power connotes one party forcing another party to do something the latter would rather not do, whereas Emerson (1962) identifies the relational nature of power in the exchange process (as does Wrong), and Wrong (1968) conveys the sense of politics as a struggle involving power. What emerges from a consideration of these three perspectives, and of the resource exchange view of organization, is an image of organizational politics as having to do with behavior of organizational members which is imposed on another party to the exchange, is judged unacceptable by that party, and (implicitly) is resisted by that party. In terms of this definition, recognition of the behavior as an imposition and as unacceptable by one or more parties to the exchange qualifies the behavior as political in the eyes of these parties. Resistance to the behavior assessed as political is incorporated into the definition in the form of intent. Actual resistance is likely to be determined by variables such as the power difference between the parties involved, as well as the anticipated or perceived consequences of the political behavior.

We perceive political behavior to be associated with the negotiation phase and sub-phases of an exchange. Political behavior is expected to occur when one or more parties attempt to exchange resources or to limit, resist, or escape from a given resource exchange agreement in ways which are imposing to other parties to the exchange and likely to be resisted if recognized.

Operationalizing Political Behavior.

We have suggested three types of behavior relevant to the two-phase exchange process. We expect political behavior to be most prevalent and most pertinent to the negotiation phase of the exchange process, and administrative behavior as most prevalent and pertinent to the enactment phase of the process. We expect to find discretionary behavior as pertinent and as occuring in both phases of the process. It becomes important to define these behaviors operationally in order to make explicit the distinctions among the three behavior types and to allow us to explore them empirically. The definitions derive from the considerations of exchange, contract and power discussed earlier and are as follows:

Administrative Behavior. The activities and actions of organizational members (individuals as well as formal and informal coalitions) when they use resources (for example, money, time, manpower) to enhance or protect their share of an exchange (involving themselves and other organizational members) in ways which are organizationally prescribed or routine.

Discretionary Behavior. The activities and actions of organizational members (individuals, as well as formal and informal coalitions) when they use resources (for example, money, time, manpower) to enhance or protect their share of an exchange (involving themselves and other organizational members) in ways which are nonorganizationally prescribed or nonroutine. Such nonprescribed or nonroutine behaviors reflect a consensus within the organization or between the parties to the exchange that the behaviors, while informal, are acceptable or are behaviors to which other parties to the exchange are indifferent.

Political Behavior. The activities and actions of organizational members (individuals, as well as formal and informal coalitions) when they use resources (for example, money, time, manpower) to enhance or protect their share of an exchange (involving themselves and other organizational members) in ways which would be resisted, or ways in which the impact would be resisted, if recognized by the other parties to the exchange.

Examination of these definitions of behavior reveals a major distinction between administrative and discretionary behavior on the one hand, and political behavior on the other hand. Administrative and discretionary actions and activities are viewed by parties to the exchange as *consensus* behavior. There is agreement that the behavior is legitimate in terms of the exchange. Political actions and activities, however, are resisted or will be resisted if their intent is recognized, by one or more parties to the exchange. There is a lack of consensus, a *non-consensus* about the legitimacy of the behavior among parties to the exchange. While political behavior represents non-consensus behavior as we have defined it, it must be emphasized that no evaluative connotations are intended for the concept of political behavior (Mowday, 1976; Porter, 1976). That is, political behavior is neither good nor bad. Evaluation of behavior, political or non-political, as good or bad requires an assessment of its outcomes as it relates to the exchange itself and to the parties to the exchange. Political behavior may result in benefits or costs (or both) to the party invoking it and to one or more of the other parties. The perceptions of each of the parties to an exchange are important if we are to establish that a behavior is political, discretionary or administrative.

Defining political behavior in the context of a resource exchange view of organization has several advantages. It allows us to deal with political behavior at several levels or organizational analysis: individual, unit/group, and multi-unit levels. It avoids the need to describe and analyze political behavior with reference to theoretical abstractions such as "*the* organization", and "*the* organization's goals and desired outcomes". It enables us to treat political behavior not as an isolated or separate phenomenon, but as an integral part of a model of organization which focuses on resource exchange between and among organizational members.

Other attempts have been made to capture the meaning of organizational politics and of political behavior in organizations. Mayes and Allen (1976) have categorized other definitions of organizational politics in the literature into those describing it as a process involving claims against the resource sharing system, as conflict over policy preferences, or as self-serving behavior. Given an assumption that organizations are marketplaces for resource exchange we would describe all behavior as primarily self-serving in the sense that exchanges are entered into first for what they have to offer and second for what must be given in return. Behavior is self-serving, but it can also be intended to serve others. Self-serving behavior is political as we define it when the intent or the perceived intent is not to serve others, or is to misserve others. In similar vein, claims against the resource system and conflict over policy preferences may or may not be political, depending on whether the behavior is viewed as consensual by the parties involved.

Mayes and Allen provide their own deductive definition of organizational politics as "the management of influence to obtain ends not sanctioned by the organization or to obtain sanctioned ends through non-sanctioned influence means" (Mayes and Allen, 1976:8). The definition makes a step toward a more analytic treatment of the concept than had earlier definitions. Introducing the notion of non-consensus *means* and non-consensus *ends* provides for the possibility of differences in tactics and focus of political behavior. However, the definition is limited in our view, by exclusive emphasis on self-serving behavior and by being tied to considerations of *the* organization, issues we have discussed earlier. Nevertheless, the links between this definition and our own become clear if we modify the Mayes and Allen approach by replacing *the* organization by "other parties to an exchange" and by interpreting the "management of influence" to mean the use of power. The use of non-sanctioned means (to sanctioned ends) and the pursuit of non-sanctioned ends (by sanctioned means) then become specific types of political behavior available to a party or parties involved in negotiating an exchange. Porter's (1976:5) definition of organizational politics as self-interested behavior outside that required or desired by the organization, or forbidden by the organization, also has ties with our approach if one relinquishes notions of *the* organization and behavior forbidden (by the organization) in favor of concepts such as coalitions, exchange processes and consensus and non-consensus behavior.

THE STUDY

The exploration of our model of organizational politics was conducted in two technological institutes, one in Australia, the other in Canada. These two educational institutions are similar along several dimensions although differing susbstantially in some of their structural characteristics. Focus in this study was on the departmental or unit level of analysis.

The Organizations Studied

Both organizations are institutes of technology offering courses in several disciplines and subdisciplines. The Australian institute has four faculties or schools (Business, Applied Science, Engineering and General Studies). The Canadian institute has four faculties or divisions (Business, Engineering, Health Services and a Core Division comprising departments of Physics, Chemistry, Mathematics and English). The current full time enrollment figures are 4000 (Australian) and 3100 (Canadian). Both institutes have a fundamental emphasis on teaching rather than research (with consequent heavy teaching loads), and instructors stress pragmatism and technology rather than theoretical aspects of the various subjects they teach. The Australian institute offers a three-year degree program and a two-year diploma program; the Canadian institute offers a two-year diploma program.

There are several structural differences between the two organizations. In 1973, the Australian institute was incorporated with other such institutes into a national network of Colleges of Advanced Education which are federally funded. The Canadian institute became an autonomous organization within its education system in 1974, and is funded by the province in which it is located. The faculty in the Australian institute are not formally unionized; the faculty below department head in the Canadian institute are unionized. A union of administrative staff also exists in this latter organization. The Australian institute is in the midst of an extensive appraisal of its structure and decision-making process. Currently, key decisions concerning allocation of resources as well as major policy formulation are made by the Director of the Institute (President) in informal consultation with the Deans of the four faculties. Interestingly, the Canadian institute has been through a similar process in the past two years. It has decentralized decision-making considerably through formation of an education committee comprising the Deans of faculties, heads of key service departments (e.g., library, career programs) and an executive director who links with the Principal of the Institute and his executive committee. This formally constituted committee has considerable discretion with respect to allocation of resources.

In general it would appear that the Canadian institute has a more extensively developed formal structure than its Australian counterpart, and is also in the process of implementing formal performance evaluation procedures and systems for long-range planning, which are not in evidence in the Australian institute.

METHOD

The Sample

The total sample of respondents, twenty-two at the Canadian institution and eleven in the Australian, was reduced, for purposes of the study, to twenty respondents, ten from each institute. This was done as a control device to attempt a closer match of respondents in terms of functions and responsibilites. For reasons of time and access, different strategies of data gathering were employed at each institution. In the Australian sample an in-depth study of one faculty (Dean, department heads and individual faculty members) as well as three service departments located in other faculties was performed. In the Canadian institution, a cross-sectional study of Deans and department heads in all faculties and general service areas was undertaken.

The sample of respondents from the Canadian institution included in this report represents department heads in the faculty corresponding to the Australian institution as well as those of service departments to this faculty. The major difference in terms of hierarchical level and function, therefore, is the inclusion of respondents in non-administrative positions in only one sample. It should be emphasized, however, that a departmental or group level of analysis was the emphasis in both samples, and that, in effect, both "line" and "staff" positions were studied in each institute.

Data Collection

The steps employed in the study are diagrammed in Figure 1 to enhance understanding of the procedures we followed.

A patterned interview was undertaken with each of the participants in the study. The interviews were tape recorded. The questions were of two main types. First, background information questions were asked to elicit demographic data on respondents, to set the general tone for the interview (i.e., the department/group focus) and to make the respondents feel at ease with the

Figure 1

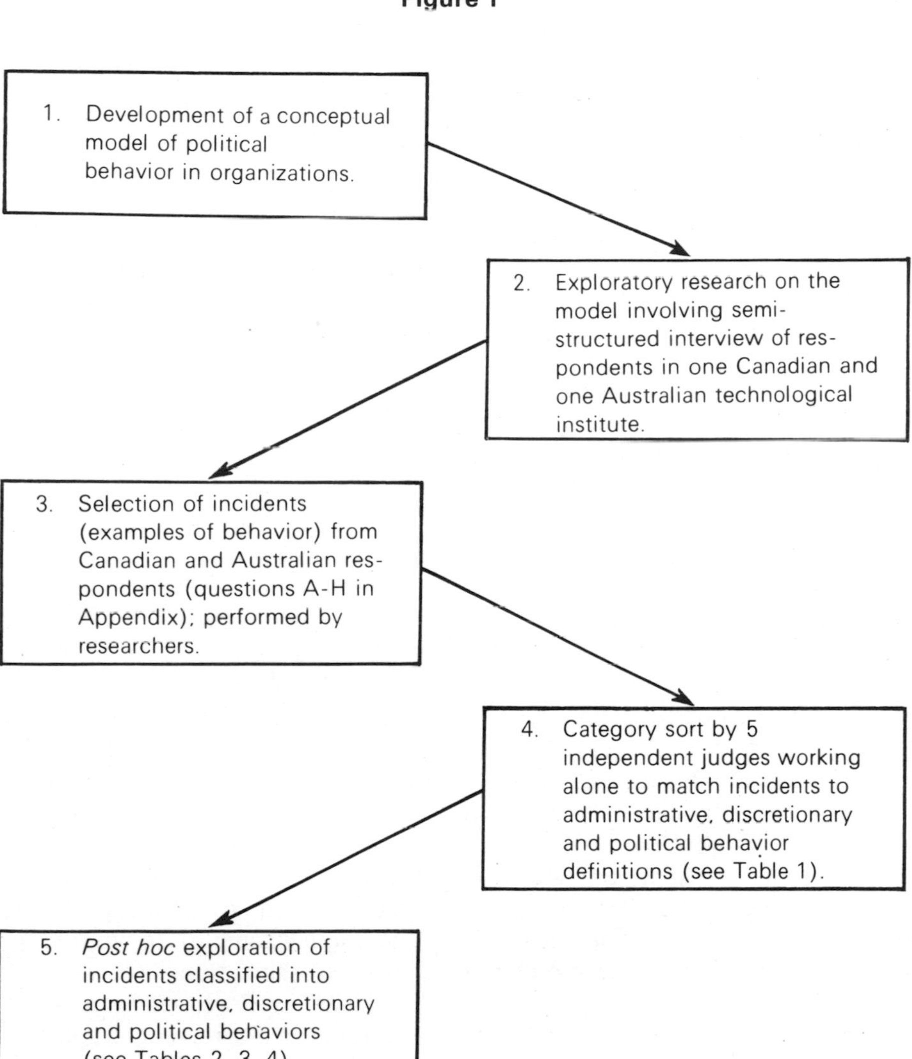

1. Development of a conceptual model of political behavior in organizations.
2. Exploratory research on the model involving semi-structured interview of respondents in one Canadian and one Australian technological institute.
3. Selection of incidents (examples of behavior) from Canadian and Australian respondents (questions A-H in Appendix); performed by researchers.
4. Category sort by 5 independent judges working alone to match incidents to administrative, discretionary and political behavior definitions (see Table 1).
5. *Post hoc* exploration of incidents classified into administrative, discretionary and political behaviors (see Tables 2, 3, 4)

* Two additional steps were employed between (3) and (4) but are not reported in this paper. The effect of these steps was to "clean up" the incidents sorted by the judges in step 4, *via* the elimination of a large number of incidents.

tape recorder. Second, questions derived from the definition of organizational politics, dealing with the establishment, maintenance and alteration of resource exchange agreements among departments were asked. (These are listed in the Appendix.) These questions deal with activities which are undertaken to set up arrangements such as joint program development, service course arrangements and joint equipment usage; activities which are undertaken to maintain satisfactory arrangements of these types; and activities which are undertaken by either party to an arrangement to unilaterally alter the arrangement or to avoid its implementation. Emphasis in the interview was placed on eliciting specific examples of behavior which each interviewee was able to relate to each of these phases of an arrangement. The analysis reported here deals with responses to this series of (eight) questions.

ANALYSIS

The transcripts of the interviews from both sets of subjects were analyzed for actual examples of departmental behavior provided in response to these questions (see Appendix). One hundred fifty-nine such examples were obtained, typed on separate sheets, numbered randomly and presented to a group of judges for content analysis. This part of the analysis was performed in order to determine whether independent judges, given no information other than the examples of behavior, would be able to group them into categories resembling administrative, discretionary and political behavior, as well as being able to determine the similarities and overlaps between such categories. The content analysis and associated retranslation by a different set of judges derived six dimensions of behavior which, though of value, did not yield the categories of interest in this study and are not reported in this paper. What we report herein is the outcome of a classification exercise by a third set of judges asked to categorize a subset of examples of behavior according to the operational definitions of political, administrative and discretionary behavior which we provided. The behavioral incidents to be classified were items which had survived the initial judging and retranslation process and which we considered to be unambiguous and unidimensional as a result of the earlier two judgement stages. We assigned five judges to work independently at this final task,[3] and instructed them to attempt to place the examples in one of four categories—administrative behavior, discretionary behavior, political behavior, or "unclear"; the latter category for items which the judges could not comfortably fit into the other three categories.

The prior analyses, omitted from this paper as indicated above, had the effect of reducing the set of examples given to this group of judges down to 60 incidents (slightly more than one-third of the original sample). In order to give greater confidence in interpretation of the classifications (in terms of administrative, discretionary and political behavior), we included for analytical purposes only the items on which either all, of four out of five, judges agreed on a given categorization. This left slightly less than half of the items for purposes of discussion and analysis (29 out of 60). If a simple majority-rule for inclusion of

[3] All judges were members of the Commerce Faculty at U.B.C., with teaching and research interests in the behavioral area.

items had been adopted, 56 out of 60 items would have survived, indicating almost unanimous agreement among judges on classification. We felt more comfortable applying the "80 per cent or greater" inclusion rule in terms of the degree of confidence it allowed us in interpreting our results. Nevertheless, the impact of this decision in reducing the sample size should be recognized.

As presented in Table 1, the final items were almost evenly split between the two institutions (14 Canadian and 15 Australian) reflecting the even distribution in the set of sixty items examined by the judges.[4]

DISCUSSION

As indicated in the Appendix, the questions asked of respondents focused on specific examples of behavior which occurred when departments set up, carried out, resisted or unilaterally changed arrangements betweeen themselves and other departments. (We did not mention to our interview subjects our administrative/discretionary/political behavior distinctions. They were not aware that the study focused on political behavior.) The incidents categorized by the independent judges on the basis of the definitions we provided have several interesting characteristics which we explore in this section of the paper.

It must be borne in mind that the nature of the data and the small size of the sample make generalization inappropriate. The discussion which follows is, like the study, intended to be exploratory and illustrative of what we perceive to be a potentially rich perspective on behavior in organizations. The ideas and interpretations offered are not made in the usual sense of being generalizable to other situations, but rather as bases for further research in the area. This *caveat* is critical for the reading of the remainder of the paper.

As a first step in interpreting data, we observe from the Appendix and Tables 2–4 that, as would be predicted by our definitions of political and nonpolitical behavior, items provided in response to questions eliciting examples of activities involved in *enacting* or *implementing* arrangements (question B) only appear in the administrative and discretionary categories. The judges did not perceive these activities to be political in terms of the definition provided. Examples dealing with the *setting up* of arrangements also fall into these two categories, and not that of political behavior. Finally, although some items in response to

Table 1

BEHAVIORAL CATEGORIES BY COUNTRY OF INSTITUTION

	Administrative	*Discretionary*	*Political*
Canada	4	2	8
Australia	5	5	5

[4] A chi-square test found no differences between institutions in terms of the behavioral categories.

questions involving *unilateral change* of arrangements (questions C,D,E,G,H) and some activities aimed at *increasing* the share of resources (question F) are classified as discretionary or administrative, the majority of examples provided were perceived to be political. In other words, the enactment phase behaviors analyzed were judged as either administrative or discretionary. Most negotiation phase (and subphase) behaviors were judged political, but a few behaviors generated in response to "negotiation phase" interview questions were classified by judges as discretionary or administrative. This finding highlighted

Table 2

REPRESENTATIVE EXAMPLES OF ADMINISTRATIVE BEHAVIOR (Questions which elicited the response are indicated)

(F)	When there is a general requirements for more funds, we build the arguments on the size of the department—staff numbers, student numbers, number of programs offered, service courses provided to others and so on.
(A)	For example, we're giving a course; we're already providing training for real estate salesmen for industry in cooperation with the university, and our students have gone out in the industry and have done exceptionally well. We have the industry actually recruit our students for jobs in various aspects of real estate where students have had no specific real estate training. So it's a question here of showing what we have done and what we can do, what our strengths at the Institute are.
(E)	We've had a problem with a number of requests for servicing involving non-educational activities. People were coming to us direct to develop publicity materials and that sort of thing and it became quite embarrassing to have to refuse a Dean. In that case, I approached our Dean and the registrar, and they issued a formal statement saying that we were not to do these thing unless authorized by the registrar.
(G)	I would venture to say six months, it has got to be almost six months ago, two faculties came to the Education Committee with recommendations that they revert from the quarter system to semester system. These things were tabled and left hanging and all the rest of it. And they were lifted from the table and a decision was made. And the decision that was made bounced back on us in the Education Committee. Then a committee was struck to look at it again and the committee came in with recommendations, came back to the Education Committee. Finally one of the two faculties said: "Look we've got to go with it, the decision was made it is done."
(A)	We use the Educational Development Committee fairly extensively. We have extended the committee recently by appointing what we term Educational Development Unit liaison officers, who are people in each department to liaise between the Educational Development Unit and their department.
(B)	We have improved the equipment circulation service and I have figures every month on cost of staff; statistics every month as to what equipment was used by what department as well as periodic reports from supervisors and complaints or comments from the various departments—we monitor the situation that way.

the need for an examination of the examples for possible similarities in the political, discretionary and administrative behaviors linked to the negotiation phase, as well as an assessment of whether there were differences between such administrative and discretionary behaviors and those linked with the enactment phase.

Examining for patterns within categories, it appears from the examples provided in Table 2 that there are differences in focus within the category of administrative behavior. The focus varies from construction of arguments to acquire resource increments through the formal mechanisms of the organization, to public relations exercises, to use of the formal hierarchy to protect one's department against encroachment, to formal integration mechanisms, to system performance monitoring. In each of the examples, a different use is made of the administrative system. Some refer to internal (to the department) mechanisms; others, which are external, refer to formal interdependencies within the organization. It is interesting to note that these uses of "administrative" behavior are not judged as political, since, as described, they do not constitute actions and activities which other parties to an exchange do, or would find to be unacceptable and so a cause for resistance. That is, they are consensus behaviors.

However, the examples of administrative behavior generated in response to negotiation phase questions were not anticipated, given the conceptual framework discussed in the initial portion of the paper. While no conclusive statements can be made on this observation given the sample sizes in the study, it does emphasize the need for a careful test of the assumptions we make about behavior and the exchange phases in developing our conceptual framework. The observed external focus of such behavior also highlights the need to assess perspectives of all parties to an exchange if we are to accurately capture the nature of the three categories of behavior we have developed.

Similarly, the examples of discretionary behavior in Table 3 show differences in focus. There appear to be parallels to the situations involving administrative behavior. Internal activities, such as the establishment of new teaching programs, and external activities with varying degrees of (informal) interdependencies, e.g., joint program development and the gathering of *ad hoc* feedback on performance, all fall within the category of discretionary behavior as judged in this study. The same broad dichotomy of focus, internal *versus* external (interdependence), is not in evidence within the category of political behavior. The thrust of each instance of political behavior is clearly external to the particular department or unit; that is, it is directed toward other departments. Examples from Table 4 include attempts to increase resources available to a department, efforts to resist resource increments to others, and reactions against imposition of change by others. That is, the focus of the political behavior example is on negotiation with other units not enactment of previously negotiated contracts nor the administration or operation of a particular subunit.

Interestingly, the items in this study which have been judged as political describe behavior which is strikingly similar to that discussed by Pfeffer (1977) in his treatment of power and its use in maintaining and allocating resources. For example, Pfeffer talks about the way in which subunits can achieve power through alliances with internal and external groups (Pfeffer, 1977:259). Both

Table 3

REPRESENTATIVE EXAMPLES OF DISCRETIONARY BEHAVIOR (Questions which elicited the response are indicated)

(G) The elaborate laboratory set-up we have now and the radical revisions in our beginning course's educational methods were effectively the ideas of one person and the team of staff he got working for him. From that beginning on his own initiative, we put in a special proposal to the government funding body to fully fund the preparation of the necessary special materials for this course, which was granted for one year. At the end of that time it was so successful that we were able to convince the institute to pick up the tab for the on-going costs in future years.

(B) For instance, at the graduate diploma level, we make sure we only have people teaching who can relate to students. This is because when I came most of our department confirmed everyone else's prejudices of our being a soft area. So we've been very conscious of the fact that we've had to market ourselves.

(A) We recently developed a joint program with another faculty. That was quite an exciting thing as there seems to be some traditional feelings that the two faculties don't get on well. We were able to win support in principle for that combined degree, and then we were able to win support right down the line that it was a worth while thing.

(A) It's happened with another department this last spring; they decided they would like an elective course for their second-year students—the first-year students get math as a requirement, but an elective for their second-year students. So the department head came to me and said, "Would this be possible?", and I went back to my department and asked were they willing to staff it in spite of their overload. The department is overloaded relative to institute. They said yes—on a one-year basis they would try it. And so I went back to the other department and said "Yes". Then I got the instructor who agreed to teach it, and we talked to them. It's a very sort of unstructured process. . . .

(A) They say what they think they would like and we say whether we think this is pedagogically possible in the time allotted. Then there is a lot of compromise and then a course outline and then it starts.

(B) The other way, from that Faculty servicing us, is most inefficiently operated at the moment, and that's a criticism of ourselves. We look for occasional *ad hoc* feedback by bumping into someone in the hall and by being reasonably friendly with the people who take classes, to every now and then just have a talk and say: "How is it going, do you have any particular problems?"

such alliances are described as political behavior in items reported in this study. The hiring of auxiliary people and $2500 subscription is an example. As a second example, Pfeffer talks about the use of committees to legitimate allocation decisions in organizations (Pfeffer, 1972:242). A reported behavior in our study describes the use of a committee and the timing of a committee meeting to "push through" a unilateral decision to reduce the number of hours taught in a particular course.

Thus, in terms of our definition of political behavior, we see examples of

Table 4

REPRESENTATIVE EXAMPLES OF POLITICAL BEHAVIOR
(Questions which elicited the response are indicated)

(F) You have to cheat a little, be a little unethical perhaps. Here is an example. We need something here in the department right now we should have. However, the commercial outlet that supplies it will not supply it to an academic institution. OK, right now we are speaking to a person who is in industry downtown, who can get it. So we are saying, "You take the $2,500 subscription and we will share the cost with you, and you give us 50 % of the material because they send things in multiple copies. You give us the material—they don't really want it. Alright, at the same time I mentioned this to a university director here in the city. And he said, "When you get it, I want to share the cost too." So now we have three people, so we are reducing the cost. The only thing anyone here is going to see is "Hey, we have got access to this information." The Bursar will see it, because suddenly he is going to transfer money to some industry for a service to the department. The only person that will not see is the Institute that is supplying the material. As far as they are concerned it is coming to an industry.

(F) We do need staff. Our service has grown and needs for it have grown and we've asked for staff and we were frustrated in our request for fulltime staff members last year. We've been running with auxiliaries. I made damn sure we spent every cent we had in anything related to staff. As a matter of fact, I tried to overspend. Not in a wasteful sort of way, because the need is there and the services have been valuable, but I just made damn sure that every cent was spent. So that, in fact, is going to be a bottom line. At least it will be completely absorbed in this sort of thing and it took a fair amount of work on my part in some cases to get this money spent. It is very difficult within the institute bureaucracy to hire auxiliary people, it took a hell of a lot of work but I was able to and spent just about every cent that I had and you know some of them are full time regular positions. So that's the thing—spending money, plus actually soliciting the departments we're to serve, to say "For God sakes, let your department heads and Deans know that you want this service if you actually want it. I'll work for you if you work for yourself." This sort of thing. And so this information now is pumping up to Deans, "Yes, we do need a full-time person in a permanent position instead of this auxiliary situation."

(D) The Dean of one Faculty actually put to the Senate (in other words, the top academic group), that courses which involved a statistical content should be taught, as a matter of principle, by his faculty. And he then went even further to actually nominate subjects which he felt they ought to be teaching, which included, among others, marketing research. Now, his argument was based on the fact that you could always get the applied knowhow, a veneer of that, but you can't get the real theoretical stuff, you know, you've got to have a full mathematical type degree. Where of course, we argue, our students don't have to know how to prove a formula. What we do want is people who know how to apply it. And so there is a fundamental division in philosophy. Now, when he presented that, it was thrown out, and it was just agreed not to discuss it as being not worthy of discussion by this board. That, in fact, people accepted the principle that the course leaders know what are the needs of the courses. However, it is recognized at the same time that anybody who can contribute to a

Table 4 (*Contd.*)

course should be given that opportunity, because otherwise we could end up having mathematicians in every single department. So, in the sciences, all their people became unemployed.

(C) I went to see the Graduate division at the time, on my own and told them this proposal was going to cost them $5,000 to $6,000 a year. In my view, it's a worse deal. In other words, I attempted to sabotage what they were doing by a direct approach to the President of the Institute. But it didn't work. He had been bought off or didn't understand the issues. I don't quite know what, but as far as I was concerned, we lost that fight.

(E) If a system is introduced and I don't want to carry it out, I can tie it up from the purchase order end, the shipping end, the receiving end, the supplier end. It's tight knots from that point of view as far as once the item finally arrived, if it did, you know through the technical delays, this sort of thing, I can just keep on going. The unit comes in, it's say not approved, has to go back, comes in. You know you can use that type of thing. Budget, transfer many different ways; the institute is an incredibly complex place and the bureaucracy can work against you but it can also work for you, if you want it to. Basically that's what I would do, use bureaucracy to kill it or at least slow it down until finally people got so frustrated they just say "Oh, the hell with it."

(H) Some people use the staff society (a union) to resist change.

(H) For example, if I wanted to prevent the implementation of some recent recommendations, all I would have to do would be to go around and tell people it was the greatest load of crap that had ever been written and to ignore it, seeing I was on the committee that wrote it. I wouldn't do that, of course. You could, in my view, sabotage it quite easily. There's other people trying to do that, so I don't need to.

(H) In response to a recent report suggesting changes to be made in the institution, I set out on paper my own objections. I then circulated that to as wide an audience as possible within the organization. I am looking for support so as to be able to say "This group opposes it," not just "I oppose it."

(C) But if in fact I'm servicing somebody else's thing and they say, we want it that particular way well hopefully, the conflict is somehow resolved, you know, in a mutually satisfactory way. If it really came to the crunch, where we're told things, then I guess we would threaten as we did, in fact at the Senate, that "O.K., if that's the way you want it, we'll employ our own people. We'll get a statistician in here, don't you worry about it any more, you look after your place and we'll look after ours." And so in an ultimate situation, the people who direct the programs, who are ultimately responsible for them, would argue that if they won't cooperate with us, that we'll do it our way.

(D) One of the departments cut their math hours from 5 hours to 4 hours in quarter A, and 3 hours in quarters B and C, and this was done without any consultation with anybody. In fact, I didn't know anything about it, until one of my instructors said: "Hey, how come I've only got 3 on my time table." In that case it was hopeless. It was partly a case which fell through the cracks in the system. (The Senior Education Committee had just started.) The Acting Dean of our faculty was told about 3 o'clock in the afternoon that the Committee had an emergency meeting to be held at 4:30, could he come? He was not told the agenda. He said, "No, I have

Table 4 (*Contd.*)

another meeting, I can't come." At that meeting they got this through the Committee. The Executive Director of the Committee should have killed it at that stage but he didn't. It went to the Academic Sub-Committee of the Board that night and to the full Board 2 days later and it was done. I think it was an intentional strategy partly due to anxiety and pressure in the department itself. They were under pressure to reduce the physical sciences content. I think it was due in part to a personality clash between the previous Head of our department and the Head of that department. I think it was partly a convenient thing for them to do, if they could get it that way. Kind of, "We'll take what we want if we can, or we'll justify it if we have to."

actions which reflect non-consensus behaviors. However, it should be noted in this context that the nature of exchange agreements, and the negotiating and enactment of such agreements, involves at least two parties. In all of the examples in this study, given the methodology employed, we are only dealing with one perception of the particular exchange, that of the reporter of each example.[5] Potentially, focus on a particular exchange as the research emphasis and obtaining the perceptions of the other parties to the exchange would lead to a more complete understanding of the behavior and to the delineation of networks in which perceptions as to the intent or result of particular actions would likely vary considerably among network members.

For example, take the case of a multilateral exchange involving five parties, A–E. A's intent in the exchange may be political, but only perceived to be so by B; parties C, D and E may perceive A's behavior as discretionary. Such multiple and conflicting perceptions of behavior are to be expected in complex systems, and reflect the nuances of coalition formation and operation, and the networks of interdependencies in such systems. The description of such networks of perceptions would, in effect, provide us with interesting snapshots of significant organizational exchanges processes: we would be able to more fully explore the exercise of power, perceptions of power bases, rationales for particular courses of action, the nature of the formal administrative system and how it operates, potential "bugs" or "loopholes" in enacted contracts represented in control or budget systems, etc. Even with the one-sided perspective which our examples provide, this richness comes out in several of the examples classified as representative of political behavior. As an illustration, take the item in which the individual boasts that he can tie things up in a number of ways in order to prevent implementation (Table 4). His intent is readily discernible, yet given his knowledge of the operation of the formal administrative system of the organization, and his potential ability to shrug off complaints by others by making reference to "red-tape" and "bureaucracy", he can keep such intent well hidden. In fact, others may perceive the problem to be one of too much "bureaucracy", and not due to the exercise of power by the individual reporting

[5] To this extent, we have a perspective of political behavior from one vantage point only, that of the department represented by the interviewee. More precisely, we have an interpretation of the nature of this behavior once-removed, since ascribing the behavior as political is done by a consensus of judges studying a behavior incident. To have asked the interviewee if the behavior was political would have been disruptive in this study, since it would have signalled our intent and biased the outcomes.

the incident. Their response might be very different if the political nature of the behavior was recognized. Such covert behavior (behavior which would be resisted but is not since it is not recognized) would seem to capture the essence of what Bachrach and Baratz (1962) refer to as the "hidden face of power". The behavior by the department which ties up the bureaucracy has a non-consensus intent but it is also of a nature that it is not resisted because it is so well hidden that it is not recognized for what it is. Clearly, the methodological problems involved in exploring this notion of power are formidable. It remains, nevertheless, an intriguing area of political behavior for further investigation.

Contrasting with this "hidden power" activity is behavior which is more openly political. It is behavior which imposes, is not consensual, but is sufficiently overt that it can be recognized by other parties. Resistance by the other party to the exchange may follow, depending on circumstances and variables not captured in this study.

Instances of such behavior are given by some items in Table 4. One example deals with the recognition that some people use the union to resist changes: this is overt behavior, visible to other parties, and thus methods of resistance to it may develop. Similarly, the example of the use of the committee system to push through a change, although partially hidden in the particular example, is overt behavior capable of being resisted.

An important issue relating to the operational definitions of administrative, discretionary and political behavior concerns ability to discriminate among the three classes of behavior. This issue can be approached in two ways. Some evidence of discrimination is provided by the five independent judges completing their tasks with a relatively high degree of interjudge agreement. As indicated above, twenty-nine of the sixty items met the stringent inclusion rule of unanimous or 80 % agreement among judges; another twenty-seven items were agreed to by three of the five judges. A 60 per cent agreement rule, therefore, would have included 56 out of the 60 items.

Additional evidence is provided by examination of the behaviors themselves. Administrative and discretionary behaviors have two characteristics not shared by political behavior. First, they represent consensus behaviors; behaviors which the parties to an exchange either tacitly or formally agree are appropriate or acceptable. Political behavior is non-consensus behavior; it is behavior which at least one party to the exchange does not perceive to be appropriate or acceptable. The second characteristic concerns the process aspect of the behaviors: the acts or procedures that are involved in their performance. Administrative and discretionary behaviors are, in some sense, voluntary processes: parties to an exchange act in ways they either wish to or normally do. Disagreeable or unusual actions and procedures are not involved. The very essence of political behavior, on the other hand, is that it represents an exercise of power, the imposition of the will of one party on one or more others, forcing them to do things they would not otherwise do. Administrative behavior is distinguished from discretionary behavior on the basis of its routineness.

Further insights into the nature of what we perceive to be the process of political behavior in organizations can be garnered from items excluded from the original set by judges on the grounds that they were multidimensional. These items would seem to have a mix of administrative, discretionary and political behavior and indicate the dynamic nature of the process, as evidenced, for example, by the following illustrations:

> The senior person in part of our department is very keen to have another senior person to assist her. She didn't know that I had arrived at this same decision, privately too, and had already started the machinery in motion—because I didn't want her to be disappointed if we missed out. She came to discuss it with me, and I told her that I'd already put something in train to this effect—and that I thought I had a good chance of success if I did. It's now been stymied temporarily. So, I've said to her, 'Now, you've got to bring pressure to bear on the Dean.' He happened to wander into her office the week after he and I had had a contretemps—and he didn't know that I'd filled her in totally on the picture. So he said, 'How are things going?', and she hit him right between the eyes with 'I need another senior lecturer!'

And, from a service department head:

> One of the nuts I've been trying to crack is Department X. There is a tremendous amount of potential for visuals and for various other things in that Department. Their teaching methods in my opinion are quite archaic. I started off with the Department meeting. I threw out a few pieces of bait, in terms of what we could do and this sort of thing. I identified, from comments within the meeting, that there were some people who were fairly interested. Then I provided follow-up with one of those individuals. In fact, I went up and did some slides for them of Frank Lloyd Wright. Then I sat down with him knowing that he has a good rating with his instructors, knowing that his approach is reasonably well received by the students. I believe that if I can get that person singing the praises of the sort of thing I've done for him, then in fact I've got a good number of the department because there are some other people on the verge. So we are doing exhaustive research for him in terms of finding what packages are available, we're servicing him to death. Bring the stuff in, look at it, great, if it's not great, fine, talk with our graphic art shop designer. 'We'll make it for you'. We're servicing him to death . . . . Unless something fouls it up, which could be one of the segments of our service falling down and really annoying the person, we are going to be in that department.

As the above examples indicate, the administrative, discretionary and political behaviors do not necessarily occur on their own. Rather, we see evidence in these examples of the behaviors occurring in a sequential fashion. It is clear to us that the study of this mix, the nature of the sequencing, and interrelationships between the behaviors is an exciting and potentially fruitful area for future research.

We would also envisage within organizational contexts, different mixes of administrative, discretionary and political behavior. Potentially, these could be reflected in the form of profiles, empirically derived, which would depict this mix. (For example, Behavior emphasis: Situation A, administrative high, discretionary moderate, political low; Situation B, administrative low, discretionary moderate, political high; etc.) Our expectation is that several variables, such as managerial values, core technology and organizational structure, would be possible correlates of, influences on, or outcomes of this behavioral mix. We anticipate that such mixes would differ in appropriateness within different organizational contexts. For example, an over-emphasis on administrative programmed behavior (and by implication on contract enactment) may be dysfunctional when a task process is unpredictable. On the other hand a high incidence of political behavior may be the appropriate organizational response to rapidly changing environmental conditions.

CONCLUSION

This exploratory study has provided some interesting insights into political behavior in organizations. While the number of subjects as well as the number of organizations involved was too small to make any meaningful inferences, we can suggest, in a tentative way, that the institute members in each organization encounter similar types of problems and respond in similar kinds of ways to such problems. Much more detailed and extensive research is needed to substantiate this observation.

Some insights into the implications of organizational politics and to the distinction we have suggested between administrative, discretionary and political behavior have been gained in the study. We are encouraged by the finding and intend to pursue several avenues of further investigation, which we hope will lead eventually to the development of a predictive model of behavior. As indicated earlier, the analysis employed in the study was extremely labor intensive, such that replication in a large number of organizations and involving a large number of respondents poses problems of cost and time. As one approach to further study of political behavior, we intend to utilize the preliminary results obtained as a means to constructing a different data gathering methodology which will attempt to capture patterns we perceive in the responses through clustering or factoring techniques. From questionnaire data, it should be possible to construct behavioral profiles which measure the relative "amounts" of the multiple categories of behavior as seem to be apparent in some of the incidents reported. We shall also attempt to explore the multidimensionality and sequencing of behaviors we have observed. Given the unobtrusive nature of political behavior and the importance of understanding its process, and the interdependence of parties whose behavior we study, it remains crucial, nevertheless, to pursue other "softer" techniques of research (such as interviews and participant observation) in our subsequent research on this concept. Further, the effect that political behavior has on other aspects of organization is a critical area of future research, the major area of interest being perhaps its impact in terms of organizational effectiveness.

The study of organizational politics is exciting. We believe that studying its occurrence, as well as its antecedents and consequences, will be an important field for organizational research in the years ahead.

REFERENCES

Bachrach, P. and M. S. Baratz. "The Two Faces of Power." *American Political Science*
1962 *Review*. 947–952.

Baldridge, J. F. *Power and Conflict in the University*. New York: John Wiley.
1971

Barnard, C. I. *The Functions of the Executive*. Cambridge, Mass.: Harvard University
1938 Press.

Blau, P. M. *Exchange and Power in Social Life*. New York: John Wiley.
1964

Burns, T. "Micro Politics: Mechanisms of Institutional Change." *Administrative Science*
1961 *Quarterly*. 6:257–81.

Child, J. "Organization Structure, Environment and Performance: The Role of Strategic
1072 Choice." *Sociology*. 6:1–22.

Cyert, R. and J. G. March. *A Behavioral Theory of the Firm*. Englewood Cliffs, N. J.:
1963 Prentice-Hall.

Dahl, R. A. "The Concept of Power." *Behavioral Science*. 2:201–218.
1957

Dimitriou, B. "The Interpenetration of Politics and Planning." *Socio-Economic Planning*
1973 *Sciences*. 7:55–65.

Emerson, R. M. "Power–Dependence Relations." *American Sociological Review*.
1962 27:31–41.

Freund, J. E. *Mathematical Statistics*. 2nd Edition, Englewood Cliffs, N. J.: Prentice-
1971 Hall.

Georgiou, P. "The Goal Paradigm and Notes Towards a Counter-Paradigm."
1973 *Administrative Science Quarterly*. 16:216–229.

Hall, R. H. *Organizations: Structure and Process*. 2nd Edition, Englewood Cliffs, N. J.:
1977 Prentice-Hall.

Harvey, E. and R. Mills. "Patterns of Organizational Adaptation: A Political Perspective."
1970 In M. Zald (ed.), *Power in Organizations*: 181–213. Nashville, Tenn.: Vanderbilt University Press.

MacMillan, I. C. "Organizational Politics–A Prerequisite Perspective for General
1977 Managements." In M. E. Nasser *et al*. (eds.), *Organizational Behavior: Readings for Management*: 93–110. New York: McGraw-Hill.

March, J. G. "The Business Firm as a Political Coalition." *Journal of Politics*.
1962 24:662–678.

March, J. G. and H. A Simon. *Organizations*. New York: John Wiley.
1958

Mayes, B. T. and R. W. Allen. "Toward a Definition of Organizational Politics." Paper
1976 presented at the Summer, 1976 meeting of the Academy of Management. Kansas City, Missouri.

Mechanic, D. "Sources of Power of Lower Participants in Complex Organizations."
1962 *Administrative Science Quarterly*, 3:349–64.

Mowday, R. "The Exercise of Influence in Educational Organizations." Paper presented
1976 at Annual Meeting of the Academy of Management. Kansas City, Missouri.

Peery Jr., N. "Technical Rationality and Political Behavior Within Organizations."
1975 Proceedings of Academy of Management 35th Annual Meeting, Summer 1975, 179–181.

Pettigrew, A. M. *The Politics of Decision Making*. London: Tavistock.
1973

Pfeffer, J. "Power and Resource Allocation in Organizations." In B. M. Staw and
1977 G. R. Salancik (eds.). *New Directions in Organizational Behavior* 235–265. Chicago, Ill.: St. Clair Press.

Pfeffer, J. and G. R. Salanick. "Organizational Decision Making as a Political Process:
1974 The Case of a University Budget." *Administrative Science Quarterly*, 19:135–51.

'Pondy, L. R. "Toward a Theory of Internal Resource Allocation." In M. N. Zald (ed.),
1970 *Power in Organizations*. Nashville: Vanderbilt University Press.

Porter, L. W. "Organizations as Political Animals." Presidential Address, Division of
1976 Industrial-Organizational Psychology. American Psychological Association 84th Annual Meeting, Washington, D. C.

Robbins, S. P. *The Administrative Process: Integrating Theory and Practice*. Englewood
1976 Cliffs, N. J.: Prentice-Hall.

Simon, H. A. *Administrative Behavior*. 3rd Edition, New York: The Free Press.
1976.

Thompson, J. D. *Organizations in Action*. New York: McGraw-Hill.
1967

Wergin, J. F. "Evaluation of Organizational Policy Making: A Political Model." *Review*
1976 *of Educational Research*. 46:75–84.

White, P. E. "Resources as Determinants of Organizational Behavior." *Administrative*
1974 *Science Quarterly*. 19:366–79.

Wildavsky, A. *The Politics of the Budgetary Process*. Boston: Little, Brown.
1964

Wrong, D. H. "Some Problems in Defining Social Power." *American Journal of*
1968 *Sociology*. 73(6):673–81.

Appendix

PATTERNED INTERVIEW QUESTIONS

A. What kinds of activities or things did your Department or would your Department concentrate on to set up an arrangement with other Departments? (Tell me what it would do now if you can't recall activities involved in the past.) By activities I mean anything you would consider as important to ensure you reached an arrangement suitable to your Department, the strategies you would employ, the issues you would consider, etc.

B. Suppose your Department had established a satisfactory arrangement with another Department in the organization. If we look at what your Department does to carry out the terms of the arrangement, can you think of what such an arrangement might look like for your department? What activities would your Department concentrate on to maintain the arrangement?

C. Let's look at a situation now where your Department wants to change an existing arrangement with another Department: one your Department was satisfied with but isn't now. Can you think of an example of such a situation relating to your department? What activities would your Department concentrate on in trying to change the arrangement?

D. Let's consider a different case now. Suppose that another Department has an arrangement with yours. Your Department is happy with the arrangement, but the other Department wants to change or even terminate the arrangement. What activities would your Department concentrate on to try to maintain or continue the arrangement?

E. Suppose you had an arrangement with another Department and you don't want to carry out the terms of the arrangement. You aren't trying to change the arrangement now, but to avoid carrying it out. Can you think of some examples of this? What activities would your Department concentrate on to resist implementing the arrangement?

F. Suppose it is budget time and your Department wants to change the size of the allocation of money, supplies and equipment, academic or support staff that you had been allocated. What kinds of activities would the Department concentrate on to try to accomplish this?

G. In general, in this organization, what do people do when they want changes made in the organization either within the Department, the faculty, or the institution as a whole?

H. In general, in this organization, what do people do when they want to prevent changes being made? Again, either in the Department, the faculty or the institution as a whole?

Comparing the Incomparable —Study of Employment Agencies in five Countries*

ERHARD BLANKENBURG

West-European industrial countries are facing similar problems of unemployment, and they have agreed on a common concept of "active labor market policy" as an attempt to fight long-term unemployment. However, the administrative set-up to implement this policy is different from one country to another.

This paper reports on some of the results of the comparison of local labor market administration in the Federal Republic of Germany, England, France, Italy, and Sweden. Differences are analyzed as far as legal rules and authority are concerned, and they are followed into the organizational set-up of placement services. Results are reported only insofar as this is necessary to give a rationale for the methodological approach of the study. Since there is no correspondence of organizational boundaries of labor market agencies in the respective countries, comparison has to start with task definitions and the analysis of task contingencies. The explanation of national differences lies in a configuration of variables extending beyond the organizational boundaries of labor market administration. In order to integrate explanatory variables, the typological concept of "administrative culture" is introduced.

Because of the incomparabilities of the organizational structures, standardized methods are infeasable. Therefore, the paper argues that the comparison of national institutions should be based on a "methodology of Verstehen."

OBJECT, METHODOLOGY AND PARADIGMATIC TRADITION OF CROSS-CULTURAL ORGANIZATIONAL COMPARISON

Social science in our age has grown with exponential speed. One of the organizing principles of this growth is that differentiation leads to ever new

* The paper outlines the approach taken in a five country comparison of employment agencies. A comprehensive report on the study will be published 1978/79. National reports have been written by Horst Hart for Sweden, Uta Krautkramer for the Federal Republic of Germany, Janet Lewis for the United Kingdom, Gianpietro Mazzoleni for Italy, Martine Morel for France. A grant of the Stiftung Volkswagenwerk enabled us to finance the cross–national field work.

specialized fields. Hardly have comparisons of organizations within one cultural context been developed as a subfield of organization sciences, when a new subfield emerges: that of intercultural comparison of organizations. At first glance, it may appear as if "culture" has been introduced as just another variable. But this holds true only as long as intercultural comparisons stay within the methodological and theoretical paradigm of "comparative organizations". This field has assembled a specific set of methods from the traditions of business administration, socio-psychology and sociology, and developed a limited number of reserach questions. The emergence of a field of "intercultural comparison of organizations" stays within this consensus on object and methodology of organizational research as long as "culture" is treated as just another variable. If the concept of "organization" is conceived in formal terms irrespective of historical patterns and task contingencies, very little variance is likely to be found in the "cultural" variable.

Continuing such paradigmatic traditions into intercultural comparisons, the question is asked whether generalizations found in a number of organizations in one country hold true in others as well. While most comparative organizational studies have been developed in a culturally homogenous environment, comparison across countries now tests whether the generalization of such studies holds true in different cultural environments. Thus, one may ask whether the achievement motive of managers in steel companies in India is as pronounced as that in Australia or the United States. Or, one may ask whether there are more levels of hierarchy in the French factory than can be found in Great Britain or Germany. Such studies fit into the paradigmatic tradition of socio-psychological or sociological research on organizations trying to arrive at generalizations about "how organizations work." Here research follows the operationalization of formal characteristics with an attempt to formulate these at a level so general as to be applicable to a large variety of organizations. The result will tell whether standardized indicators of behavior patterns of formal organizational characteristics undergo cultural variation or not. "Culture" in this understanding is reduced to a variable in a set of standardized indicators, as they have been developed in a culturally homogenous environment (largely in the Anglo-Saxon tradition of instrumental pragmatism).

It should not be surprising that, such research disproves that much cultural variation exists (England and Negandhi, 1978). Such a finding is the result of a specific set of methods and a limited number of research questions. If we compare steel factories in different countries, and translate achievement scales into another language, we might indeed find behavior regularities across countries. However, this is due to the imitation of technology as well as the limited scope of reality which we measure by our indicators. What is specific about different "cultures" is largely outside of the differences regarded by formal explanatory models. Cultural differences might be such that the units of analysis have to be defined differently for each country; that standardized indicators do not fit into other cultural contexts; and that the meanings of questionnaire responses vary with language and traditions (Brossard and Maurice, 1976).

Therefore, this study does not follow the paradigmatic tradition of studies in "comparative organizations." Many of these studies treat organizations as boundary-defined entities. This is not a self-evident assumption since the boundaries of an organization are very often not clearly marked. The persons who are included on the pay-roll might not be identical with those in the organization chart. Different goal orientations might lead to a number of subdivisions and overlaps. Changing task descriptions might shift the boundary of an organization altogether. The ambiguity of boundary definitions might be less in economic organizations, where production goals are relatively well-defined. This study, however, looks at agencies of public administration, which derive their authority from complex legal prescriptions. Here the goals of agencies are very often multifunctional. The boundaries might be different from one country to another; what is called an "employment agency" in one country, might be under the authority of several agencies in another. Many agencies in the government bureaucracy are part of a chain of decisions and implementation processes with rather complicated legal boundary definitions. Therefore, they can much better be understood as part of "organizational networks" which as a whole fulfill the tasks which we want to study.

Our organization comparison therefore starts with an analytical definition of its units of analysis. How this definition is arrived at is a consequence of the goals of the study: as we are trying to explain the implementation process of "labour market policy", we chose a functional definition of a certain set of tasks, and then tried to find the agencies which are responsible for them. Analytically, the focus is on "task contingencies" rather than on formal organizational contingencies. This approach enables us to better grasp the contextual quality of what "culture" is about.

In this paper we do not try to give a comprehensive summary of the study of labor administration. Rather, we want to develop the reasons for a methodological approach to cross-cultural comparison away from established explanatory paradigms. As has already been outlined, the analysis starts with the tasks of labor administrations and its contingencies. We then compare the different institutional arrangements, concentrating here on the placement activities and on three of the five nations compared. The summary fashion in which this is presented is meant to give an exemplification of the methodological approach. The analytical concepts which developed from the comparison are then outlined.

This attempt at not following established explanatory models has consequences on the methodology (which are outlined in the concluding remarks). The restrictions of using only those variables which allow for standardized operationalization are not accepted. Therefore a descriptive approach in trying to discover a wide range of data is used. The attempt to describe complex configurations which make "culture" distinguishable leads to description rather than measurement; the number of characteristics to be taken into consideration at the same time leads to a methodology of discovery rather than to one of testing theories.

ORGANIZATIONAL STUDY OF IMPLEMENTATION

There have been a number of studies of employment agencies at the local level. These include the classical studies by Blau (1955) and Francis and Stone (1956). Both studies criticized models of formal organizations, such as the ideal-type construction of Max Weber's "bureaucracy". Both studies analyzed interactions among placement officials as well as their encounters with the agencies' clients. The behavior patterns found were labeled as informal organizations and they led to an incorporation of behavioral data into general models of bureaucracy. This might be called a process of "paradigmatic enrichment" as any model-building involves a selection of variables from complex reality; every critique of such models will follow the path of enriching them. Both studies developed aspects of a general theory of organization. Their conceptual level is so general as to be applicable to all bureaucratic organizations in general. Blau explicitly states, in his methodological epilogue, that he initially intended to study a set of different organizations but problems of access happened to lead to a study of employment agencies.

In a later study of Blau and Schönherr (1971) the process of paradigmatic reduction which followed can be observed. Trying to formulate a general theory of the structure of organizations, Blau and Schönherr followed the standards of scientific measurement. They used structural variables as their main indicators which can be coded from organization charts, thus reducing their reality to formal characteristics. The tasks of the organizations under comparison are mentioned only as a matter of courtesy. The analysis aims at general conclusions about organizational size, structural differentiation and decentralization irrespective of what organizations do and with which environment they interact.

Studies of interaction of employment agencies with what we call core actors form another extension of the paradigmatic limits of what is operationalized as the structure of organizations. Schmidt and Kochan (1976) do not accept placement agencies as organizationally bounded to be their unit of analysis. Rather, they take exchanges between employment services and employers as units of their analysis. Aldrich (1976) uses frequency of interaction as a measurement to define a more inclusive unit of analysis which he calls organizational network. These studies still reduce reality in taking "interaction" rather formally, and in not giving much information on the characteristics of the units at both ends of interaction. Nevertheless, these studies are nearer to the type of problem definition which is need in cross-national research, because they do not take organizational boundaries as self-evident, but rather define them according to task definitions and interaction patterns.

In a study of this type, organizations have different task descriptions from one country to another. The tasks and scope of authority of a German *Arbeitsamt* includes processing unemployment claims as well as placement and job counseling; these are located in different agencies in England, France and Sweden. Training facilities, which are at the core of labor market policy, are organized privately according to the subsidiary principle in Germany; they are integrated into the general school system and intra-firm training in Sweden; they are organized as a unitary, centralized service in France; and there is an attempt to organize them similarly in England. Thus, the unit of analysis of comparison is an analytical construction. It is defined by a set of tasks which are the basis for labor market policy. Thus, we start by defining these tasks, then stating general task contingencies of labor market policy in order to finally compare the different solutions which national administrations choose in order to overcome them.

This does not imply taking employment agencies as purely instrumental. Organizations are instrumental as one facet among many, such as trying to survive, maintaining the support of staff and of environmental forces, and pursuing long-term and short-term goals. Introducing "policy implementation" as the explanandum of this study, we cannot be satisfied by measuring a few output indicators. Policy definitions are complex in nature: they contain general statements of intent on a very abstract, sometimes symbolic level; they might be operationalized in terms of political programs, always including standards for the performance of routine tasks as well as goals for special measures. Only by looking at the combined effect of the different tasks which employment agencies perform, can we understand the way labor market policy is implemented.

A CROSS-CULTURAL STUDY OF EMPLOYMENT AGENCIES

Employment agencies are peculiar among public administration institutions in that they have to mediate more than they can govern. Since their task is to achieve a match between the supply and demand for labor, they have simultaneously two types of clients with partly opposing interests: job seekers and employers. This explains some of the contingencies of labor administration. Its penetration of labor markets is only partial and its means of implementation are rendering services and providing subsidies rather than making authoritative and binding decisions. Employment agencies act in an interorganizational network where their policy is determined by general economic conditions and the climate of industrial relations.

Limitations on the effectiveness of labor market policies, which stem from the contingencies of employment agencies, can hardly be overcome by political "fiat". Nevertheless, politicians have raised their expectation of labor administration due to the pressure of unemployment problems. With economic and technological change in western industrial societies proceeding at a rapid pace, all European countries are experiencing a rise in unemployment independent of the business cycles. This has had long-term effects. During the 1960's and early 1970's (before the recession following 1973), European countries provided their labor market administrations with increased power to interfere in the labor market. The formulation of a policy normatively labelled "Active Labor Market Policy" was stimulated and coordinated by OECD experts. Comparisons of the measures of labor market policies used in northern European countries shows that the OECD exchange of their international "mandarins" led to highly congruent policy recommendations.

All countries which took part in this mutual imitation process introduced major changes in their administrative structures. Some countries (like France and England) built up new, autonomous organizations separate from the traditional agencies of the department of labor. Some (like Germany and Sweden) shifted the goals and capacities of their traditional administrative structures. A comparison in these four countries—some results of which are reported here—analyzes the implementation of institutional change on a local level. A parallel project is being undertaken in Italy, where the traditional pattern of the labor bureaucracy (relative style, combining unemployment insurance and bureaucratic placement procedures) still prevails.

Conceptually, the study starts out with task contingencies of labor market policy and the resulting limits to labor market administration. The next step is to define the actors in the field. In a comparative study, this can be done only by functionally defining the boundaries of the policy system. Those agencies are defined as *core actors* which provide placement services, unemployment insurance, further training and target programs for improving the labor market structure. *Relevant actors* are those with whom the core agencies have to interact continuously in order to achieve their goals. As one of the contingencies of this policy field is high interdependence with employers, trade unions and local government, all countries have some sort of institutionalized participation by relevant actors in the management of labor market agencies.

In this study, representatives of core actors and relevant actors were interviewed about their perception of labor market problems, their own goals and the goals of the other actors. As information in such interviews is complex, they cannot be standardized, interviews. Interpretation has to take into consideration the gaps between the formulation of abstract goals and actual activities. In addition, the different interviewees may have different perceptions of the same problem. By confronting them, the researchers are trying to interpret formal structures as well as informal relations.

The study's findings show that, despite the congruent policy statements and the similar goals of labor market agencies in the 1960's, actual implementation has led to quite different administrative structures. Intra-agency traditions, as well as institutional differences in the relevant environment, lead to a number of national differences. Analyses of these differences, however, can only be undertaken on the level of descriptions. When comparing (five) cases of organizational change, quantification does not seem to be appropriate. Rigid measurement of indicators which could be used in all countries alike would lead to a substantive loss in information. Therefore, the aim is analytical description, making use of a case study approach and a rather pragmatic compromise between comparative intention and adaptation to the peculiarities of each national case. This leads to a methodological point with theoretical consequences. Comparing functionally equivalent institutions cross-nationally has to take into account what one might call "national administrative cultures", a typological label for dealing simultaneously with more variables than we have cases to compare.

THE CONCEPT OF "ACTIVE LABOR MARKET POLICY"

The term "Active Labor Market Policy" has been a very successful label, even though its meaning has been manifold and often not spelled out at all. In 1964, the OECD Manpower and Social Affairs Committee formulated its "Recommendation on an Active Manpower Policy" which suggested the following means of implementation:

1. offering retraining and further training for those skills which became obsolete by production changes and sectorial changes in the economy;
2. offering subsidies for regional mobility to move the labor force from backward regions to those of high labor demand;

3. integrating handicapped groups into the labor force;
4. reintegrating women into the labor force; and
5. providing for higher mobility of capital to areas where a supply of labor can be found.

It is quite obvious that this program was aimed at a situation with a generally high level of employment, and with a small, but hard core of unemployed. These could not easily be placed in jobs in their regions or with the qualifications they offered. In those days, the general demand for labor was high, so the main tasks of labor policy were to activate labor market resources and to reduce the mismatch of demand and supply on the labor market by encouraging mobility. Under such favorable conditions, labor market problems were somewhat marginal to the issues of day-to-day policies. Full employment has been a favorable condition for concepts of "active labor market policies" to be designed. There was a consensus about the goal of full employment; there was a shared understanding that the main obstacles were to be found in maladaptations of demand and supply in the labor market; and there was a coordinated set of means of implementation to meet these problems by increasing the mobility of the work force across regional, sectorial and occupational skill barriers. The term "active" emphasizes two aspects of its general philosophy: that labor market policy should no longer leave market mechanisms to themselves as the classical "human capital" approach to manpower policy would have done, and that labor administration should no longer see its role in merely reacting to changes on the labor market, but rather seek to "actively" monitor such changes in a desired direction.

However, the 1960's were a time of limited labor market problems and a time of basic optimism in many policy fields. This caused politicians to create an expectation level as high as is indicated by the label "active labor market policy". The impact of their *Zeitgeist* becomes apparent if we look at the parliamentary debates which accompany the passing of the Labor Promotion Act (AFG) in the Federal Republic of Germany in 1969. These debates were praised to the effect that through an "active labor market policy" the goal of full employment was very near to being realized. Unemployment risks, at that time, were seen as resulting solely from imbalances of labor markets by regions and by economic sectors. Matching job seekers to existing vacancies was the main problem rather than the creation of jobs. This optimism was based on fifteen years of experience with overall high employment and demand for foreign labor, which was only clouded by regional development problems and crises in individual sectors such as unemployment resulting from the decline of mining in the Ruhr-area. The very mild recession in 1967–68 led only to a temporary rise in unemployment figures and stabilized the optimistic mood even more.

Six years later, labor market problems changed completely. A world-wide recession following the oil crisis in 1973 showed that any labor market policy is limited as soon as global demand is lacking. But even if the priority is placed on general economic policy and its effect on the level of employment, recent experience casts doubt on the effectiveness of existing methods of implementing policy with respect to matching the supply of labor over the long term with the qualification criteria of its demand. Today, job creation is in operation and at the same time there are job offers which cannot be filled. Plans for further training are being put into effect at the same time as some of the most highly trained individuals, i.e., academics, are threatened by unemployment. Thus, we now are faced with problems of global demand, as well as with problems of change in the structures of labor demand and supply. Labor market problems have increased to a degree which had not been foreseen by legislators at the end of the 1960's.

Even if the expectations of labor market policy in the late 1960's are now regarded as having been unrealistically high, the use of the concepts of "active labor market policy" can nevertheless be seen as a remarkable success story. In a number of countries, among them Germany, France and England, a process of major organizational changes was enacted. While in Germany this was done by revising the statutes and enlarging the existing National Labor Agency, in France and in the United Kingdom a new institutional infrastructure was built. Due to the common stimulus of the OECD Committee on Manpower Policy (which was then headed by Gösta Rehn from Sweden), there is a high similarity of the guidelines for this process of organizational change. Its main postulates are:

1. increasing the penetration rate of placement by labor administration, and getting away from the "dole" image of unemployment benefit offices;
2. improving statistical information about and scientific services for ongoing changes and future trends in labor market developments;
3. empowering administrative bodies to implement measures for guiding labor market developments such as further training/retraining, mobility inducements, job creation, etc.; and
4. integrating conflicting social interests into the administrative set-up by offering trade unions, as well as employer organizations, some forms of participation.

Based on the experiences of Swedish labor market policy, which had been formed along these lines in 1949, the German *Bundesanstalt für Arbeit* revised and enlarged its administrative set-up; the *Agence Nationale pour 1'Emploi* in France was founded in 1967 and took over the former unemployment administration; and the English Manpower Services Commission was founded in 1973 taking over the placement services of the Department of Labor and changing its set-up completely.

In all cases a strategy of organizational change was followed. In some countries this was done by founding new institutions, in others by changing the laws, regulations and organizations from within. There was a constant information exchange about the developments in the other countries, communications being provided by the OECD and by direct links. But, in each of the cases, the institutional result of this reform movement took a different shape. With basically similar concepts in mind and the same means of implementation at hand, the labor market administration in each country was shaped by legal and political tradition and by the strategy of organizational change chosen.

CONTINGENCIES OF LABOR MARKET POLICY

From the period of the 1960's (when the institutional infrastructure of "active labor market policy" was designed) to the 1970's (when it was put into operation) the scope of labor market problems has changed considerably. The rapid environmental change is one of the contingencies faced by all the labor market administrations. This is due to two major reasons. Labor market policy, more than other policy fields, is characterized by constant and very quick changes in the scope of problems and in the feasibility of measures. Questioning labor agencies about their current main concerns leads to an enormous variety of regional differentiaion; half a year later the researcher might be faced with a complete change in priorities in the targets of administrative action. This is one of the features of labor market policy; that its problems vary not only according to local conditions but also within short time periods. The best "policy" in such a situation must be to create an infrastructure of agencies and options for action which can react in a flexible way. In such a policy field, legal regulations can provide authority for measures, but they should leave open, when and to what degree that authority is used.

Such a task description does not fit into the traditional thinking of administrators, who perceive themselves as simply executing directives while the responsibility for their underlying policy rests with the legislative bodies. Labor policy needs institutions which can handle political decisions within the framework of general goals rather than an executing body which implements clearly prescribed operations. Its administration therefore needs a high degree of discretion in determining whether and when to use the means of implementation available to it. The use of such discretion presupposes a constant flow of information on current labor market developments. Therefore, information gathering forms a considerable part of the work of all labor administration. Central evaluation facilities are a necessary tool of labor market policy.

Labor market developments are also highly dependent on general economic policy. Any decision in the national or regional economy affects labor market problems, and very often such effects are felt more strongly than any action undertaken explicitly under the label "labor market policy". On the national level, labor market problems derive from the fluctuations of global demand. On the regional level, the maintenance of existing jobs and the creation of new ones are the major determinants of the scope of labor market problems, but neither keeping nor attracting industries is within the scope of influence of labor administrations.

Placement activities and the impact of administrative actions only partly penetrate labor markets. Most labor mobility takes place without the aid of administrative agencies, because:

1. on internal labor markets within big firms, internal careers and firm-run training programs are offered, especially for further training;
2. on segmented job markets specialized search procedures are used to obtain highly skilled and professional employees. The higher the skill level needed for a job, the scarcer such a skill is on the labor market and the more likely it is that placement will be handled outside of the public agencies; and
3. on all labor markets, for all skill levels, informal search procedures, advertising and other direct attempts are used to fill jobs.

Even though it is true that in all countries a sifting out of jobs and job seekers occurs, leaving the less desirable to the public agencies, there are differences in the degree of penetration of labor markets by different placement agencies. There are differences, too, in the degree of involvement of labor market administration in the politics of maintaining and creating jobs. Starting from an analysis of their traditional tasks, hypotheses need to be formulated as to which of the institutional set-ups is most apt to overcome the contingent limitations of employment administration.

TYPOLOGY OF EMPLOYMENT ADMINISTRATION TASKS

There are marked differences from country to country in whether and how the different tasks of employment administration are distributed over several institutions. In all countries, the employment administration includes the traditional tasks of making regulations and processing unemployment insurance claims and it is centered around the services of placing people into jobs. To these traditional tasks the objectives of an active labor market policy, such as furthering occupational mobility, maintaining and creating workplaces are related. Thus, we have to include regulatory, service-oriented, and goal-oriented activities as the core of employment administration.

Unemployment Insurance

Traditionally, labor administrations were predominantly institutions for handling the unemployed and processing insurance claims. Whenever there is much unemployment, this task is of primary importance; in times of full employment, personnel capacities are free for other tasks. Handling claims for unemployment benefits is an activity governed by rules and burdened by paperwork. As with any insurance, the prerequisites for a claim have to be checked, the amount of the claim has to be computed, payments have to be handled and the main prerequisite (that of being unemployed) has to be continuously checked. Handling such claims is *regulation-oriented* and is handled by a strict legal program.

Regulatory Tasks *vis-à-vis* Employers

In some countries (like France and Italy) labor inspectors are perceived as being a part of labor administration. Labor inspectors have to survey all laws applicable to employers regarding safety regulations, minimum working conditions, employment restrictions, etc. A similar *regulatory orientation* is involved in the process of granting loan subsidies, apprentice-subsidies, etc., in almost all countries. Even if its powers are generally considered to be very weak, labor administration is found to have a norm-control task in the studies of all countries.

Mediating Tasks

One of the prerequisites to claim unemployment benefits is that the claimant be a job seeker and be willing to accept any adequate job which is offered. While related to regulatory decisions discussed above, this is a situation which is basically service- and client-oriented; matching job seekers to existing job offers requires a consulting situation where neither side withholds information for tactical reasons. Placement, as well as job counseling, make up a large part of the activity of labor market agencies and can best be dealt with in a supportive atmosphere with a minimum of legal regulations.

Policy Tasks

Within the same administrative frame, goal-oriented instruments have to be applied; facilities for training and retraining have to be set up; jobs for the handicapped have to be created, relief work and subsidized positions have to be organized. Such policy-implementing tasks are clearly related to placement and to the information gathered by registering the unemployed. Training and retraining proposals can be the result of unsuccessful placement attempts. Job creation measures or loans subsidies can be the result of having too many long term benefit claimants. If unemployment is high, placement and counseling activities can aim at reducing the work force by discouraging marginal workers. In times of full employment attempts may focus on activating potential members of the labor force. Any such measures are dependent on information obtained from unemployment and placement statistics, and are implemented in placement and job counseling. The policy, however, is determined on a more general level as a result of negotiating with potential employers and mobilizing financial resources.

In the German case, all three administrative activities are combined within one administrative agency. In Sweden, insurance tasks are separated from client-oriented and goal-oriented activities while the means for accomplishing the latter is wider than in any other country. In France and England, all three activities are handled by separate organizations which operate in close cooperation. In all countries these *core actors* are linked by

Figure 1

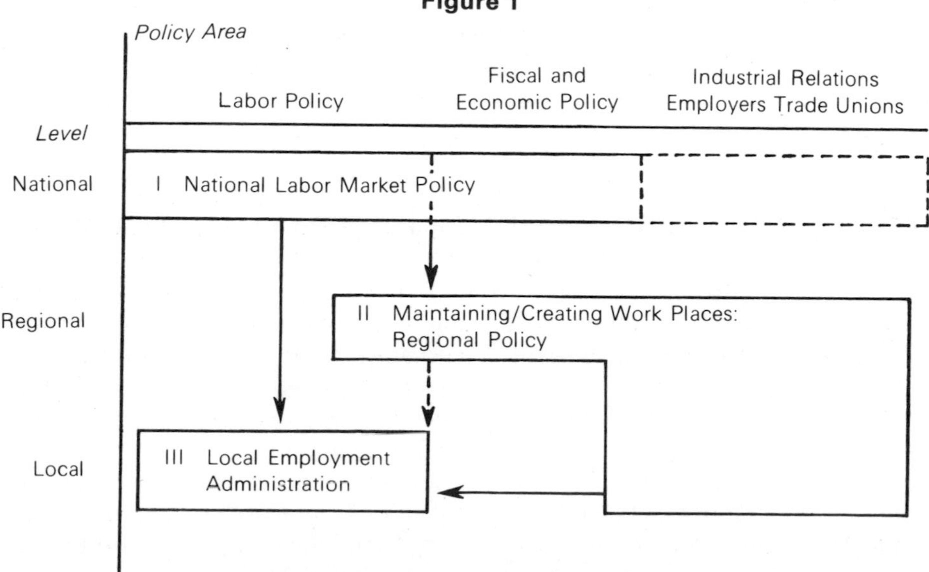

relationships—partly formal, partly informal—to trade unions, chambers of commerce, employers' associations, local governments and regional administrative bodies. This environment of *relevant actor* relationships is more important the more we get into policy-oriented activities. Providing places for further training and retraining, creating work places and providing apprenticeships for the young are activities of vital importance for an active labor market policy, but these activities transcend the authority of administrative core actors; thus the dependence on cooperation with a wide range of relevant actors.

Apart from the limitation of authority on a horizontal basis, local labor market administration faces a number of national and regional interdependencies. Here again, boundaries are defined by interpreting the perceptions of actors. It is useful to distinguish three "games" in which labor market policy is involved.

Game I is the national level of formulating overall goals which are related to general fiscal and economic policy. All countries which explicitly aim at a more active labor market policy (that is, four of the countries being studied, Italy being the exception) have a separate administrative body outside of the federal ministries which acts as the top hierarchical level of employment administration; its offices on the local level are under bureaucratic control. However, in some countries, the core actors are dispersed over separate organizations with separate agencies and independent lines of hierarchy. Nevertheless, in all cases employers and trade unions exert a strong influence on labor market policy.

The network of relevant actors is repeated on the local level. Trade unions and employers' organizations, regional and local government, schools and training institutions all belong to the set of actors in local labor market policy. Local networks, however, are very often too limited in size to plan and implement strategies for industrial settlements and commercial development. Thus, a number of links are imbedded in a regional network referred to here as "Game II". From the view point of local actors, Game II is mainly concerned with creating and maintaining jobs. A number of persons are present in more than one game, very often the boundaries between games are not distinct. Employment administrations as well as interest groups are institutionalized on all three levels with predominantly hierarchical patterns of communication within each of their own setups.

INSTITUTIONAL ARRANGEMENT OF THE PLACEMENT SITUATION

Nobody would assume that the level of unemployment in a country could be explained by the methods and quality of placement services of the employment agencies. However, it is certainly observable that under high unemployment the behavior patterns of placement agencies are different from those during times of full employment. One must ignore the differences in the level of employment in order to better serve the purpose of comparing institutional arrangements. The focus is on the national differences in the institutional arrangements of placement which are independent of the employment situation. In the following section placement procedures are compared in England, Italy, and the Federal Republic of Germany. Data on Sweden and France is left out because these would lead to a detailed discussion of national peculiarities of employment administrations. We here describe only parts of the data in three countries and to the extent necessary for showing how much variance national administrative cultures show in spite of the task contingencies outlined above. The differences analysed are a result of legal and administrative traditions, the characteristics of which recur in other public administrations in these countries.

Italy

Placement in Italy is governed by strict legal regulations which date back to the fascist laws of 1938, and were not significantly changed (in 1949) following the war. They require that placement in any job be solely under the control of the public labor administration. Except for the cases excluded by law, all placement has to be carried out by public administration which is bound by rules designed to provide a non-discriminatory, strictly legal treatment. Job seekers are placed according to their qualifications when they register with the employment administration. They are also assigned a priority for placement which can be changed according to social criteria (the number of children, exceptional need, etc.). Following these ranks, job seekers are assigned to the next employer, who has previously registered his need for labor. Further restrictions are the result of labor protection laws. Dismissals are governed by legal restrictions, while trade unions seek to preserve the *status quo* of employment in their firms. Even if dismissals for economic reasons were legally possible, the trade unions would react to any such attempts by going on strike. Therefore, employers complain that neither reducing the number of jobs nor dismissing any workers holding a job in their firm is possible. The only exception is that new employees do not have to be kept if after the first month it becomes apparent that their qualifications do not meet the requirements of the job.

There is no doubt that legal regulations directly restrict the employers' alternatives. However, a number of informal practices allows them to succeed in gaining some leeway. The employer may seek a number of unskilled workers through advertisement. These persons, who are hired for short-term employment, are recruited from outside neighboring regions and they are not registered with the local employment agency. After learning something about their qualifications, the employer recommends to those whom he wants to keep on the job, that they register with the local employment agency for a particular certification. Then he asks the agency for placement of the desired number of workers, indicating that they are desired for "confidential jobs", under which condition he is allowed to name specific people to fill the jobs. As a rule, the administration does not raise any objections to hiring "confidential personnel", because they are glad to have any placement.

Another form of circumventing the ranks set by the placement administration is by calling for qualifications which are rarely available. For example, a machine operator with good knowledge of Rumanian can be requested. Since this combination of skills is very rare, somebody who meets the requirement, will bypass all other machine operators who have been ranked on the list. (Since academic unemployment is rising, this usage has become risky, however. Often students are clever enough to meet even extraordinary qualification criteria, and can thus spoil the arrangements between employers and certain job-seekers. In such cases, the student who is placed usually takes the job for a month, and then the original game may be repeated).

Big firms have another way of avoiding the risk involved by taking workers based on their ranks on the lists. By law, small firms with up to three employed persons may hire people without consulting placement services. Big firms therefore subcontract with a greater number of small firms and, after a certain period of subcontracting they are allowed to take their labor into the firm. Since this way of circumventing the law was used to a considerable extent, it was restricted in 1970 by requiring a clearance certificate for taking labor from small firms into bigger firms. However, the labor administration rarely withholds such a clearance, as this would cause conflicts not only with some of the powerful employers, but with the workers holding jobs as well.

In a strictly regulated system, the placement situation reduces client contacts by the placement agent to a minimum. Decisions are made on the basis of written forms, the allocation of job is carried out with lists in a bureaucratic manner. Client contacts are reduced to the calling up of persons to be placed and to the allocation of vacancies. An important role for handling conflicts which might arise and for correcting the output of this bureaucratic placement process lies with an administrative board at the local employment agency. Here employers' associations and trade unions, as well as administration representatives, discuss complaints. This provides informal means for the rank order to be changed. It enables job seekers to increase their chances for placement without having an arrangement with one of the employers. Members of the board favor their clientele, be this on the basis of family relations, or by affiliation to trade unions, church or political parties.

It was not difficult for our interviewer to get interviewees to talk about the informal ways of circumventing the bureaucratic and legal rules of the placement administration. In general, employers as well as trade unionists and even administrators share the perception that the legally prescribed system "cannot work" and that an attempt to implement it strictly would lead to a further reduction of mobility and to an even lower employment level. The attitude towards the administrative system of placement is fatalistic and clever at the same time—there is a general accusation of the inflexibility to the address of the political system which cannot be changed. On the level of personal interaction, ever new ways of circumventing the system are found.

The Federal Republic of Germany

In the Federal Republic of Germany, public agencies have a placement monopoly as well; only the employment administration is allowed to run placement activities on a continuous basis, and exceptions have to be authorized by the national employment agency. However, this does by no means prevent employers from looking for labor on their own initiative, either by informal recruitment or by public advertisement. It is not even mandatory to register any new employment contracts with the labor administration, a condition which makes it hard to guess to what degree the labor administration is actually involved in influencing labor mobility. Employment administration, according to the goals of active labor market policy, tries to increase its penetration rate and can only do so by making its services attractive enough to induce employers and job-seekers to use them voluntarily. This rise in the penetration rate of labor markets has been achieved by employment agencies in the previous years. This is due partly to a higher level of unemployment, which has involved all levels of qualifications, and partly to public relations attempts to get away from the image of an "administration for unemployment compensation". Nevertheless, the majority of employers interviewed still share the perception that employment agencies offer rather unqualified workers and that those who are placed by the administrations are not the most able ones. Correspondingly, job seekers feel that being placed by the employment administration might be seen as an indication of inferior ability, so they consider it preferable to find a job by other means.

These disadvantages of the "dole" image are reinforced by the combination of placement activities and decisions on unemployment compensation within one administrative agency. If a placement agent offers a job to an unemployed person, and if the person refuses the job without giving good reasons, his unemployment compensation may be cancelled or temporarily discontinued. The decision depends on an evaluation of whether the job offered is adequate and the conditions are acceptable. It is up to the discretion of the placement officer to judge whether job seekers can be considered as being willing to work.

The placement officers in the German placement administration exert considerable power over job seekers who claim unemployment compensation. Furthermore, placement is organized in a way which maximizes the delimiting power of the placement agent. Each agent is assigned an area of responsibility based on qualifications, for which he administers a file where vacancies as well as job seekers are registered. He is the only person who has access to information both on the qualifications needed and offered. The ranking of candidates for placement is determined by his own judgement of whether and to what extent the two sides match. As a result, a placement agent may indicate to an employer for example, that he "might have to pay a little more" in order to get a qualified person or that a high turnover "might be due to certain deficiencies in the labor conditions". Similarly, he can put pressure on job seekers to change their expectations by declaring that "the desired kind of position" or "that a certain salary level" is "not available anywhere". Implicit in such mediation is the threat that a placement might not be feasable under certain desired conditions; for the unemployed this includes the potential reprisal of withholding unemployment compensation.

In the description of the placement situation it is important to remember that the disciplinary power of the officer towards employers is minimal compared to that towards the job seekers. It is significant that contact to employers occurs usually by telephone, while job seekers have to pay personal visits to the placement officer. While matching information from both sides the placement agent has a considerable delimiting power, he has no authority to compel any party to sign an employment contract. Decisions on contracts remain with employers and job seekers, the role of the placement agent is strictly one of mediation.

The consolidation of information in one person means that the agency has to divide labor by defining the authority of each agent based on specific qualifications and economic sectors. The consequence is that within the agency the service provided to white-collar and blue-collar workers differs. Furthermore, in spite of many qualifications cutting across economic sectors, they may end up in the files of only one agent. For example, there may be vacancies for car drivers in different sectors, but as vacancies are scarce, each agent keeps those he receives to himself. The overall effect—due to the specialization of placement officers by qualification—is a decrease of potential mobility across sectors. A special problem arises in the placement of unqualified young people, as they have no previous classification and thus fall under the authority of a specialized youth placement officer. However, he does not have a continuous clientele of employers and thus depends on colleagues to provide him with a share of vacancies. Thus, the consolidation of mediation in one person and the consequent division of labor according to qualifications and economic sectors increases the difficulties in integrating newcomers into the labor force.

England

The dysfunctions of the "mediating monopoly" have led many countries to introduce self-service into the general placement activity. Trying to reach a higher level of mobility in the labor market, the Manpower Services Commission in the United Kingdom increased the availability of access and decreased some of the barriers. Local employment agencies were decentralized and access was eased by introducing "job shops" where vacancies are openly displayed. The shops can be entered easily and can be left without any embarrassment. If the job seeker finds a vacancy he is interested in, he can get the address at a placement agent nearby. Usually the agent checks with a telephone call to the employer whether the opening still exists and this provides an opportunity for a minimum of mediating interaction. If a job seeker's situation is more complicated, or if he wants to register as unemployed, he is sent to a "second tier", a personalized placement service. Here placement interaction comparable to that of a German *Arbeitsamt* is possible. The agent, however, does not have his own file of vacancies, but can only consult a central file for the entire office. This seems to be an unavoidable consequence of the self-service model; registration of vacancies is separated from placement and there is a special division which files the qualification criteria of vacancies and forwards these to the self-service and the personalized placement offices, and sometimes even to job-shops in the neighborhood as well. Service is oriented towards processing vacancies as rapidly and widely as possible without an individual placement officer gaining first priority on a new vacancy. Only positions requiring very specialized qualifications or vacancies which have been set aside for disabled job seekers are exluded from this open availability of information.

In England there is no monopoly on placement for public administration. Certain occupations (such as office personnel) are handled through private placement agencies, which display their offers in openly accessible shops similar to those in the public sector. There is also competition in some parts of the labor market, even among separate public agencies. For example, besides job-shops there is a separate organization called "Careers" which provides counseling and placement service for persons leaving school. Competition for the scarce vacancies is demonstrated by the attempts of both agencies to market vacancies and to stimulate employers to create jobs and training positions. It is doubtful whether such activities increase the overall demand for labor, but they do increase the speed of announcing vacancies because there are several agencies trying to register them "before the others get a hold of them".

A certain amount of further competition arises between the job-shops and a specialized public agency, entitled "Professional and Executive Register" (PER), which caters to professionals and executives. This is a specialized part of the public employment administration for job seekers with higher qualifications. The separation of qualifications is not always clear—there is an overlap of medium level positions which could be registered by a job-shop as well as by PER. Registration for unemployment compensation should be done, however, at only one of these organizations, which gives rise not only to competition but also to conflicts in jurisdiction. PER charges a fee of a month's salary from employers, which is about half the price of commercial agencies. The orientation of PER officials, however, is influenced very much by the motive of at least covering the costs of the services. Being primarily interested in placement success, they place the better qualified first, in order to keep employers from consulting other agencies. In their orientation, if not in their actions, general employment services give more consideration to social conditions. Disabled and needy job seekers would never have a chance if the pressure for successful placement were increased by the motive of covering the costs of the agency.

In England (as everywhere) the legal claim for unemployment compensation depends on the unemployed person's being available for employment. However, the processing of forms and payments is under the authority of a separate agency, the "benefit offices". The prerequisite for compensation is registration with the employment services, and "no objection" with respect to availability. However, in reality, objections due to "unavailability" are rarely made. This cannot be ascribed solely to the separation of placement and unemployment insurance, for even in a single agency like the German *Arbeitsamt* there is a similar role separation between the placement officer who gives his evaluation, and a separate division which implements the non-payment of benefits. The permissive practice in English employment administration seems to be rooted mainly in the orientation of placement agents who, in contrast to their German colleagues, do not like to use the power of reprisal which is available to them, and who do not perceive themselves as public officials using their authority. It would be hard to differentiate between the effects of organizational separation and of the ideological orientation of agents. The remarkable fact is that they correspond in being more permissive in England, and more authority-oriented in Germany.

ANALYTICAL CRITERIA FOR COMPARISON

Observation of the institutional arrangements of job placement and its operational link to unemployment insurance, shows the central and traditional tasks of employment administration. To these, more and more policy tasks have been added. Expectations of politicians as to the range of goals which should be achieved by employment administration largely neglected the relative lack of power which the mediating situation creates for the employment agents. Under the market conditions of unemployment, vacancies are scarce. Thus, inducing employers with incentives and good service to use the facilities offered, is the main way to increase the administration's mediating authority. Also, to a limited degree sanctioning power can be used by withholding payments of permits.

After characterizing the institutional arrangements of regulatory and service oriented tasks, we can now proceed to the analysis of policy goals. It is on the basis of routine activities that the administration has to develop policy-oriented activity. Structural conditions for performing policy tasks vary as much as the institutional arrangements of placement services do. Here, many of the traditional concepts of organizational sociology help in the analysis. However, this does not imply adopting the operationalization which is common for these concepts. Having defined the unit of analysis by comparable tasks forces us to seek for new operationalizations for these concepts. The standardized measurement of organizational variables very often leads to a point that cannot be strictly compared. By finding the reasons for these incomparabilities we discover the essential aspects in the cultural comparison of institutions.

DECENTRALIZATION *VERSUS* CENTRALIZATION

It is not astonishing that a great deal of organizational literature is concerned with the issue of centralization and decentralization. It is one of the recurring problems of intra-agency disputes about organizational design. In a comparison of agencies in different countries the issue becomes more complex, because the boundaries of organizational tasks are not uniformly defined. In addition to differences about centralization of control *versus* local autonomy and the incorporation of tasks within one organization, there are different ways to attribute these tasks to the individual administration agencies. The regional extension of labor markets varies with scarcity and level of qualifications, while professional and executive jobs usually require a large degree of regional mobility. Thus, part of the placement activities need a national exchange of information, and part of them can be satisfied in local labor market regions.

The same holds true for the difficult tasks centering around maintaining and creating work places. Industrial location decisions certainly consider the basic economic conditions which cannot be influenced by regional incentives. Local authorities tend to compete for investors by offering similar favors and incentives, and, in the course of negotiations, they often withhold information for tactical reasons. Local employment administration in most countries does not participate in this game. Being part of a hierarchy of national agencies limits their activity in industrial settlement. It is of secondary importance compared to that of local governments, chambers of commerce and regional political bodies. Employment administrators could only then participate in this game, if they became part of the local power structure.

Confronted with the alternative of giving authority to administrators to integrate economic settlement policies and considerations of employment structure into the local policy networks, or to have a separate employment agency with rather narrow tasks but nationally integrated policies, none of the five countries under comparison chose the first alternative of local autonomy and of a decentralized broad range of competence.

There is a feed-back, however, because decentralized data gathering caters to the centralized decision-making process. Data on the employment level, on employment structures, and on mobility, are gathered by the local administrative agencies in all European countries. This statistical information is forwarded along hierarchical channels and evaluated by central agencies. Their policy recommendations and guidelines are based on the data of the individual employment agencies and on scientific research. These guidelines are then fed back down the hierarchy of control. However, universal as this model may be in general terms, the pattern of central coordination differs very much according to the range of competence and uniformity of employment services. Unemployment insurance for example is linked to a separate chain of organizational control as is the case in France and Sweden; it has recently been separated at the local and regional level in England; and is part of the encompassing service in Germany and Italy. Special policy targets such as relief work or youth unemployment programs in England are delegated to separate task force organizations with field offices of their own besides those of the general employment administration; they are pursued by regional offices in France and from there more closely linked to the local political game than to the employment administration on the local level; they are tightly integrated into the day-to-day placement operations of the Swedish agencies; and the German administration leaves parts of the special policy measures with regional offices and has decentralized other parts to the local level, keeping them organizationally separated from placement activities. Without going into further details a general point concerning comparability should be made: the allocation of tasks varies along vertical and along horizontal lines, and with these the boundaries vary of what is nationally regarded as the core of the employment administration. The degree of centralization and decentralization can be different with regard to different tasks, thus forming complex patterns which, as a whole, should be compared.

The challenge for coordination of employment policies is too great for any one organization to master. Not only should there be an integration of economic, fiscal, educational, and employment policies, but also of the diverging needs for coordination on national, regional and local levels. In the cases studied here this matrix of coordination has been recognized at the national policy level, with more or less fragmented structures at the local level.

PATTERNS OF ORGANIZATIONAL CONTROL

The description of placement in Germany and Italy has served as an example of how bureaucratic activity is controlled by legal regulations. As we have seen, there is a plausible correlation between the attempt to control the abuse of unemployment insurance and the concentration of placement information on the desks of placement agents. This attempt prevents the German and Italian administration from introducing self-service into placement (in contrast to the three others). Again, the attempt to control is correlated to the degree of legalistic prescription, but with remarkable differences between German and Italian administration. How can a high degree of legalism be made compatible with policy tasks? The German AFG may serve as an example. It does not leave much discretion to the administration to decide on the policy relevance of further training measures, for example. While, in Italy, legalism implies the absence of goal-oriented activities of employment administrations, the German *Bundesanstalt für Arbeit* formulates its policy in the form of laws, regulations, and continuous amendments thereof. The labor promotion act (AFG = *Arbeitsförderungsgesetz*) is an encompassing codification of organization and policy measures of employment administration. Every member of the unemployment insurance has the right to claim a subsidization of further training. The agencies are therefore legally bound, if the individual prerequisites are given. This is not directly a consequence of the text of the law which prescribes that a claim for subsidization can be made, if the further training measure is considered "in accordance with improving the chances of the applicant on the job market". While this general clause would leave some discretion in less legally-oriented cultures, German courts ruled in a number of cases that rejection of a claim for further training has to be very well founded in order to be legally sustained. Thus, the indicator for the degree of legal binding has to include the handling of legal rules on the level of administrator as well as on the level of the interpretation.

Strict binding of administration by legal regulations causes problems of flexibility in a rapidly changing task environment. This is demonstrated by the great number of amendments which the AFG underwent since having been enacted eight years ago. Less legalized bureaucracies adapt to task changes by issuing guidelines or allocating funds within the administrative hierarchy. Clearly this increases the speed of adaptation. The degree of legalism can then be measured by finding the level at which the rules for recurring activities and the decisions for special policy measures are made. However, the concept of "levels" can be attached to quite different meanings according to the legal culture of the respective country. Institutional alternatives may perform equivalent tasks, legal terminology may hide actual behavior patterns. Therefore, measurement of legalism has to be validated by several related indicators, such as "amount of procedural rules", and the "degree of precision of binding rules versus discretion".

One of the functional alternatives to legal rules are central administration guidelines. They are formulated at the national level and forwarded to the local employment agencies. In Germany, in addition to the legal prescriptions, guidelines are so numerous and detailed as to fill a bookcase in the office of a placement agent. Standard letters suggesting a polite form of addressing clients, and even the amount of time to be spent on the counseling of each client are prescribed in detail. It is not astonishing that many of the placement agents become disoriented in the mass of prescriptions and their constant amendments, and finally tend to neglect many of them altogether.

Studying an administration in only one country normally provides some data of internal control for the researcher to work with. On cross-national comparison, however, these often do not match from one country to another. Again, the German case shall serve as an illustration. When new guidelines are issued, reports on their implementation are fed back to the national offices, preparing future adaptations of guidelines with respect to their feasibility. These hierarchical feedback mechanisms provide some data on the performance of the German administration. However, there are no equivalent performance indicators available in other countries which would make cross-national comparisons possible. While in the German labor administration the individual agent's performance can be measured by the number of his successful placements, the self-service section of English, Swedish, and French labor administrations does not allow for such statistics because there is no way of accounting for placements actually made with the help of the services.

These examples illustrate that it is rarely possible to compare the same type of decisions across all five countries. If only those indicators are used for which there is comparable data in all countries, the major cultural characteristics of the control patterns in each of the administrations under study might be missed. In the light of the incomparabilities of national traditions, different indicators often have to be used from one case to another, in order not to miss the essentials of cultural differences altogether.

ORGANIZATIONAL NETWORKS

The employment administrations serve two types of clients with partly opposing interests. Collective bargaining and labor disputes engage them in one of the most crucial organized conflicts of society. Therefore, being dependent on a complex political environment, employment agencies gain some autonomy from general administration. At the same time they attempt to establish institutional links with trade unions and employers' associations as these are the most powerful organizations in their political environment. The major variable for the feasibility of such participation is the degree of cooperation in industrial relations. In some countries (like Italy, France, and England) institutionalized participation is restricted to the national level and is mainly concerned with policy recommendations. In Germany, tripartite boards exist at the national, regional, and local level, and have the authority to accept or reject guidelines at the national level, to pass the budget, and to control personnel decisions at each level. The competence of these boards is not restricted to controlling the management of agencies. It could rather be described as a quasi-legislative body making management decisions. At the local level the range of budgetary and personnel decisions is limited by the framework which is given within the hierarchical set-up of the administrative structure. The activity of local boards varies from one agency to the next; regular meetings take place about four times a year. As could be expected, agency heads present their management proposals generally without giving alternatives. They use their boards for legitimizing decisions, and they use board members as multiplicators in order to get collaboration with the interest organizations of their clients.

While the German system of management by participation involves participation bodies only in decisions on the agencies' general policies, Swedish administration uses a model of participation at the operational level. In addition to boards for general policy recommendations, the interaction of the agency with its environment takes place by placement agents. Department heads participate in personnel decisions of big employers, in training schools and in regional policy committees. Operational participation works best with bigger firms which have a separate personnel department and thus, a bureaucratic counterpart for designing a coherent employment policy. Here the administrative agents take part in consultations on decisions about the employment structure, about dismissals and the creation of work places. Legal means, like prescribing a certain structure of employment, are rarely used. In most cases, participation itself leads to mutual information and agreement on general employment decisions. The difference of participation at the operational level can best be exemplified with respect to the integration of the disabled into the labor force. While in Germany there is a legal prescription on the percentage of disabled persons to be employed (which can be lowered by paying a certain sum for any such work place), the Swedish model of participation institutionalizes "adaptation groups" in bigger firms in which management, labor unions and employment administration are represented. They look into the possibilities of creating work places for disabled persons and work out firm-specific plans for such employment. Participation is used as a functional equivalent to legal rulings, being much nearer to operational feasibility, more flexible for matching work place offers to local needs and more informative, thus giving administration better means of control.

In the countries compared, employment agencies generally try to establish institutional participation of their relevant environment. Linking the activities of an employment administration to its environment can be seen as one of the contingencies of an administration which is mainly mediating between two types of clients. The forms of such organizational networks, however, vary with the degree of social contact in the conflict between trade unions and employers. What the term "organizational network" means is something quite different in each of the five administrations studied.

This again leads to the point that a specific feature of employment administrations can only be understood by putting it into the context of wider cultural data. The organization which trade unions follow and the degree of cooperation in industrial relations determine the limits and the possibilities of employment administrations to integrate their policies with those of their political environment. The data which enters into the comparison of the relations among the core actors of employment administrations, as well as their relations with relevant actors of their environments are so manifold, that one cannot do more than describe them and give plausible explanations for the elements of which each national configuration is composed.

VERSTEHEN AS A METHOD FOR COMPARING THE INCOMPARABLE

We have been talking of understanding patterns and configurations which can be described as administrative culture. This outline does not present all of the findings. Rather, it demonstrates the kind of results desired: which features of the context of societal institutions are relevant for the way in which employment administration is set up; and the way employment administrations implement what is labelled as "active labor market policy". To answer these questions we first had to elaborate on the task contingencies which are inherent in what labor market policy wants to achieve: mediating between two types of clients; adapting to changing employment situations; performing bureaucratic tasks such as the red tape of unemployment insurance together with more client-oriented tasks such as counseling and placing job seekers. These contingencies limit the possibilities of employment administration in meeting the expectations which policy makers raised when formulating the goals of an active labor market policy.

However, in spite of the features of employment administration which are contingent on their tasks, there are great differences between the different European countries in the way administration is set up. In order to describe these differences fairly unstandardized methods were used. Even when comparing agencies in one country, there might be some questions concerning the validity of indicators (for example, the critique of using indicators for hierarchical levels which Argyris (1974) put forward). These difficulties are increased, if cross-national comparisons are attempted. Societal meaning of hierarchical levels can be so different that a comparison of such formal indicators might lead into understanding different cultures, but would mislead, if results are interpreted without taking configurative variables into consideration (Brossard and Maurice, 1976). In this study one step further towards incomparability has been taken. With regard to policy goals and their implementations, functional equivalents which can only be understood in the context of a structural configuration, called administrative culture, have been considered.

When talking of "culture" (in analogy to "political culture" as used by Almond and Verba (1963)) typologies for comparison are used. While Almond and Verba relied on surveys which at least guarantee a comparable data basis, and while they interpret attitudes and behavior patterns which uniformly relate to individuals as unit of analysis, the use of the term "culture" in this paper refers to a configuration of institutions and to the laws and links which rule their interactions. The range of authority of an organization was found to be culture bound, just as the way agencies are directed by political programs and environmental pressures, the degree of their legalistic orientation, the range of their discretionary power and their patterns of intra-organizational control. The term "administrative culture" in employment agencies includes their relations to relevant actors such as trade unions, employers, local government and regional planning. Employment administration is dependent on the way labor relations are constituted in a country and these change with the type of trade union which prevails. Administrative culture is a term summarizing patterns of behavior and configurations of societal institutions.

What is an adequate method to use in the study of administrative culture? Structural configurations can be described; their relation to the implementation to policy goals can be made plausible, but they cannot be measured in any strict sense. The methods used here for data gathering have been analyses of policy statements, organization charts and internal documents. These, given some knowledge of formal organizational structures, were used in order to design focused interviews, which were aiming at reconstructing the self-perception of the actors in the field of study. Not even the samples of persons to be interviewed could be standardized. As the number and competence of institutions concerned varies from one country to another, our researchers had to follow the task descriptions of what was analytically defined as "employment administration", and had to identify the core actors as well as those of the relevant environments with the "snowball-technique" of the reputational method.

Our interviews aimed at reconstructing the logic of action in which the actors see themselves (Crozier and Friedberg, 1977). Such information can be contradictory. The self-perceptions of interviewees are not always consistent, nor do they always fit together. Contradictions and different perceptions from the point of view of different actors are ubiquitous elements of any institutional configuration. Understanding culture implies understanding the contradictions which it entails. Thus, understanding means more than just following the information given by interviewees. It includes the confrontation of different points of view, making contradictions "meaningful" from the point of view of an outside analyst. For comparison, a further step is needed. Some heuristic device is needed in order to distinguish relevant data for the description of what makes for the national differences of administrative cultures from irrelevant data. The descriptive data was ordered along the lines of analytical criteria such as "patterns of centralization", "patterns of control" and "patterns of linkage with relevant organizations of the environment".

Trying to understand such configurational structures in several countries leads to case studies as a basis for comparison. The number of variables which is necessary to describe these configurations will always be bigger than the number of cases to be compared. Epistemologically, administrative cultures are singular events. They form unique configurations. Certainly, in characterizing such configurations analytical criteria of general applicability such as can be tested in deductive-nomological models of explanation are used. But we resist standardization of their measurement, as the use of standardized indicators would overly restrict the reality we want to focus on.

It could be argued that such an understanding of culture is the first step for designing more strictly comparable research. It is a necessary step. Only if proceedings are free from measurement technology, will we be able to discover which features are relevant for cultural comparison. If we put these into a testable "model", we will again have to reduce reality to indicators which can be measured in a standardized way. The more standardized, the more comparison is narrowed down. The more complex the concept of culture gets, the more we have to reconstruct the logic of a system using what one might call a methodology of *verstehen*. This methodological paradigm is not to be confounded with the "operation" of "verstehen". Abel (1948) criticized that understanding does not add to our store of knowledge, but rather "consists of the application of knowledge already validated by personal experience". However, used as a method of successive steps in describing and comparing, each of the many operations of *verstehen* in the course of an accumulative process of research adds to our knowledge and to the validity of our concept of "culture".

REFERENCES

Abel, Theodore. "The Operation Called Verstehen." Am. Soc. 54.
1948

Aldrich, Howard. "Resource Dependence and Interorganizational Relation."
1976 *Administration and Society*. 4:419–453.

Argyris, Chris. *The Applicability of Organizational Sociology*. London: Cambri-
1974 dge University Press.

Blau, Peter, *The Dynamics of Bureaucracy*. Chicago: University of Chicago
1955 Press.

Blau, Peter, and Richard Schönherr. *The Structure of Organizations*. New York and
1971 London: Basic Books.

Brossard, Michel, and Marc Maurice. "Is There a Universal Model of Organizational
1976 Structure?" *Int. J. Soc.* 6:41–75.

Crozier, Michel, and Erhard Friedberg. *L'Acteur et le Systeme*. Paris.
1977

England, George, and Anant Negandhi. "National Context and Technology as
1977 Determinants of Employer's Perceptions." Paper presented at Honolulu, Hawaii.

Francis, Roy, and Robert Stone. *Service and Procedure in a Bureaucracy*. Minneapolis,
1956 Minn.: University of Minnesota.

Gabriel, Almond, and Sidney Verba. *The Civic Culture*. Princeton: Princeton
1963 University Press.

Schmidt, Stuart, and Thomas Kochan. "An Application of a 'Political Economy'
1976 Approach to Effectiveness." *Administration and Society*. 7:455–473.

Institutional Goals and Organizational Functioning: A Critical Evaluation

Continuing our previously established pattern, we provide, in this Chapter, a critical evaluation of the papers presented in Section III. The commentators are:

(1) William H. Money, Kent State University
B. R. Baliga, University of Wisconsin, Eau Claire
(2) F. Musschoot, Rijksuniversiteit
(3) Makoto Takamiya, International Institute of Management

Comments on Endruweit's paper

PROBLEMS IN CROSS-CULTURAL RESEARCH IN COMPLEX ORGANIZATIONS—*William H. Money & B. R. Baliga*

The author's work attempts to contribute both to the theoretical development in cross-cultural research and an understanding of the methodological problems involved which restrict our understanding of the impact of culture upon organizations. It is a comparative case study of the German and United States police experience. However seen in a broader sociological framework, the authors analyses may be viewed as a limited examination of the organizational methods of executing social control forces within a society.

However, the work cannot be viewed as a strict comparison of the similarity and the differences in the enforcement of the legal environment and customs of particular societies. No attempt to provide for potential differences in these legal restrictions and charges for the control systems examined is presented in this work. The author does note the overall similarity in the goals of these organizations, but makes no serious attempts to identify or explain specific differences that will either support or constrain specific organizational activities.

The data presented are a comparative analysis of fifteen organizational characteristics. The variables have not been specifically categorized as to their structural or process impact upon the organizations. In addition, their interaction effects have not been specifically examined by the author. Furthermore, different units of analysis are compared with one another and the data for the analysis were collected in different ways in different types of units.

Thus, it is extremely difficult to view this work as a direct analysis of the organizational characteristics of these institutions. The German organizational sample may be viewed as a sample drawn from a large (single) organization. Its form represents that developed in multidivisional organizations such as the multinational corporations operating in a world environment. In contrast, the three organizations in the United States (Illinois State, Chicago, and Evanston Law enforcement departments) are only three cases (perhaps non representative) of the hundreds of agencies charged with enforcing law and maintaining social order in the United States. Many individual characteristics such as size or budget autonomy can restrict the operations and activity of the individual police organizations. Thus, the limited sample may not be representative of the overall U.S. experience, if such a global experience can be said to exist.

Because of these sample constraints, a second set of comparative analysis cannot be undertaken by the author on this data. The author can, however, examine internally the interrelationships among the variables and advance the understanding of each one of these organizations. The German case would certainly be much stronger than the U.S. case where such an analysis can be undertaken with a greater degree of reliability and external validity.

The author's conclusion that the cultural environment may be an important explanatory variable in understanding the role of organizations is questionable given the relatively poor quality of the data. A refinement and expansion of the study may indeed prove this to be the case but with evidence currently presented the conclusion is unwarranted.

In sum, the paper highlights the dilemmas confronting the researcher of complex organizations in cross-cultural settings. Resource and other (cultural?) considerations make it extremely difficult to obtain comparable units of data. For instance, an organization that may be considered as small and insignificant in one cultural setting may be considered relatively large in another cultural setting. While environmental forces may choose to ignore the former organization they may exert considerable pressure on the latter. The relatively larger organization may also exert, in turn, sufficient pressure on the environment to have significant impact. The question then arises: Are Organizations that have the same 'absolute' size (number of personnel, capital investment to cite a couple of measures) similar in cross-cultural contexts? Unless research workers in the cross-cultural area confront such issues squarely and develop appropriate methodology to deal with them, cross-cultural studies of the type undertaken in Endruweit's paper will forever remain the target of attack by the more rigor oriented researchers in the organizational behavior area. Issues of validity and reliability will always be raised. We feel that rather than focus on the conclusion drawn from the study, readers would do better to ponder over the problems involved and develop insights that will prevent recurrence of such problems in the future.

Comments on Frost and Hayes' Paper

AN EXPLORATION IN TWO CULTURES OF POLITICAL BEHAVIOR IN ORGANIZATIONS—*F. Musschoot*

The primary focus of the investigations is managerial behavior in negotiation activities (formulating, changing, and defending a contract). In order to test the model, semi-structured interviews were used. The information obtained from the interviewees (retrospective communications) was analyzed and classified in categories. In a real negotiation situation there are at least two participants playing their respective roles and defending the interests of their group (concern).

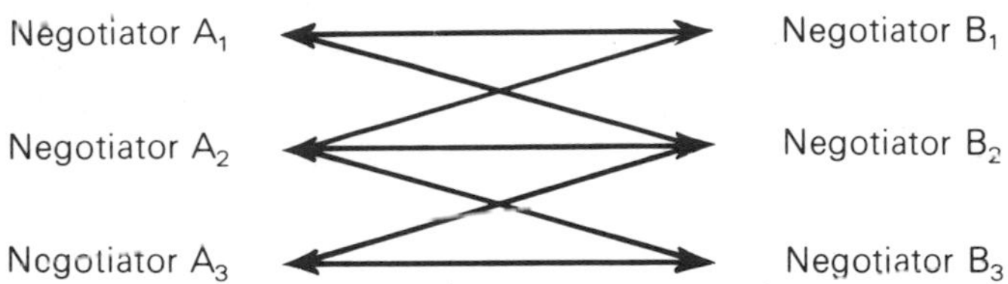

In this interaction situation, attitudes and behavior may alternate slowly, rapidly, or not at all. In a negotiation situation the participants judge each other. They estimate how intelligent, how well informed and how sincere they are. Some will encourage the other(s) to do all the talking and afterwards, in a group discussion, try to discriminate against their opinions. There is nothing unethical in this; it is an essential attitude in business and in politics.

There is a great risk of misrepresentation and misinterpretation in using information from one participant in the negotiation context (for example, A_1 in the scheme).

Analysis information is given in terms of verbally expressed behavioral categories: administrative, discretionary and political. But what were, in the reality of the professional content, the exact role positions? The negotiating psychological situation is quite different when one has the power and freedom to make decisions and when one is mandated by a group (colleagues). If I am a bachelor and I want to sell my house, I do not have to be afraid of opposition. But when I am representing my faculty at a meeting where I am supposed to obtain a maximum of financial support, I will be seriously constrained by my colleagues. History shows that understanding of leadership and behavior requires not only knowledge of the man, but also of the content in which he exercises his leadership.

Managers (also deans) must assess where their organization is going and, with their staff in particular, they should involve the staff members that are closest to them, such as fellow directors and department heads. They must deal with stresses and perhaps conflicts that the future, whether next year or tomorrow, is bound to bring. In interpreting interview data the question must always be asked: "Is it possible to analyze the interviews in such a way as to find indications about group pressure, influencing the managerial behavior categories?"

The exploration of the model was carried out in two technological institutes: one in Australia, the other in Canada. As far as testing the model is concerned, the choice of the institutes is less important than the two cultures. It is doubtful whether the decision to choose two countries with an Anglo-Saxon cultural background and a democratic regime was a happy one.

In an exploration study the interviews should be conducted in a rather standardized manner. However, this does not imply that exactly the same things should be done and said with each individual. The standardization sought is such that each interviewee should be given the greatest possible opportunity to reveal those aspects of his experience which are psychologically significant to him. We have the impression, and it is only an impression, that the interviewers provided insufficient opportunity to discuss the underlying questions influencing the behavior categories.

Despite this, and the fact that the authors proved once again that interviewing can be used as an objective, the method is a very positive point. We cannot obtain reliable material for cross-cultural studies solely through the use of questionnaires. There is not only the translation problem, but without interviews and observation in realistic situations, we risk misunderstanding the real sense of human behavior.

Comments on Blankenburg's Paper

COMPARING THE INCOMPARABLE—*Makoto Takamiya*

A cross-cultural comparison of employment agencies is obviously an important area for both academic and practical purposes. Blankenburg's paper provides interesting methodological and theoretical insights to this important but rarely explored area. The following discussion will be addressed only to the major defects of the paper and possible strategies to eliminate them.

Instead of using the conventional approach of choosing an organization as a unit of comparison, Blankenburg first conceptualizes "employment administration tasks" and then attempts to compare "institutional set-ups" designed differently in each country to perform these tasks. These cross-national variations of the institutions result from national peculiarities: "labor market contingencies" and international imitation processes (see Figure 1).

Based on this model, three research tasks emerge: (1) to construct analytical concepts for the tasks of the agencies which are applicable to all five countries: (2) to systematically compare differences of the institutional set-ups in five countries along common dimensions; and (3) to analyze labor market contingencies, national peculiarities and international imitation processes to explain why the same tasks are performed in different organizational set-ups.

Conceptualization of Our Tasks. Blankenburg proposes a three-way typology

Figure 1

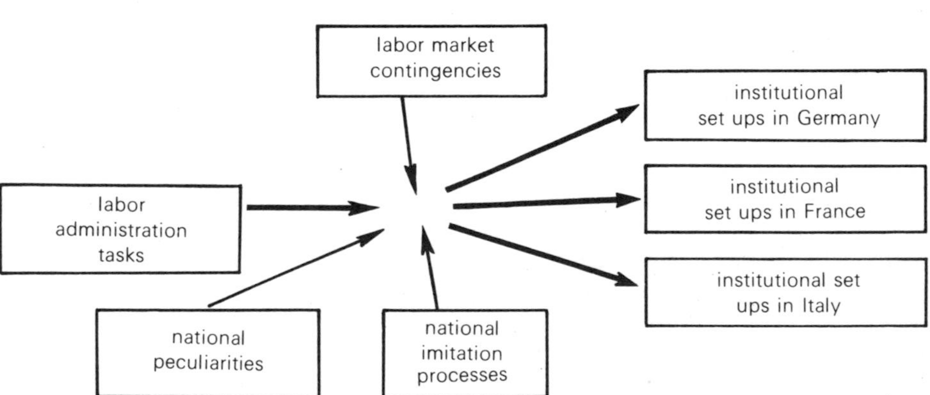

of labor market tasks: regulatory tasks (unemployment insurance and regulation of employees); client oriented mediating tasks; and goal oriented policy tasks. If one starts from these tasks and looks for responsible institutions in each country, as Blankenburg sets out himself to do, the problem will be far more complicated than the paper suggests. Many of these tasks are in fact undertaken by private institutions to various degrees and in a variety of ways. The matching of personnel to positions is done heavily by personnel departments of companies and by placement offices of educational institutes. Training may be conducted largely within the company or by professional and vocational schools, and, as in Japan and in some industries in the U.S., even unemployment compensation or its functional equivalents are paid by employers. If one chooses to study cross-national differences of institutional set-ups which perform common societal tasks, the extent and practice of the operation of these private institutions, as well as their relations with governmental employment agencies, should be compared across countries. Blankenburg, unfortunately, confines his arguments only to governmental agencies. This makes his approach, which he claims to be unique, not very different from the conventional comparisons of organizations.

Cross-Cultural Comparisons of the "Institutional Set-Ups". Blankenburg's allusions to the cross-national differences of institutional set-ups are scattered throughout his paper. They can be summarized as in Table 1. Two defects are apparent from Table 1. First, the comparison along six dimensions is not done across all five countries. Although Blankenburg stresses the degree of centralization as an important criterion for comparison, no statement can be found in the paper explicitly comparing five countries along this dimension. Second, his choice of these dimensions is rather arbitrary. The literature on organizations has found a number of crucial organizational variables. A brief listing of these variables relevant to this study may include, for example, the size of the agencies, the number of agents per unemployed worker (or per worker), the degree of bureaucratization, the relative emphasis of the agencies on the three different tasks (e.g., in terms of resource allocation), etc. Since a complex organization, such as an employment agency, can be compared in a number of ways, which often results in quite different conclusions, the researcher should be very careful in choosing the dimensions for comparison. One straightforward strategy is to systematically survey the literature and make an exhaustive list of possible dimensions and find relevant ones.

Analysis of the Causal Relations. Very little analysis is conducted as to how national peculiarities, labor market contingencies and international imitation may have led to different institutional set-ups for each country. Instead of relabeling national characteristics as "administrative culture", one has to examine in detail what national differences are relevant and how they affect the set-ups. "Labor market contingencies" and international imitation effects may vary with countries. This makes it necessary to examine how they differ and what impact this difference has on the institutional set-ups.

Comparison of Performance of the Agencies. As Blankenburg aims at

Table 1

Countries	*Organizational set-ups for three tasks*	*training facilities*	*institutional arrangement of the placement activities*	*centralization decentralization*	*degree of bureaucratic control*	*relations with relevant actors*
Germany	One administrative agency	private institutions	placement activities are exclusively done by Gov't, but employers can seek workers by themselves	degree of centralization depends upon tasks; no conclusive comparison	high	tripartite body to determine general policies
France	Insurance tasks are separated from client-oriented tasks	centralized	same as in Germany		?	tripartite body only at the national level
England	same as above	limited centralization	Self-Service oriented Private companies are allowed to engage in placement mediation		?	participation at the national level
Sweden	all three are separated	integrated to school system and intra-firm training	same as in Germany		low	tripartite participation at the operational level
Italy	?	?	Strictly legally controlled with some informal escape		very high	participation at the national level

when "formulating hypotheses as to which of the institutional set-ups is most apt to overcome the contingent limitations of employment administration", some judgment on the degree of success of the agencies in each country must be made. The measure of success is certainly difficult to obtain but one can use multiple measures to reach a better picture of the reality. For instance, a random listing of possible measures might include employers' evaluations of the service of the agencies, the comparison of job standards before and after training, evaluation by the unemployed on the efficiencies of the unemployment insurance administration, the degree to which the agencies' regulations of employers are observed, etc.

A careful application of various measures may enable one to reach such a finding as: "as compared to France, Germany is relatively successful in regulatory tasks but unsuccessful in mediating tasks"; and then possibly to trace the reason of such a phenomenon to the different institutional arrangements.

Problems and Prospects in Cross-Cultural Organizational Studies

In this concluding chapter we turn now to the two remaining questions which were introduced in Chapter I: what theoretical and methodological shortcomings exist in the field of cross-cultural studies of organizations; and where do we go from here? We limit ourselves to identification of the most promising theoretical and methodological features in the rapidly growing research area of *comparing organizations*, cross-nationally or cross-culturally. The reader interested in more general aspects of comparative social science must be referred to the significant contributions of other authors (e.g., Dujker, 1955; Rokkan, 1962, 1965, 1968; Merritt and Rokkan, 1966; Berstecher, 1970; Przeworski and Teune, 1970; Szalai and Petralla, 1977; and Malpass, 1977).

THE TREND TOWARDS OPEN SYSTEMS PERSPECTIVES

The plea for a treatment of organizations in an open systems approach is by no means new. It can be traced back to Köhler's (1938) discussion of living organisms as parts of a larger functional context. But it was von Bertalannfy (1950) who first focused scientific attention on the difference of treating living and physical entities as open or closed systems, a line of thinking that first came to fruition in the field of organization research with the seminal socio-technical systems study by Trist and Bamforth (1951). Since then we can note the growing theoretical concern with the input-output relationships of organizations and their environment (Katz and Kahn, 1966; Emery, 1969).

The inadequacy of treating organizations as closed systems irrespective of their environmental interaction became abundantly evident with the research lines of the comparative management tradition (see Chapter I) which, by necessity, shifted the focus of attention from merely intra-organizational structures and processes to external environmental factors and their impact on internal properties and functioning. The central question was: what are the major pan-cultural environmental variables that are potentially relevant to issues of organizational functioning? This, in the context of organization studies, might be considered as an equivalent problem to the long standing tradition of cultural anthropologists in their search for "cultural universals" (Kluckhohn, 1962).

Hellpach (1953), and independently from him, Kluckhohn (1954) and

Kluckhohn and Strodtbeck (1961) have developed conceptual notions of cultural values and value orientations which are considered to be fundamental in their function in constituting the predominant image of a given culture's population about the nature of its world, life, and social coherence. Hellpach calls a culture's "guiding value" (Leitwert) its dominant orientation which has an impact on all social spheres, behavior and institutions. The basic cultural value orientations of Clyde and Florence Kluckhohn and Strodtbeck towards human nature, the man-nature relationship, time, activity, and predominant characteristics of social relations (man-man) are quite similar. They are assumed to reflect specific culture responses to universally existing basic human problems.

Although theories of cultural value orientations were developed in the early 1950's, it took until the 1970's when publications began to appear, empirically and theoretically exploring their organizational relevance (England and Koike, 1970; Evan, 1974–1975). However, even these efforts cannot be considered as comprehensive attempts to relate differences in cultural value orientations to various aspects of internal organizational structuring and performance. Given the widespread common sense assumption that values have impact on behavior, which is backed up by theoretical reflection (Evan 1974–1975) and growing empirical evidence (England, 1975), the research line of comparative value studies and organizational behavior appears to have a promising future.

The model by Farmer and Richman (1964) was expressly formulated for the purpose of studying managerial efficiency under varying environmental conditions. "Where environments do vary, as is the case between nations, it is necessary to examine the external pressures, or constraints, upon internal management" (1964:56). Farmer and Richman proposed to systematically measure the "macromanagerial structure", i.e., the constraining environmental factors consisting of educational (e.g., literacy), sociological (e.g., attitude towards scientific method), political and legal (e.g., political stability, foreign relations), and economic characteristics (e.g., market economy, labor market) in their impact on managerial performance.

While Farmer and Richman's important attempt to classify national environmental characteristics for purposes of systematic comparisons still remained on a rather global level, further refinements could be drawn from both organization theory and comparative management research. Dill (1958), in his study of Norwegian firms, had already conceptualized "task environment" of companies in terms of their customers, suppliers, competitors, and regulatory groups (such as governments, unions, interfirm associations). Negandhi (1975) incorporated both Dill's task environment and Farmer and Richman's classification of environment in his model of determinants of organizational patterns and effectiveness. However, by including traditional "closed systems" variables such as size, technology, and ownership as well as cultural ones (categorized as societal variable), his conceptualization provides the possibility of linking "culturological" perspectives through societal features of the Farmer and Richman variety with Dill's task environment and internal "closed systems" variables. No doubt, the aspirations are ambitious and we have not seen enough hard nosed measurement attempts yet. However, the prospects look promising.

Lamenting with Roberts (1970) the careless use of an implicit notion of culture to explain empirically identified differences, Evan (1974–1975) suggests following Kroeber and Parsons' (1958) proposal to differentiate between culture and society or social system as a first step towards reducing conceptual ambiguities. The term "culture" would thus refer to content and patterns of values, ideas, and symbols, and "society" would be used to indicate the relational system of interaction between individuals, groups, and organizations. In pursuing this line of reasoning, Evan then proceeds to identify socio-structural or institutional domains of organizational environments which he considers important for organizational functioning: familial, economic, political, educational, religious, and legal institutional spheres, which could, be further supplemented by such institutional fields as military, technological and scientific institutions. The problem then, of how to link the concepts of norms, roles, organizations and institutions in comparative analyses of organizational functioning could be solved by adopting certain linkage mechanisms between the macro and micro levels of analysis. Evan suggests four such mechanisms: Merton's (1957) operationalizations of social structure (role sets, status sets, status sequences); and his own concept of organization set. By employing these conceptualizations in comparative studies of organizations, he contends, one may be able to overcome the static and atomistic nature of most organization research.

It was without these specific theoretical considerations that some recent French organization studies began to consider the *interactive* effects of industrial organizations and their specific national institutional environment (Daubigney and Silvestre 1972; Silvestre, 1974; Brossard and Maurice, 1974). Confronted with their findings that a pairwise (same sector, size, and local labor market) comparison of French and German firms consistently showed higher levels of hierarchization and higher pay differential in French companies, they turned to the differential educational and industrial relations systems as potential explanatory reasons. The educational system apparently plays an important role in providing differentially trained labor and in providing conditions for differential degrees in the division of labor and respective remunerative reinforcing mechanisms which are upheld by specifics of the industrial relations system and pay bargaining. Thus, a given organizational system, in a nucleus, reflects the social stratification of the national environment. On the other hand, it may very well be that economic organizations, by virtue of their significance in maintaining the viability of the whole societal system, reinforce established educational system features.

What emerges from these attempts at conceptualizations and theoretical propositions? It appears that the field has made considerable theoretical progress during the last decade. A large variety of conceptual tools is available to promote successful efforts to come to grips with the essential notion of understanding organizations as open systems in cross-national (cultural) research. But little is implemented as yet. What needs to be done is further operationalization of the concepts at hand to systematically measure environmental features in order to be able to asses their impact on organizational functioning. How it is to be done is the methodological problem.

METHODOLOGICAL PROBLEMS

If one accepts the foregoing analysis of the general trend from closed system thinking to open system thinking and its conceptual implications, there still remains the question of what methodological issues are posed and how different or similar they are from general methodological issues commonly faced in social science inquiry. We will comment on this latter question generally and then move to a consideration of the specific methodological issues posed by the theoretical developments.

It seems obvious that the separation between theoretical and methodological problems flowing from open system thinking is arbitrary in many respects. Methodological advance must necessarily await the theoretical developments that take us to the stage of having a reasonably well-developed taxonomy of important environmental variables and reasons for expecting them to affect the internal properties and functioning of organizations in certain ways. Research efforts which fail to recognize this interdependence between theoretical and methodological problems are incomplete at best, and add findings but not knowledge at worst. It is almost a truism in this field, as in many others, that what we may perceive as methodological problems are really theoretical problems in disguise—at least, they have large theoretical components.

With this premise, it seems important to emphasize that the set of methodological problems that face students of organizations, as they shift from closed system to open system thinking and as they move from national to international studies, are not different in kind from those faced by all social scientists. In fact, one can be carried a great distance by attending to a general set of social science inquiry procedures. An abbreviated list of such general procedures might be phrased as follows:

1. Making national comparisons of the impact of environmental variables on organizational functioning implies that scientifically one is seeking underlying causation for observed similarities and differences. While some correlates of this general reason for making comparative studies are identified in chapter 1 of this volume, we would emphasize that one should have a basic rationale for comparing the impact of environmental variables on organizational functioning among countries. Preferably, there should be articulated expectations or hypotheses involving variables at the national level. While the purpose and content of the study will dictate what national level variables are considered important, one should not lose sight of the fact that it is only these expectations about variables at the national level which provide real intellectual justification for doing comparative studies. As such, they should be articulated as fully as possible prior to conducting a comparative study.
2. We must determine what it is that we ought and want to know, why we want to know it (largely theoretical issues), and design the research accordingly (largely methodological issues and/or issues of research design).

3. One must obtain useful and relevant data since the meaning of our results can never transcend the quality of the data we have (largely methodological, measurement and issues of operationalization).
4. We must interpret results in such a way that meaning flows from them (a combination of theoretical, analytical and methodological issues).

When one moves from single country studies to comparative studies among several countries, certain methodological issues take on increased salience. Fundamentally, one is faced with the additional tasks of: (1) assuring that equivalent samples are studied in each country; (2) formulating meaningful questions for the respondents and ascertaining that they are equally meaningful in all countries participating in the study; (3) developing understanding and interpretation of obtained results which are a function of all countries under study as opposed to one's own unicultural view.

Acceptance of the earlier theoretical analysis about the need to identify relevant environmental variables that affect organizational functioning makes it logically imperative that the first and major methodological question is: How do we identify, measure and operationalize the theoretically suggested environmental variables in a way that lends itself to cross-cultural (national) comparison? There seem to be two related issues to this question. Assuming that theory identifies the set of potentially relevant environmental variables, we are still faced with the problem of assessing or measuring them and the problem of doing so in a pancultural way. We would argue that these two issues are highly interdependent and that any solution must encompass both issues.

While there has been a great deal written in comparative methodological literature about the Emic-Etic distinction and the phenotypic-genotypic distinction, both are quite similar to, if not identical with, the old ideographic-nomothetic controversy. Gordon Allport (1966) made it abundantly clear over a decade ago that the science of behavior must necessarily combine knowledge obtained from both ideographic and nomothetic approaches. We see no reason whatsoever for disregarding this advice when we are concerned with the issue of assessing environmental variables that affect organizational functioning in universal ways. This is also why we have included both research strategies in this volume. Methodological precision will necessarily come from attempts to measure environmental variables in a given country and from attempts to do the same thing in a set of countries. It is certainly true that seeking a general and equivalent set of indicators across many countries is a larger task than doing inter-institutional comparisons within only one country, but in principle nothing is changed. The taxonomic problem is the same and only the matter of equivalence across countries is more complicated.

Cross-cultural researchers have devised a set of methodological strategies to deal with the equivalence issue which would seem useful for consideration by organizational analysts. As Malpass (1977) has suggested, there are three approaches for coping with this problem: (1) "while ideally one might randomly select local populations to represent the various levels of the independent variables to be investigated, this can seldom be done in practice"; (2) "investigate a *pattern* of differences among local populations"; and (3) "not to investigate mean differences but to investigate differences in patterns of *relations* among variables". These latter two strategies are really analytical strategies for at least partially getting around the possibility of non-equivalence, and essentially suggest that some degree of non-equivalence can be tolerated if one shifts analysis strategy slightly. Of course, direct approaches to the equivalence issue would would seem preferable and should be pursued. Again, this is the old issue of combining knowledge gained from both ideographic and nomothetic approaches, and we again emphasize the merits of such combination. In this context it would be profitable to further develop methodologies that incorporate feedback cycles into the process of research itself. Group Feedback Analysis (Heller, 1969), which feeds findings immediately back to respondents in an effort to understand the "true meaning" of the results obtained, appears to have potential in overcoming, or at least alleviating, equivalence problems, and thus, helps to bridge the apparent dichotomy of ideographic and nomothetic approaches.

Thus, it would seem that few, if any, new methodological issues are presented by shifting from a closed system approach to an open system approach. The central methodological problem remains that of assessing environmental variables. Equivalence is important but it can be obtained under certain analytical procedures. These methodological considerations and the theoretical issues posed suggest certain steps that should be taken and it is to these we turn.

WHAT LIES AHEAD?

It appears that consequences must be drawn on two levels—the conceptual-methodological level and the research organizational level. Both imply a shift in forms and emphasis as well as attitude among students of organizational behavior. First, we finally ought to rule out the abuse of "culture"—or "national environment" for that matter—as undifferentiated residual categories that acquire an explanatory *deus ex machina* function whenever we fail to explain variance with the set of variables we happend to include in our design. Rather, the remaining explanatory gap should provide sufficient incentives to search specific environmental dimensions that might relate to the phenomena under study.

This is, of course, more easily said than done. The bulk of comparative (in our case cross-cultural) literature and the above theoretical reflections provide abundant testimony to the inherent difficulties of conducting research along these lines. A first step in the right direction might well be to make use of the suggestion to differentiate between culture as referring to distinct sets of dominant values and value orientations of various populations and groups on the one hand, and society or social system on the other, as a term denoting the specific surrounding institutional setting of focal organizations. This would enable us to gain insights into the interaction patterns of these two environmental system levels and their joint impact on organizations. The process of operationalizing social system and cultural dimensions in the attempt to link them systematically to organizational features and dynamics might conceivably follow a dialectic that swings from the failure to apply meaningfully standardized measures cross-nationally back to ideographic, qualitative case descriptions of organizations in their "natural" setting, and move forward again with improved conceptual tools to nomothetic approaches.

Another issue that has found only limited attention but may be of great theoretical and practical significance, is the impact that organizations have on their societal and cultural environment. We noted the French organization studies that theorized on the function which industrial organizations have in maintaining certain features in the French educational system and the corresponding impact on professional selection standards and value judgments about remunerative policies. However, the problem acquires an international dimension. The world-wide growth of multinational companies might well be assumed to have important consequences on business behavior in their countries by virtue of the implied international transfer of managerial values and practices (Negandhi, 1975). Certainly both national and international impacts of organizations on their environments deserve added attention.

Consequences for organizational forms of comparative research seem necessary as well. Increased attention to specific linkages between focal organizations and particular dimensions of their environment in cross-national (-cultural) studies overtaxes the expertise of a single researcher. Multi-national team research is required instead of individual safari trips for multi-national comparative data gathering. Multi-ethnic teams will ensure higher degrees of "enculturation" of comparative research design and instrumentation simply because the differential experiences of team members and their insights into their own national societies and cultures will serve as filters to inappropriate operationalizations and procedures. But genuine multi-national collaborative research is cumbersome. It requires social skills and cooperative attitudes far beyond national team research efforts. Thus, the dynamics of the research process in international teams itself acquires particular significance. Decisions must not be made unilaterally but consensually. And here it may often be that consensus decisions become compromise decisions diluting what some team members may perceive as necessary theoretical succinctness. From this it follows that scientific leadership in multinational (often also multi-disciplinary) teams demands far more than disciplinary expertise (Fourcade and Wilpert, 1976).

Motivation of members in an international team to carry out joint decisions will often depend on their own scientific and professional stakes in the research project. This can be maximized by designing the research in such a way that it allows for intra-national as well as international comparisons; in other words, that national sub-studies can survive as pieces of research in their own right. This means that the magnitude of a genuine collaborative international research project will be standard national study multiplied by the number of participating countries, plus the international transactions in developing, designing, coordinating, evaluating and publishing the overall international study. Traditionally, national and international funding agencies and research promoting institutions are simply not accustomed to the size and costs of such research ventures. Hence, a decentralization of funding through various channels will frequently be necessary. In any case, international cooperation, coordination (project meetings) and evaluation should, in general, be funded from some central source. That is usually not perceived to fall into the responsibility of national funding agencies. But this is also the point where funding bodies must realize the tremendous potential that can be mobilized through supporting the international overhead of otherwise decentralized funding of national substudies. By picking up a fraction of the grand total of multination research costs a multiplication of research output is achieved. It is from continuing the general orientation in theorizing about organizations as open rather than closed systems and linking them systematically to specific, measured environmental dimensions combined with different organizational forms of doing research on organizations that we can hope to make further progress in the attempt to answer the still open question: To what degree and in which ways are organizations culture- and society-bound?

REFERENCES

Allport, G. W. 1966 "Traits Revisited." *American Psychologist*, XXI(1):1–10.

Berstecher, D.: 1970 *Zur Theorie und Technik des internationalen Vergleichs. Das Beispiel der Bildungsforschung:* 123 Stuttgart: Ernst Klett.

Bertalannfy, v. L. 1950 "The Theory of Open Systems in Physics and Biology," *Science*, 3:23–29.

Brossard, M., and M. Maurice. 1974 "Betriebliche Organisationsstrukturen im interkulturellen Vergleich," *Soziale Welt*, 25(4):432–454; also: "Existe-t-il un modèle universel des structures d'organisations?" *Sociologie du Travail*, 4:402–425.

Daubigney, J. P., and J. J. Silvestre. 1972 "Comparaison de la hierarchie des salaries entre l'Allemagne et la France," Manuscript, Laboratoire d'Economic et de Sociologie du Travail, Aix en Provence.

Dill, W. R. 1958 "Environment as an influence on Managerial Autonomy," *Administrative Science Quaterly*, 2:409–443.

Duijker, H. C. 1955 "Comparative Research in Social Science with Special Reference to Attitude research," *International Social Science Bulletin, UNESCO*, 7(4):

Emery, F. 1969 *Systems Thinking*. London: Penguin.

England, G. W., and R. Koike. 1970 "Personel Value Systems of Japanese Managers," *Journal of Cross-Cultural Psychology*, 1:21–40.

England, G. W. 1975 *The Manager and His Values: an International Perspective from the United States, Japan, Korea, India and Australia.* Cambridge, Mass.: Ballinger Publ.

Evan, W. M. 1974/5 "Culture and Organizational Systems," *Organization and Administrative Sciences*, 5(4):1–16.

———. 1976/7 "Social Structure and Organizational Systems," *Organizational and Administrative Sciences*, 7(4):53–72.

Farmer, R., and B. M. Richman. 1964 "A Model for Research in Comparative Management," *California Management Review*, VII(2):55–68.

Fourcade, J.-M., and B. Wilpert. 1976 *Group Dynamics and Management Problems of an International Research Team*, Berlin: IIM-preprint series.

Heller, F. A. 1969 "Group Feedback Analysis: A Method of Field Research," *Psychological Bulletin*, 72(2):108–117.

Hellpach, W. 1953 *Kulturpsychologie.* Stuttgart:

Katz, D., and R. L. Kahn. 1966 *The Social Psychology of Organizations.* New York: Wiley.

Kluckhohn, C. "Values and Value Orientations in the Theory of Action: An Exploration
1954 and Classification," In: T. Parsons, and E. A. Shils (eds.) *Toward a General Theory Action:* 388–433. Cambridge, Mass.:

———. "Universal Categories of Culture," In: S. Tax, (ed.), *Anthropology Today*:
1962 304–320. Chicago, London.

Kluckhohn, F. R., and F. L. Strodtbeck. *Variations in Value Orientations*. Evanston, Ill.:
1961 Row, Peterson & Co.

Köhler, W. *The Place of Values in a World of Facts*. Liverright.
1938

Kroeber, A., and T. Parsons. "The Concepts of Culture and Social Systems," *American*
1958 *Sociological Review*, 23:582–583.

Malpass, R. S. "Theory and Method in Cross-Cultural Psychology," *American*
1977 *Psychologist*, 1069–1079.

Merrit, R., and S. Rokkan, *Comparing Nations: The Use of Quantitative Data in Cross-*
1966 *National Research*. New Haven: Yale Univ. Press.

Merton, R. K. *Social Theory and Social Structure*, rev. ed. Glencol, Ill: The Free Press.
1957

Negandhi, A. R. *Organization Theory in an Open System*. New York, London: Dunellen.
1975

Roberts, K. H. "On Looking at an Elephant: An Evaluation of Cross-Cultural Research
1970 Related to Organizations," *Psychological Bulletin*, 74:327–350.

Rokkan, S. "The Development of Cross-National Comparative Research: A Review of
1962 Current Problems and Possibilities," *Social Sciences Information sur le Sciences Sociales*, 1(1):21–38.

———. "Trends and Possibilities in Comparative Social Science: Report on an
1965 International Conference," *Social Sciences Information sur le Sciences Sociales*, 4(1):139–165.

———. *Comparative Research Across Cultures and Nations*. Paris, The Hague:
1968 Monton.

Przeworski, A., H. Teune. *The Logic of Comparative Social Inquiry*. New York: Wiley-
1970 Interscience.

Silvestre, J. J. "Industrial Wage Differentials: A Two-Country Comparison,"
1974 *International labour Review*, 110:495–514.

Szalai, A., and R. Petralla. *Cross-national Comparative Survey Research: Theory and*
1977 *Practice*. Oxford, New York: Pergamon.

Trist, E. L., and K. W. "Some Social and Psychological Consequences of the Long Wall
1951 Method of Coal Getting," *Human Relations*, 4:3–38.

NAME INDEX

Abegglen, J. C. p. 216
Abel, Th. p. 296
Adam, R. p. 239
Adamek, R. p. 176
Adizes, I. p. 73
Ahn, C. p. 177
Ajiferuke, M p. 3, 64, 188
Albrow, M. p. 227
Aldag, R. p. 90
Aldrich, H. E. p. 64, 276
Alkers, H. A. p. 45
Allen, R. W. p. 251, 256, 257
Allen, S. A. p. 219
Allport, G. W. p. 311
Almond, G. p. 295
Appelbaum, R. P. p. 143
Anderson, R. p. 218
Aquilar, F. J. p. 94, 100
Argyris, C. p. 65, 105, 201, 295
Arm W. p. 237, 240
Armstrong, D. M. p. 105
Astrachan, B. p. 227, 245, 247
Azumi K. p. 227

Bachrach, P. p. 268
Baldridge, J. F. p. 252
Baliga, B. R. p. 299
Bamforth, K. W. p. 307
Baratz, M. S. p. 268
Barnard, C. L. p. 252, 253
Barret, G. V. p. 3, 64
Barret, H. p. 3
Bass, B. p. 50, 64
Becker, S. W. p. 192, 227, 243, 246
Beer, S. p. 227
Bem, D. J. p. 21
Benedict, R. p. 117, 216
Beres, M. E. p. 7, 11, 139, 147, 211, 214
Berger, P. L. p. 107
Berkowitz, N p. 212
Bernstein, P. p. 73
Berry, J. W. p. 107
Berstecher, D. p. 307
Von Bertalanffy, L. p. 4, 307
Bittner, E. p. 226
Blandin, S. p. 7, 133, 134, 135
Blankenship, L. V. p. 53
Blankenburg, E. p. 8, 273, 302, 303
Blau, P. M. p. 201, 202, 227, 229, 232, 244, 245, 252, 275, 276
Boddewyn, J. p. 2, 3, 64, 188
Bordua, D. J. p. 243; 246, 247
Brogden, H. E. p. 22
Brossard, M. p. 201, 274, 295, 309
Brown, B. p. 7, 133, 134, 135
Burger, P. O. p. 139
Burns, T. p. 5, 251

Campbell, J. P. p. 42
Camstock, D. E. p. 196
Cantril, H. p. 179
Caplow, T. p. 4, 232, 241
Casey, T. W. p. 103, 109
Cattel, R. B. p. 39
Champan, S. G. p. 238, 241
Champion, D. J. p. 227, 228, 243
Chandler, A. D. p. 207
Chattopadhyay, P. p. 23, 44
Chie, N. p. 216
Child, J. p. 12, 55, 58, 103, 207, 243, 252
Cicourel A. V. p. 104
Clark, A. W. p. 23, 65
Click, J. p. 115
Cole, M. p. 115
Crombie, A. D. p. 225
Crozier M. p. 50, 296
Cummings, L. p. 65
Cyert, R. M. p. 91, 100, 252, 253

Dahl, R. A. p. 254, 255
Dasen, P. R. p. 107
Daubigney, J. P. p. 309
Davis, K. p. 127, 128
Davis, St. M. p. 3, 10, 185
Desai, K. G. p. 182
Dewar, R. p. 42
Dill, W. R. p. 4, 89, 90, 175, 308
Dimitriou, B. p. 252, 253
Docherty D. p. 49
Doktor, R. p. 139
Doob, L. W. p. 116
Downey, H. K. p. 90
Dore, R. p. 63
Drabek, T. E. p. 227, 232, 243, 244, 245, 246
Dujker, H. C. p. 307
Duncan, R. p. 90, 192
Dunnette, M. D. p. 42
Durheim, E. p. 245

Earle, H. H. p. 226
Eldridge, J. E. T. p. 225
Emerson, R. M. p. 254, 255
Emery, F. E. p. 4, 175, 246, 307
Endruweit, G. p. 8, 12, 225, 299
England, G. W. p. 8, 9, 10, 11, 19, 20, 21, 22, 24, 42, 45, 127, 175, 177, 212, 215, 274, 308

Estafen, B. D. p. 109
Etzloni, A. p. 65, 77, 228, 239
Evan, W. M. p. 77, 139, 155, 171, 308, 309

Faison, J. p. 127, 135
Farmer, R. N. p. 2, 108, 308
Farrow, D. p. 50
Feest, J. p. 243
Feldman, A. S. p. 179
Festinger, L. p. 142
Fiedler, F. D. p. 172
Fillol, Th. R. p. 184, 185
Fine, K. S. p. 73
Fisher, L. P.
Fisher, L. p. 192
Flaes, R. M. B. p. 73
Flores, G. p. 73, 130, 185
Fokking, P. p. 49
Forde, D. p. 149, 156
Foucault, M. p. 206
Fourcade, J. M. p. 49, 313
Francis, R. p. 275
Freeman, J. p. 233, 234, 245
Friedberg, E. p. 50, 296
Friedson, E. p. 205
Frost, P. J. p. 8, 10, 231, 251, 300,

Galtung, J. p. 229
Gammage, A. Z. p. 241, 242
Gangulli, A. C. p. 182
Gardener, R. E. p. 245
Garfinkel, H. p. 104
Gay, J. p. 115
Georgiou, P. p. 252
Germann, A. C. p. 232
Ghiselli, D. E. p. 12, 24, 58, 64, 109, 112, 113, 129, 139, 185, 212
Gilpatric, R. J. p. 245
Gladwin, T. p. 121
Glick, J. p. 115
Glueck, W. F. p. 74
Goodman, P. S. p. 139
Gordon, G. p. 192, 193, 196
Gourley, G. D. p. 225, 231
Granick D. p. 58
Greenwood, J. M. p. 184, 185
Grochla, E. p. 245
Grosset, S. p. 58
Grunow, D. p. 244, 245

Haas, E. p. 202, 227, 232, 243, 244, 245, 246
Hage, J. p. 42, 227, 245
Hair, F. D. p. 218, 219
Haire, M. p. 3, 12, 24, 58, 64, 109, 112, 113, 129, 139, 185, 212, 215
Hall E. T. p. 115, 116, 117
Hall, R. H. p. 202, 227 232, 253
Hallowell, A. I. p. 116
Hannan, M. T. p. 233, 234, 245
Hansen, D. C. p. 235
Harbison, F. p. 175, 185
Harmon, H. H. p. 30
Harre, R. p. 104
Harvey, E. p. 4, 251
Hayes, D. C. p. 4, 8, 10, 251, 300
Hegner, F. p. 244, 245
Heider, F. p. 141
Heller, F. A. p. 7, 12, 51, 52, 54, 65, 128, 130, 185, 312
Heller, W. p. 139, 172
Hellpach, W. p. 307, 308
Hesseling, B. p. 140
Hesseling, P. p. 211, 215
Hickson, D. J. p. 4, 103, 196
Hill, W. p. 227, 242
Hoefert, H. W. p. 228
Hofstede, G. A. p. 63, 180, 212, 215
Hoft, W. p. 49
Holbeck, J. p. 192
Holmstrom, M. p. 183, 184
Hoover, J. D. p. 7, 73, 130
Hsu, F. L. K. p. 116

Indik, B. p. 4
Inkeles, A. p. 142

Jacob, B. M. p. 177
Jacob, P. E. p. 177
Jain, S. p. 185
James, M. p. 49
Johnson, N. J. p. 202
Jones, E. E. p. 143
Josh, V. p. 185

Kahn, R. L. p. 307
Kaiser, p. 30
Karlsson, L. E. p. 73
Karpik, L. p. 203
Kassem, S. p. 63, 215
Kast, F. E. p. 5
Katz, D. p. 307
Kavrohn, D. p. 74
Kefalas, A. p. 91, 94, 100
Kelley, L. p. 212
Kendall, p. 62, 80, 81
Kerlinger, F. N. p. 155
Kervasdoue, J. de p. 8, 191, 218
Kieser, A. p. 55, 58, 103
Kiesler, C. A. p. 42
Kimberly, J. R. p. 8, 191, 200, 208, 218
Klecka, C. p. 155
Kluckhohn, F. p. 22, 307, 308
Kluckholn, C. p. 140
Koch, J. L. p. 50
Kochan, T. p. 276

Kohler, W. p. 307
Koike, R. p. 308
Koontz, H. p. 4, 109, 119, 120
Kosiol, E. p. 227
Kraut, A. J. p. 180
Kroeber, A. L. p. 140, 309
Krupp, S. p. 227
Kuhn, T. p. 106
Kuhne, R. J. p. 73

Lammers, C. J. p. 201
Larson, R. C. p. 234
Lau, S. p. 114
Lauter, P. G. p. 185
Lauterbach, A. p. 185
Lautmann, R. p. 243
Lawrence, P. R. p. 5, 58, 89, 90, 91, 93, 133, 175, 194, 196, 246
Lawler, E. E. p. 42, 170
Lee p. 22
Levinson, D. J. p. 142, 227, 245, 247
Likert, R. p. 4
Litterer, J. A. p. 244
Locke E. A. p. 21
Lomax, A. p. 149, 156, 157, 212
Lorsch J. W. p. 5, 89, 90, 91, 93, 133, 175, 194, 196, 219, 246
Luchmann, N. p. 227, 234, 244, 245, 246
Luckman, T. p. 107

McCall, R. B. p. 270
McKelvey, B. p. 200
MacLntire, A. p. 225
MacMillan, L. C. p. 251
Malpass, R. S. p. 307, 311
Mandelbaum, D. G. p. 184
March, J. G. p. 21, 91, 100, 141, 144, 146, 232, 251, 252, 253
Martyn-Johns, T. A. p. 7, 9, 11, 103, 135
Maruyama, M. p. 106, 109, 110, 111, 116
Maslow, p. 116, 170
Mastermans, M. p. 106
Maurice, M. p. 201, 274, 295, 309
Mayes, B. T. p. 251, 256, 257
Mayntz, R. p. 227, 236, 246
Mays, R. p. 49, 54
McCabe, S. p. 23, 65
McClelland, D. C. p. 179
McEwen, W. J. p. 244, 246
McKelvey, B. p. 200
Mechanic, D. p. 251
Merritt, R. p. 307
Merton, R. K. p. 309
Meyer, M. W. p. 245
Miles, R. E. p. 53, 58, 63, 64
Miller, J. A. p. 50
Miller, J. G. p. 4, 5, 127
Mills, R. p. 251
Miner, J. B. p. 211, 212, 213
Mintzberg, H. p. 21
Moberg, D. L. p. 50
Moch, M. p. 196
Money, W. H. p. 211, 218, 299
Moore, B. E. p. 139
Moore, R. p. 139, 171, 179
Morris, M. D. p. 183
Mott, P. E. p. 245
Mowday, R. p. 256
Mulder, B. p. 132
Mumford, E. p. 73
Munson, P. A. p. 227
Murdock, G. P. p. 149
Murphy, G. p. 141
Musschoot, R. p. 299, 300
Myers, C. A. p. 175, 179, 185

Nakamura, H. p. 111
Narain, D. p. 3, 185
Nath, R. p. 3
Negandhi A. R. p. 1, 4, 8, 9, 10, 11, 13, 64, 109, 139, 144, 175, 176, 215, 274, 308, 313
Neuhaser, D. p. 218, 227, 243, 246
Northrop, F. S. C. p. 111
Novick, D. p. 245

Obenhaus, V. p. 149, 156
Oberg, W. p. 175, 176
Obradovic, J. p. 132
O'Donnell, C. p. 109, 119, 120
Ornati, O. A. p. 179
Orne, M. T. p. 23

Parsons, T. p. 2, 77, 228, 309
Peck, R. F. p. 139
Peery, Jr. N. p. 252, 253
Perrow, C. p. 4, 59, 77, 175, 195, 228
Petralla, R. p. 307
Pettigrew, A. M. p. 251, 252
Pfeffer, J. p. 64, 251, 263, 264
Pfeiffer, D. K. p. 227, 245, 246
Pondy, L. R. p. 44, 252
Porter, L. W. p. 12, 24, 58, 64, 109, 112, 113, 129, 139, 185, 212, 246, 251, 256, 257
Portwood, J. p. 7, 11, 139, 211, 214
Prasad, B. p. 64
Pratt, R. C. p. 177
Przeworski, A. p. 307
Presthus, R. p. 246
Pugh, D. S. p. 228, 229

Redding G. p. 7, 9, 11, 103, 109, 117, 135
Reiss, A. J. p. 243, 246, 247
Reseer, C. p. 212
Richardson, S. A. p. 227, 243
Richman, B. M. p. 2, 108, 308
Ritchie, J. B. p. 58, 63

Robbins, S. P. p. 251
Roberts, K. H. p. 13, 55, 139, 140, 171, 309
Rodgers, W. B. p. 245
Roemer, M. I. p. 220
Roig-Amat, B. p. 49
Rokkan, S. p. 307
Rosenthal p. 24
Rosenzweig J. E. p. 5
Ruedi, A. p. 58
Rummel R. J. p. 30
Ryterband E. C. p. 3

Salancik, G. R. p. 251
Sasaki, N. p. 127, 133
Saunders, C. B. p. 237, 239, 240, 242
Scheewind, K. A. p. 39
Schmidt, St. M. p. 65, 147, 276
Schoderbek, P. p. 91, 94, 100
Schoenherr, R. p. 201
Schollhammer, H. p. 2
Schon, D. A. p. 65
Schonher, R. p. 276
Scott, W. R. p. 196
Secord, P. F. p. 104
Sefer, B. p. 133
Servan-Schreiber, J. J. p. 12, 58
Sharma, K. L. p. 185
Sills, D. L. p. 77
Silverman, D. p. 22, 104, 243
Silvestre, J. J. p. 309
Simon, H. A. p. 21, 77, 141, 144, 146, 232, 252, 253, 254
Simonetti, S. H. p. 180
Singer, M. p. 184
Sirota D. p. 184, 185
Sithi-Amnuai, p. 116
Slocum, J. W. p. 90
Slotkin J. S. p. 179
Smith, Br. p. 226
Snow, C. C. p. 64
Solomon, R. p. 50
Sowle, C. R. p. 226
Spray, S. D. p. 176
Staehle, W. H. p. 49, 127, 130
Stalker, G. M. p. 5
Sterling, J. W. p. 237
Steudler, F. p. 206
Stodgil, R. M. p. 4
Stodtbeck, F. L. p. 22, 308
Stone R. p. 275
Storey, R. p. 90
Strauss, G. p. 65
Stumper, A. p. 231, 232
Sturtevant, W. C. p. 106
Suharto p. 216
Szalai A. p. 307

Takamiya M. p. 299, 302
Tandon, P. p. 23, 24
Tannenbaum, A. S. p. 228
Terreberry, S. p. 243, 245
Teune, H. p. 307
Thiagarajan K. M. p. 3, 24
Thompson, J. D. p. 4, 59, 60, 77, 89, 90, 91, 100, 175, 244, 246, 252
Thorelli, H. B. p. 4
Tompkins, S. S. p. 213
Tosi, H. p. 90
Tschanett, E. p. 226
Trist, E. L. p. 4, 175, 246, 307
Troub R. M. p. 7, 73, 130

Udy, S. H. Jr. p. 228, 235, 247

Valenzi, E. p. 50
Vanek J. p. 73
Van Doorn, J. p. 201
Verba, S. p. 295
Vroom, V. H. p. 58, 170

Wagenführ, H. p. 244, 245
Waldmann, P. p. 236
Wallat, G. p. 234, 236
Wanous, J. p. 212
Watson, N. A. p. 237
Weber, M. p. 111, 149, 155, 156, 157, 212, 275
Weick, K. p. 22, 42
Weinshal T. D. p. 49, 64
Wergin, J. F. p. 251
Wheelright, E. p. 23, 44
White P. E. p. 252
Whitehall, A. M. p. 8, 139
Whitehead C. J. p. 7, 73, 130
Whitehill, A. M. p. 177
Whitely, W. T. p. 7, 12, 22, 44, 127, 128
Whyte, W. F. p. 139, 185
Wildavsky, A. p. 251
Williams L. K. p. 139, 215
Wilpert B. p. 7, 12, 51, 52, 54, 65, 128, 130, 185, 313
Wilson, J. Q. p. 225, 226, 234
Witkin H. A. p. 111
Woodward, J. p. 4, 5, 59, 129, 175
Worthley, R. p. 212
Wright, G. N. p. 109, 115
Wrong D. H. p. 254, 255

Yetton, Ph. W. p. 58

Zald, M. M. p. 218, 219
Zaltman, G. p. 192
Ziegler, R. p. 236
Zimblist, A. p. 73
Zurcher, L. A. p. 185

SUBJECT INDEX

Active labor market policy p. 277-279
Administrative behavior p. 255, 263, 269
Adopted values p. 19

Causality paradigm p. 113
Choice behavior p. 21
Closed—systems approach p. 4
Cluster analysis p. 21
Comparative Management p. 2, 13
Comparative Management, Behavioral Approach p. 2-3
Comparative Management, Economic Development Orientation p. 2
Comparative Management—Environmental Approach p. 2-3
Comparative Studies, future of p. 216
Conceived values p. 19
Confucianism p. 111
Construct paradigms p. 107
Contingency approach, p. 50
Contingencies of Labour Market Policy p. 279-280
Convergence Hypothesis p. 10-11
Cross Cultural differences p. 104
Cross-Cultural studies p. 1, 4, 8
Cross cultural studies, future of p. 312-314
Cross-Cultural studies, historical perspectives p. 1-2
Cross-Cultural studies, methodological problems p. 310-312
Cross-cultural studies; perspectives p. 307-309
Cross-Cultural studies; reasons for p. 8-10
Cultural influence on individuals p. 144-145
Cultural Influence, process of p. 144
Culture, Impact of p. 12
Culture, measurement of p. 149-151

Decision-making patterns, differences in p. 12
Discretionary behavior p. 255-256, 263, 269

Employee's commitment to industrial life p. 179
Employment agencies, organizational networks p. 293-294
Employment agencies, patterns of control p. 291-293
Employment agencies, decentralization versus centralization p. 290-291
Employment agencies, criteria for comparison p. 289-290
Employment agencies, England p. 288-289
Employment agencies, Germany p. 286-288
Employment agencies, Italy p. 285-286
England's Model p. 19, 20, 21, 22
Ethnomethodology p. 104

General-systems approach p. 4-5
German and U.S. police, age structure p. 236-237
German and U.S. police, budget autonomy p. 233-234
German and U.S. police, compulsary formal training p. 240-241
German and U.S. police, continuation training p. 241-242
German and U.S. police, educational requirements p. 231-239
German and U.S. police, level of organization p. 230-231
German and U.S. police, number of organizations p. 232-233
German and U.S. police organizational differences p. 229-230
German and U.S. police, organization size p. 231-232
German and U.S. police, place of training p. 241
German and U.S. police, police density p. 232
German and U.S. police, recruiting requirement p. 237
German and U.S. police, selection process p. 240
German and U.S. police, selectivity p. 239-240
German and U.S. police, structure of formal training p. 241
Goal hierarchy p. 79, 84, 87

Health care in France p. 204-207

Individual Behavior, Influence on an organization p. 146-147

Leitwert p. 308

Management practices and Culture p. 11-12
Management styles and decision making p. 185
Managerial Values p. 12
Measurement of values, p. 24, 29
Mediating tasks p. 281
Metaparadigms p. 106, 107
Models of Culture p. 10-11
Moralism p. 22
Multiple Causation p. 4
Mutual causal paradigm p. 109

Open-systems approach p. 4
Operative values p. 19
Organizational behavior, contingency approach p. 49-50

Organizational goals p. 12, 78
Organizational structure p. 12
Organizational theory; recent changes p. 3-4

Paradigm p. 104, 106
Paradigm differences and control p. 121-122
Paradigm differences and directing and leading p. 120-121
Paradigm differences and organizing p. 119
Paradigm differences and planning p. 119
Paradigm differences and staffing p. 119-120
Paradigm differences, causality p. 109-114
Paradigm differences, empirical support p. 109
Paradigm differences, morality p. 117-118
Paradigm differences, probability p. 115
Paradigm differences, self p. 116-117
Paradigm differences, time p. 115-116
Peruvian co-determination system p. 73
Policy tasks p. 281-283
Political behavior p. 256-257, 263-269
Politics in organizations p. 252
Power equilization, Peruvian process p. 74, 77, 86
Power equilization, Yugoslav process p. 74-77
Power in organizations p. 254-255
Pragmatism p. 22
Pragmatists, classification of p. 30, 31

Reference group, p. 176-178
Reference groups, importance of p. 216
Regulatory Tasks p. 281
Resource distribution in an organization p. 252-253
Role of the contract in organizations p. 253-254

Social structure and the perceived role of work p. 153
Socio-cultural Variables p. 3
Sub-cultural differences p. 12

Undirectional causal paradigm p. 109
Unemployment Insurance p. 281

Values p. 19
Values, properties of p. 22
Value systems p. 19, 20, 21, 22, 43, 44, 45
Value systems, Influence on development of p. 22

Weak values p. 19
Workers' concern for public Issues p. 178-179
Worker satisfaction p. 181
Work values p. 179
Work values, black-white differences in p. 157-161
Work values, European differences in p. 162-163, 165
Work values in European and African Cultures p. 155-157
Work values, individual p. 153-154
Work values, influences on p. 151-152

Yugoslav self-determination system p. 73

Zadryga p. 132

DATE DUE

JUN 27 1990			
MAR 1 1991			